Relax.

You've opened the right book.

Once upon a time, people were wrong. They thought the automobile was an electric death trap that would never replace the buggy, the Internet was only for academic shut-ins, and people who used study guides were simply *cheaters*. Then cars stopped exploding every time you started the engine, people realized you could use computers for more than just calculating the digits of *pi*, and the "cheaters" with the study guides ... well, they started getting it. They got better grades, got into better schools, and just plain ol' got better. Times change. Rules change. *You snooze, you lose, buggy drivers.*

SparkNotes is different. We've always been thinking ahead. We were the first study guides on the Internet back in 1999—you've been to SparkNotes.com, haven't you? If not ... why?! You'll find busy message boards, diagnostic test prep, and all kinds of tools you'll need to get your act together and your grades up. And if your act's already together, SparkNotes will help you brutalize the competition. Or work for peace. Your call.

We're inexpensive, not cheap. Not only are our books the best bang for the buck, they're the best bang, period. Our reputation is based on staying smart and trustworthy—one step ahead, making tough topics understandable. We explain, we strategize, we translate. We get you where you want to go: smarter, better, faster than anyone else.

If you've got something to say, tell us. Your input makes us better. Found a mistake? Check www.sparknotes.com/errors. Have a comment? Go to www.sparknotes.com/comments. Did you read all the way to the bottom? Awesome. We love you. You're gonna do just fine.

SPARKNOTES®

guide to AP*

U.S. History

SPARK PUBLISHING

Spark Publishing
A Division of Barnes & Noble
120 Fifth Avenue
New York, NY 10011
www.sparknotes.com

Library of Congress Cataloging-in-Publication Data

SparkNotes Guide to AP U.S. History. p. cm.
ISBN-13: 978-1-4114-0517-2 (pbk.)
ISBN-10: 1-4114-0517-X (pbk.)
1. United States—History—Outlines, syllabi, etc. 2. United States—History—Examinations—Study guides. 3. Advanced placement programs (Education)—Examinations—Study guides. 4. College entrance achievement tests—Study guides. I. SparkNotes LLC. II. Title: SparkNotes Guide to AP U.S. History.

E178.2.S73 2008
973.076—dc22

2007049276

Please submit changes or report errors to www.sparknotes.com/errors.

Printed and bound in USA

10 9 8 7

Acknowledgments

SparkNotes would like to thank the following writers and contributors:

Greg D. Feldmeth, MA
Assistant Head of School, Advanced Placement U.S. History Teacher, Polytechnic School, Pasadena, California

Kelly McMichael, PhD
Professor of History, Texas Christian University

Greg Cantrell, PhD
Professor of History and Erma and Ralph Lowe Chair in Texas History, Texas Christian University

Ashley Laumen
Teaching Assistant, Department of History, Texas Christian University

Sean Taylor, PhD
Visiting Assistant Professor of History, Minnesota State University Moorhead

Timothy Buckner
Teaching Assistant, Department of History, University of Texas at Austin

Paul Rubinson
Teaching Assistant, Department of History, University of Texas at Austin

Joshua Cracraft
Graduate Student, American History, Brandeis University

Andrew Jones
BA, International Studies, Oglethorpe University; MA, Slavic Languages and Literature, Ohio State University; MS, Journalism, Boston University

Christian Lorentzen
AB, Classics, Harvard University

Contents

Chapter 3: Seeking Independence: 1763–1783 39

Chapter 4: Building a Nation: 1781–1800 53

Chapter 5: Republican Agrarianism: 1800–1824 69

Chapter 6: Jacksonian Democracy: 1824–1848 83

Chapter 7: A Growing Nation: 1820–1860 97

Introduction

If you're looking at this book, you're probably considering taking the Advanced Placement U.S. History Exam. And there are many good reasons to do so: AP Exams give you the opportunity to earn valuable course credit or advanced standing in college, as well as the opportunity to impress on college admissions officers that you are a serious and dedicated student. AP Exams offer one of the few chances to prove to colleges that you are already capable of doing college-level work.

In fact, the expectations placed on students taking AP Exams have become so high that it's easy to become overwhelmed or intimidated. We're here to tell you that the exam is manageable. We're here to help.

First, we'd like to update you on the latest changes to the AP U.S. History Exam. In May 2006, a new exam was administered to include the addition of the Pre-Columbian period. The College Board (the test administrators) have also merged two test topics together to form "Social Change, and Cultural and Intellectual Developments." Our book includes these changes, so there will be no surprises on test day.

This book provides an in-depth review of the material you'll need to master before taking the AP U.S. History Exam. The chapters are divided into time periods so that you can easily navigate through the sections. We recommend that you sharpen your U.S. history knowledge by reviewing each chapter, focusing on the areas you need to brush up on. As you will see, throughout the text, important names, events, amendments, treaties, etc., are bolded for quick scanning and reviewing. Don't forget to review the Timelines and Major Figures sections at the end of the chapters.

In addition to studying the subject review, it is crucial to work on practice exams. The practice exams in this book will help you become comfortable with the test. More important, they can help you understand what's not on the exam, so you don't waste your time striving for some elusive ideal of "college-level preparation." Practice exams help you to see the test as it really is, so you know exactly what to expect.

Before launching right into the practice exams, we'll give you an overview of how the test is structured and precisely what kinds of questions you'll see on it.

FORMAT OF THE EXAM

The Advanced Placement U.S. History Exam is three hours and five minutes long and is divided into two parts:

- A 55-minute Multiple-Choice section, which counts for 50 percent of your score
- A 130-minute Free-Response section, which counts for 50 percent of your score

The Multiple-Choice Section

Format

Section I of the exam contains 80 multiple-choice questions, which you are given 55 minutes to complete. The questions test your knowledge of material usually covered in an introductory U.S. history college course.

The multiple-choice questions are either questions or incomplete statements, followed by five suggested answers. The exam-graders penalize you a quarter of a point for each wrong answer, so you should only guess if you can eliminate two or more of the answer choices.

Topics of Questions

The multiple-choice questions fall into four basic topics:

- **Political Institutions, Behavior, and Public Policy.** Approximately 35 percent of the questions (or 28 questions) address political institutions and public policy.
- **Social Change and Cultural and Intellectual Development.** Approximately 40 percent of the questions (or 28 questions) address social and cultural change.
- **Diplomacy and International Relations.** Approximately 15 percent of the questions (or 12 questions) address diplomacy and international relations.

- **Economic Developments.** Approximately 10 percent of the questions (or 8 questions) address economic change.

  Roughly one-half of the questions cover the period 1790–1914, at least one-third of the questions deal with the period from 1915 to the present, and the remainder focus on the Pre-Columbian period to 1789. Approximately 65 percent of the questions (or 52 questions) ask you to simply recall facts, while the remaining 35 percent ask you to analyze a set of circumstances and draw conclusions.

The Free-Response Section

Types of Questions

Section II of the exam is a 130-minute Free-Response section broken into three individual parts:

- **Part A.** Part A consists of one document-based essay question (DBQ). This question usually focuses on a specific time period and requires the student to both analyze and interpret the documents provided, as well as to apply his or her own knowledge of the time period to construct a coherent essay. The documents, including charts, graphs, cartoons, pictures, and articles, are unlikely to be familiar to the student. Part A begins with a required 15-minute reading period during which students are encouraged to analyze the documents and plan their answers. The College Board suggests that students spend 15 minutes reading and planning and 45 minutes writing the response.
- **Part B.** Part B consists of two groups of two standard essay questions of which the student will choose one to answer from each group. Suggested time allotment for Part B is 5 minutes of planning and 30 minutes of writing for each question.

  Generally, the four questions included in Part B move chronologically; questions in group 1 of Part B address issues that occurred before those addressed in group 2. Neither the DBQ nor those questions in group 1 and 2 of Part B exclusively address issues that occurred from 1980 to the present.

Scoring

In general, in order to receive a 3, you must answer 60 percent of the multiple-choice questions correctly. In the Free-Response section, Part A counts for 55 percent of your total Section II score, and Part B counts for 45 percent. Each essay is scored on a scale from 1 to 9:

8–9 High score

6–7 Medium-high score

5 Medium score

3–4 Medium-low score

1–2 Low score

Answers to the questions in this section will be judged on the strength of the thesis developed and the quality of the argument, rather than on factual information. For example, if you incorrectly identify the date of a battle in the Civil War in one of your essays, you will not be penalized.

SCORING

The AP Exam is scored on a five-point scale:

5 Extremely well qualified

4 Well qualified

3 Qualified

2 Possibly qualified

1 No recommendation

HOW TO PREPARE FOR THE EXAM

The AP U.S. History Exam not only tests your knowledge of facts but also your ability to analyze a set of facts and draw conclusions. These skills are tested in both sections of the test and are by far the most important skills you need in order to get a high score. In other words, it's not enough that you know the dates of the major battles in the Civil War. You have to understand why the Battle of Gettysburg was so crucial to the outcome of the war. Dates and presidents and other facts are important as well, but how you pull all that data together is what the exam-graders are really looking for.

This is a skill that you can improve. The best way is to take a lot of practice tests. That's why we've included two full-length tests in this book. The more familiar you are with analysis questions, the better you'll become at them. While some multiple-choice questions ask you to analyze a set of facts and draw conclusions, these skills are primarily tested in the Free-Response section of the exam. The more practice you have writing timed essays, and developing quality thesis statements and supporting arguments, the better off you'll be on test day.

STRATEGIES FOR TAKING THE EXAM

The Multiple-Choice Section

- Skim the questions first so that you know what sorts of things you'll be reading for.
- Answer the questions you feel confident with first; skip harder questions and save them for last.
- Guess on questions when you can eliminate at least two wrong answers.
- Mark the questions you can't answer with a check—tackle all of these questions after you've gone through all of Section I.
- Cross off wrong answers on the test itself.

The Free-Response Section

- Underline key words in the question (often the prompt gives you important pieces of guidance on purpose or on kinds of things to look for).
- Read the prompt carefully; underline and mark the key parts of the question.
- Brainstorm ideas for your thesis and the evidence you will use to support it.
- Outline your essay in the form of a thesis supported by reasons and evidence.
- Reread the prompt to make sure you haven't missed part of the question.
- Don't get hung up on perfect wording, spelling, etc.
- Don't get upset if you can't remember exact dates or names—you won't be penalized for that in this section.
- If you run out of time, at least try to put down an outline of what you would have written for the essay. You won't get full credit, but you may be able to pick up a point or two.

GET ONLINE

Don't forget to visit us online. Go to **testprep.sparknotes.com** to take a free AP U.S. History diagnostic test. Our powerful test prep software will pinpoint your problem areas and help you overcome your weaknesses. Based on the results of your diagnostic test, we will build you a personalized study plan that links to the U.S. history topics you need to review. We recommend that you take the diagnostic test before you take the practice exams in this book. That way, you'll know which topics you need to brush up on, and you can use our book to reivew. You should also take advantage of the message boards, where you can chat about your anxieties and share study tips with fellow test-takers.

REGISTERING FOR THE EXAM

Contact your school's AP coordinator or guidance counselor for help registering for the test. If you are homeschooled or your school does not administer the test, contact AP Services for information about registering to take the exam at a school in your area.

AP Services
P.O. Box 6671
Princeton, NJ 08541-6671
(888) CALL-4-AP; (609) 771-7300
Email: apexams@info.collegeboard.org
Website: www.collegeboard.com/ap/student

PART I

U.S. HISTORY REVIEW

CHAPTER 1

Colliding Cultures: Pre-Columbian Period to 1700

PRE-COLUMBIAN AMERICA

Between 15,000 and 30,000 years ago, bands of hunters from northeast Asia pursued mammoths and other big game across a frozen patch of land known as **Beringia**, unwittingly becoming the first Americans. This land bridge has since disappeared and become the salty **Bering Strait** that divides Siberia from Alaska. Cold weather and harsh conditions drove these hunters south in search of food and a better climate. Gradually, they spread across North and South America and formed various Native American tribes. Historians have learned about these people from the artifacts they left behind, including stone tools and weapons, bones, pottery, ancient dwellings, and bits of textiles and basketry.

Central and South American Natives

By the time Christopher Columbus first set eyes on the New World, more than 50 million people lived in North and South America. About 4 million of those people lived in what is now the United States. The richest, most complex native civilizations developed near the **Isthmus of Panama**, the thin strip of land that divides North and South America. There were four major civilizations there:

- **The Mayas**, who lived just north of the Isthmus of Panama, developed a sophisticated approach to mathematics and astronomy and a calendar more accurate than that of Europe.
- **The Toltecs**, who lived in the center of present-day Mexico, had conquered most of Central America by the tenth century.
- **The Aztecs**, who frequently made ritual human sacrifices, founded Tenochtitlán, now known as Mexico City, in 1325.
- **The Incas**, or **Quechua** people, who inhabited the Andes Mountains, developed elaborate road systems and a strong central government.

These four civilizations distinguished themselves from other Native American societies in South America. They are considered advanced civilizations for the following accomplishments:

- Establishing permanent cities
- Developing large-scale agricultural techniques to raise such crops as maize (corn), beans, squash, chili peppers, avocados, and pumpkins
- Building giant pyramids, courts for ceremonial games, and other monumental architecture
- Engaging in complex commercial and military practices

North American Natives

In North America, three distinct native civilizations emerged:

- **The Adena-Hopewell** culture of the Northeast, which had reached its peak by the seventh century, long before European conquest. European settlers later encountered their distant descendants in the **Iroquois** and **Pequot** tribes.
- **The Mississippian** culture of the Southeast, which developed sophisticated agricultural practices and created temple mounds akin to the pyramids built in South America. The Mississippians thrived until the fifteenth century, when European diseases wiped them out. The **Creeks**, **Cherokees**, **Choctaw**, **Chickasaws**, and **Seminoles** all descend from this culture.
- **The Pueblo-Hohokam** people of the Southwest, who developed elaborate irrigation systems. Their descendants include the **Hopi**, **Zuni**, and **Anasazi** tribes.

None of these native cultures developed to the same degree of sophistication as that of the Mayas, Aztecs, or Incas. However, most of the native peoples in North America were able to maintain large agricultural systems, build ceremonial mounds or pueblo dwellings, and develop elaborate clan structures.

EARLY EUROPEAN EXPLORATION

During the fourteenth, fifteenth, and sixteenth centuries, Europe underwent a period of fast-paced change and development known as the **Renaissance**, meaning "rebirth." Rampant disease, political fragmentation, and religious hysteria had plagued Europeans throughout the medieval period between the fifth and the thirteenth centuries. The Renaissance, however, featured the following:

- The revival of learning, with emphasis placed on ancient Greek and Roman scholarship
- The growth of major European cities
- The development of trade and capitalistic economies
- The rise of new and powerful monarchies

Increased power and wealth in the hands of the monarchies eventually led to an interest in exploration and expansion.

Columbus's Voyages

Italian-born **Christopher Columbus** learned to sail from Portuguese seamen. After years of sailing on Portuguese ships, Columbus hatched his own plan to lead an expedition westward in the hopes of finding a faster route to Asia across the Atlantic. He eventually received financial backing from King Ferdinand and Queen Isabella of Spain in exchange for the gold, spices, and silk he promised to bring back from the Orient.

The Voyage of 1492

Columbus and eighty-seven other men set sail aboard three ships: the *Nina*, *Pinta,* and *Santa Maria.* After a rocky thirty three-day voyage, they landed on an island in the Bahamas. They named it **San Salvador**. Columbus called the friendly island people *los indios* (Indians) because he believed he and his men had landed on an island in the East Indies.

Columbus then sailed southward down to Cuba and to the island of **Hispaniola** in search of the mainland. When one of his ships sank, he decided to return home. Leaving forty men behind, Columbus seized a dozen natives to give to the king and queen of Spain and sailed back across the Atlantic.

Columbus's Return Trips to America

Columbus returned to Spain a hero and prepared for a second voyage. He sailed back to the Americas in 1493 with seventeen ships, more than 1,200 men, and instructions from the king and queen to treat the Indians well. Unfortunately, the forty men Columbus had left on Hispaniola after his first voyage had raped and murdered many Indians and had plundered their villages. The natives had struck back in return and killed ten Spaniards. Columbus counterattacked with crossbows and guns and loaded five hundred natives on a ship bound for the slave markets in Spain. He made two more voyages to the Caribbean in the next decade but refused to believe he had discovered anything other than outlying parts of Asia.

Spanish Exploration

By the early sixteenth century, Spain had begun an inland conquest of the Americas mainly to search for gold, silver, and other riches. Spanish conquistadors, or "conquerors," penetrated much of present-day Latin America and established a vast new world empire for Spain by the 1530s. The following men were the most famous of these conquistadors:

- **Hernando Cortés**, who conquered the Aztecs at Tenochtitlán with only 600 men in 1519.
- **Francisco Pizarro**, who defeated the Incas in 1532 with fewer than 200 soldiers.
- **Hernando De Soto**, who explored the present-day southwestern United States with 600 men in 1539.

"Biological Exchange"

An enormously influential exchange occurred when the Europeans landed in the Americas, generally to the benefit of Europeans and detriment of the native peoples. Sugar and bananas crossed the Atlantic, while pigs, sheep, and cattle arrived in the Americas. However, European diseases such as typhus, influenza, measles, and smallpox also crossed the Atlantic and devastated the Native American population.

Subjugation of the Native Americans

The Spanish explored all of South and Central America and eventually became the privileged landowners of the newly discovered continent. They created the *encomienda* system, in which favored Spanish officers controlled land and the nearby native villages. These officers protected the villages but also demanded tributes from the natives in the form of goods and labor.

Not surprisingly, a bipolar society emerged in Spanish America, with affluent Europeans at the top and poor, subjugated natives at the bottom. By the mid-1500s, much of the Native American population had died from disease, violence, or overwork. To replace this labor force, the Spanish began importing slaves from Africa.

Challenges To Spain's Empire

Spain also dominated much of southern and western North America during the colonial period, but not without serious competition from the French, the Dutch, and the English. The French challenged Spanish claims first, most significantly when explorer **Jacques Cartier** made three voyages into present-day Canada in the 1530s. Religious civil wars in France halted further attempts to colonize North America until **Samuel de Champlain** founded "New France," a territory that covered much of eastern Canada in the 1600s.

Spain also suffered from Dutch and English pirates who plundered Spanish ships as they crisscrossed the Atlantic. War eventually erupted between Spain and England in the mid-1500s, ending with England's defeat of the Spanish Armada in 1588. British naval supremacy opened the way for English colonization of the New World.

ENGLISH DOMINANCE IN NORTH AMERICA

Early English attempts at colonization proved unsuccessful and expensive, but colonists soon managed to establish themselves in the wilderness of North America. By the eighteenth century, England had replaced Spain as the dominant colonial power on the continent.

The Colonization Movement

Several factors made the acquisition of New World colonies a virtual necessity for England:

- Spanish gold and silver from the New World had flooded Europe and created a severely inflated economy.
- England did not have any colonies that produced gold and therefore suffered greatly from the inflation.

- English farmers had begun growing foods, such as corn and potatoes, in the Americas that helped to eliminate starvation but contributed to the population boom.
- The increased population combined with extreme inflation fueled the unemployment rate in England and led to overcrowding in English cities.

With a depressed economy, high unemployment rates, and a growing population, England needed somewhere to send its citizens to discover riches and relieve the cities of their unemployed masses.

"The Lost Colonists"

In 1578, Queen Elizabeth I granted Sir Humphrey Gilbert a royal patent to explore and claim new territories in North America. Gilbert hoped to transplant Britons to the Americas to acquire wealth for himself and for England. On his first voyage in 1583, he managed to claim some land in Newfoundland but had to turn back as winter approached. Tragically, he and his ship vanished on the return trip.

The next year, Gilbert's half-brother **Sir Walter Raleigh** petitioned the queen for a commission in his own name. In 1587, Raleigh sponsored an expedition of 117 men, women, and children who settled on Roanoke Island off the coast of North Carolina. The Spanish–English War prevented any further ships from sailing to **Roanoke**, and three years passed before another English ship arrived in 1590. Strangely, the sailors found the settlement abandoned. To this day, historians do not know what happened to those "Lost Colonists."

Managing the Costs of Colonization

New World colonization soon became so expensive that no single individual could fund expeditions. Instead, English entrepreneurs formed **joint-stock companies** in which stockholders shared the risks and profits of colonization. These stockholders expected to earn a return on their investments in the form of gold and silver, wines, citrus fruits, olive oil, and other spoils that would result from colonization. Some of the larger companies, such as the **Virginia Company**, acquired patents from the monarchy and held monopolies on large tracts of land.

Jamestown

In 1607, three ships carrying almost 100 men reached the Chesapeake Bay. These settlers chose a highly defensible site along the James River in present-day Virginia and established the small settlement of **Jamestown**.

First Encounters

The Jamestown settlers faced extreme difficulty from the outset, and many men fell to disease, starved to death, or died in skirmishes with Native Americans.

Only the adventurer **John Smith**'s military expertise and leadership saved the colony. By the time another English ship arrived in 1609, only fifty-three of the original 100 colonists remained. Unfortunately, the ship carried 400 more settlers without any supplies. Overwhelmed and suffering from battle injuries, Smith abandoned the colony and returned to England.

The "Starving Time"

Smith's departure and the advent of winter marked the beginning of the **"starving time"** in Jamestown. Weak from disease and hunger, the 450 colonists destroyed the town for firewood and then barricaded themselves inside their fort to evade hostile natives. Once inside the fort, they resorted to eating dogs, rats, and even one another after food supplies disappeared. Only sixty people survived the winter. As the survivors prepared to abandon the colony the following spring, four English ships arrived with 500 more men and supplies. Settlers struggled for two more years until colonist **John Rolfe** discovered a new American treasure: tobacco.

Cash Crop: Tobacco

Rolfe discovered that the soil in and around Jamestown was perfectly suited for growing tobacco, and England and the rest of Europe couldn't buy enough of it. In fact, so many Europeans smoked or sniffed tobacco that Jamestown had exported thirty tons' worth of leaves to England by 1619. As a result, the little colony prospered and so did Virginia Company investors. At last, stockholders and the monarchy found it profitable to fund expeditions to the Americas. More important, the discovery of tobacco solidified England's position in North America.

To glean a share of the wealth, Parliament and the Crown forbade the colonists from shipping their tobacco anywhere but England. Even with the limited market, tobacco generated enough profit that the colonists grew richer too. Women eventually joined the farmers in Virginia as the colony flourished. Some Jamestown settlers also brought back black **indentured servants** (not slaves) who became the first Africans in North America. Laws distinguishing between servants and slaves developed gradually in the 1600s.

Bacon's Rebellion

Historians have long looked on **Bacon's Rebellion** as the first manifestation of "revolutionary" feelings. In 1676, colonists in Virginia, especially on the western frontier of the colony, had come under attack from some of the Native American tribes in the area. The royal governor, Sir William Berkeley, ordered an investigation into the attacks and arranged several meetings between the colonists and the Indians. **Nathaniel Bacon**, a farmer and landowner—and Berkeley's cousin—was unhappy with these efforts. He and several other farmers felt that the government was not protecting them. They coalesced into a loosely organized army and began attacking largely peaceful Indian camps throughout northern Virginia.

Berkeley, in trying to keep the peace, labeled Bacon a rebel. Bacon and his forces surrounded the government buildings in Jamestown and forced Berkeley to flee the city. Shortly thereafter, Bacon died and Berkeley was able to return to power. He promptly hung several of Bacon's compatriots.

The Pilgrims

The **Pilgrims**, who eventually established **Plymouth Colony**, belonged to an uncompromising sect of Protestant Puritans in England who challenged the Anglican Church's authority. Also known as **Separatists** because they had separated from the Anglican Church, these Pilgrims formed a Puritan church under their own covenant. Doing so was considered treasonous at the time, since the church and state were intertwined. To avoid imprisonment or persecution, the Pilgrims fled to Holland in 1607.

New World Freedom

Although the Dutch tolerated Puritan religious practices and allowed them to worship freely, the Pilgrim separatists found themselves relegated to performing the lowest-paying jobs. Living in poverty and finding that their children were assimilating into Dutch culture, the Pilgrim congregation made a drastic decision to leave Europe and establish a Puritan colony in the New World. Although the king of England didn't relish the idea of a faith-based settlement in North America, he agreed not to interfere.

The Mayflower Voyage

Securing a land patent from the Virginia Company, the Pilgrims created their own joint-stock company and prepared for the trans-Atlantic voyage. In 1620, 102 men, women, and children crowded aboard the *Mayflower* and set sail for America. Several non-Puritan settlers joined them, including a cooper named **John Alden** and a hired soldier named **Miles Standish**, both of whom played a crucial role in the founding of the colony. During the voyage, the Pilgrims were blown off course. Reaching Cape Cod instead of Virginia, they attempted to head south but had to turn back because of rough seas. The Pilgrims decided to stay on Cape Cod at a place they called Plymouth.

Assistance from Native Americans

The *Mayflower* remained in New England that first winter and provided shelter to the Pilgrims while they tried to build houses on land. Exposure to the elements, malnutrition, and illness soon began to take their toll, and more than half of the Pilgrims died that first winter. The settlers made friends with their neighbors, the Wampanoag Indians, who helped the remainder survive. One Wampanoag named **Squanto** helped the Pilgrims grow maize the next year. By the following autumn, the Pilgrims had their own bumper crop of corn and were well on their way to self-sufficiency. To celebrate their bountiful first harvest, the Pilgrims held a feast and invited their Wampanoag neighbors. This feast served as the inspiration for the modern-day Thanksgiving holiday.

The Mayflower Compact

By the early seventeenth century, the king had divided English territorial claims in North America between two chartered joint-stock companies, the **London Virginia Company**, which had jurisdiction over the land from present-day North Carolina to New Jersey, and the **Plymouth Virginia Company**, which controlled the land from New York to Maine. Each company would then issue patents to groups of settlers, allowing them to establish settlements on company land.

The Pilgrims arrived in what is now Massachusetts with their patent from the Virginia Company to settle in Virginia, not Plymouth. Without a patent to settle in the Plymouth territory, technically, no one controlled them, and the Pilgrims formed their own government under the **Mayflower Compact**. Forty-one men signed the compact, elected a simple government, and agreed to obey its laws.

Massachusetts Bay Colony

Within a few years, a new colony of Puritans overshadowed the smaller Plymouth Colony. In 1629, a group of Puritan merchants and country gentlemen obtained a royal charter to found the **Massachusetts Bay Company**. The stockholders elected **John Winthrop**, a prosperous and respected lawyer and landowner, to serve as governor of the new colony. Unlike all previous charters from the king, the articles included the provision that the government of the Massachusetts Bay Colony could be located in the colony itself rather than in England. Winthrop and a group of 1,000 Puritans settled in Boston and Salem, Massachusetts, in 1630.

Reform vs. Separation

Winthrop's settlers were Puritans, but as they were not members of the Separatists' extreme sect, they were not Pilgrims, like the people of Plymouth. Instead, the Puritans in Boston and Salem believed that the Anglican Church had become too much like the Roman Catholic Church and needed to be purified in order to restore strict biblical interpretations. In short, they were **Reformists**, not Separatists.

"City upon a Hill"

Winthrop remained the leader of the Massachusetts Bay Colony for twenty years until his death in 1649. During this time, the colony grew rapidly, as nearly 20,000 Puritans fled England for the Salem and Boston areas within the first ten years of the colony's existence. This contingent of Reformists planned to establish a shining example of Puritanism for the world and to change the Anglican Church through the example of their good works and holy lifestyle.

Winthrop laid out this philosophy of setting an example for others to follow in a famous sermon. While still aboard the ship *Arbella* on the way from England, Winthrop delivered the sermon that has since been hailed one of the most influential speeches in American history. Winthrop told the settlers they would be casting off all the evil and past wrongdoings of Europe and starting a new

chapter in human history. He also proclaimed that the New World held the potential for greatness, saying, "We must consider that we shall be a city upon a hill. The eyes of all people are upon us." Winthrop's **"City upon a Hill"** sermon thus pronounced the colony a beacon of godliness for the world.

Halfway Covenant

The foundation of the Puritans in the New World was shortly thereafter marked by an important change in the church: how membership was conferred. Until 1677, membership in the Puritan church was restricted to those who could give verbal testimony of their "experience of Grace." Even those baptized had to pass this testimony before being accepted as full members of the church. In 1662, however, came the publication of the **Halfway Covenants**, adopted to allow certain people to retain a limited degree of church privileges, including baptizing their children, without becoming offical members. In 1677, this new practice was adopted and greatly increased the sizes of congregations in the New World.

The Middle Colonies

In the seventeenth century, most colonists believed the church instilled moral behavior and respect for authority and created better citizens. The governments relied on the church and protected its existence in a reciprocal relationship. As a result, each of the early English colonies established its own state-sanctioned church. All the early colonial leaders in the southern Virginian colonies and the northern Puritan colonies believed everyone in the colony should practice the same religion to maintain unity. They also reasoned there would be no religious persecution if there was only one faith to follow. In other words, each colony would be harmonious without any religious or civic disagreements.

The middle colonies, comprising New York, New Jersey, Pennsylvania, and Delaware, however, did not establish state-sanctioned religions. In refusing to do so, they opened the doors to people from a multitude of nationalities and faiths.

The mid-Atlantic region, unlike New England and the southern colonies, drew many of its initial settlers from war-torn or intolerant countries in Europe. Those who fled to the middle colonies of the New World included:

- Dutch Mennonites
- French Huguenots
- German Baptists
- Portuguese Jews
- Dutch Reformed
- Lutherans
- Quakers

All of these groups had borne the brunt of religious exclusion in Europe and were not eager to repeat the experience in the New World. They joined Anglicans already living in the middle colonies and simply agreed to disagree. Also in the mix were the indigenous people and the African slaves (with their own religious practices). The middle colonies became a mosaic of nationalities and religious practices.

New York. Originally called New Netherlands, the English renamed the colony New York after defeating the former Dutch owners in 1664. New York City eventually became a port of entry and home for people of all nationalities. In a census taken in 1770, for example, there were eighteen different churches to support a population of 22,000 people: three Dutch Reformed, three Anglican, three Presbyterian, two Lutheran, one French Huguenot, one Congregational, one Methodist, one Baptist, one Quaker, one Moravian, and one Jewish temple.

New Jersey. The colony of New Jersey developed more slowly than the colony of New York, but its diversity was just as great. By 1701, the colony had forty-five different congregations. Most were unable to afford individual churches, so they frequently shared houses of worship.

Pennsylvania. William Penn formed the colony of Pennsylvania to provide a safe haven for the persecuted of both the Old and New Worlds. A Quaker himself, Penn believed that force would never convert anyone. Many persecuted peoples, such as the Amish, Dunkers, Schwenkfelders, and Mennonites, found freedom in Pennsylvania.

Delaware. Scandinavian Lutherans and Dutch Reformed were the first to settle Delaware, and English Quakers and Welsh Baptists soon followed. Although Delaware was one of the most diverse colonies, the Anglican Church had a strong following there by the end of the eighteenth century.

TIMELINE: 30,000 B.C.–1676

30,000–15,000 B.C.	Asians begin several migrations over Bering Strait.
5000 B.C.	Maize cultivation begins in southern Mexico.
700 B.C.	Olmec people flourish along Gulf of Mexico.
100 A.D.	Hopewell culture sets up massive trading network.
300	Mayan city of Tikal features 20,000 residents and many temples.
500	Teotihuacan's population reaches 100,000 at peak of culture.

600	Hohokan civilization develops in present-day Arizona and New Mexico.
900	Anasazi build cliff villages in American southwest.
1000	Leif Erikksson and Norsemen attempt a settlement (Vinland) in Newfoundland.
1125	City of Cahokia (near present-day St. Louis) has 15,000 residents and 100 temple mounds.
1300	Europe experiences the Renaissance.
1325	The Aztecs found Tenochtitlán (later known as Mexico City).
1440	Johann Gutenberg invents the moveable-type press.
1492	Christopher Columbus lands on an island in the West Indies and names it San Salvador.
1493	Columbus returns to the Americas on his second voyage.
1521	Hernando Cortés conquers the Aztecs.
1532	Pizarro defeats the Incas.
1539–1542	Spanish explorer Hernando De Soto and 600 soldiers trek through what later becomes the southern United States.
1587	Sir Walter Raleigh founds Roanoke, off the coast of North Carolina.
1588	England defeats the Spanish Armada.
1607	The Virginia Company founds Jamestown.
1609–1610	Colonists in Jamestown suffer the "starving time," an extremely harsh winter.
1612	Colonist John Rolfe begins growing tobacco in Virginia.
1620	Pilgrims sail to America on the *Mayflower* and found the colony of Plymouth in Massachussetts. They also sign the Mayflower Compact, establishing their own government.
1629	The Massachusetts Bay Colony obtains a royal charter and elects John Winthrop as governor. Winthrop gives his "City upon a Hill" sermon.

1636	Roger Williams founds Providence in Rhode Island, the first settlement to legislate freedom of religion.
1662	Halfway Covenant enacted.
1664	English settlers conquer the Dutch settlement of New Netherlands and rename it New York.
1676	Bacon's Rebellion occurs.

MAJOR FIGURES

John Alden. Although not a Puritan himself, John Alden sailed across the Atlantic on the *Mayflower* with the Pilgrims and helped found and lead Plymouth Colony.

Nathaniel Bacon. A farmer and landowner, Bacon formed a loosely organized army and rose up against Native American camps in Virginia. Later known as Bacon's Rebellion, this was the first sign of colonial rebelling.

Jacques Cartier. A French explorer, Cartier made three early voyages into present-day Canada in the early 1500s.

Samuel de Champlain. A French explorer, Champlain founded "New France," present-day eastern Canada, in the 1600s.

Hernando Cortēs. A Spanish conquistador, Cortés conquered the Aztecs and took their capital of Tenochititlán (Mexico City) in 1521.

Christopher Columbus. An Italian explorer, Columbus discovered the New World in 1492 when he landed on an island in the Caribbean.

Hernando De Soto. A Spanish explorer and conquistador, De Soto trekked through the present-day southwest of the United States for Spain in the mid-1500s.

Francisco Pizarro. A Spanish explorer and conquistador, Pizarro conquered the Incas in the 1520s and claimed all the land from Panama to Peru for Spain.

Sir Walter Raleigh. Half-brother of Sir Humphrey Gilbert, Raleigh obtained a royal charter in 1587 to found the colony of Roanoke in Virginia. The colonists, however, mysteriously disappeared between the time of settlement and 1590.

John Rolfe. A colonist of Jamestown, Rolfe saved the colony in Virginia when he discovered tobacco. His discovery also gave England further cause to establish more colonies in North America. Rolfe also promoted peaceful relations with the Indians by marrying Pocahontas.

John Smith. A mercenary, Smith took command of the Jamestown colony in the early 1600s and thus saved the colonists from starvation and hostile Native Americans.

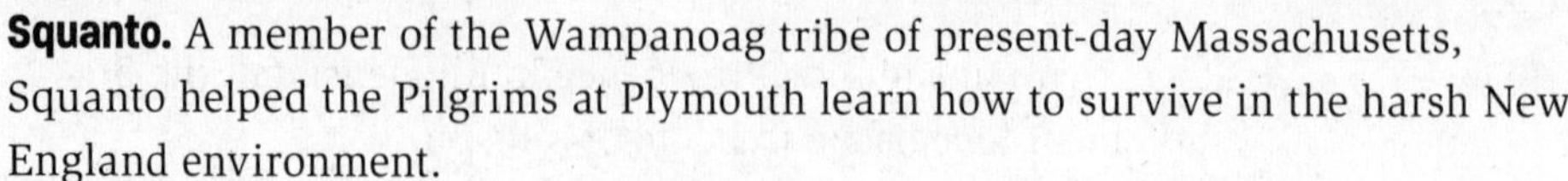
Squanto. A member of the Wampanoag tribe of present-day Massachusetts, Squanto helped the Pilgrims at Plymouth learn how to survive in the harsh New England environment.

Miles Standish. A soldier hired by the Puritans who sailed to North America on the *Mayflower*, Standish proved instrumental to the early success of Plymouth Plantation.

Amerigo Vespucci. An Italian explorer, Vespucci published a wildly popular account of his voyages in the New World near the North American continent in 1503. A German mapmaker named the newly discovered continents after him to honor his achievements.

Roger Williams. A cast-out from Puritan Salem and Plymouth because of his radical religious beliefs, Williams founded his own colony of Providence, which became the first permanent settlement in Rhode Island.

John Winthrop. A prosperous and respected lawyer and landowner, Winthrop served as the governor of the Massachusetts Bay Colony. He claimed that Americans stood distinct from Europeans and had an opportunity to usher in a new age for humanity in his famous "City upon the Hill" speech.

CHAPTER 2

Colonial Life: 1700–1763

SOUTHERN COLONIES

The southern colonies included Maryland, Virginia, North Carolina, South Carolina, and Georgia. These colonies all boasted plenty of good, cleared land and a mild climate conducive to growing staple and exotic cash crops. Tobacco became the staple crop and the economic foundation of Virginia and North Carolina. South Carolinian soil, though unfit for tobacco, was perfect for growing rice and indigo, a dye used to dye textiles blue. The southern colonies also produced lumber, tar, pitch, turpentine, furs, and cattle.

Work in the Southern Colonies

The production of cash crops required large amounts of land and a large work force. Colonists had plenty of land, but not enough labor. **Indentured servants** performed much of the labor during the early years of colonization. These servants, mostly paupers from England, Ireland, and Germany, got their name from the indenture, or contract, they signed, binding themselves to work for a period of four to seven years to pay for their transportation to the New World. Many of northern Europe's poor voluntarily indentured themselves in order to acquire their own land after their contract had been fulfilled. Indentured servants accounted for roughly half of all white settlers living in the colonies outside New England.

Until the latter half of the 1600s, white indentured servants were the dominant source of labor in the Americas, and it was not until the 1680s and 1690s that slave labor began to surpass the use of white indentured servants. Although **African slaves** cost more initially than indentured servants, they served for life and thus quickly became the labor force of choice on large plantations.

Life in the Early Colonial South

In the early 1600s, most southern colonists lived in utter poverty, and men outnumbered women three to one. Southern colonists suffered high mortality rates because of the many mosquito-borne illnesses that plagued the land. As a result, the average southern man could expect to live only forty years, while southern women usually did not live past their late thirties. Moreover, one-quarter of all children born in the southern colonies died in infancy, and half died before they reached adulthood. Most southern colonists lived in remote areas on farms or plantations with their families, extended relatives, friends, and slaves. The Anglican religion dominated the region, although most southerners did not attend church regularly, if at all.

By the 1700s, life had settled down for the southern colonists, and more rigid social classes had formed. A gentry, or wealthy upper class, emerged and built large plantation homes in an attempt to imitate the lives of the English upper crust. Many of the plantation owners relied heavily on credit to maintain their leisurely lifestyles.

NORTHERN COLONIES

The northern colonies included New Hampshire, Massachusetts, Rhode Island, Connecticut, New York, Pennsylvania, Delaware, and New Jersey. Whereas southerners lived in relative isolation from one another, northern colonial life revolved around townships. Villages formed around the church, and a central green area was usually created (often called "the commons") where important business and community activities took place. People built their houses around the town center, and town growth radiated out in concentric circles. As a result, community involvement and activity became a central feature of life in the North.

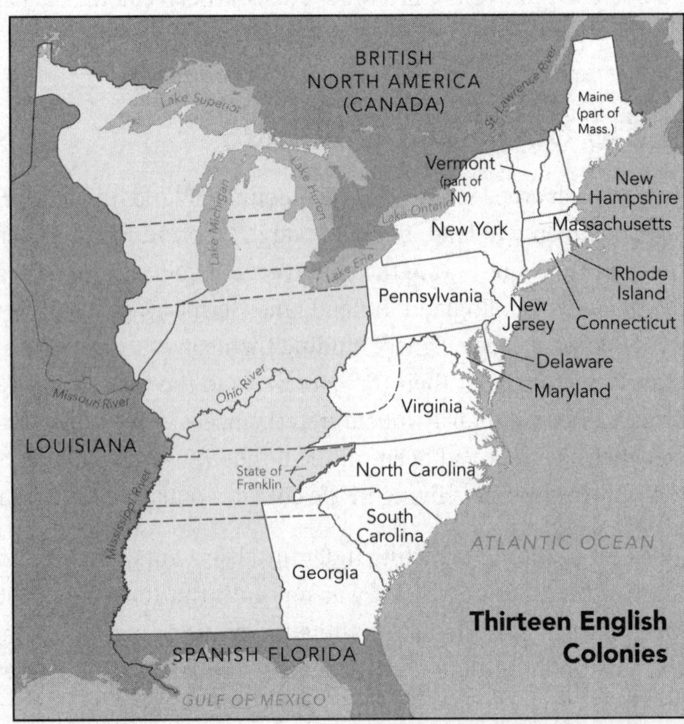

Thirteen English Colonies

Work in the Northern Colonies

Most of the land in the North was stony, sloped, and heavily forested, and people in the North couldn't sustain huge plantations as their southern neighbors could. Instead, families farmed small plots with the help of perhaps one or two servants or slaves. Additionally, the weather was too cold and harsh to support large-scale market crops. As a result, northern farmers grew crops mainly for their own consumption and sold any surplus at local markets. Crops such as barley, oats, and wheat were grown, and the colonists also raised cattle, pigs, and sheep. Many northerners became fishermen. Skilled artisans migrated to the northern colonies, developing industries that ultimately created a foundation for future manufacturing.

Ample water sources made possible the construction of mills to process grain, textiles, and lumber. In time, a strong merchant class emerged, bolstered by the shipping industry that developed in northern ports. As shipping grew, ship building also increased. Eventually, traders and bankers sprang up to run the manufacturing and shipping economy, and northern port cities such as Boston became central trading areas for the British in the Americas.

Life in the Early Colonial North

The northern climate was free of mosquitoes, so northerners enjoyed longer lives, usually living well into their sixties, as compared with their southern counterparts. Husbands and wives formed teams of production, with children adding to the number of workers. The single life was almost impossible, given both the religious climate and the physical rigors of life in general at the time.

In contrast to the southern colonies, religion permeated the lives of northern colonists and exercised a pervasive influence over the people. Towns and communities were built around the church, and in most colonies, the church and the state remained one, controlling many aspects of life. Puritans settled in New England, both separatists and reformists, and these rigid religions dominated the region.

The Salem Witch Trials

Increasing influences from the outside world, introduced by new immigrants, among other sources, strained northern society, as the tragedy of the 1692 **Salem witch trials** made clear. Salem had been settled by Puritan reformists, and, like most people in the North at this time, they still believed in the supernatural. By 1691, nearly 300 primarily middle-aged women in New England had been convicted of witchcraft. Of those, more than thirty were hanged.

The episode in Salem was far more intense than any other witch hunt in North America. It began during the winter of 1691–1692, when several adolescent girls accused three local women of practicing witchcraft. Similar accusations followed, and within a year nineteen women had been hanged, one man pressed to death under heavy stones, and more than one hundred others jailed.

New Roles for Women

Historians originally thought that local feuds and property disputes between the town of Salem proper and Salem Village caused the unrest. More recently, many historians have begun to believe that the trials resulted from the clash between two different sets of social values. Many of the accused women had in some way defied the traditional roles assigned to females. Some worked outside the home, while others did not attend church. Whatever the reason, no other similar outbreaks of mass hysteria occurred in New England.

COLONIAL CITIES

The thirteen British colonies developed separately and distinctly throughout the seventeenth century. In fact, the large cities of Boston, New York, Philadelphia, and Charleston had more contact with London than they did with one another. Traveling between cities on crude roads was both difficult and dangerous, which contributed to the isolation. However, taverns provided safe havens, overnight rest stops, and refueling stations. Colonists gathered in taverns to relax, drink, and gossip about politics and business. Many years later, these tendencies would prove vital to both the exchange of information about British injustices and the promotion of the efforts of the revolution.

Despite the fact that 90 percent of all colonists lived in townships and small villages in the countryside, the minority of city dwellers controlled commerce, dominated politics, and defined the cultural norms. Society was rigidly stratified in cities, with merchants at the top of the order; craftsmen, retailers, and innkeepers below them; and sailors, unskilled workers, and small artisans at the bottom. Over time, class stratification became more pronounced, and wealth became concentrated among a select few. All of the colonists, however, hungered for English luxury goods. Imports increased through the years as the Americans purchased more and more goods such as mirrors, silver-plated items, spices, linens, wigs, clocks, tea sets, books, and other household items.

SLAVERY

Slavery had virtually disappeared in Western Europe by the 1500s, and only Spain and Portugal still practiced slavery. Unfortunately, they brought slavery with them to the New World, where it established a strong foothold.

The First Slave Traders

The Portuguese were the first Europeans to trade with Africa and the first to reap the enormous profits to be made in the slave trade. By the time Columbus sailed for the Americas, the Portuguese had taken about 25,000 Africans to work on sugar plantations. The Spanish recognized the labor potential of slaves and began importing them to the New World to mine for gold and silver.

The Middle Passage

Other European countries also became involved in the slave trade. In addition to the Spanish and Portuguese, the English, French, and Dutch actively bought and sold Africans into slavery. These Europeans used extreme violence and brutal tactics to acquire their slaves.

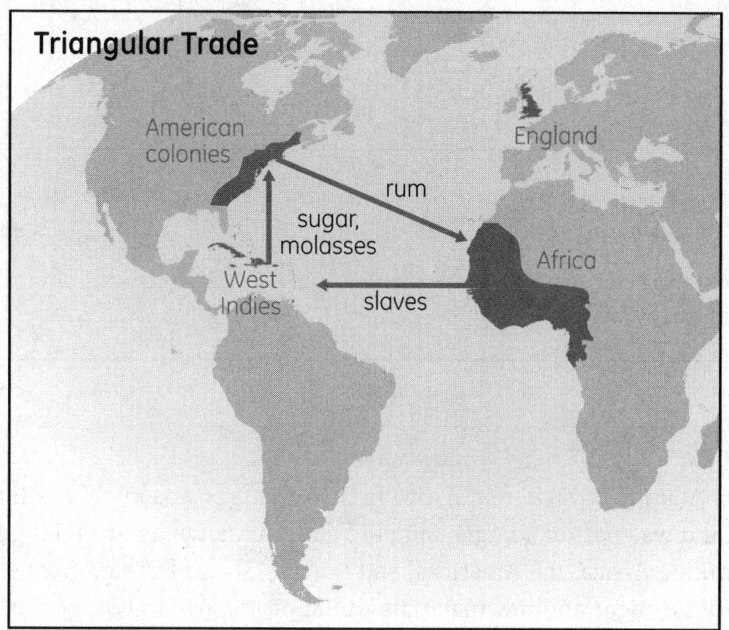

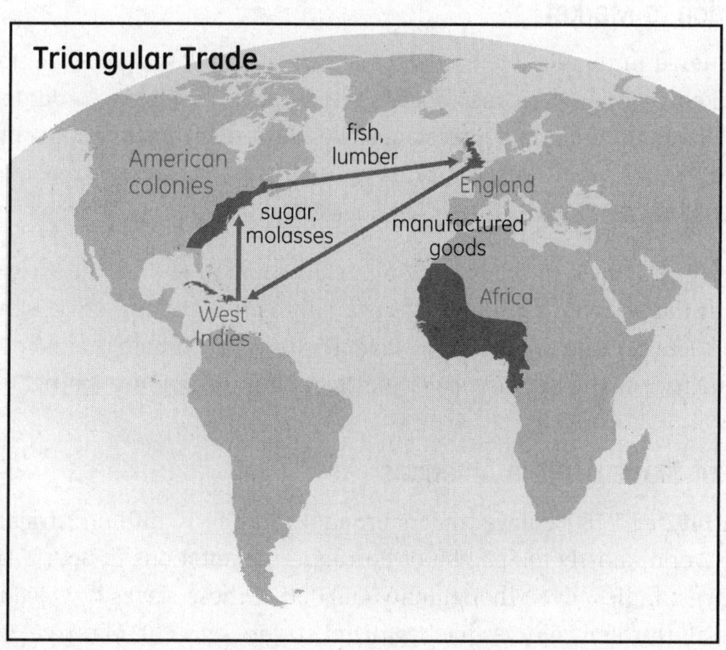

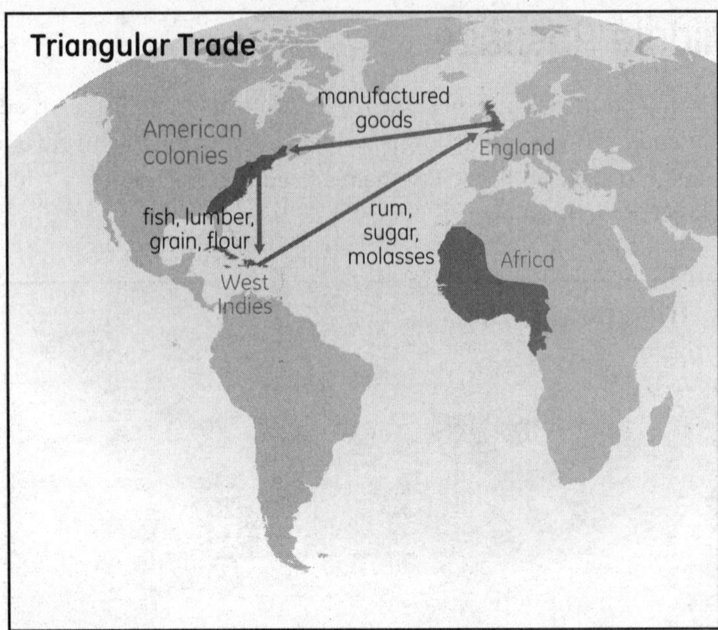

The Triangular Trade

The trans-Atlantic voyage from Africa to the Americas was known as the **Middle Passage** and was part of a larger shipping pattern known as the **Triangular Trade**, linking Africa, the Americas, and Europe. Slaves traveled from Africa to the Americas; sugar and raw materials would be shipped to Europe; tobacco, timber, and foodstuffs would be shipped from North America to the West Indies.

From Africa to Market

Slaves suffered unimaginable hardships on the Middle Passage. Slave traders often packed as many Africans aboard their ships as possible in order to maximize profits. In addition to depression, slaves suffered from smallpox, measles, gonorrhea, syphilis, yellow fever, scurvy, and dysentery. On average, about 12.5 percent of the captive slaves died during the voyage.

Once they had arrived in the New World, slaves had to endure the **"seasoning"** process, or the period ranging from a few months to a year in which slavers prepared them for sale and life as a slave. Historians estimate that 30 percent of imported Africans died of disease or maltreatment during "seasoning."

Growth of Slavery in the Americas

Between 1492 and 1808, slave traders brought roughly 10 million Africans to the New World, mostly to Spanish or Portuguese plantations in South America and the West Indies. Even though only 400,000 of these slaves traveled to North America, all thirteen colonies had legalized slavery by 1750. Many colonial farmers came to prefer slavery as rising wages in England made it more and more difficult to find indentured servants.

In time, slavery became more acceptable and developed into a key aspect of the economy and American society. States developed laws to keep African Americans under control: Whipping, branding, dismembering, castrating, or killing a slave became legal under certain circumstances. Laws also stripped slaves of the freedom of movement, freedom of assembly, and the right to earn money or pursue an education. White Americans feared a slave rebellion above all else, especially considering that slaves outnumbered whites in some areas. Slave revolts in Charleston, South Carolina (1739), and New York City (1741) fueled these fears.

THE ENLIGHTENMENT

During the flurry of exploration and colonization in North America in the seventeenth and eighteenth centuries, Europe was experiencing a scientific revolution known as the **Enlightenment**. Scientists had abandoned the old Ptolemaic view of an earth-centered universe in favor of Copernicus's heliocentric (sun-centered) model. Isaac Newton had published his theory of gravitation, which laid the foundation for a scientific vision of the universe and argued that events occur in accordance with natural laws. More important, people were using reason and the study of mathematics to understand the working of the universe and the world around them.

Philosophers of the Enlightenment such as John Locke believed that the American experience embodied the ideas of the Enlightenment. The old barriers of birth and wealth did not apply as much in the New World as they did in Europe, and people of all classes could succeed if they worked hard.

John Locke's Contract Theory of Government

John Locke applied the new scientific understandings of the world first presented in the Enlightenment to the study of society and government. Locke came up with an idea he called the **Theory of Contract under Natural Law**, in which he argued that kings and queens did not hold their positions because of God's divine will but because of an accident of birth. In other words, kings had simply gotten lucky. Locke further explained that all humans had certain natural rights, such as the rights to life, liberty, and property, and that no government could deny its constituents these rights.

Locke's theory on government had an enormous influence on American political thought. Locke argued that the people "contracted" with the government to protect their interests. If the government failed to do so, then the government had broken the contract and should be disbanded. Colonists quickly picked up on this idea, eventually using it to justify the American Revolution against England. In fact, Thomas Jefferson used very similar language in the Declaration of Independence when he wrote that everyone had the right to "life, liberty," and the pursuit of happiness."

Benjamin Franklin

Benjamin Franklin, one of the "founding fathers" of the country, personified the ideas of the Enlightenment. Franklin owned his own print shop, published his own newspaper, and had published his *Poor Richard's Almanac* all by the time he had turned twenty-six. Franklin's business was so successful that he retired when he was only forty-two, and he devoted the rest of his life to science and public service. Among other things, Franklin did the following:

- Founded a library and invented a new kind of stove
- Started an academy that eventually became the University of Pennsylvania
- Formed a debating club that eventually became the American Philosophical Society
- Wrote a treatise entitled *Experiments and Observations on Electricity,* based on his own electrical experiments
- Studied medicine, meteorology, geology, astronomy, and physics
- Served his country as the colonial agent in London and then as the American ambassador to France during the Revolutionary War
- Served as a representative at the Continental Congresses and the Constitutional Convention

---

Franklin was a living example of Locke's ideas of the possibilities that society and government had to offer.

THE GREAT AWAKENING

With so many new scientific and philosophical ideas springing out of the Enlightenment, many American colonists turned away from religion. In the 1730s, however, a renewed spirit of evangelism swept through the colonies in the Great Awakening. In an attempt to reassert the doctrines of Puritanism, the leading preachers and theologians of the **Great Awakening** appealed very strongly to colonists' emotions.

George Whitefield

The Great Awakening began in different cities in the colonies, but all the revivals shared a high level of emotionalism. Preachers such as **George Whitefield** tried to replace the cold and unfeeling doctrines of Puritanism with a religion more accessible to the average person. The twenty-seven-year-old Wesleyan minister noted upon arriving in the colonies from England that American congregations lacked passion because "dead men preach to them."

Planning to reignite the fires of religion in the New World, Whitefield settled in Philadelphia in 1739 and began attracting crowds of more than 6,000 people. Before long, he was holding revivals from as far south as Georgia all the way up to New England. Young and charismatic, Whitefield staged performances for his audiences by acting out the miseries of hell and the joys of salvation. People flocked from miles around to hear him speak, and he urged them to experience a "new birth," or a sudden, emotional moment of conversion and forgiveness of sin. Audiences swooned with anticipation of God's grace, some people writhing, some laughing out loud, and some crying out for help.

Jonathan Edwards

Jonathan Edwards was another noteworthy preacher and theologian during the Great Awakening. He believed that his parishioners, especially the young, lived too freely, spending their time drinking and carousing while the older churchgoers had become preoccupied with making and spending money. Edwards wanted to touch the hearts of those in his congregation and "fright persons away from hell." He would therefore fill his sermons with vivid descriptions of the torments of hell and the pleasures of heaven. By 1735, he reported that "the town seemed to be full of the presence of God; it never was so full of love, nor of joy."

Unlike Whitefield, Edwards never resorted to theatrics; instead, he entranced audiences with the seriousness of his message, as in his most famous sermon **"Sinners in the Hands of an Angry God,"** which marked the pinnacle of the Great Awakening movement and is recognized as one of the most famous sermons in American history.

Impact of the Great Awakening

The Great Awakening had an enormous impact in the American colonies, especially along the western frontier and in the South. Common folk responded with great enthusiasm, and the Baptists and the Methodists, two popular Protestant denominations, grew enormously as a result.

Ironically, even though revivalists such as Whitefield and Edwards had hoped they would encourage a more pious lifestyle, the colonists concluded that salvation was available to all, not merely to a few chosen elect, as the Puritans had always claimed. Consequently, the Great Awakening helped democratize religion in the colonies and ultimately took power away from churches and ministers. Moreover, the Great Awakening renewed interest in intellectualism and prompted the founding of new universities and the distribution of books.

BRITISH RULE

By the 1750s, the American colonists, feeling more unified by such intellectual currents as the Enlightenment and the Great Awakening, had developed a unique culture of their own. Although the individual colonies developed distinctive religious, social, and demographic characteristics, they all shared a basic sense of unity that grew stronger through the coming years of economic and political upheaval.

The colonists had effectively governed themselves throughout most of the seventeenth and eighteenth centuries. For the most part, the British government had left the colonists to fend for themselves during this **Age of Salutary Neglect**, neither imposing new taxes nor enforcing those on the books. Therefore, the colonists resented Britain's attempts to exert more influence over the colonies in the mid-1700s.

British Trade with the Colonies

Although the British had granted the colonies a fair amount of autonomy, they had always attempted to control trade to and from North America. The British imposed laws and taxes to ensure that all trade with the colonies would benefit Britain and to ensure that the colonists could not take trade matters into their own hands.

The Mercantile System

Under the Mercantile System, power and wealth went hand in hand. In other words, the leaders of mercantilist countries (countries with large import and export operations) believed that power derived from a full national treasury. To acquire and keep gold and silver, the mercantilist powers had to limit foreign imports and preserve a favorable balance of trade. To do this, England, France, Spain, Portugal, and the Netherlands did the following:

- Encouraged their domestic manufacturers to produce as many goods as possible
- Developed and protected their own shipping industry
- Acquired colonies to provide raw materials
- Sold finished manufactured goods to the colonists

Under mercantilism, great powers needed to acquire colonies to produce raw materials such as grain, sugar, rice, timber, and tobacco. Each colony also provided the mother country with an exclusive market for its manufactured goods.

To safeguard its monopoly in North America, Britain began regulating colonial trade in the 1660s and declared that Americans could only ship their products directly to England. Royal officials could then levy taxes on those goods before shippers sent them elsewhere.

Navigation Acts

The **Navigation Act of 1660** marked England's first real attempt to regulate colonial trade by stipulating that all goods exported from the colonies had to be carried on English ships. The act also declared that colonists could only trade certain raw materials, such as sugar, cotton, tobacco, wood, pitch, and tar, with England or other British colonies. The **Second Navigation Act of 1663** required that colonial ships unload their cargo upon arriving in England so that each item could be taxed.

Restraining Acts

The **Restraining Acts of 1699** followed the Navigation Acts and protected manufacturers in England by banning factories in the colonies. Although colonial industry hadn't even begun to develop by this point, Britain didn't want colonial manufacturers to compete with domestic manufacturers in England. The Restraining Act also banned the export of woolen products in order to protect the English wool industry and later forbade the export of beaver hats and processed iron.

The Colonists' Response

Most colonists willingly complied with the Navigation and Restraining Acts, simply happy they had achieved a relatively high standard of living in such a short amount of time. More important, the restrictions on manufacturing affected few Americans because manufacturing hadn't ever taken root.

Moreover, the mercantile system showered the colonists with benefits. Even though the British levied taxes on American raw materials, they also kept prices on those materials high by eliminating foreign competition. Britain even paid subsidies to American shipbuilders and tobacco and rice farmers. In short, both sides benefited handsomely from the arrangement.

The Molasses Act

Despite economic benefits, some colonists had begun to complain about their subservient position within the mercantile system by the 1730s. The Navigation and Restraining Acts hit those who conducted trade in the West Indies hardest. In 1733, Britain passed the **Molasses Act** to curtail colonial trade with the West Indies by imposing a huge tax on sugar and molasses imported into the colonies. The act would have seriously disrupted colonial trade, but the royal officials in North America never strictly enforced it. This wavering policy led many Americans to question Britain's intentions and wisdom regarding the regulation of colonial trade.

Colonial Governments

King George III owned all the colonies, but Americans enjoyed an unprecedented degree of autonomy. All but one of the colonies had erected its own government with a bicameral legislature comprising an upper and lower house. The king appointed a governor and the members of the upper house in eight of the thirteen colonies. Wealthy land-owning colonists chose the members of the lower house. The colonies of Pennsylvania, Delaware, and Maryland were owned by individuals. These individuals, such as William Penn in Pennsylvania, held the royal charter and appointed legislators. In the corporate colonies of Rhode Island and Connecticut, owned by joint stock companies, wealthy land-owning white men elected all government officials.

Voting and Representation

Colonial governments modeled themselves after the English system with two exceptions:

- A greater percentage of the population could vote in the colonies than in England.
- The colonists rejected the British concept of **"virtual representation."** In England, elected members of Parliament claimed to represent all their constituents because they supposedly represented the interests of all royal subjects no matter where they lived. The colonists disagreed; they felt that delegates should represent only those who had elected them.

All in all, the representative colonial legislatures enjoyed a great deal of freedom, and the king permitted the autonomy as long as colonial laws didn't interfere with Parliament's.

THE FRENCH AND INDIAN WAR

For most of the colonial period, Britain and France remained at peace with each other, their colonial empires developing in relative isolation. Beginning in the 1680s, however, the European powers waged several wars for control of North America:

- The War of the Palatinate (King William's War), from 1689 to 1697 in New England and Canada
- The War of the Spanish Succession (Queen Anne's War), from 1702 to 1713 throughout the western frontier of the colonies from St. Augustine in Florida to New England

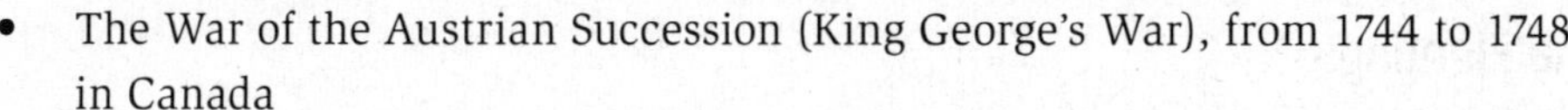

- The War of the Austrian Succession (King George's War), from 1744 to 1748 in Canada
- The Seven Years' War (the French and Indian War, which actually lasted nine years in the colonies), from 1754 to 1763 throughout New England and Canada

---

The British and American colonists fought side by side against the French in all four wars, gaining much western land and parts of Canada as a result.

The French in America

The French established their presence in the New World in the 1670s. Their mercantilist empire spanned from India to Africa to the Americas. The French king expected his North American settlers to export furs and grains back to France and then purchase French manufactured goods. By 1682, the French had sailed from Canada down the Mississippi, claiming land on both sides of the river and founding the city of New Orleans.

By 1743, the French had reached the Rocky Mountains and had claimed the entire interior of North America for themselves. To consolidate their claim, they built a string of forts that ran from Quebec to Detroit and down to New Orleans. The British, however, refused to recognize French territorial claims or the legality of the forts.

Indian Alliances

Both the British and the French knew that they would need the help of the local Native Americans with the skirmishes in the Americas. The British had established effective trading practices with the native tribes, but the French promised them friendship and equality and demonstrated a greater sensitivity to the Native Americans' cultures. French fur trappers, for example, frequently married Indian women and adopted native customs, while the Jesuit priests refrained from using force when trying to convert them to Catholicism.

The War Begins

The **French and Indian War** (known in Europe as the Seven Years' War) began in 1754 when the governor of Virginia sent a young lieutenant colonel in the Virginia militia named **George Washington** to warn the French that the disputed Ohio Valley territory had been settled at France's peril. Washington carried the message to a French fort but was rebuffed. Soon afterward, he organized a force of volunteers, defeated a small French garrison, and built a modest outpost he called Fort Necessity. The French returned in greater numbers and attacked the fort, eventually forcing Washington to surrender and withdraw to Virginia. Washington's surrender triggered a series of Indian raids along the frontier, in which the Native Americans sought revenge for 150 years of bad treatment by the British.

The Fighting

Fighting raged for two years between the British and the French in the colonies before the war erupted in Europe. In 1756, the colonial war finally spilled over into Europe, when Austria and Russia and eventually Spain formed an alliance with France. Britain allied with Prussia in return. King George II named William Pitt the head of the war ministry, and Pitt tried to keep the focus of the war in North America. He sent large numbers of British troops to the colonies but also encouraged the colonists to enlist, demanding that they defend themselves against the French. Pitt's tactics worked, and the British eventually gained the upper hand. France simply couldn't match Britain's powerful navy or the number of troops stationed in North America.

The French and Indian War climaxed in 1759 when the British defeated the French at Quebec and effectively eliminated France's influence in North America. News of the battle reached London along with news of a similar victory in India, in which British forces had significantly reduced the number of French outposts. Outgunned and outnumbered, France formally surrendered in the Americas in September 1760. It took three more years before Britain could declare victory in Europe.

The War Ends

The **Treaty of Paris**, or Peace of Paris, ended the French and Indian War and gave Britain undisputed control over all of Canada and almost all of present-day United States, from the Atlantic to the Rockies. Britain decided to keep everything east of the Mississippi and gave Spain everything west of the Mississippi, including the key port city of New Orleans in exchange for Florida. Britain also gained control of several former French colonies in the Caribbean. In short, Britain reigned supreme over North America east of the Mississippi after the conclusion of the war.

Impact on the Colonies

The French and Indian War had a tremendous impact on the colonists and on England. Britain's debt skyrocketed because it had had to borrow so much to fund the war, and Parliament decided to raise colonial taxes to pay off that debt. At the same time, Pitt's insistence that the colonists defend themselves added to the colonists' sense of independence from England. Success on the battlefield contributed to the colonists' belief that their reliance on England was coming to an end. Ultimately, the war boosted the new Americans' sense of unity and distinctiveness from Britain.

TIMELINE: 1692–1763

1692	Several people are tried and convicted of witchcraft in Salem, Massachusetts.
1699	Britain passes the Restraining Acts to restrict manufacturing in the North American colonies.
1714	George I takes the British throne, beginning the Hanover dynasty.
1733	Britain passes the Molasses Act to tax sugar, and molasses is imported into British colonies.
1734	The Great Awakening begins.
1739	A gathering of slaves headed for the South kill more than twenty whites in the Stono Rebellion in South Carolina.
	George Whitefield begins preaching in America.
1741	Jonathan Edwards, a leading theologian, preaches his famous "Sinners in the Hands of an Angry God" sermon.
1743	Benjamin Franklin sets up the American Philosophical Society.
1750	Slavery is legalized in all thirteen British colonies.
1755	The French and Indian War begins.
	Franklin's Albany Plan, which sought to link all thirteen colonies in a loose union, is rejected.
1759	Britain captures Quebec.
1763	The Treaty of Paris ends the French and Indian War.

MAJOR FIGURES

Jonathan Edwards. An eighteenth-century theologian and philosopher, Edwards delivered rousing speeches throughout the American colonies during the Great Awakening to frighten colonists into worshipping God. Historians consider his most famous speech, "Sinners in the Hands of an Angry God," to be one of the most influential sermons in American history.

Benjamin Franklin. A founding father and example of an Enlightened soul, Franklin ran a successful publishing company, published several scientific treatises, made significant advances in the field of science and medicine, and served as the U.S. ambassador to France during the Revolutionary War.

John Locke. A philosopher of the Enlightenment, Locke theorized that people enter into contracts with their governments to ensure the protection of their natural rights. His ideas formed much of the intellectual backbone that justified the American Revolution.

George Washington. A young Virginia planter and militia officer, Washington served in the French and Indian War in 1754. He later became commander in chief of the American forces during the Revolutionary War and first president of the United States in 1789. Although he lost most of the battles he fought, his leadership skills were unparalleled and were integral to the creation of the United States.

George Whitefield. A dynamic minister during the Great Awakening, Whitefield relied on dramatics to scare people into believing in God.

Chapter 3

Seeking Independence: 1763–1783

EMERGENCE OF AMERICAN NATIONALISM

The American colonists were jubilant at the end of the French and Indian War in 1763, celebrating both their defeat of the French and the resulting access to the unexplored western frontier. With a new sense of confidence as they looked out across the vast and fertile new territory, Americans saw their future. However, obstacles remained in the colonists' path as they sought to claim the land and the freedom that they believed was rightfully theirs.

Pontiac's Rebellion

Although Britain and the colonists had defeated the French and Native American forces in 1763, they continued to fight Native Americans along the western frontier for several more years. Many of the tribes in the Ohio Valley banded together under the leadership of Ottawa chief **Pontiac**, a former ally of the French who resented American colonial encroachments on Indian lands.

By October, Pontiac's men had killed more than 2,000 British soldiers and American settlers and destroyed all but three British outposts in the region. Pontiac eventually signed a peace treaty in 1766, but the British knew that more conflict would arise as long as colonial farmers kept pushing westward in search of new land.

The Proclamation of 1763

To prevent further bloodshed between whites and Indians, Britain issued the **Proclamation of 1763**, which prohibited colonists from settling west of the Appalachian Mountains. Only licensed trappers and traders would be allowed to venture farther, while those colonists who'd already settled beyond the mountains would have to relocate.

Although Britain had hoped the proclamation would help and protect Americans, most colonists were outraged at the policy, especially after they had shed so much blood during the war to win the land in the first place. In addition, many Americans believed that despite the proclamation, they had the right to expand westward. Feeling bitterly betrayed, many hardy colonists ignored the proclamation and crossed into the Ohio Valley anyway.

British War Debt

Britain's victory in the French and Indian War had cost a fortune, nearly bankrupting the government. To refill the treasury and pay off debts owed to creditors, Prime Minister **George Grenville** convinced Parliamentarians to raise taxes both at home and in the colonies. Even though Britons paid significantly higher taxes than the Americans, colonists balked at the thought of higher taxes. They also resented **King George III**'s decision to permanently station 10,000 British regulars in North America to control his newly acquired territories.

The Sugar Act. The first tax hike came in 1764 when Parliament passed the Sugar Act to tax molasses and other imports, such as textiles, wines, coffee, indigo, and sugar. Colonists, of course, hated the Sugar Act because it was the first tax Parliament had ever levied on them solely to raise revenue.

The Currency Act. Parliament also passed the Currency Act in 1764, which prohibited the colonists from printing their own cheap paper money. The Currency Act, combined with new taxes and stricter enforcement, shocked the American economy.

The Stamp Act Crisis of 1765. Although the Sugar and Currency Acts did increase revenue, Britain needed much more money in order to pay off war debts and keep troops posted in the colonies. To make up the difference, Grenville next proposed the Stamp Act to tax printed matter and legal documents in the colonies, such as newspapers, pamphlets, almanacs, bonds, licenses, deeds, diplomas, and even playing cards. Americans despised the Stamp Act more than the Sugar Act or the Currency Act because it taxed items they deemed necessities. More important, they also hated the tax because it challenged colonial assemblies' exclusive power to levy internal taxes.

Quartering Act. Parliament passed the **Quartering Act** in 1765, forcing colonists to supply, feed, and house the unwanted British soldiers, even in their own homes if necessary. Colonists resented this act as a direct affront to their civil rights and personal liberties.

The Regulator Movement

Following the American colonial tradition of self-government, groups of backcountry settlers in North Carolina sought to restore law and order and establish institutions of local government. Named the **Regulators**, these citizens, led by both wealthy planters and small farmers, created their own association in 1767 to "regulate" legal issues in the backcountry sections of the colony. Upset by unruly bands of outlaws and disgusted with the colonial assembly's failure to establish a level of legal stability, they arrested criminals and established local courts to end legal disputes. Colonial governors and legislatures allowed this form of vigilante justice to operate, recognizing the Regulators' authority in the western regions of the colonies. The use of violence eventually alienated many former supporters, however, and seven leaders were executed by order of governor William Tryon in 1771, ending the Regulator Movement.

The Issue of Representation

Many Americans protested under the cry of **"No taxation without representation!"** Prime Minister Grenville shot back that all members of Parliament represented the interests of all British subjects in the empire no matter where they lived. Colonial critics ridiculed this doctrine of **"virtual representation,"** believing that a small body of men could never satisfactorily represent people they knew nothing about.

The Sons of Liberty

A group of educated colonists known as the **Sons of Liberty** began to hold meetings in public places under trees they dubbed "Liberty Trees" to discuss the Stamp Act and possible courses of action. They eventually organized a massive **Stamp Act Protest** in Boston in August 1765 and burned Boston's stamp agent in effigy as it swung from the city's Liberty Tree. Riotous mobs later destroyed the stamp office and ransacked the homes of the local customs officer and royal governor, Thomas Hutchinson. Colonists also terrorized royal tax collectors to the point that many of the collectors fled the colonies to return to England.

Building Colonial Unity

Opposition to the Stamp Act united colonists, who initiated a widespread **boycott** of British goods in the hopes that desperate British manufacturers would pressure Parliament to repeal the tax. Mutual opposition to the Stamp Act also made colonists realize that they had more in common with each other than they did with Britons. To foster colonial unity, the Massachusetts House of Representatives issued a letter inviting the different colonial assemblies to a meeting. Nine of the colonies responded and sent delegates to New York to attend the **Stamp Act Congress** in October of 1765.

The twenty-seven men who gathered at the congress registered their complaints in the **Declaration of the Rights and Grievances of the Colonies**, petitioning King George III and Parliament to repeal the Stamp Act. Under pressure from

British manufacturers and unwilling to enforce the collection of an incredibly unpopular tax, Parliament ultimately consented and repealed the Stamp Act. At the same time, however, it quietly passed the **Declaratory Act**, asserting Parliament's right to tax the colonies in "all cases whatsoever." The Declaratory Act allowed Parliament to save face and provided a temporary solution to the brewing crisis.

RESISTANCE BECOMES REBELLION

In 1767, Parliament passed the **Townshend Acts,** which levied taxes on virtually all imports entering the colonies from Great Britain. Although the taxes did increase revenue, they sparked another round of fiery protests from the colonists.

Samuel Adams Fuels the Revolution

The ardent Bostonian revolutionary and Son of Liberty **Samuel Adams** launched a citywide propaganda campaign to protest the Townshend taxes. He distributed pamphlets, letters, and essays on the injustices of British rule, all of which quickly spread throughout the colonies. Within just a few years, colonists in most every major city and town from the South to New England had formed their own campaigns.

The Boston Massacre

Bostonians hated royal encroachments on colonial liberties and took their resentment out on the British soldiers garrisoned in the city. Crowds taunted and jeered at the troops for months until the tense situation finally exploded. On March 5, 1770, several British soldiers fired into a crowd of rock-throwing colonists, killing five Bostonians. News of the **Boston Massacre** spread rapidly through the colonies. Hoping to avoid further bloodshed, Parliament repealed all the Townshend duties except for the tax on tea, mostly as a symbol of royal authority.

Taxing Tea

The new Prime Minister, Frederick Lord North, eventually, even drastically, reduced this last tax on tea in order to help the failing East India Company unload its surplus of tea. North also believed that the tax reduction would appease the Americans and restore good relations between Britain and the colonies. Yet colonists resented the reduced tax because they believed it was a British trick to bribe the colonies, grant a monopoly to the East India Company,

and ultimately control all colonial trade. Many worried that if Britain successfully regulated the tea trade, they might also try to control other commodities in the future.

The Boston Tea Party

Rebels such as Sam Adams churned out more propaganda in response to the reduced tax and urged colonists to boycott tea. Port officials throughout the colonies refused to allow East India Company tea ships to unload their cargoes, forcing them to sail back to England. In Boston, however, Governor Hutchinson wouldn't allow the tea ships to return, either, forcing them to remain in port.

The Bostonian Sons of Liberty ended the stalemate on the night of December 16, 1773, when, disguised as Mohawk Indians, they boarded the tea ships and threw several hundred chests of tea into the harbor. Several hundred spectators watched the **Boston Tea Party** unfold and wondered how Britain would respond to such blatant defiance of royal authority.

The Intolerable Coercive Acts

Outraged, King George III and Parliament immediately passed the **Coercive Acts** to punish Bostonians and exact payment for the thousands of pounds of lost tea. These acts included:

- **The Boston Port Act**, which closed Boston Harbor until the city had repaid the East India Company for the tea. The act paralyzed Boston's maritime economy.
- A new **Quartering Act** requiring Bostonians to house and feed several thousand British soldiers sent to enforce the Coercive Acts.
- **The Massachusetts Government Act**, which cancelled city elections and indefinitely closed town meetings.

Britain hoped their harsh punishment would make an example of Boston and convince Americans in the other colonies to obey the Crown in the future. Instead, the Coercive Acts fostered a greater sense of unity among the thirteen colonies because many thought the punishment too great for the crime. Colonists everywhere rallied to Boston's aid, delivering food and winter supplies from as far away as Georgia.

British Acts and Colonial Response	
British Act	**Colonial Response**
Writs of Assistance, 1760	Challenged laws in Massachusetts Supreme Court, lost case
Sugar Act, 1764	Weak protest by colonial legislatures
Stamp Act, 1765	Virginia Resolves, mobs, Sons of Liberty, Stamp Act Congress
Townshend Duties, 1767	*Letters from a Pennsylvania Farmer,* boycott, Boston Massacre
Tea Act, 1773	Boston Tea Party
Intolerable Acts, 1773	First Continental Congress

The First Continental Congress

Most colonial leaders agreed that the Coercive Acts required a unified response from all of the colonies. Twelve colonies (Georgia abstaining) sent a total of fifty-five delegates to the **First Continental Congress** in Philadelphia in 1774 to draft an official protest. A few of the delegates hoped the Congress would become a colonial parliament of sorts and proposed measures that would lead to colonial government, but the majority rejected their proposals. Most delegates wanted Congress only to resolve the brewing crisis in Boston, not to establish a colonial government or start a rebellion.

Declaration of American Rights

Delegates at the First Continental Congress drafted the **Declaration of American Rights** in 1774, which declared that Parliament had no authority over internal colonial affairs. They also created the **Continental Association** to coordinate a stricter boycott on all British goods throughout the colonies. Association committees eventually became the backbone of the Revolution.

An infuriated King George III heard of the colonial meeting and the Declaration of American Rights and remarked, "New England colonies are in a state of rebellion," and that "blows must decide whether they are to be subject to this country or independent."

THE REVOLUTION BEGINS

By 1775, resentment toward Britain had calcified into the desire for rebellion. Many cities and towns organized volunteer militias that drilled openly in public common areas while King George III grew increasingly intolerant of American resistance to royal authority.

Lexington and Concord

On April 15, 1775, a British commander dispatched troops to arrest Samuel Adams and John Hancock and to seize the arsenal of weapons cached in Concord, Massachusetts. Militiamen from nearby Lexington intercepted them and opened fire. Eight Americans died as the British sliced through the line and moved on to Concord. The **redcoats** arrived in Concord, however, only to find the Concord militia waiting for them. Militiamen fired their muskets from the protection of the forest trees and stone walls into the organized columns of bright red uniforms, killing seventy British soldiers and forcing the British to retreat back to Boston.

The Second Continental Congress

Almost immediately after the **Battle of Lexington and Concord**, thousands of militiamen surrounded Boston to prevent the British troops from leaving. Meanwhile, delegates from all thirteen colonies gathered once again in Philadelphia at the **Second Continental Congress** to discuss the battle and its consequences. Because most delegates still desired reconciliation with King George III and Parliament, they agreed to sign a petition professing their love for King George III in a document called the **Olive Branch Petition**. They beseeched the king to recall the troops in Boston to restore peace between the colonies and Britain. King George III ultimately rejected the petition. After the British defeat at the Battle of Bunker Hill, King George III officially declared the colonies in a state of rebellion. Any hope of reconciliation and a return to the pre-1763 status quo had vanished.

Washington Takes Command

Even though delegates at the Second Continental Congress had signed the Olive Branch Petition, they also agreed to bolster colonial defenses in case of war. They set aside funds to organize an army and a small navy and also selected **George Washington** to command the newly christened **Continental Army** surrounding Boston.

Independence

Their Olive Branch petition rejected, delegates at the Second Continental Congress finally elected to declare independence from Britain on July 2, 1776. They then selected **Thomas Jefferson** to draft the congress's official **Declaration of Independence**.

Life, Liberty, and the Pursuit of Happiness

Jefferson kept the Declaration relatively short because he wanted it to be direct, clear, and forceful:

> We hold these truths to be self-evident, that all men are created equal, that they are endowed by their Creator with certain unalienable rights, that among these are Life, Liberty, and the pursuit of Happiness.

Drawing from the writings of John Locke, Jefferson argued that governments exist in order to protect the rights of the people and that the people have a right and even a duty to overthrow governments that fail their mandate.

A Long Train of Abuses

Jefferson further justified the Revolution by detailing King George III's "abuses and usurpations" against the American colonies, including the following:

- Shutting down representative colonial legislatures
- Refusing to allow the colonies to govern themselves
- Assuming judicial powers and manipulating the court system
- Conspiring with Native Americans against the colonists
- Restricting trade
- Imposing unjust taxes
- Coercing American sailors to work on British ships
- Taking military actions against Americans
- Refusing to allow colonists to redress grievances

Jefferson argued that the colonists should establish a new government as the United States of America in order to protect their rights.

AMERICANS IN REVOLT

All thirteen colonies immediately prepared for war after the Battle of Lexington and Concord. New militias formed throughout America, usually for the sole purpose of defending local communities from British aggression. Other units, however, rushed to join their comrades, who were cornered by British troops in Boston. Under the strict command of George Washington, Nathaniel Greene, and the German Baron von Steuben, this ragtag collection of undisciplined militiamen eventually became the well-trained **Continental army**.

Common Sense

The radical English author and philosopher **Thomas Paine** helped turn American public opinion against Great Britain and solidify the emerging colonial unity. In

January 1776, he published *Common Sense,* a pamphlet that denounced King George III as a tyrannical "brute." He called on Americans to unite and overthrow British rule so that they could usher in an era of freedom for humanity. Within only a few months of its first printing, Americans had purchased more than 100,000 copies of the pamphlet.

Women in the War

Most American women supported the war effort as well. Some particularly daring women chose to serve as nurses, attendants, cooks, spies, and even as combatants on the battlefields. The majority of women, however, fought the war at home by managing the family farms and businesses. Making yarn and homespun necessities such as socks and underwear to send to militiamen and supporting the boycott on British goods were significant contributions by female Americans.

Sadly, the Founding Fathers never recognized women's tremendous wartime efforts. Despite Abigail Adams's private plea to her husband, John Adams, to "remember the ladies" when making new laws, women didn't receive the right to vote or to even own property at war's end.

The Loyalists

Although most Americans supported the decision to break away from Great Britain and declare independence, about one-fifth of the colonists chose to remain loyal to the Crown. Some, including many lawyers, Anglican clergymen, and royal officials, felt that challenging British rule was unconscionable, while others simply wished to maintain the status quo. **Loyalists** lived throughout America but, the majority lived in the lower southern colonies. More than 100,000 Loyalists fled to Canada, England, and the West Indies before and during the war. Loyalists who stayed in the colonies faced persecution and even death.

Native Americans

Most Native Americans were particularly afraid of future American expansion onto their lands and therefore sided with Great Britain in the war. The influential Mohawk chief **Joseph Brant**, for example, successfully convinced the Iroquois, Creek, Cherokees, and Choctaw, among others, to raid American settlements and outposts in the West.

African Americans

Blacks generally supported the British because an American victory would only keep them enslaved. Although approximately 5,000 blacks did serve in militias for the United States, most fled to British encampments and Loyalist areas to escape bondage. As a result, both northern and southern colonies lost tens of thousands of slaves during the war. Those blacks who didn't have the opportunity to escape remained enslaved despite Jefferson's belief that "all men were created equal."

The Undecided

Finally, some men and women neither supported nor opposed the revolution and opted instead to wait and see what would happen. Because civilian casualties remained low throughout the war, sitting on the fence proved to be a good alternative to fighting for those who didn't much care which side won or lost. Patriotic colonies often tried to reduce the number of free riders by passing laws that essentially ordered, "You're either with us or against us," and many townships prosecuted able-bodied men who failed to join militias.

WASHINGTON WINS THE WAR

The odds stood in favor of the British at the beginning of the war because they had the world's most powerful navy, a huge standing army in North America, and a large force of German Hessian mercenaries ready to fight. They soon discovered, however, that fighting in North America was exceedingly difficult. Though George Washington had to rely on a small, inconsistent volunteer force, he could also rely on local militias that used hit-and-run guerilla tactics to confuse the orderly columns of British regulars.

Washington wisely understood that he needed only to outlast the British—not defeat them in every engagement. He knew that Britain would eventually grow tired of fighting an unpopular war so far away from home. Washington focused primarily on outrunning the British, forcing his adversary to chase his Continental army from colony to colony. This tactic worked brilliantly, considering the Americans didn't have any key strategic areas they needed to defend.

Battle of Saratoga

The first military success for the colonists came at **Saratoga** in upstate New York in October 1777, when more than 5,700 British troops surrendered to American forces. This victory turned the war around for the Americans because it demonstrated to France that Britain might actually lose the war. By the following year, the two sides had formed the **Franco-American alliance** and had agreed to fight the British together until the United States achieved independence.

French Intervention

Many historians believe that the colonists could not have won the war without French assistance. France, for example, sent fresh troops and supplies to North America to take pressure off the outnumbered Continental army. More important, however, France's participation expanded the scope of the war. Before long, Britain found itself pitted against the Spanish and the Dutch as well as the French and the Americans and fighting battles in North America, Europe, the Mediterranean, Africa, India, and the West Indies.

Battle of Yorktown

Washington, meanwhile, continued to engage the British in North America, first in a series of western campaigns and then in Georgia and South Carolina. Eventually, he moved back northward to join French forces surrounding Britain's General Cornwallis at **Yorktown**, Virginia. Cornered and greatly outnumbered, Cornwallis surrendered to Washington on October 19, 1781, and thus ended the Revolutionary War.

The Treaty of Paris

Once the fighting had stopped, the Continental Congress sent John Adams, John Jay, and Benjamin Franklin to negotiate a permanent settlement. They eventually signed the **Treaty of Paris** on September 3, 1783, in which Great Britain recognized the United States as an independent nation and established a western border along the Mississippi River. The last British troops left New York, and the Continental army disbanded.

TIMELINE: 1763–1783

1763	Peace of Paris ends French and Indian War.
	Pontiac's Rebellion occurs.
	Parliament issues the Proclamation of 1763.
1764	Parliament passes the Sugar and Currency Acts.
1765	Parliament passes the Quartering and Stamp Acts.
	The Stamp Act Congress convenes in New York.
	Stamp Act riots and protests spread throughout colonies.
1766	Parliament repeals the Stamp Act and passes the Declaratory Act.
1767	Parliament passes the Townshend Acts and suspends the New York legislature.
1768	British soldiers occupy Boston.
1770	Boston Massacre occurs.
	Parliament repeals Townshend Acts but keeps the tax on tea.
1772	Samuel Adams forms the Committee of Correspondence.
1773	Boston Tea Party occurs.

1774	Parliament passes the Coercive or "Intolerable" Acts.
	The First Continental Congress convenes and drafts the Declaration of American Rights.
1775	Battle of Lexington and Concord occurs.
	The Second Continental Congress convenes.
	Battle of Bunker Hill occurs.
	Paul Revere warns minutemen of redcoats' approach in his Midnight Ride.
1776	Thomas Paine writes *Common Sense*.
	Congress votes for independence; Thomas Jefferson writes the Declaration of Independence.
1777	Battle of Saratoga brings first military success for the colonists.
1778	France and the United States form the Franco-American alliance.
1781	Washington accepts Cornwallis' surrender at Yorktown.
1783	The Treaty of Paris ends the Revolutionary War.

MAJOR FIGURES

Samuel Adams. Cousin to John Adams, Adams was a failed Bostonian businessman who became an ardent political activist in the years leading up to the Revolutionary War. He organized the first Committee of Correspondence and was a delegate to both Continental Congresses in 1774 and 1775.

Joseph Brant. A Mohawk chief and influential leader of the Iroquois tribes, Brant was one of the many Native American leaders who advocated an alliance with Britain against the Americans in the Revolutionary War. Although he had no love for the British, he and other tribe leaders feared the land-hungry American settlers even more.

George Grenville. Prime Minister of Parliament at the close of the French and Indian War, Grenville was responsible for enforcing the Navigation Laws and passing the Sugar, Stamp, Currency, and Quartering Acts in the mid-1760s. He wrongly assumed that colonists would be willing to bear a greater tax burden after Britain had invested so much in protecting them from the French and Native Americans in the previous decade.

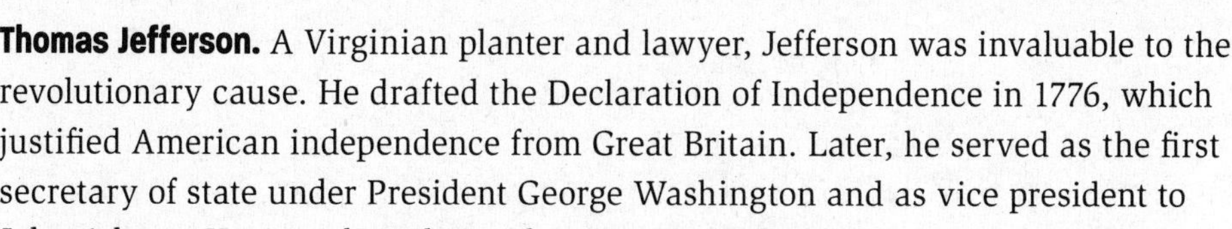

Thomas Jefferson. A Virginian planter and lawyer, Jefferson was invaluable to the revolutionary cause. He drafted the Declaration of Independence in 1776, which justified American independence from Great Britain. Later, he served as the first secretary of state under President George Washington and as vice president to John Adams. He was elected president in 1800 and 1804.

King George III. Having inherited his father's throne at the young age of twelve, George III was King of Great Britain throughout the French and Indian War (the Seven Years' War), the American Revolutionary War, the Napoleonic Wars, and the War of 1812. After the French and Indian War, the king's popularity steadily declined in the American colonies. In the Declaration of Independence, Thomas Jefferson vilifies George III and argues that his neglect and misuse of the American colonies justified their revolution.

Thomas Paine. An exile from England, Paine was a radical philosopher who supported republicanism and civic virtue. His 1776 pamphlet Common Sense was a bestselling phenomenon in the American colonies and convinced thousands to rebel against the "royal brute" King George III.

Pontiac. An Ottowa chief, Pontiac was disillusioned by the French defeat in the French and Indian War. Pontiac briefly united various tribes in the Ohio and Mississippi Valleys to raid colonists on the western frontiers of British North America from 1763 to 1766. He was eventually killed by another Native American after the British had crushed his uprising. Parliament issued the Proclamation of 1763 to prevent any future tribal insurrections against British colonists.

Chapter 4

Building a Nation: 1781–1800

THE ARTICLES OF CONFEDERATION

Delegates at the Second Continental Congress drafted the **Articles of Confederation** to create the first national government of the United States. The Articles loosely bound the thirteen states in a confederacy that eventually proved incredibly weak.

A Weak National Government

Wary of strong central governments after their interactions with Britain, delegates at the Second Continental Congress made certain that the new national congress created under the Articles of Confederation would have very little authority over state legislatures. Instead, drafters hoped that Congress would act as a collective substitute for a monarch, or a multiperson executive. The Articles stipulated that Congress could do the following:

- Negotiate treaties, declare war, and make peace
- Coin money
- Issue loans
- Maintain an army and a navy
- Operate a postal service

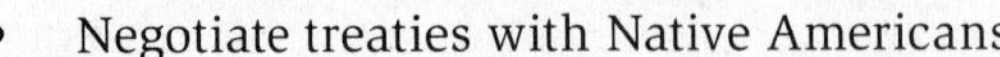

- Negotiate treaties with Native Americans
- Resolve disputes among the states
- Govern western territories for the benefit of all states

The Articles clearly stated that the individual states reserved all powers not specifically granted to Congress. Representative governments in the states would levy their own taxes, for example, and then use a percentage of the duties collected to pay their share of national expenditures. Over time, this unfolded as an ineffective way of bankrolling a federal government, primarily because many of the states refused to pay their fair share.

Moreover, Congress had been granted no rights to control interstate commerce. States were thus given a free hand to draft conflicting and confusing laws that made trade across borders difficult. Finally, any changes to the Articles of Confederation required unanimous agreement from all states in the Union, an event that was unlikely to occur even on the smallest issue.

Governing Western Lands

After the Articles of Confederation went into effect, Congress passed two landmark laws to govern American territories in the West:

- **The Land Ordinance of 1785**, which helped the government survey western lands. The law created townships, each six miles square, that were divided into thirty-six square-mile sections and auctioned to the highest bidder so that any American could settle in the West.
- **The Northwest Ordinance of 1787**, which stipulated that a western territory could apply for full statehood as soon as it had the same number of people as the least populous of the original thirteen states. The ordinance made certain that new states would receive equal footing with older states and that all citizens of the territories would have the same rights as the citizens of the states.

Continental Dollars and Depression

The new Congress immediately set to printing paper currency in order to pay for the Revolutionary War. The money became the standard currency in the United States during the war, but when hard times hit and inflation skyrocketed, these Continental dollars became "not worth a Continental." Many Americans, especially farmers, faced hardship as the economy slid into depression. Congress requested that states increase taxes to help pay for a new national currency, but most states refused and printed their own paper money instead. This, too, quickly succumbed to inflation, and by the end of the war Americans had fistfuls of a variety of worthless money.

Shays's Rebellion

Frustration with the economic depression boiled over in 1786. Farmers throughout the colonies were suffering intensely after the Revolution, mainly due to the worthless Continentals they were forced to use as money. Most of the state legislatures refused to provide any assistance to these impoverished farmers and, in some cases, even raised taxes. Unable to find any relief, and still intoxicated from their success in the Revolution, many farmers grabbed their muskets once again and marched on the various state capitals to demand new governments.

The most notorious of these small uprisings was **Shays's Rebellion**. Led by Revolutionary War hero Daniel Shays, protesters attacked Massachusetts's courthouses to prevent local judges from foreclosing on farms. The state legislature ultimately used militia troops to crush the uprising. Still, Shays's Rebellion awakened legislators in Massachusetts and throughout the states to the inadequacies of the existing political system.

FORMING A MORE PERFECT UNION

With Congress's permission, delegates met in Annapolis, Maryland, in 1786 and again in Philadelphia in 1787 to discuss revising the Articles of Confederation. The delegates, however, soon realized that the Articles needed to be scrapped entirely to create a stronger central government.

The Framers

The fifty-five men who gathered at the **Constitutional Convention** in Philadelphia came from the upper echelons of society. Most had attended college and had become wealthy planters, lawyers, and merchants but generally understood that they served all classes of Americans. On the other hand, the delegates did want the new government to protect individuals' rights to acquire and hold wealth. Interestingly, most all of the attendees had not been heavily involved in the Revolution: **Thomas Jefferson**, **John Adams**, Samuel Adams, and Patrick Henry were all absent. Nevertheless, most did have experience writing their own state constitutions. Delegates unanimously selected **George Washington** to chair the convention.

Creating a New Government

The men gathered in Philadelphia quickly realized the Articles of Confederation should be scrapped and replaced with a new constitution to create a stronger national government. Even though this decision violated Congress's mandate merely to *revise* the Articles, most delegates feared the Union would collapse without a stronger central government. The delegates drafted a new **Constitution** to create a republican government consisting of three distinct branches:

a legislative branch (Congress), an executive branch (the president), and a judicial branch (headed by the Supreme Court). The delegates felt that this **separation of powers** into three different branches would prevent tyranny over the states.

Virginia vs. New Jersey

Both Virginia and New Jersey submitted proposals for a new national legislature, plans that divided delegates and nearly deadlocked the convention. The **Virginia Plan** called for the creation of a bicameral national legislature, or a new Congress with an upper and a lower house, in which the number of representatives per state would be apportioned based on that state's population. Many of the more populous states supported this **"large state plan"** because it would give them more power.

New Jersey, on the other hand, proposed the creation of a unicameral legislature in which all states large and small would have the same number of representatives. This **"small state plan,"** or **New Jersey Plan**, would have tipped the balance of power to favor the smaller states over the larger ones.

The Great Compromise

Eventually, the delegates settled on a **"Great Compromise"** to please both Virginia and New Jersey. They decided that the new Congress would have two houses, a Senate in which all states would be equally represented by two senators, and a lower House of Representatives in which the number of delegates would be apportioned based on state population. State legislatures would appoint senators every six years, while the people would elect representatives to the House of Representatives every two years. The new Congress retained all the powers it had under the Articles of Confederation but also had the power to levy taxes.

The Three-Fifths Compromise

Even at this early date, the slavery issue divided the northern and southern states. States with large slave populations wanted slaves to count as people on the official census so that they could have more representatives in the House. States with smaller populations wanted to exclude slaves altogether. Delegates finally made the so-called **Three-Fifths Compromise** to count slaves as three-fifths of a person for both taxation and representation. They also agreed to discuss banning the slave trade in 1808.

The Presidency

After they had created the legislative branch, the delegates moved on to creating a strong executive branch. Most agreed that the Articles of Confederation had left Congress too weak to maintain unity among all thirteen states. To amend this, delegates outlined the powers of a new executive or president of the United States. Elected to a term of four years, the president had the following authority:

- To serve as commander in chief of the army and navy
- To appoint judges to all federal courts
- To veto legislation passed by Congress

Just as important, the House of Representatives could also impeach the president for treason, bribery, and other "high crimes and misdemeanors" because the delegates wanted to make sure the president never became a king.

The Electoral College

Fearing that the democratic "rabble" would elect an uneducated man to the presidency, the Constitution's framers stipulated that the people would only indirectly elect presidents. Instead, state legislatures would choose a select body of educated men to cast the final votes for the president in the **Electoral College**.

In theory, voters in the college would vote according to the outcome of the popular vote in their states; however, should the people elect a person deemed unqualified for the presidency, electoral voters could change the vote to ensure that only the "best man" become president.

The Judiciary

Finally, the delegates turned to creating a judicial branch. They created a system of federal circuit courts headed by a Supreme Court that outranked all other courts in the nation. The Senate had to approve of all presidential appointments to the Supreme Court, particularly since justices would serve life terms. The Constitution also stipulated that Congress's first duty would be to create the federal court system.

Checks and Balances

Despite separation of powers, most delegates wanted to include other safeguards in the Constitution to prevent tyranny. They therefore created a system of **checks and balances** so that each branch of government had the ability to check the powers of the others in order to prevent one branch from dominating the others. The president, for example, has the right to appoint Supreme Court justices, cabinet members, and foreign ambassadors, but only with the approval of the Senate. On the other hand, he reserves the right to veto all congressional legislation. Congress, too, could override a presidential veto with a two-thirds majority vote.

RATIFYING THE CONSTITUTION

Even though the delegates at the Constitutional Convention in Philadelphia had succeeded in drafting a new Constitution to replace the Articles of Confederation, they still had to convince state legislatures to approve the radically different document.

The Articles of Confederation stipulated that all thirteen states must unanimously ratify the Constitution in order for it to take effect. To circumvent this undoubtedly impossible task, the Philadelphia delegates included in the Constitution a section outlining a new plan for ratification. When only nine of the states ratified the document at special conventions with elected representatives, the Constitution would replace the Articles in those nine states. The delegates figured correctly that the remaining states would be unable to survive on their own and would therefore have to ratify the Constitution as well. In effect, the framers of the Constitution chose to appeal to the American people to ensure ratification.

Federalists vs. Anti-Federalists

Debates immediately erupted throughout the thirteen states as to whether or not the new Constitution should replace the Articles of Confederation. The Federalists, or those who supported ratification, generally came from the more educated and wealthier classes and included leaders such as John Adams, George Washington, Benjamin Franklin, **James Madison**, and **Alexander Hamilton**, among others.

The Anti-Federalists favored a weaker central government in favor of stronger state legislatures. Not all of them liked the Articles of Confederation, but none of them wanted the new Constitution either. Generally from the poorer classes in the West but also with the support of patriots such as Samuel Adams and Patrick Henry, the Anti-Federalists feared that a stronger national government would one day destroy the liberties Americans had won in the Revolutionary War. They particularly didn't like the fact that the new Constitution didn't delineate any specific rights for the people.

A Federalist Victory

Elected conventions in several of the smaller states quickly ratified the Constitution because it gave these states more power in the new legislative branch than they currently enjoyed under the Articles of Confederation. Other ratifying conventions didn't end so quickly or peacefully. Riots broke out in several cities throughout the United States in 1787, and public debates between Federalists and Anti-Federalists became heated. By the summer of 1788, nine of the states had ratified the Constitution, thus making it the supreme law of the land according to the ratification rules. Legislators in the four remaining states—New York, Virginia, North Carolina, and Rhode Island—hated the new Constitution but knew that they couldn't survive without the other nine.

The Federalist Papers

Debate continued to rage in the Anti-Federalist stronghold of New York. To support the Constitution, Alexander Hamilton, James Madison, and **John Jay** published a series of anonymous essays now known as *The Federalist Papers*. Written as propaganda, these essays extolled the benefits of a strong central government and allayed fears about any loss of civil liberties. Historians and political scientists now regard the essays, well written and extremely persuasive, as some of the finest writings on the Constitution and republicanism.

The Bill of Rights

Anti-Federalists in New York finally agreed to ratify the Constitution as long as the new Congress would amend the Constitution to outline specific rights and liberties reserved for the people. Madison himself wrote these ten amendments, collectively known as the **Bill of Rights**. Congress ratified the bill as the first ten amendments to the Constitution, including the following:

- **The First Amendment**, which protects freedoms of religion, speech, and the press
- **The Second Amendment**, which guarantees the right to bear arms
- **The Fifth Amendment**, which guarantees due process of law in criminal cases and freedom from self-incrimination
- **The Sixth Amendment**, which guarantees the right to a speedy trial by an impartial jury
- **The Ninth Amendment**, which stipulates that the people have other rights besides those specifically mentioned in the Constitution or Bill of Rights
- **The Tenth Amendment**, which awards all powers not specifically given to Congress to the individual states

---

WASHINGTON'S PRESIDENCY

Voters in the Electoral College unanimously elected George Washington the first president in 1789 and made John Adams the vice president. Washington proved a firm, dignified, and conscientious leader. He felt his responsibility acutely, tried to remain within his branch of power, and never interfered with Congress. Washington created the first presidential cabinet to advise him. He named Alexander Hamilton secretary of the treasury, Thomas Jefferson secretary of state, and Henry Knox secretary of war.

Creating the Judiciary

Even before ratifying Madison's Bill of Rights, Congress had to create the judiciary branch of government as stipulated in the Constitution. To do so, Congress passed the **Judiciary Act of 1789**, establishing a federal court system with thirteen district courts, three circuit courts, and a Supreme Court presided over by six justices. Congress, however, did not want the federal court system to have too much power over local communities and therefore designated that federal courts would primarily serve as appeals courts for cases already tried in state courts.

Hamilton and the Economy

Hamilton hoped to use his position as secretary of the treasury to stabilize the economy and establish a solid credit. His sound fiscal policies enabled him to achieve these goals and strengthen the national government at the expense of the individual states.

Establishing Public Credit

Hamilton knew that the United States needed capital to develop economically and to convince the rest of the world that the new government would honor debts incurred during the Revolution and under the Articles of Confederation. By 1789, the United States owed roughly $51 million, and Hamilton argued that the government should pay back the entire sum as soon as possible. He also wanted the central government to assume all the states' debts and repay creditors "at par," or with interest.

Hamilton believed that the new government should sell bonds to encourage investment from citizens and foreign interests. Congress initially fought **assumption** and **funding-at-par** but eventually conceded. These policies gave the United States a sound credit rating, allowed foreign capital to flow into the country, and stabilized the economy.

The Excise Tax

To raise money to pay off these debts, Hamilton suggested Congress levy an excise tax on liquor. Because farmers often converted their grain harvests into alcohol before shipping to save cost, many of the congressmen from agrarian states in the South and West opposed the plan and denounced it as an attempt to make northern investors richer. Congress eventually compromised and agreed to assume all federal and state debts and to levy an excise tax in exchange for making the southern city of Washington, D.C., the nation's capital.

The National Bank

Next, Hamilton proposed to create a privately funded **Bank of the United States** to safely store government funds and tie wealthy Americans' interests to the stability of the federal government. Although the Constitution said nothing about creating a national bank, Hamilton argued that the document's **"elastic clause"** allowed the government to pass all laws "which shall be necessary and proper."

Moreover, as a **"loose constructionist,"** he generally believed that the Constitution permitted everything it did not expressly forbid. Washington agreed and authorized creation of the bank.

Hamilton's Economic Vision

Hamilton went on to create a broad economic plan, which was primarily designed to encourage industrial growth. He asked Congress to issue protective tariffs on foreign goods, provide subsidies, and bestow awards to encourage the formation of new businesses. Hamilton's goal was to change an essentially agricultural country into a nation with a self-sufficient industrial economy.

Jeffersonian Opposition

Secretary of State Thomas Jefferson opposed nearly every measure Hamilton proposed. As a **"strict constructionist,"** Jefferson believed that the Constitution forbade everything it didn't expressly permit. He therefore vehemently opposed the formation of a Bank of the United States because it seemed to benefit only the wealthy in the Northeast. He also argued against the excise tax because it unfairly punished southern and western farmers.

The Birth of Political Parties

Hamilton and Jefferson had diametrically opposed visions for the United States. Whereas Hamilton wanted a diversified industrial economy, Jefferson wanted a self-sufficient, agricultural nation. Jefferson in particular despised the thought of large cities and instead wanted a republic consisting of small farmers. These philosophical debates between Hamilton and Jefferson, combined with their own personal animosity for each other, split Washington's cabinet and even Congress during Washington's presidency. Eventually, two distinct political parties emerged from the feud: Hamiltonian **Federalists** and Jeffersonian **Democratic-Republicans**.

Federalists	Democratic-Republicans
Led by Adams, Hamilton, and Marshall	Led by Jefferson and Madison
Associated with aristocracy	Associated with the masses
Encouraged the development of industry	Encouraged the development of agriculture
Favored an alliance with Great Britain	Favored an alliance with France
Championed a strong central government at the expense of individual states	Championed a weak central government in favor of strengthening the states

The Indian Intercourse Act

Congress passed the **Indian Intercourse Act** in 1790. The Intercourse Act stipulated that Congress would regulate all trade with Native Americans and that the United States would acquire new western lands only via official treaties. Not surprisingly, most American farmers ignored this bill and continued to steal Indian lands in the Ohio Valley. Native Americans naturally fought back in several particularly bloody skirmishes on the frontier. The fighting ended only after American forces routed the most powerful tribes at the **Battle of Fallen Timbers** in 1794.

The Whiskey Rebellion

A small band of Pennsylvania farmers marched toward the national capital in Philadelphia to protest Hamilton's injurious excise tax, causing rumors of another revolution to spread throughout the countryside. In response, Washington organized an army of 13,000 and marched to western Pennsylvania to end the so-called **Whiskey Rebellion** before it grew. The farmers quickly disbanded in awe of the massive display of federal force.

The French Revolution

Washington also had many foreign crises to address, most notably the **French Revolution.** In 1789, the French overthrew King Louis XVI to the exultation of most Americans. Thomas Jefferson and his supporters in particular believed that a firm friendship with a republican France would only benefit both peoples. When the revolution turned bloody, however, and war erupted between France and Great Britain, American support for France waned.

Many of the Jeffersonian Democratic-Republicans continued to back the French and believed that the United States should honor the 1778 Franco-American alliance. More conservative Americans, such as Hamilton and the Federalists, believed that the United States should ally itself with Britain.

Neutrality and Citizen Genêt

Washington finally ended the debate when he issued his **Neutrality Proclamation of 1793**, which pledged mutual friendship and the desire to trade with both nations. France's ambassador Genêt, however, ignored Washington's proclamation and continued to pursue an alliance anyway. The **Citizen Genêt Affair** outraged Federalists and Democratic-Republicans alike because it illustrated France's blatant disregard for Washington. Jefferson, though also displeased and embarrassed, eventually resigned his cabinet post for having initially supported the ambassador.

Jay's and Pinckney's Treaties

To prevent another war with Britain, Washington also dispatched Supreme Court Chief Justice John Jay to London in 1794 to negotiate a settlement concerning British troops still stationed on American soil. Britain eventually agreed to withdraw its troops from the Ohio Valley and pay damages for American ships the Royal Navy had illegally seized in the year after the Revolutionary War. In exchange, the United States agreed to pay outstanding pre-Revolutionary War debts to British creditors. **Jay's Treaty** angered many Democratic-Republicans who viewed the agreement as a solid first step toward a new Anglo-American alliance, which they opposed. A year later in 1795, Washington's diplomats also ended border disputes with Spain. Known as **Pinckney's Treaty**, the agreement gave Americans access to the Mississippi in exchange for promises of nonaggression in the West.

Washington's Farewell

Tired of the demands of the presidency, Washington refused to run for a third term, and in 1796 he read his **Farewell Address** to the nation. In the speech, he urged Americans not to become embroiled in European affairs and, in response to the growing political battles between Jefferson and Hamilton, warned against the dangers of factional political parties, which could ruin a nation.

ADAMS AND THE FEDERALISTS

By the end of George Washington's second term, the ideological and personal differences between Thomas Jefferson and Alexander Hamilton had expanded beyond the cabinet to divide politicians throughout the country. By 1796, these two factions had coalesced into two distinct political parties. Unfortunately, neither party realized that both had the best interests of the country at heart. Debates quite often became heated and even violent as the two parties battled for control of the government.

The Election of 1796

Two strong candidates emerged in the months prior to the election of 1796:

- Vice President John Adams for the Federalists
- Former secretary of state Thomas Jefferson for the Democratic-Republicans

Adams won the most electoral votes and became president, while runner-up Thomas Jefferson became vice president. The presence of a Democratic-Republican in the upper echelons of the Adams administration made it difficult at times for the new president to promote his strongly Federalist agenda.

Undeclared Warfare with France

The first test of Adams's mettle came in 1796, when France ended diplomatic relations with the United States in response to improved Anglo-American relations outlined in Jay's Treaty with Britain. Washington's Neutrality Proclamation and Jay's Treaty had both stunned France, which had expected the United States to honor the Franco-American alliance made during the Revolutionary War. Consequently, French warships began seizing hundreds of American merchant ships and millions of dollars' worth of cargo without cause or compensation.

The XYZ Affair

Hoping to avoid war with France, Adams sent ambassadors to Paris to normalize relations in 1797. When the emissaries arrived, however, the French officials, nicknamed by the American press X, Y, and Z, demanded a bribe of a quarter of a million dollars before they would even speak with the Americans. The **XYZ Affair** outraged Congress and the American public and prompted many to cry, "Millions for defense, but not one cent for tribute!" Adams's popularity skyrocketed when he refused the request and prepared for war. Although Congress never officially declared war with France, both countries waged undeclared naval warfare in the Atlantic for several years.

The war ended shortly before Adams left office, when he signed the **Convention of 1800**, in which he promised U.S. merchants would not seek payment for seized cargo in exchange for the annulment of the Franco-American alliance.

The Alien and Sedition Acts

Adams's sudden boost in popularity in the wake of the XYZ Affair gave Federalists in Congress the confidence to boldly strengthen the federal government. In 1798, Congress passed the **Alien and Sedition Acts** in part to prevent French revolutionaries from entering the United States but also to cripple the Democratic-Republicans:

- **The Alien Act** extended the time required for foreigners to become American citizens from five years to fourteen years and gave Congress the power to expel aliens. This act was aimed directly at Irish and French immigrants, who mainly supported the Democratic-Republicans.
- **The Sedition Act** banned public criticism of the president and Congress and was used to silence Democratic-Republican newspapers.

The Virginia and Kentucky Resolutions

Instead of weakening the Democratic-Republicans, the Alien and Sedition Acts only made them stronger. For the first time, Jeffersonians organized as a true opposition party in Congress: They formed caucuses, selected party leaders, and promoted a platform. They also challenged Federalists for the previously nonpartisan position of Speaker of the House.

Democratic-Republicans across the country vehemently protested the Sedition Act as a violation of their First Amendment right to free speech. Vice President Jefferson and James Madison even anonymously drafted the **Virginia and Kentucky Resolutions** later that year, in which they proclaimed the Alien and Sedition Acts null and void in those states. The resolutions argued that because the states had formed a compact in creating the Union, the states thus reserved the right to nullify any congressional laws they deemed unconstitutional.

Jefferson and Madison's Virginia and Kentucky Resolutions were two of the most influential American works written before the Civil War. Arguing that member states had the authority to nullify unconstitutional acts of Congress, the resolutions effectively claimed the power of judicial review for the states, not the Supreme Court. The resolutions also sparked the first debate over whether the states or the federal government had the final authority. Future Democrats—the political descendents of the Democratic-Republicans—would continue this line of reasoning.

TIMELINE: 1781–1798

1781	The Second Continental Congress ratifies the Articles of Confederation.
1785	Congress passes the Land Ordinance of 1785.
1786	Shays's Rebellion occurs.
	Protesters attack courthouses in Massachusetts.
	Delegates meet to discuss revising Articles of Confederation in Annapolis, Maryland.
1787	Congress passes the Northwest Ordinance of 1787.
	The Constitutional Convention is held in Philadelphia, Pennsylvania.
	Alexander Hamilton, John Jay, and James Madison begin writing the *Federalist Papers.*
1788	Nine states ratify the new Constitution.

1789	George Washington becomes the first president.
	Congress passes the Judiciary Act of 1789.
1790	Congress passes the Indian Intercourse Act.
1791	The Bill of Rights is ratified.
	The Bank of the United States is created.
	Congress levies an excise tax.
1792	Washington is reelected.
1793	Washington issues the Neutrality Proclamation.
	The Citizen Genêt affair outrages the American public.
1794	A band of farmers marches to the capital to protest the excise tax in the Whiskey Rebellion.
	Fighting between Native Americans and American farmers finally ends in the Battle of Fallen Timbers.
	Jay's Treaty angers Democratic-Republicans who oppose an Anglo-American alliance.
1795	Pinckney's Treaty gives Americans access to the Mississippi.
1796	Washington reads his Farewell Address.
	John Adams is elected president.
1797	French officials demand a bribe in the XYZ Affair.
1798	Congress passes the Alien and Sedition Acts.
	U.S. wages undeclared naval war with France.
	Jefferson and Madison write the Virginia and Kentucky Resolutions.

MAJOR FIGURES

John Adams. A prominent Bostonian lawyer, Adams first became famous for defending the British soldiers accused of murdering five civilians in the Boston Massacre. He was a delegate from Massachusetts in the Continental Congresses, where he rejected proposals for home rule. He served as vice president to George Washington and was president of the United States from 1797 to 1801.

Alexander Hamilton. A brilliant New York lawyer and statesman, Hamilton at thirty-two years old was one of the youngest framers of the Constitution at the Constitutional Convention in 1787. An ardent Federalist, he supported the Constitution during the ratification debates even though he actually believed that the new document was still too weak. He helped write the *Federalist Papers,* which are now regarded as some of the finest essays on American government and republicanism. He served as the first secretary of the treasury under President George Washington and is responsible for establishing the first Bank of the United States and the national credit.

John Jay. Coauthor of The Federalist Papers, Jay worked tirelessly to convince Anti-federalist New Yorkers to ratify the Constitution. He served as the first chief justice of the Supreme Court and became one of the most hated men in America after he negotiated Jay's Treaty in 1794 with Great Britain.

James Madison. Originally a Federalist, Madison supported the ratification of the Constitution to replace the Articles of Confederation and wrote some of the best essays on American government and republicanism as coauthor of the *Federalist Papers.* He also personally drafted the Bill of Rights, afraid that the Constitution might be amended if handed to a committee. After ratification, he began supporting southern and western agrarian interests as a Democratic-Republican. While in retirement in Virginia, Madison coauthored the Virginia and Kentucky Resolutions with Thomas Jefferson in 1798. He later reentered politics and was eventually elected president in 1808 and again in 1812. As the fourth president, Madison promoted the development of southern and western agriculture as his predecessor and friend Thomas Jefferson had. He repealed the Embargo Act but supported the Non-Intercourse Act and Macon's Bill No. 2. He led the United States in the War of 1812.

Daniel Shays. A depressed western Massachusetts farmer, Shays led approximately 1,500 fellow farmers in a revolt against the state legislature in Boston in 1786. State officials easily ended Shays's Rebellion and pardoned all but two of the would-be revolutionaries. Shays escaped to Vermont and finally settled in New York. His revolt was only one of many launched against state governments in the mid-1780s and prompted prominent Americans to discuss amending the Articles of Confederation.

Chapter 5

Republican Agrarianism: 1800–1824

THE ELECTION OF 1800

As the presidential election of 1800 approached, problems mounted for President Adams and the Federalists. The Alien and Sedition Acts, Jay's Treaty, and the suppression of the Whiskey Rebellion by federal troops had all soured Americans' opinion of the Federalists. Still, Federalists nominated both **John Adams** and Charles C. Pinckney, while Democratic-Republicans selected **Thomas Jefferson** and Aaron Burr to run for president.

Jefferson Elected

Although Adams received a significant number of electoral votes, he still won fewer than either Jefferson or Burr. Both Democratic-Republican candidates had tied with seventy-three votes each, thus forcing the House of Representatives to determine the next president. Most Federalists lobbied representatives to elect Burr, but Alexander Hamilton succeeded in convincing his colleagues to vote for his archnemesis Jefferson because he hated Burr even more. As a result, Jefferson became the nation's third president and Burr his vice president.

The Revolution of 1800

Historians often refer to the election of 1800 as the **Revolution of 1800** because the Federalists ceded power to the Democratic-Republicans entirely without violence, a truly significant accomplishment given the fact that so many wars in Europe had begun when one party had refused to relinquish control to another. For this reason, the Revolution of 1800 was just as momentous as the Revolution of 1776. Whereas the American Revolution had established the United States as an independent nation, the election of 1800 proved that the new nation would survive.

Adams's Midnight Judges

Shortly before they transferred power to the Democratic-Republicans, Federalists in Congress passed the **Judiciary Act of 1801** to ensure that Federalists would continue to control the courts during Jefferson's presidency. Adams even used his last remaining hours as president to appoint a new chief justice to the Supreme Court and forty-two other **"midnight judges"** to lower federal courts.

REPUBLICANS IN POWER

Jefferson came to power promising to reduce the size of the federal government and de-emphasize industry in favor of agriculture. Jefferson argued that these actions would set the United States back on its "rightful" course toward agrarian republicanism and redefine the role of the government so it would be less intrusive in the lives of American citizens. He slashed federal spending, virtually disbanded the army and navy, and repealed almost all taxes except those on the sale of federal lands. By selling public lands, Jefferson hoped to encourage the creation of more small farms and rid the government of debt.

Marbury v. Madison

Soon after taking office, the Democratic-Republicans proceeded to repeal the bulk of Federalist legislation, including the Alien and Sedition Acts and the Judiciary Act of 1801. Jefferson and his secretary of state, **James Madison**, also refused to honor the appointments of Adams's "midnight judges." Outraged, one Federalist justice named William Marbury sued Madison, and in 1803 the Supreme Court heard the case. Chief Justice **John Marshall** sympathized with fellow Federalist Marbury but ruled in the landmark decision *Marbury v. Madison* that even though the president should have honored Adams's appointments, the Supreme Court had no power over Jefferson in this matter because the Judiciary Act of 1789 was unconstitutional. This decision allowed Marshall to simultaneously give Jefferson his victory and strengthen the Supreme Court with the power of **judicial review**, or the right to declare laws passed by Congress unconstitutional.

The Louisiana Purchase

Jefferson overstepped his authority as president again in 1803 when he purchased the vast tract of land between the Mississippi River and the Rocky Mountains from Napoleon in France. Although Jefferson knew the Constitution didn't authorize presidents to purchase land, he also realized he had to act on the unprecedented opportunity to double the size of the country for only $15 million. The **Louisiana Purchase** gave Americans control of most of the Mississippi River and ended French dreams of a North American empire.

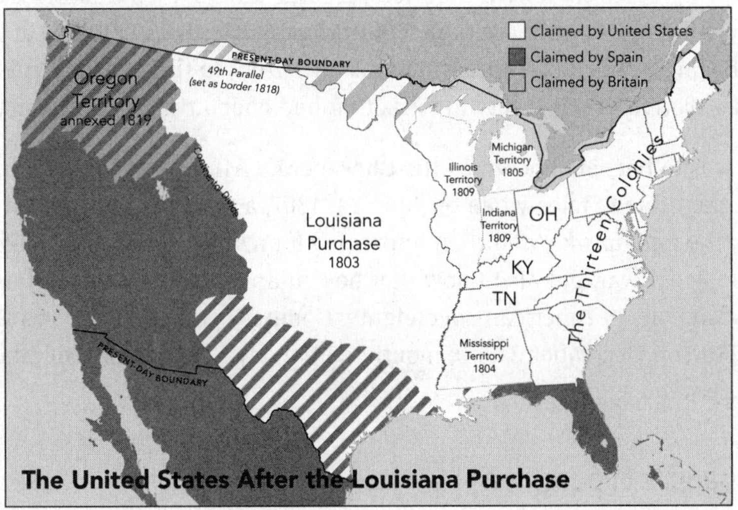

The United States After the Louisiana Purchase

Lewis and Clark

In 1803, Jefferson asked Congress to fund an exploratory expedition to the Pacific Northwest, ostensibly "for the purpose of extending the foreign commerce of the United States" mainly by finding a water route to the Pacific Ocean. Jefferson also wanted to map the unexplored Louisiana Territory and foster trade relations with the indigenous Native Americans. With Congress's approval, Jefferson assigned his secretary Meriwether Lewis and army captain William Clark to lead the **"Corps of Discovery"** expedition.

Lewis and Clark embarked on their journey from St. Louis with approximately fifty men in 1804 and returned more than two years later in 1806. They found no easy water route to the Pacific but returned with maps and information about the terrain, people, and natural resources that would fuel the pioneering spirit of countless Americans.

Embargo Act

France sold the Louisiana Territory to Jefferson primarily because Napoleon needed money to fund his war with Great Britain as he attempted to conquer the whole of Europe. Although far removed from the fighting, the war nevertheless hurt American trade across the Atlantic. Both the French and English navies frequently seized American ships looking for arms, supplies, and other contraband even though the United States had declared neutrality. Unable to

convince either side to respect American neutral shipping rights, Congress and Jefferson decided that American merchants would simply not trade with Europe anymore and passed the **Embargo Act** in 1807, prohibiting trade with Europe. Democratic-Republicans hoped that the embargo would cripple both France and England and force them to respect American shipping rights.

Impressment

Britain complicated the situation by forcing American sailors from seized ships into military service on British warships. Although Royal Navy officials claimed they only impressed their own deserters, records have shown that British officers illegally impressed more than 5,000 American men. Americans at home viewed Britain's policy of **impressment** as an affront to their hard-won liberties and as a violation of the Treaty of Paris that had ended the Revolutionary War.

In what was to become known as the **Chesapeake Affair**, war fever raged once again in the United States when on June 22, 1807, a British ship attacked a U.S. warship, the *Chesapeake*, and then impressed four American sailors. Jefferson wanted to avoid war, but also knew that he couldn't simply ignore Britain's blatant violations of American sovereignty. Congress passed Jefferson's Embargo Acto of 1807 on December 22, six months to the day after the British attacked the *Chesapeake*.

The Embargo's Impact

The Embargo Act crippled the American economy far more than it hurt Britain or France, as American exports fell from $109 million to $22 million in the first year alone. Depression followed soon after, when farmers in the West and South couldn't sell any grain, cotton, or tobacco to the lucrative markets abroad. Rumblings of secession even spread throughout the hardest-hit areas in the northern states. Still, Jefferson refused to lift the embargo, and it remained in effect until Congress finally repealed it in 1809.

The Election of 1808

The depression caused by Thomas Jefferson's Embargo Act weakened the Democratic-Republican Party in the 1808 national elections. Although **James Madison** still managed to defeat the Federalist candidate Charles Pinckney for the presidency, the party lost seats in Congress. As Jefferson's chosen successor, Madison carried out his fellow Virginian's policies throughout both of his presidential terms.

Tecumseh and the Prophet

One of Madison's greatest challenges during his first term involved the growing Native American threat to American settlers in the West. American farmers had eagerly pushed westward into the Mississippi River basin since Jefferson's Louisiana Purchase, despite Congress's promise to respect Native American territory in the Indian Intercourse Act of 1790. Frustrated, two Shawnee brothers named

Tecumseh and Tenskwatawa, nicknamed the Prophet for reportedly having a series of "visions," succeeded in creating a pan-Indian alliance called the **Northwest Confederacy** (including the Shawnee, Cherokee, Choctaw, Chickasaws, and Creeks, among other tribes), which sought a return to traditional ways of Native American life. Fearing another Native American uprising, Madison ordered Indiana Territory Governor **William Henry Harrison** to destroy the Confederacy, which he did in 1811 at the **Battle of Tippecanoe**.

THE WAR OF 1812

By 1810, many of the older and experienced statesmen in Congress had retired, leaving their seats open to a young and passionate new generation. Most of these young congressmen came from the southern and western states and yearned for action. These **"War Hawks,"** like **John C. Calhoun** and **Henry Clay**, had ordered Harrison to defeat Tecumseh and the Prophet and clamored for a new war against Great Britain. Although President Madison hoped to avoid war, he eventually caved to pressures from the War Hawks and requested that Congress declare war against Britain in June of 1812.

Non-Intercourse Act and Macon's Bill Number 2

Because the Embargo Act had failed, Congress passed the **Non-Intercourse Act** in 1809 to reopen trade with every country *except* France and Britain. When this too failed, Congress then passed **Macon's Bill Number 2** in 1810 to entice Britain and France into recognizing American shipping rights. The bill stipulated that the United States would reward the first of the two to respect American shipping by reinstating the embargo on the country that did not.

Hoping to bring the Americans into the war, Napoleon ordered French ships to respect American merchants, thus forcing Madison to reinstate the embargo on trade with Britain. After two more years of British aggression on the Atlantic and in the West, Madison eventually had no choice but to heed War Hawk demands and ask Congress to declare war on Britain.

Causes of the War of 1812

Americans clamored for war with Britain in 1812 for two reasons: to defeat the British-backed Native Americans in the Ohio Valley and to defend American shipping rights and end the practice of impressments. Despite these goals, many Americans in the West also wanted war in order to seize more land, particularly in British Canada.

A Stalemated War

The war itself went badly for the United States. Thanks to Jefferson's belief in frugal government, the U.S. Navy consisted of just a few ineffective gunboats, and the army had very few men, weapons, or supplies. American forces had

some success in the Northwest but couldn't manage to punch through the British blockade of the eastern ports or prevent the burning of Washington, D.C. The war, for all practical purposes, was a stalemate, and both countries signed the **Treaty of Ghent** in 1814 to end it. The treaty essentially stipulated that neither side had gained or lost any territory, and neither side mentioned impressment or the illegal seizure of American ships. Ironically, American troops under the command of General **Andrew Jackson** won a resounding victory in early January 1815 at the **Battle of New Orleans**, just days after diplomats had signed the peace treaty.

The Hartford Convention

While the American and British delegations negotiated the treaty in Ghent, Federalist delegates from five New England states met in Hartford, Connecticut, to discuss their dissatisfaction with "Mr. Madison's War." In fact, some felt so outraged that they proposed secession from the Union. After meeting for several weeks, delegates at the **Hartford Convention** settled on merely petitioning Congress with a list of four major grievances:

- The federal government should compensate New England shippers for profits lost during the war.
- The Constitution should be amended so that states can vote on important decisions that affect the entire Union, such as the admission of new states and declaring war.
- The executive office should be changed so that presidents can only serve one term and cannot come from the same state as the previous president.
- The Three-Fifths Clause should be stricken from the Constitution.

The Hartford Convention's list of demands reflected northern dissatisfaction with the federal government and the war. Of the first five presidents, only one of them—John Adams—had not been a member of the so-called **Virginia Dynasty,** which consisted of Washington, Jefferson, Madison, and Monroe, all from Virginia. This strong southern representation in the White House frustrated many New Englanders, who felt that they had been left out of the political loop. This frustration was the true driving force behind the delegates' list of demands.

Unfortunately for the Hartford delegates, their petition arrived in Washington, D.C., just as news of Jackson's victory in New Orleans arrived and the Treaty of Ghent was signed. The effect on the Federalists was devastating as the country voiced its support of the war and of the government. The Federalist Party never recovered from the stigma of disloyalty.

THE "ERA OF GOOD FEELINGS"

Despite the fact that the United States had gained nothing from the War of 1812, Americans felt intensely patriotic when the conflict ended in 1814. Jackson's victory at the Battle of New Orleans made Americans particularly proud, as if they had won a "second war for independence" against the most powerful army in the world. This newfound American spirit also boosted the popularity of the War Hawks, such as Clay and Calhoun, who emerged as the nation's new congressional leaders in the postwar era.

Democratic-Republican **James Monroe** easily defeated his weak Federalist opponent, Rufus King, in the election of 1816. In doing so, Monroe not only effectively killed the Federalist Party but also ushered in an era of domestic tranquility and single-party rule. One newspaper in Boston, the *Columbian Centinel*, dubbed these virtually controversy-free years the **"Era of Good Feelings."** The name stuck.

Clay's American System

As the leader of the War Hawks, Speaker of the House Henry Clay proposed a three-pronged **"American System"** to improve the national infrastructure of the United States. Clay's nationalistic system included:

- Improving the financial sector of the economy. Under his leadership, Congress created the **Second Bank of the United States** in 1816 to offer easy credit and stabilize the economy.
- Protecting struggling American manufacturers from the postwar influx of cheap British goods. He pushed the **Tariff of 1816** through Congress to place a 20 percent tax on all foreign goods. This also happened to be the first tariff Congress passed to protect industry rather than merely to increase revenue.
- Connecting the country via a system of roads and canals built with money raised from the new protective tariff. These **internal improvements** would help farmers ship their crops and goods to the East and manufacturers to ship their products to the West.

Postwar Expansion

The Era of Good Feelings at home affected foreign policy as well. Most significantly, the United States ended decades of hostility with Great Britain with the following agreements:

- **The Rush-Bagot Agreement** in 1817, to demilitarize the Great Lakes region
- **The Treaty of 1818**, to establish a clear border between the United States and Canada from Minnesota to the Rocky Mountains at the forty-ninth parallel. The treaty also specified that the United States would jointly occupy the Oregon Territory in the Pacific Northwest (present-day Oregon, Idaho, Washington, British Columbia, and part of Montana) until 1828.

New States

Settlers carved out three new territories in the Deep South after the war:

- Louisiana became a state in 1812.
- Mississippi became a state in 1817.
- Alabama became a state in 1819.

Seizing Spanish Florida

General **Andrew Jackson**, meanwhile, illegally seized Spanish Florida on the pretext that Spain had plotted with the Seminole Indian tribe against the United States. Spain ultimately ceded Florida to the United States in 1819 in exchange for Washington's retraction on claims to Spanish Texas.

The Monroe Doctrine

In 1823, John Quincy Adams devised the **Monroe Doctrine**. It represented the Monroe administration's most significant foreign policy achievement. The Monroe Doctrine stipulated the following:

- European powers had to stay away from the New World.
- Old World powers could keep the colonies they currently had but could not establish any new ones.
- America would support the growth of democracy throughout the western hemisphere.

British policy-makers had originally suggested the Monroe Doctrine to Monroe and Adams because they wanted to protect their West Indian colonies from the continental powers in Europe. Secretly, the British also feared American

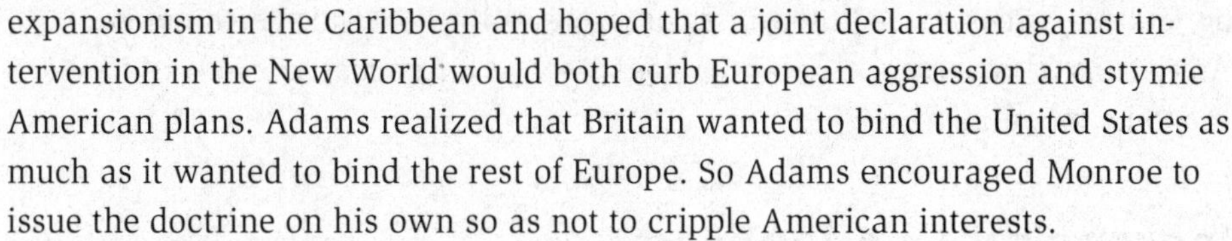

expansionism in the Caribbean and hoped that a joint declaration against intervention in the New World would both curb European aggression and stymie American plans. Adams realized that Britain wanted to bind the United States as much as it wanted to bind the rest of Europe. So Adams encouraged Monroe to issue the doctrine on his own so as not to cripple American interests.

Even though the British failed to contain the United States, they still supported the Monroe Doctrine anyway and used Royal Navy warships to enforce it. The Monroe Doctrine allowed new Latin American democracies to flourish without fear of war with Spain, France, or Portugal.

John Marshall and the Supreme Court

The Supreme Court issued a series of rulings during the Era of Good Feelings that also increased the power of the federal government. The Court, still dominated by diehard Federalist chief justice **John Marshall**, upheld federal power more out of Hamiltonian beliefs in strong government than out of love for the new nationalism. The rulings included the following:

- *Dartmouth College v. Woodward,* that states could not nullify or amend legal contracts (1819)
- *Cohens v. Virginia,* that the Supreme Court had the authority to review decisions reached in the supreme courts of the individual states (1821)
- *McCulloch v. Maryland,* that neither Hamiltonian "loose" interpretations of the elastic clause nor the Bank of the United States violated the Constitution (1819)
- *Gibbons v. Ogden,* that Congress had the authority to regulate interstate commerce (1824)

Marshall's rulings during these early years played a huge role in consolidating the power of the federal government over the individual states and ensured that Federalist ideals would live on despite the party's early death.

The Panic of 1819

A string of crises beginning at the end of Monroe's first term quickly dampened the "good feelings" of the era. The first crisis hit in the **Panic of 1819** and was caused at least in part by a change in credit policies of the Second Bank of the United States (SBUS) toward a more conservative lending policy. The bank was concerned about the practices of the rough-and-tumble **wildcat banks** in the West that were lending money quickly and without as much concern for regulations as other banks. The SBUS called in loans made to these banks, forcing the banks to call in loans they had made to thousands of pioneers along the frontier, mainly farmers. The new policies, combined with price declines in many

agricultural areas, forced thousands of farmers off their land. The number of Americans in poverty and debtor prisons swelled for almost a decade until the economy rebounded.

Increasing Sectionalism

Sectional tensions also arose in 1819 when the Missouri Territory applied for admission to the Union as a new slave state. Even though Missouri had met all of the qualifications, the northern-dominated House of Representatives denied the territory statehood because they didn't want to tip the sectional balance in the Senate in favor of the South with twelve slave states to only eleven free. The House then passed the **Tallmadge Amendment** in 1819 to gradually free slave children and declare that settlers couldn't take any more slaves into the territory.

The Missouri Compromise

Southern elites were outraged at what they acutely believed to be northern attempts to eliminate slavery. By 1819, they had become almost completely dependent on slave labor to produce cotton and reasoned that if slavery couldn't expand westward, then the southern way of life would certainly die. In other words, they feared that northerners in the free states would hem them in geographically and suffocate them economically. People in the South also feared that banning slavery in Missouri would set a precedent for all other new states. As a result, they rejected the Tallmadge Amendment in the Senate and then deadlocked Congress for several more months until House Speaker Henry Clay proposed the **Missouri Compromise**. Both southerners and northerners agreed to the following:

- Missouri would be admitted as a slave state.
- Maine would simultaneously be admitted as a free state to maintain the sectional balance.
- Slavery was declared illegal north of the 36° 30' parallel west of Missouri.

Impact of the Compromise

The Missouri Compromise of 1819 saved the Union from a potentially divisive issue. Most southerners liked the compromise because the slave South could expand westward. Northerners, on the other hand, also liked the compromise because slavery South of the 36° 30' parallel kept slavery contained in the South and out of most lands acquired in the vast Louisiana Purchase, which was a free

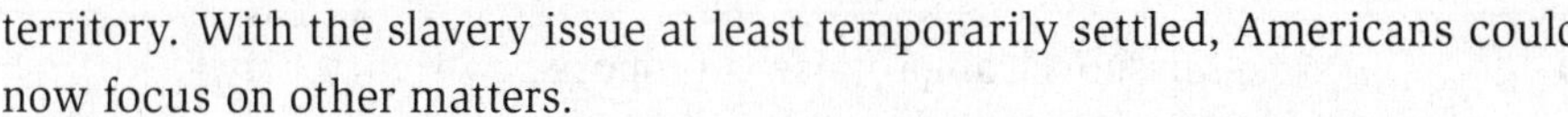

territory. With the slavery issue at least temporarily settled, Americans could now focus on other matters.

TIMELINE: 1800–1824

1800	The Convention of 1800 ends the war with France.
	Thomas Jefferson is elected president of the United States.
1801	Congress passes the Judiciary Act of 1801.
1802	Congress repeals the Judiciary Act of 1801.
1803	Jefferson purchases Louisiana Territory.
	Supreme Court hears *Marbury v. Madison*.
1804	Jefferson is reelected.
	Lewis and Clark explore Louisiana Territory.
1807	The Chesapeake Affair incites war fever.
	Congress passes the Embargo Act.
1808	James Madison is elected president of the United States.
1809	Congress repeals the Embargo Act.
	Congress passes the Non-Intercourse Act.
1811	The Battle of Tippecanoe is fought.
1812	United States declares war on Great Britain.
	Madison is reelected.
1814	New Englanders discuss secession at Hartford Convention.
	Treaty of Ghent ends War of 1812.
1816	Congress passes the Tariff of 1816.
	James Monroe is elected president.
1818	General Andrew Jackson invades Florida.
1819	The Panic of 1819 ends the "Era of Good Feelings."
	Spain cedes Florida to the United States.
	The House passes the Tallmadge Amendment.
	The *McCulloch v. Maryland* ruling increases the power of the federal government.
	Dartmouth College v. Woodward rules that states cannot amend legal contracts.

1820	The Missouri Compromise is proposed by Henry Clay.
	Monroe is reelected.
1823	John Quincy Adams devises the Monroe Doctrine.
1824	The *Gibbons v. Ogden* ruling gives Congress authority to regulate interstate commerce.

MAJOR FIGURES

John C. Calhoun. Even though Calhoun served as vice president to both John Quincy Adams and Andrew Jackson, he also led the movement to nullify the 1828 Tariff of Abominations in South Carolina. Shortly after Congress passed the tariff, he wrote *The South Carolina Exposition,* which urged South Carolina legislators to declare the tax null and void in the state. The Exposition and Nullification Crisis was the greatest challenge the nation had yet faced and illustrated the emerging sectional differences. Calhoun is also regarded as one of America's finest political theorists.

Henry Clay. Also known as the Great Pacificator, this Kentuckian served as Speaker of the House of Representatives, secretary of state to John Quincy Adams, and later as a U.S. senator. He was the father of the American System to promote higher tariffs and internal improvements at government expense. He earned his nickname for devising both the Missouri Compromise of 1820 and the compromise Tariff of 1833 to end the nullification crisis. In 1834, Clay allied himself with Daniel Webster of New England to form the Whigs, a progressive new political party supporting internal improvements, limited westward expansion, and reform. Even though he never served as president (he ran and lost three times), historians regard him as one of America's greatest statesmen.

William Henry Harrison. A former governor of Indiana Territory and an army general, Harrison rose to national stardom when he defeated the Northwest Confederacy at the Battle of Tippecanoe in 1811. He became the first Whig president when he defeated incumbent Martin Van Buren in the election of 1840. Harrison's election marked the beginning of the Second Party System in American politics (Whigs vs. Democrats), but he died after less than a month in office. He was also the grandfather of Gilded Age president Benjamin Harrison.

Andrew Jackson. Hero of the Battle of New Orleans and of the Creek War, Jackson entered the national political arena when he challenged John Quincy Adams for the presidency in 1824. After a controversial loss, he ran again in 1828 and won. His presidency was plagued by one crisis after another, from the Bank War to the Nullification Crisis, to the forced removal of thousands of Native Americans from their homes. Jackson's presidency has become associated with a surge in democracy, westward expansion, and a strengthened federal government.

John Jay. Coauthor of *The Federalist Papers,* Jay worked tirelessly to convince Anti-Federalist New Yorkers to ratify the Constitution. He served as the first

Chief Justice of the Supreme Court and became one of the most hated men in American after he negotiated Jay's Treaty in 1794 with Great Britain.

James Monroe. Without any serious Federalist competition, the Democratic-Republican Monroe was elected president in 1816 and ushered in the "Era of Good Feelings." An excellent administrator, Monroe bolstered the federal government and supported internal improvements. His first term went so well that he ran virtually uncontested in the election of 1820. The good times ended, however, during the Missouri Crisis of 1819 and 1820, which split the United States into North and South. He is most famous for his 1823 Monroe Doctrine, warning European powers to stay out of the affairs of Latin America.

John Marshall. Chief justice of the Supreme Court, Marshall was instrumental in establishing judicial review, in which the Supreme Court rules whether laws passed by Congress are constitutional. Marshall also served as a captain in the Continental army under George Washington and spent the winter in Valley Forge in 1777.

Tecumseh. A member of the Shawnee tribe, Tecumseh and his brother, Tenskwatawa, organized many of the tribes in the Mississippi Valley into the Northwest Confederacy to defend their lands from white American settlers. Even though the tribes had legal rights to their lands according to the Indian Intercourse Act of 1790, the Democratic-Republican War Hawks in Congress ordered General William Henry Harrison to wipe out the Confederacy. Tecumseh and his brother were defeated at the Battle of Tippecanoe in 1811.

Chapter 6

Jacksonian Democracy: 1824–1848

THE ELECTION OF 1824

Four major candidates contended for the presidency in the election of 1824:

- **John Quincy Adams**, the son of former president John Adams, represented New England.
- **Andrew Jackson**, the champion of the common man, drew widespread support from the West and South.
- William Crawford, a southern planter, advocated states' rights.
- **Henry Clay**, who championed the American System, appealed to wealthier Americans.

The fact that four candidates had decided to run for the presidency was proof that the Missouri Compromise of 1820, which allowed slavery in the South and prohibited it north of the 36° 30' parallel, had replaced the "Era of Good Feelings" with sectionalism and divisiveness. Americans held many differing views regarding the direction in which the country should move.

The American System

Henry Clay ran on the **"American System"** platform, which sought to improve the fledgling United States in the following ways:

- Promoting internal improvements, such as building canals and national roads
- Raising **protective tariffs** on foreign goods to help domestic manufacturers
- Establishing a **Bank of the United States** to stabilize the economy

The American System dominated the election of 1824. Candidates Clay and Adams both endorsed the system, but Jackson opposed it.

Adams's Corrupt Bargain

After a vicious campaign, Jackson emerged as the most popular candidate, garnering 99 electoral votes to Adams's 84, Crawford's 41, and Clay's 37. Because no single candidate received the necessary clear majority in the Electoral College, it fell to the House of Representatives to decide which of the top three candidates would become the next president. As Speaker of the House, Clay threw his support to Adams in exchange for becoming the next secretary of state. Clay's support brought Adams to the presidency, but many Americans joined Jackson in denouncing Clay and Adams's **"corrupt bargain."** His reputation ruined, Adams had very little influence during his four years as president.

THE RISE OF MASS DEMOCRACY

By the 1830s, most states had eliminated voting qualifications, such as literacy tests and property ownership, so that all white males could vote. As a result of this trend toward **universal manhood suffrage**, the number of voters increased dramatically, from 350,000 in 1824 to more than 2.5 million by 1840.

The Election of 1828

By 1828, political leaders such as Adams and Clay, who promoted policies focused on internal improvements to the country, had split from Jackson's Democratic-Republicans (eventually to become known simply as Democrats) and formed their own National Republican Party. Adams and Jackson faced off once again in the presidential election of 1828. Not surprisingly, the tainted Adams lost, winning only New England.

Politics of Personality

Jackson believed that his landslide victory in 1828 had given him a mandate from the people to do whatever he deemed right. As a result, he greatly expanded the powers of the presidency. For example, Jackson vetoed bills he personally disliked, unlike previous presidents who had only vetoed bills they thought unconstitutional. Jackson also strengthened the federal government at the expense of individual state governments.

The Spoils System

Jackson believed that political power should rest with the people in a democracy. He used this belief as a justification for replacing many career civil servants in the capital with his own political allies. This action marked the rise of the **spoils system** in nineteenth-century American politics, a system in which presidents award the best appointments in government to their friends and supporters. While previous presidents had practiced this system to a lesser degree, Jackson was the first to publicly attempt to justify and defend it.

THE NULLIFICATION CRISIS

The tariff issue once again shot to the political foreground in 1828, when Congress unexpectedly passed the Tariff of 1828, setting duties on imported goods at nearly 50 percent, a great increase from the current duties. Jackson actually disliked the tariff and knew it would be unpopular but had pushed for its passage before his election to the presidency to further discredit Adams. As soon as he entered the White House, however, the so-called **Tariff of Abominations** (the Tariff of 1828) became his problem.

Calhoun's South Carolina Exposition

As a westerner, Jackson had no love for the new tariff, which hurt the agricultural South and West, but he didn't seek its repeal either. Jackson's vice president, **John C. Calhoun**, hated the Tariff of Abominations so much that he anonymously encouraged his home state to nullify the law in a pamphlet published in 1828 called *The South Carolina Exposition and Protest*. Calhoun argued that states could nullify any act of Congress they deemed unconstitutional because the states had created the central government and therefore had greater power. Calhoun believed the South Carolina legislature should nullify the new tariff because the tariff protected textile manufacturers in northern states and hurt southern cotton-producing states when the price of cotton abroad rose.

The Tariff of 1832

Though the southern states protested vehemently against the Tariff of 1828, the tariff generated large revenues that helped the government pay many of its debts. With federal finances in better shape, Jackson signed the lower **Tariff of**

1832. Calhoun and South Carolinians, however, continued to protest. Although they despised the tax itself, they resented federal supremacy over the states even more. Consequently, legislators in South Carolina declared the new tariff null and void in the state and even threatened to secede if Jackson tried to enforce tax collection.

The Nullification Proclamation

Jackson was outraged at South Carolina's challenge to the authority of the federal government, and he issued his own **Nullification Proclamation**, dening any state's right to nullify federal laws. Moreover, he declared nullification treasonous and threatened to hang the nullifiers himself. He organized a corps of army troops loyal to the Union and then railroaded the **Force Bill** through Congress in 1833, justifying the use of military force to collect tariff duties in South Carolina.

The Compromise Tariff of 1833

Just as violence seemed imminent, the "Great Compromiser," Henry Clay, proposed and passed the **Compromise Tariff of 1833**, which reduced tariff rates over the next ten years. Since no other state supported South Carolina, state legislators reluctantly decided to accept the new tariff. They did, however, nullify the Force Bill out of spite.

JACKSON'S BANK WAR

By 1832, the **Second Bank of the United States** had become the most important financial institution in the nation. Many Americans, however, hated the bank, especially farmers and land speculators who could not repay their loans after the agricultural market crashed during the Panic of 1819. Jackson himself had lost most of his money in 1819 and blamed the country's financial problems on the bank.

Henry Clay, afraid that Jackson and the Democrats might not renew the bank's charter in 1836, when it would otherwise expire, attempted to renew the charter several years early, in 1832. Clay also hoped to make the bank a key issue in the presidential election later that year. Congress passed a bill renewing the bank's charter, but Jackson vetoed it. Jackson believed that the strong national bank did the following:

- Unfairly stifled competition from smaller state banks and private banks
- Violated the Constitution, which states that only the federal government could regulate currency
- Encouraged speculation that eventually caused panics and depressions
- Oppressed the poor while making rich financiers even wealthier

The Election of 1832

Clay succeeded in making the bank one of the most important issues in the election of 1832. Three candidates contended for the presidency that year:

- Andrew Jackson ran on the Democratic ticket against the bank and lower tariffs.
- Henry Clay, representing the National Republicans, pressed for the bank, higher tariffs, and internal improvements.
- William Wirt, running for the **Anti-Masonic Party**, opposed the Order of the Masons.

Clay's plan to win the presidency by supporting the bank backfired. Jackson won the election easily with the votes of millions of recently enfranchised voters in the poorer areas of the West and South who hated the bank.

Although never a major party, the **Anti-Masonic Party** was the first third party to run a candidate in a presidential election and the first to specify its aims in a detailed party platform. The Anti-Masonic Party's primary objective was to end the Freemasonry movement, a secret society with religious overtones found throughout the United States. The party tried to capitalize on the public's fear of conspiracies and secret societies at the time.

Jackson Kills the Bank

Jackson interpreted his sweeping victory as a mandate from the people to destroy the Bank of the United States, and he did so by withdrawing all federal money and depositing it into smaller state banks instead. Afraid that the bank's death would encourage investors to over-speculate in western lands, valuing them more than they were worth, Jackson also issued a **Specie Circular** in 1836 that required all land to be purchased with hard currency.

INDIAN REMOVAL

Jackson, bowing to pressure from western settlers, convinced Congress to pass the **Indian Removal Act** in 1830, which authorized the forced relocation of tens of thousands of Native Americans to the "Great American Desert" west of the Mississippi, a land so inhospitable that most believed no white settlers would ever want to settle there.

Native American Resistance

The Native American tribes affected by the Indian Removal Act did not move quietly. The U.S. army encountered some of the heaviest resistance from the Fox

and Sauk in the Old Northwest region near the Great Lakes. Chief Black Hawk and his warriors resisted resettlement for two years until American troops ended the **Black Hawk War** in 1832. The Seminoles in Florida resisted relocation for seven years in the **Seminole War**.

Cherokees Fight the Law

The Cherokee tribe in Georgia also refused to comply with the new law. As one of the so-called Five Civilized Tribes, the Cherokee had actually taken great strides to assimilate into white southern culture. Most worked as farmers and some even owned large slave plantations. Instead of fighting for their homes, however, they challenged the law in court. Chief Justice John Marshall ruled in the following:

- *Cherokee Nation v. Georgia*, that the United States could not remove the Cherokee because they legally owned their lands as a separate nation independent from the United States (1831)
- *Worcester v. Georgia*, that Georgia could not force its laws on the independent Cherokee (1832)

The Trail of Tears

Jackson blatantly ignored the Court's rulings and forced the Cherokee to cede their lands and relocate to the Arkansas Territory. More than 12,000 Cherokee walked the **"Trail of Tears"** with the Choctaws, Chickasaws, Creeks, and conquered Seminoles. Thousands died from hunger, cold, and disease during this humiliating journey.

VAN BUREN, HARRISON, AND TYLER

Jackson, who had become old and weak, declined to run for a third term in 1836. His bold policies against nullification and the central bank had prompted his political opponents to form the new **Whig Party**, led by former National Republican leader Henry Clay. Like the National Republicans, the Whigs supported the American System, promoting internal improvements, creating protective tariffs, and supporting the bank.

Election of 1836

Four major candidates competed for the White House in 1836:

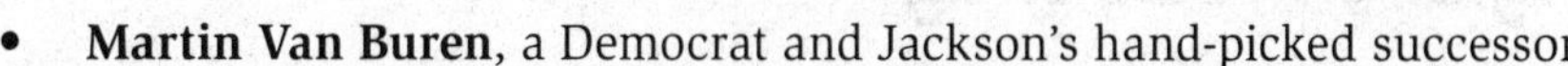

- **Martin Van Buren**, a Democrat and Jackson's hand-picked successor
- **Daniel Webster**, a prominent statesman from New England and Whig leader
- Hugh Lawson White, a Whig from Tennessee
- **William Henry Harrison**, yet another Whig and a famous war hero

The Whigs ran three candidates against Van Buren in the hopes that one of them could garner enough votes to oust the Jacksonian Democrats from the White House. The three candidates competing against each other, however, merely scattered Whig votes so that none of them had enough to defeat the popular Van Buren. As a result, Van Buren easily defeated his opponents to become the eighth president.

The Panic of 1837

Van Buren's presidency was blighted by the Panic of 1837 and the ensuing depression. Jackson's Specie Circular, issued just before he left office, required the payment of public land to be in gold or silver rather than paper money. This caused a run on banks, especially those in the West, as thousands tried to withdraw their money in gold and silver coins. Commodity prices fell, hundreds of banks shut down, and millions of Americans found themselves out of work or too poor to farm.

In response, Van Buren forced Congressional Democrats to pass a **Divorce Bill** to separate federal money from unstable banks and to redeposit it in a new and independent treasury. Van Buren hoped that such a move would restore Americans' faith in the economic stability of the government. But the depression only worsened and contributed to Van Buren's growing unpopularity.

The Hard Cider Election of 1840

The Depression ruined Van Buren's chances of reelection in 1840. Nevertheless, the Democrats nominated him again for lack of a better candidate. The Whigs, meanwhile, had grown wiser in the last four years and decided to focus their efforts on a single candidate instead of three. In the 1840 election, the Whigs nominated war hero William Henry Harrison. The Whigs appealed to common voters in the West and South by touting Harrison as a log-cabin-born, hard-cider-guzzling frontiersman. This strategy worked, and Harrison easily defeated Van Buren, much to the jubilation of Henry Clay and Daniel Webster. Yet, fewer than thirty days after taking the oath of office, Harrison died.

John Tyler's Presidency

Harrison's relatively unknown running mate, **John Tyler**, became president and proceeded to pursue his own agenda. Tyler, a former Democrat who'd only joined the Whig Party to oppose Jackson, had no love for federally funded internal improvements, higher protective tariffs, or a national bank. Instead, the new president tried to reduce tariffs, give more power to the individual states, and even vetoed a Whig bill to revive the Bank of the United States. Furious at Tyler's betrayal, Whig leaders officially expelled him from the party in 1842.

MANIFEST DESTINY AND POLK

In 1845, a New York newspaper editor wrote, "Our manifest destiny is to overspread the continent allotted by Providence for the free development of our yearly multiplying millions." The American public quickly latched on to **Manifest Destiny** and the belief that Americans had a mandate from God to spread democracy throughout North America. Thousands of settlers poured from the growing urban regions in the East to California, Oregon, and Texas. This belief in Manifest Destiny spread all the way to the highest levels of government, where congressmen and presidents traded, bought, annexed, and even went to war for new lands.

The Webster-Ashburton Treaty

The **Webster-Ashburton Treaty** of 1842 marked the government's first step toward fulfilling America's perceived destiny. The treaty, between the United States and Great Britain, settled the boundary disputes between the United States and Canada over the ore-rich Great Lakes region. It also stipulated that both countries would jointly occupy the Oregon Territory.

Texas

Texas declared independence from Mexico in 1836 and immediately requested annexation by the United States. Northern Whigs and others opposed to the expansion of slavery protested the creation of another slave state and blocked the southerners' move to annex Texas. Moreover, Congress had promised noninterference to Mexican officials during the war and thus couldn't legally annex Texas. Mexico, meanwhile, tried several times to retake its rebellious state over the next decade, with no success.

Britain's Plans for Texas

Forced to protect themselves without any assistance from the United States, Texans negotiated trade and security treaties with several European powers. Britain

in particular became very interested in Texas because an independent Texas would help them as follows:

- Halting American expansion
- Weakening the Monroe Doctrine, which might eventually allow Britain to found new colonies in North America
- Providing another source of cotton for British textile manufacturers

Election of 1844

Texas became the hottest issue in the election of 1844 after American policy-makers discovered Britain's plans. The election also focused on Oregon, tariffs, and the increasingly heated slavery issue. The major candidates of the election included the following:

- Henry Clay, a veteran Whig statesman, who ran on a platform against the annexation of Texas
- **James K. Polk**, a Democratic lawyer and Tennessee planter, who ran on a platform in favor of annexation
- James G. Birney, the new **Liberty Party** candidate, who was an abolitionist and ran on an antislavery platform

Texas Joins the Union

Polk barely won the election, with only 40,000 more popular votes than Clay. Sitting president John Tyler interpreted the victory as a mandate from the people to annex Texas. Before leaving office, Tyler asked Congress in 1845 for a joint resolution to annex Texas. Unlike the usual two-thirds vote of the Senate that was needed to ratify a treaty, the resolution required only a simple majority of each house. The resolution passed, and Texas was added to the Union as a slave state later that year.

Outraged, Mexico immediately withdrew its ambassador to the United States. More trouble arose when the two countries became embroiled in a border dispute. Americans claimed that the Rio Grande River divided Texas from Mexico, whereas Mexicans marked the border at the Nueces River farther north in Texas. Both sent troops to the region, the Americans camping north of the Nueces and the Mexicans to the south of the Rio Grande. War would soon erupt.

The Polk Presidency

James K. Polk entered the White House with a three-pronged agenda. He wanted to reduce tariffs, acquire Oregon, and acquire California. Amazingly, he achieved all three goals in only four years' time.

1. **Tariff Reduction.** Polk successfully pushed the **Walker Tariff** through Congress in 1846 to reduce general tariff rates from 32 to 25 percent.

2. **Oregon.** Although the United States had jointly occupied the Oregon Territory with Great Britain for several decades, Polk wanted sole ownership of Oregon for the United States, all the way to the southern border of Alaska at the 54° 40' parallel. Most Americans supported the move for all of Oregon, particularly considering that nearly 5,000 Americans had settled there after crossing the continent on the perilous **Oregon Trail**.

   Polk pressured Britain to relinquish Oregon to the point of threatening war, but eventually signed the compromise **Oregon Treaty** in 1846 to split Oregon at the forty-ninth parallel. Britain took all of present-day British Columbia while the United States took all the territory that eventually became Washington State, Oregon, Idaho, and parts of Montana.

3. **California.** Polk's greatest ambition of all was to add California to the United States. Polk particularly desired the glittering San Francisco Bay, which could open the United States to lucrative trade deals with Asia. Unfortunately for the president, Mexico had strong territorial claims to California. Polk's designs on California, as well as the U.S. troops stationed in Texas, led to conflict with Mexico once again.

THE MEXICAN-AMERICAN WAR

President Polk sent envoy John Slidell to Mexico in 1845, hoping to smooth relations with Mexico, resolve the Texas issue, and buy California. The president authorized Slidell to purchase California and New Mexico for a total of $25 million. Mexico, of course, refused the low offer and sent Slidell back to Washington. Undoubtedly knowing full well that Mexico would refuse the offer, Polk had simultaneously sent adventurer **John C. Frémont** to California, ostensibly on a scientific survey mission. At the same time, Polk sent several U.S. Navy ships to the California coast. General **Zachary Taylor** and 2,000 troops moved from their position north of the Nueces River and encamped along the northern shores of the Rio Grande River in disputed territory.

Polk Asks for War

In April of 1846, Mexican troops crossed the Rio Grande and attacked Taylor's men camped in disputed territory. Immediately after receiving news of the Mexican attack, Polk "reluctantly" requested that Congress declare war. After much debate, Congress eventually acquiesced. As soon as Congress formally declared

war the following month, U.S. forces defeated the Mexicans quickly and easily. In a little more than a year and a half the following occurred:

- Frémont and the navy seized California.
- American troops seized most of present-day New Mexico and Arizona.
- Taylor seized all of northern Mexico after defeating an overwhelming Mexican force at the Battle of Buena Vista.
- General Winfield Scott seized Mexico City in September 1847 to end the war.

The Treaty of Guadalupe-Hidalgo

American and Mexican diplomats signed the **Treaty of Guadalupe-Hidalgo** in 1848 to end the war. In the treaty:

- Mexico ceded California and most of present-day New Mexico, Arizona, Nevada, Colorado, and Wyoming to the United States.
- Mexico abandoned its claims to Texas.
- The Rio Grande River was established as the border between Texas and Mexico.
- The United States generously agreed to pay Mexico $15 million for all lands acquired.

Lincoln's "Spot Resolutions"

Despite the American victory and the enormous territorial gains that came with it, Polk faced severe criticism for the war in Washington. Whig congressman **Abraham Lincoln** continually badgered Polk about the exact spot where the Mexicans had engaged Taylor. These **"spot resolutions"** damaged Polk's reputation and led many to believe that the president had intentionally provoked the Mexicans in order to seize California.

The Legacy of the Mexican-American War

The vast majority of Americans had supported the war despite the $98 million price tag and the loss of approximately 12,000 men. However, the war was never perceived as a moral crusade based on the defense of democratic principles, because the United States hadn't fought for independence, freedom for oppressed peoples, or to save democracy. Rather, Americans had gone to war primarily in

the name of Manifest Destiny, to expand and acquire more land. At war's end, most Americans felt jubilant that the United States finally spread from coast to coast. The ever-present issue of the expansion of slavery into the new territories, however, would quickly sour the spoils of victory.

TIMELINE: 1824–1848

1824	The disputed presidential election of 1824 is dominated by the American System.
1825	House of Representatives chooses Adams for the presidency.
1828	Congress passes the "Tariff of Abominations."
	Andrew Jackson is elected president.
	John C. Calhoun publishes *The South Carolina Exposition.*
1830	Congress passes the Indian Removal Act.
1832	Jackson thwarts attempts to recharter the Bank of the United States.
	Congress passes the Tariff of 1832.
	Jackson is reelected.
	Jackson issues the Nullification Proclamation.
	The Black Hawk War ends one of the most destructive conflicts between pioneers and Native Americans.
1833	Congress passes Tariff of 1833.
	Jackson withdraws federal money from the Bank of the United States, vowing, "I will kill the bank."
	Congress passes the Force Bill.
1834	The Whig Party forms.
1836	The Bank of the United States' charter expires.
	Texas declares independence from Mexico.
	185 Texans fight a 4,000-man Mexican army in the Battle of the Alamo.
	Jackson issues Specie Circular.
	Martin Van Buren is elected president.

1837	Thousands withdraw money from banks in the Panic of 1837.
	Congress refuses to annex Texas.
1838	The army forcibly removes the Cherokee on the "Trail of Tears."
1840	William Henry Harrison is elected president.
	The Liberty Party forms.
1841	William Henry Harrison dies a month after becoming president.
	Vice President John Tyler becomes president.
1842	The United States and Britain sign the Webster-Ashburton Treaty.
1844	James K. Polk is elected president.
1845	The United States annexes Texas.
1846	Congress passes the Walker Tariff.
	The United States resolves the dispute over Oregon with Great Britain.
	The Mexican War erupts.
	John Frémont seizes California.
1847	Gen. Winfield Scott captures Mexico City.
1848	The United States and Mexico sign the Treaty of Guadalupe-Hidalgo.

MAJOR FIGURES

John Quincy Adams. Son of President John Adams, Adams served as James Monroe's secretary of state and in 1824 ran against Andrew Jackson for the presidency. Because neither he nor Jackson received enough electoral votes to become president, the election was thrown to the House of Representatives. Speaker of the House Henry Clay supported Adams, possibly in exchange for the position of secretary of state. This "corrupt bargain" tainted Adams's presidency and rendered him politically impotent during his four years in office.

John Frémont. Days after Congress declared war on Mexico in 1846, Frémont seized control of the government of California and declared it an independent country. He then immediately petitioned Congress to annex California. Many accused him of being an agent of James K. Polk and believed his presence in California to have been more than a coincidence. He later ran for president

against James Buchanan and Millard Fillmore in 1856: the first presidential candidate for the fledgling Republican party.

Abraham Lincoln. A former lawyer from Illinois, Lincoln became the sixteenth president of the United States in the election of 1860. Because he was a Republican and associated with the abolitionist cause, his election prompted South Carolina to become the first state to secede from the Union. Lincoln believed that the states had legally never truly left the Union but fought the war until the South surrendered unconditionally. He proposed the Ten-Percent Plan for Reconstruction in 1863 but was assassinated by John Wilkes Booth before he could carry out his plans.

James K. Polk. An expansionist Democrat from Kentucky, Polk was elected president on a Manifest Destiny platform in 1844. During his four years in office, he lowered the protective tariff, revived the independent treasury, acquired Oregon, and seized California in the Mexican War. Many critics past and present have accused him of purposefully provoking war with Mexico as an excuse to annex everything between California and Texas.

Zachary Taylor. A hero of the Mexican War, Taylor became the second and last Whig president in 1848. He campaigned without a solid platform to avoid controversy over the westward expansion of slavery in the Mexican cession. He died after only two years in office and was replaced by Millard Fillmore.

John Tyler. The first president who was not elected, Tyler entered the White House after the death of William Henry Harrison. He had originally been a Democrat but joined the Whigs in the 1830s because he couldn't stand President Andrew Jackson's autocratic leadership style. His political ideologies never really changed, however, and he consistently shot down most Whig legislation during his four years in office. To Henry Clay's and Daniel Webster's consternation, he refused to revive the Bank of the United States and disapproved of funding internal improvements with federal money, though he did pass the protective Tariff of 1842. Outraged, the Whigs kicked him out of the party before the presidential election of 1844. In his final days as president, he successfully annexed Texas.

Martin Van Buren. Former secretary of state to Andrew Jackson, Van Buren was elected president on the Democratic ticket in 1836. Unfortunately for him, his years in office were plagued by a depression after the financial Panic of 1837. Believing that federal funds in smaller banks had made the economy worse, Van Buren pushed the Divorce Bill through Congress to create an independent treasury. William Henry Harrison soundly defeated him in the election of 1840. He also ran as the Free-Soil Party candidate in the election of 1848.

Daniel Webster. A senator from New England, Webster was an ardent proponent of the American System. He was a leading statesman in his day and eventually teamed up with Henry Clay in 1834 to form the new Whig Party. As Whigs, he and Clay campaigned for progressive new reforms and limited westward expansion.

Chapter 7

A Growing Nation: 1820–1860

THE MARKET REVOLUTION

Between the 1820s and 1860, the **Industrial Revolution** transformed the national economy into a **market-based economy** that was heavily reliant on exportation of goods, especially cotton in the South, and the manufacturing of goods in the North. Internal improvements in transportation as well as new inventions spurred industrial and agricultural production and made transporting goods from one part of the country to another much easier.

The Southern Agricultural Revolution

Although textile manufacturing flourished in Great Britain, it lagged far behind in the United States, primarily because Americans lacked a source of cheap cotton. Southern planters had attempted to grow cotton in the eighteenth century but had almost completely switched to rice and tobacco by the dawn of the nineteenth century because growing cotton required too much labor.

The Cotton Gin

Inventor **Eli Whitney** made growing cotton more profitable with the automatic **cotton gin,** which he invented in 1793. Whitney's cotton gin vastly reduced the amount of labor required to harvest cotton and transformed the southern

economy virtually overnight. Planters quickly abandoned tobacco and rice for the suddenly profitable cotton. Cotton production in turn spurred the construction of textile factories in the North.

Interchangeable Parts

Several years after inventing the cotton gin, Whitney perfected a system to produce a musket with **interchangeable parts**. Before Whitney, craftsmen had made each individual musket by hand, and the parts from one musket would not necessarily work in another musket. With interchangeable parts, however, all triggers fit the same model musket, as did all ramrods, all flash pans, all hammers, and all bullets. Manufacturers swiftly applied the concept of interchangeable parts to mass-produce other identical goods.

The Western Agricultural Revolution

Many of those new products in turn revolutionized agriculture in the West. John Deere, for example, invented a horse-pulled **steel plow** to replace the difficult oxen-driven wooden plows farmers had used for centuries. The steel plow allowed farmers to till more soil in less time for less money without having to make repairs as often.

McCormick's Mechanical Mower-Reaper

In the 1830s, another inventor, Cyrus McCormick, invented a **mechanical mower-reaper** that quintupled the efficiency of wheat farmers. Often credited as the cotton gin of the West, the mower-reaper allowed farmers to grow large quantities of wheat instead of less profitable corn. As in the South, western farmers raked in huge profits as they acquired more land to plant greater quantities of wheat. More important, farmers for the first time began producing more wheat than the western markets could handle. Rather than letting it go to waste, they sold crop surpluses to the wageworkers in Northeast cities, which in turn helped those cities grow.

The Transportation Revolution

Western farmers, southern cotton growers, and northern manufacturers all relied on new forms of transportation to move their goods north and south, east and west across the country. Henry Clay's American System inspired state legislatures to construct a number of roads, canals, and other internal improvements to connect the Union.

Roads. Many northern states built turnpikes and toll roads during these years, the most famous being the **Cumberland Road,** or National Road, stretching from Maryland to St. Louis, Missouri, by the time construction finished in 1852. Other well-known roads include the Wilderness Road and the Lancaster Turnpike.

Canals. The **Erie Canal** that spanned the length of New York also helped northerners transport goods from the Great Lakes region to the Hudson River and ultimately the Atlantic. The canal also helped give birth to cities like Chicago, Cleveland, and Detroit, as ships from the Atlantic could now reach far inland. Other northern states built similar canals, usually to link the agricultural West with the industrial East.

Steamboats. The newly invented steamboat permitted fast, two-way traffic on all of these new waterways as well. For the first time in history, mariners didn't have to rely on winds and currents and could travel directly to any port at any time. Within a couple decades of their invention in 1807, steamboats chugged along all the major rivers and canals, and eventually on the high seas.

Railroads. Railroads were another conduit for moving people and goods quickly and cheaply. Prior to the 1850s, most railroads consisted of short lines linking local cities. Railroad construction expanded rapidly in both New England and the Northwest in the 1850s, with 31,000 miles of track in operation by 1860. The South, which was the least industrialized section of the nation, had fewer railroads than the North.

NORTHERN SOCIETY

The market revolution and surge in manufacturing had a tremendous impact on northern society. New York, Boston, Philadelphia, Baltimore, Pittsburgh, and other major cities sometimes tripled or even quadrupled in size between 1820 and 1860 as people left their farms to find work in urban areas. Smaller towns also experienced population growth during these years.

The Wage Labor System

As northerners continued building factories, they needed more and more workers to tend the machinery. Rather than learning a trade skill as most workers had in the past, these day laborers worked alongside scores of others, feeding or regulating a machine for hourly pay under harsh conditions. Workers toiled in textile factories for as many as sixteen hours a day, six or seven days a week. Although wealthy business owners loved the cheap labor, wage laborers suffered from poor working conditions.

Strikes and Reforms

Some workers chose to unite and strike in the 1830s and 1840s to protest inhumane conditions. The strikes caused such a stir in the national press that the government eventually took action. In 1840, for example, President Martin Van Buren established a ten-hour working day for all federal employees. Two years later, the Massachusetts Supreme Court legalized trade unions in the landmark 1842 decision ***Commonwealth v. Hunt***. Ultimately, despite the exploitation of early wage laborers, the shift away from craftsmanship toward wage labor helped give rise to a substantial and powerful middle class.

German and Irish Immigration

Mass immigration from Ireland and Germany was another factor in the urbanization phenomenon. More than 100,000 Irish came to the United States every year in the late 1840s and 1850s to escape the Potato Famine in Ireland, which ultimately killed more than a million people. Most of these immigrants settled in New York, Boston, and later Chicago, but Irish districts emerged in every major northern city. Germans also came en masse to the United States during the same period to escape political persecution in central Europe. These German immigrants generally had more money than the Irish and therefore mostly settled outside the congested cities.

Nativism and the Know-Nothings

A significant number of native-born Americans resented the influx of Germans and Irish. These **"nativists"** considered the Irish and Germans ignorant and inferior human beings, incapable of understanding democracy or assimilating into mainstream American culture. Many Protestants also hated the Germans and the Irish for their Catholic beliefs. The anti-immigration American Party, or **Know-Nothing Party**, was popular among nativists in the 1850s.

SOUTHERN SOCIETY

Although the North and West experienced dramatic social changes, the South for the most part did not. Rather, the southern social fabric remained relatively unchanged between 1820 and 1860 because of the region's reliance on cotton production. Cotton production proved so profitable after the invention of the cotton gin that by 1860 the South produced 75 percent of Britain's cotton supply.

Southern Social Hierarchy

Instead of evolving socially as the North had, the South continued to adhere to an archaic semi-feudalistic social order, which consisted of wealthy planter elites, slave-owning farmers, poor landless whites, and slaves.

Wealthy white plantation owners controlled the southern legislatures, represented the South in Congress, and had some of the largest fortunes in the country. Next came the white landowning subsistence farmers assisted by their one or two family slaves, followed by poor landless whites, who composed the vast majority of the southern population. Black slaves, of course, formed the base of the social hierarchy.

Justifying Slavery

Even though few southerners actually owned slaves, virtually all whites firmly believed in the superiority of their social system. Even very poor whites supported slavery because they dreamed of becoming wealthy slave owners. Whites justified slavery in many ways. Some championed the "paternal" nature of slavery by arguing that slave owners took care of the inferior race as fathers would small children. Others believed that slavery Christianized blacks and saved them from brutal lives as savages in Africa. Southerners, in general, preferred their more "humane" southern slavery to the impersonal "wage slavery" in the North.

REVIVALISM AND UTOPIANISM

A new wave or spiritual revivalism spread across America in the early to mid-nineteenth century. Many new denominations and utopian sects, including Methodists, Baptists, Shakers, Mormons, and Millerites, among others, emerged during these years.

The Second Great Awakening

A newfound sense of spirituality deeply affected Americans in the **antebellum period**. This renewed interest in religion, which began with the **Second Great Awakening** around the turn of the nineteenth century, swept across the country primarily as a reactionary response to the Enlightenment and the so-called "Age of Reason" that had inspired thinkers such as Benjamin Franklin, Thomas Jefferson, and Thomas Paine.

Hundreds of preachers, including **Charles Grandison Finney** and Timothy Dwight, set up revivalist camps in rural areas and attracted thousands of converts throughout the country. The converted often became so frenzied that they would roll, jerk, shake, shout, and even bark in excitement.

The Burned-Over District

Named for its abundance of hellfire-and-damnation preaching, the **Burned-Over District** in western New York produced dozens of new denominations, communal societies, and reform movements. This region was also burned-over (or, perhaps more appropriately, burned-*out*) from the economic changes it had undergone since the completion of the Erie Canal and the rapid development of the new market economy. Influenced by so many new ideas, visionaries, and forces, Americans in the Burned-Over District became some of the nation's greatest reform leaders.

Northern Denominations

Not all of the new Christian denominations were so "spirited." Although hellfire-and-damnation sermons appealed mostly to southerners and westerners, many northern denominations came to be highly regarded for their appeal to reason. Unitarians, Presbyterians, and Episcopalians, for example, attracted a huge following because of their belief in a loving God, free will, and denial of original sin.

Utopian Movements

In the spirit of the reform movement, more than 100,000 American men, women, and children between 1820 and 1860 searched for alternative lifestyles. Disenchanted with the world around them, utopian seekers aspired to a perfect society.

Mormons

Another new denomination from the Burned-Over District was the Church of Latter Day Saints, or **Mormon** Church. Founded by Ohioan **Joseph Smith** in 1830, Mormons believed God had entrusted them with a new set of scriptures called the Book of Mormon. Because Smith also advocated polygamy, Mormons faced intense hostility and persecution from Protestants throughout the Midwest.

When an angry Illinois mob murdered Smith in 1844, his disciple Brigham Young took charge of the church and led a mass migration to the desert around the Great Salt Lake (then claimed by Mexico). There the Mormons converted the barren lands into an oasis suitable for growing crops. Utah, the territory settled by the Mormons, eventually became a U.S. territory after the Mexican War but did not become a state until 1896, when Mormons agreed to abandon the practice of polygamy.

Other Utopian Communities

A variety of other utopian communities appeared and disappeared throughout the mid-nineteenth century. These communities included the following:

- **New Harmony,** a community of roughly 1,000 Americans in Indiana who believed socialistic communities could end poverty. The community collapsed in just a few short years.
- **Brook Farm,** a community in Massachusetts closely affiliated with the Transcendentalist movement, preached harmony with nature and modest living. This community also collapsed within a few years.
- **Oneida Community,** in Upstate New York, practiced free love, birth control, and eugenics.
- **The Millerites,** who eventually disbanded after Jesus failed to appear on October 22, 1843, as they believed he had promised he would.
- **The Shaker Movement,** located in several states and boasted more than half a million members at its height, ultimately dissolved because believers were forbidden to marry or have sex.

THE REFORM MOVEMENT

Fueled by the Great Awakening, many progressive northerners, women in particular, strived to improve society. They launched a variety of reform movements against prostitution, the consumption of alcohol, and the mistreatment of prisoners and the insane. Other reformers tried to expand women's rights and improve education. Many of these movements actually succeeded in convincing northern state legislatures to enact new laws. Southern states, however, generally lagged behind, remaining socially conservative.

Abolitionism

The abolitionist movement sought to eradicate slavery and quickly became the most visible reform movement during the antebellum period. Prominent northern abolitionists included Theodore Weld, Sojourner Truth, Frederick Douglass, Elijah P. Lovejoy, and **William Lloyd Garrison**, among many others.

Garrison and *The Liberator*

Garrison attained infamy after first publishing his antislavery newspaper *The Liberator* in 1831 and then cofounding the American Anti-Slavery Society two years later. A radical abolitionist who called for immediate emancipation, Garrison criticized the South so severely that many southern state legislatures issued warrants and bounties for his arrest or capture. Southerners feared Garrison because they incorrectly assumed he'd helped the black preacher **Nat Turner** lead a bloody slave uprising in Virginia the same year *The Liberator* debuted.

Anti-Abolitionism in the North

Not all northerners supported the abolition movement. In fact, many people actually felt ambivalent about emancipation or even opposed it outright. The blossoming trade unions and wageworkers, for example, hated abolitionists because they feared competition for jobs from free blacks. Most public figures and politicians, even Abraham Lincoln, shunned abolitionists for their radicalism and unwillingness to compromise. As a result, abolitionists at first had few friends and many enemies.

The Temperance Movement

The **temperance movement** sought to ban the manufacture, sale, and consumption of alcohol. By the 1830s, Americans had earned a reputation for hard drinking, especially in the West and South, where settlers endured extreme hardship. Factory owners in the cities also lamented that alcoholism reduced worker output and caused too many on-the-job accidents. Women, moreover, charged that drinking ruined family life and led to spousal and child abuse. As the new sense of morality spread throughout the country, more and more people campaigned against drinking.

Early Prohibition

The first chapter of the **American Temperance Society** formed in 1826 and blossomed into thousands of nationwide chapters within the following ten years. The society distributed fliers, pamphlets, and illustrations and paraded victims of abuse and reformed alcoholics through towns to preach against consumption.

The movement gained even more fame when T. S. Arthur published his novel *Ten Nights in a Barroom and What I Saw There* about the horrible effects of hard liquor on a previously quaint village. Several cities and states passed laws prohibiting the sale and consumption of alcohol, such as the so-called **Maine Law** in the northeastern state. However, no federal law or proclamation would make the sale or consumption of alcohol illegal until the 1920s.

Prohibiting Prostitution

Antebellum reformers struck out against prostitution in the rapidly growing industrial cities. Spearheaded almost entirely by upper- and middle-class women, antiprostitution societies fought not only to reduce the number of working girls on the streets but also to reform them. New York women founded the Female Moral Reform Society in 1834, which branched off to hundreds of other cities and towns by 1840. These societies also strove to end prostitution by decreasing demand. Many newspapers published the names of prostitutes' patrons, for example, while many states enacted laws to punish clients as well as the prostitutes themselves. However, the world's oldest profession continued unabated.

Prison Reform

Reformers also launched a campaign to improve prisons. Early- to mid-nineteenth-century prisons often resembled medieval dungeons and usually held only Americans who couldn't repay their debts. Over time, reformers managed to change the system. Debtor prisons gradually began to disappear as Americans realized the barbarity of locking people away for bad luck or circumstances beyond their control. More and more states also prohibited the use of cruel and inhumane punishments. Reformers also succeeded in convincing several state legislatures that governments should use prisons to help reform criminals, not just incarcerate them.

Reform for the Mentally Ill

Insane-asylum reform went hand in hand with prison reform, as most Americans at the time believed that the mentally ill were no better than animals. As a result, prisons contained thousands of mentally ill prisoners. Prison reformer **Dorothea Dix** spearheaded asylum reform by compiling a comprehensive report on the state of the mentally ill in Massachusetts. The report claimed that jailers had chained hundreds of insane women in stalls and cages. Her findings convinced state legislators to establish one of the first asylums devoted entirely to caring for the mentally ill. By the outbreak of the Civil War, nearly thirty states had built similar institutions.

Education Reform

Reformers sought to expand public education too. Most nineteenth-century Americans considered public education only fit for the poor. Wealthier Americans could, of course, pay for their children to attend private primary schools and secondary academies, but they loathed the idea of paying higher taxes to educate the poor.

Over the course of the antebellum period, more and more cities and states acknowledged that public education would expand democracy, improve productivity, and make better citizens. For example, **Horace Mann**, the secretary of the Board of Education in Massachusetts, fought for higher teacher qualifications, better pay, newer school buildings, and an improved curriculum.

The Women's Suffrage Movement

Women reformers also fought for gender equality. In the years before the Civil War, many Americans continued to believe that men and women worked in separate spheres: men outside the home, and women inside. Sometimes referred to as the "cult of domesticity," this social norm encouraged "good" women to make the home a happy and nurturing environment for their wage-laborer husbands, on top of maintaining day-to-day housekeeping.

The Seneca Falls Convention

As the American economy changed and more women left the sphere of the home for the workforce, many women began demanding more social, political, and economic rights. Prominent leaders of the women's rights movement included Lucretia Mott and **Elizabeth Cady Stanton**. These women astounded Americans and Europeans alike when they met at the **Seneca Falls Convention** in Seneca Falls, New York, in 1848. There, women leaders drafted a **Declaration of Sentiments** in the spirit of the Declaration of Independence to declare that women were equal to men in every way. Of the many sentiments declared, the call for full political suffrage shocked the world the most.

THE AMERICAN RENAISSANCE

The early nineteenth century gave rise to **Romanticism**, a cultural movement in Europe and America that revolted against the certainty and rationalism of the Enlightenment. In America, Romanticism manifested itself as a literary and artistic awakening in thought, literature, and the arts. Americans took great interest in the movement, idealizing its emphasis on the individual and the common man. Romanticism underscored feeling and emotion, in contrast with the balance, harmony, and form of eighteenth-century Classicism.

The Romantics

Romantics, such as John Greenleaf Whittier, Louisa May Alcott, and Henry Wadsworth Longfellow, tried to capture their thoughts and emotions as well as the spirit of the new America. Other social commentators included the so-called **Dark Romantics**, such as Edgar Allan Poe, Herman Melville, and Nathaniel Hawthorne, who took a more critical view of American society in the years before the Civil War.

The Transcendentalists

The New England **Transcendentalists** argued that not all knowledge comes from the senses and that ultimate truth "transcends" the physical world. Transcendentalists believed in the divinity of man's inner consciousness and thought that nature revealed the whole of God's moral law. Between 1830 and 1850, Transcendentalists such as **Ralph Waldo Emerson**, Henry David Thoreau, and Walt Whitman championed self-reliance and a rugged individuality that matched the character of the developing nation.

American Art

For the first time, American painting was reaching a level comparable to that of contemporary European artists. American artists worked within the Romantic Movement and sought to create unique aesthetic forms. Folk art attained popularity as did landscape paintings by the **Luminists** and **Hudson River School**. Americans also liked **Currier and Ives** lithographs, which portrayed rural and domestic scenes.

The blossoming artistic scene, however, belied a growing unease throughout the country. The slavery issue in particular began to occupy center stage in American politics, especially as new western states petitioned to join the Union. The disputes escalated into sporadic violence in the 1850s, pushing the North and South closer and closer to civil war.

TIMELINE: 1793–1855

1793	Eli Whitney invents the cotton gin.
1798	Whitney invents interchangeable parts for firearms.
1800	The Second Great Awakening begins.
1807	Robert Fulton invents the steamboat.
1823	Lowell Mills opens in Waltham, Massachusetts.
1825	The Erie Canal is completed.
	The New Harmony commune is founded.

1826	The American Temperance Society is founded.
1828	The first American railroad is completed.
1830	The Transcendentalist movement begins.
	Joseph Smith establishes the Mormon Church.
	Charles Grandison Finney begins conducting Christian revivals.
1831	Nat Turner leads a slave rebellion in Virginia.
	William Lloyd Garrison begins publishing *The Liberator.*
1833	The National Trades Union forms.
	Garrison and Theodore Weld found the American Anti-Slavery Society.
1834	Cyrus McCormick invents the mechanical mower-reaper.
1836	The House of Representatives passes the "Gag Resolution."
1837	John Deere invents the steel plow.
	Oberlin College begins admitting women.
	Mary Lyon establishes Mount Holyoke Seminary.
1840	Van Buren establishes a ten-hour working day for federal employees.
1841	The Brook Farm commune is founded.
1843	Dorothea Dix crusades for prison and insane-asylum reform.
	Millerites prepare for the end of the world.
1846	Mormons begin migration to Utah.
1848	The Seneca Falls Women's Rights Convention is held.
	The Oneida Community is founded.
1850	Nathaniel Hawthorne publishes *The Scarlet Letter.*
1851	Herman Melville publishes *Moby-Dick.*
1852	The Cumberland Road is completed.
1854	Henry David Thoreau writes *Walden.*
	T. S. Arthur publishes the novel *Ten Nights in a Barroom and What I Saw There.*
1855	Walt Whitman publishes *Leaves of Grass.*

MAJOR FIGURES

Dorothea Dix. A schoolteacher from Massachusetts, Dix spearheaded the campaign to establish publicly funded insane asylums to help the mentally ill. Her report on the deplorable treatment of insane women in the state's prisons convinced legislators to build the first asylums. Dix traveled tens of thousands of miles promoting her cause.

Ralph Waldo Emerson. One of America's leading essayists and philosophers, Emerson was also one of the foremost Transcendentalists in the 1830s, 1840s, and 1850s. His essays—including the famous "Self-Reliance"—made him one of the nation's most popular practical philosophers.

Charles Grandison Finney. A former lawyer, Finney applied his sharp wits and keen intellect to preach evangelism throughout the North during the 1830s. His camp-style meetings put thousands of people into a frenzy during his fifty-year crusade. He encouraged women to become church leaders and railed against the evils of slavery and alcohol.

William Lloyd Garrison. A radical abolitionist, Garrison advocated the immediate emancipation of all slaves in the United States. His infamous magazine, *The Liberator,* earned him many enemies in the South.

Horace Mann. A champion of public education, Mann supervised the creation of many new tax-supported schools as the secretary of the Massachusetts Board of Education in the 1830s. He fought for better curriculum, higher pay for teachers, and more teacher qualifications.

Joseph Smith. A New Yorker from the Burned-Over District, Smith founded the Mormon Church (Church of Jesus Christ of Latter Day Saints) after claiming to have received a new set of gospels from an angel. Smith attracted a huge following but was forced to move to the Midwest to escape persecution for his belief in polygamy. After he was murdered by a mob, his disciple Brigham Young led thousands of Mormons to the Great Salt Lake in Utah. The Mormon Church was one of the more successful new religions to sprout from the Burned-Over District.

Elizabeth Cady Stanton. One of the first American feminists, Stanton called for social and political equality for women in the nineteenth century. She helped organize the Seneca Falls Convention in 1848 and drafted the Declaration of Sentiments.

Eli Whitney. Inventor of the cotton gin and interchangeable parts, Whitney completely changed the American economy and social fabric. His 1793 cotton gin made growing cotton easy and highly profitable for southern planters, who eventually converted most of their fields to growing the crop. The surge in production also required more black slaves to pick the cotton. Southern cotton and interchangeable parts in turn stimulated the growth of textile manufacturing in the North and the birth of the wage labor system.

Chapter 8

Prelude to War: 1848–1859

SLAVERY AND EXPANSION

The new lands west of Texas that had been yielded to the United States at the end of the Mexican War rekindled the debate over the westward expansion of slavery. Southern politicians and slave owners wanted to permit slavery in the West out of fear that a ban would spell doom for the institution, as the South would lose the newly created seats in Congress. Whig northerners, however, viewed slavery as a moral evil and wanted it banned. Tensions mounted when Pennsylvanian congressman David Wilmot proposed banning slavery in the territory in the **Wilmot Proviso** in 1846, even before the Mexican War had ended. Outraged, southerners immediately killed the proposition in the Senate.

The Election of 1848

The debate over the westward expansion of slavery dominated the election of 1848 despite the death of the Wilmot Proviso, which would prohibit slavery in the western territories. Three major candidates contended for the presidency that year:

- **Lewis Cass**, the Democratic candidate, who championed **popular sovereignty**, which would allow people in the western territories to decide for themselves whether to legalize slavery.

- **Zachary Taylor**, the Whig candidate, a Mexican–American War hero who chose not to address the slavery issue
- **Martin Van Buren**, the **Free-Soil Party** candidate, who ran on an abolitionist platform

---

Van Buren's entry into the race split the Democrats and allowed Zachary Taylor to win easily. Although Taylor's silence on the slavery question quelled further discussion for a time, the issue resurfaced less than a year later when California applied for statehood. As a result, a great debate quickly divided northerners and southerners in Congress over the future of slavery beyond the Mississippi.

The Compromise of 1850

In 1850, the North and South once again agreed to compromise on the issues of slavery and California's acceptance into the Union. Although **Henry Clay** deserves most of the credit for engineering the compromise, a younger generation of politicians, such as Illinois senator **Stephen Douglas**, hammered out most of the details of the **Compromise of 1850**:

- California entered the Union as a free state.
- Northerners and Southerners agreed that popular sovereignty would determine the fate of slavery in all other western territories.
- Texas gave up territorial claims west of the Rio Grande (in New Mexico) in return for $10 million.
- Washington, D.C., abolished the slave trade but not slavery itself.
- Congress passed a new and stronger **Fugitive Slave Law**, which required Northerners to return runaway slaves to Southern plantation owners.

Although President Taylor opposed the compromise, he unexpectedly died (most likely from cholera) in 1850 before he could veto it. Instead, Vice President **Millard Fillmore** became president and signed the compromise into law in September 1850.

Significance of the Compromise

The Compromise of 1850 benefited the North far more than the South:

- California's admission tipped the precious sectional balance in the Senate in favor of the North with sixteen free states to fifteen slave states.

- California's admission to the Union as a free state set a precedent in the West against the expansion of slavery.
- Southerners conceded to end the slave trade in Washington, D.C.
- The compromise averted civil war for ten more years, allowing the North to develop industrially.

Though the compromise granted Californians popular sovereignty, meaning they were allowed to decide for themselves whether to allow slavery, Northerners knew that slavery would never take root in the West. Cotton couldn't grow in the arid western climate, and therefore the need for slaves would not be as great as it was in the South.

Northern Reaction to the Fugitive Slave Law

The new Fugitive Slave Law only fanned the abolitionist flame instead of relieving sectional tensions. Even though most white Americans in the North harbored no love for blacks, they didn't want to re-enslave those who had escaped to freedom. Consequently, armed mobs of Northerners sometimes attacked slave catchers to free captured slaves. On one occasion, it took several hundred troops and a naval ship to escort a single captured slave through the streets of Boston and back to the South to prevent mobs from freeing him. The law helped transform abolitionism from a radical philosophy into a mainstream movement in the North.

The Underground Railroad

Even though very few slaves actually escaped to the North, the mere fact that northern abolitionists encouraged slaves to run away infuriated Southern plantation owners. Despite this fury, there were those in the South who helped slaves escape to freedom. The **Underground Railroad** successfully ferried as many as several thousand fugitive slaves into the North and into Canada during these years. "Conductor" **Harriet Tubman** supposedly delivered several hundred slaves to freedom herself.

Harriet Beecher Stowe's 1852 novel *Uncle Tom's Cabin* also had a profound effect on Northerners. Stowe sold hundreds of thousands of copies within just a few months and turned many Northerners against slavery.

Pierce and Expansion in 1852

After the Compromise of 1850, Southerners quickly sought out new territories to expand the cotton kingdom. The election of **Franklin Pierce** to the presidency in 1852 only helped their cause. Pierce was a pro-South Democrat from New England and a firm believer in Manifest Destiny who also hoped to expand the United States.

Walker in Nicaragua

Pierce became particularly interested in acquiring new territories in Latin America during his presidency. He even went so far as to quietly support a coup in Nicaragua led by southern adventurer **William Walker**, who hoped that Pierce would annex Nicaragua as Polk had annexed Texas in 1844. The plan failed, however, when several other Latin American countries sent troops to remove Walker from power.

Cuba, Japan, and the Gadsden Purchase

Pierce also threatened to steal Cuba from Spain in a letter called the **Ostend Manifesto**. His plans failed when northern journalists received a leaked copy of the letter and published it in 1854. Despite these failures, Pierce acquired 30,000 square miles of New Mexican territory from Mexico in the **Gadsden Purchase** in 1853 and successfully opened Japan to American trade later that year.

THE KANSAS-NEBRASKA CRISIS

To prevent railroad developers from building a transcontinental railroad through the South and Southwest, which would aid the spread of slavery, Illinois senator **Stephen Douglas** proposed instead to build the line farther north through the vast unorganized territory west of the Mississippi River. Douglas proposed the **Kansas-Nebraska Act** in 1854 to create two new territories, Kansas and Nebraska, North of the 36° 30' parallel, as the law stipulated that developers could only lay railroad tracks in states or in federal territories. Because Douglas knew that Southerners would never approve two new free territories, he instead declared that popular sovereignty would determine whether Kansas and Nebraska would enter the Union as free or slave states.

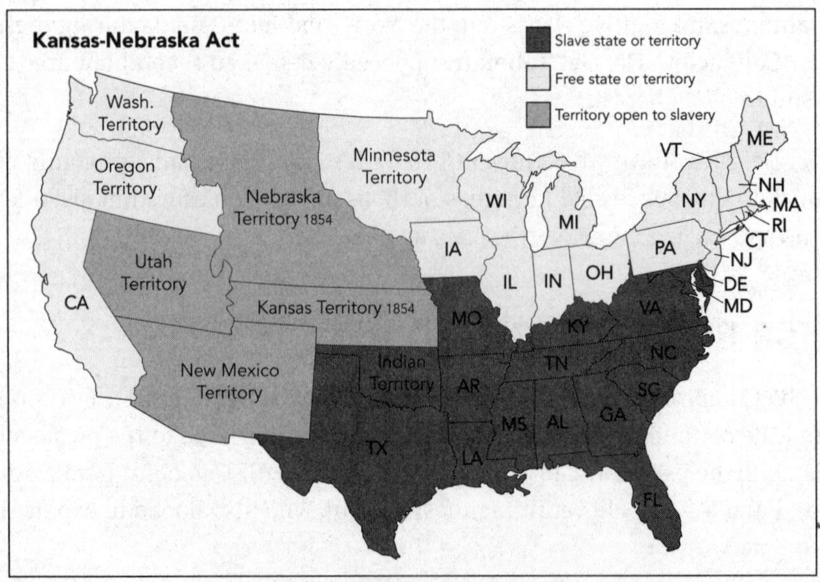

Douglas made an enormous error in proposing the Kansas-Nebraska Act. Southern Democrats and Whigs alike jumped at the opportunity to open northern territories to slavery and quickly passed the act. Northerners, however, felt outraged that Douglas and the Southerners had effectively revoked the sacred Missouri Compromise of 1820, which banned slavery north of the 36° 30' parallel. Hundreds of riots and protests consequently erupted in Northern cities, and many people began to feel that differences between the North and South had become irreconcilable.

Bleeding Kansas

As soon as Congress passed the Kansas-Nebraska Act, thousands of proslavery Missourians crossed the state line into Kansas and claimed as much land as they could. Hoping to make Kansas another slave territory, these **"Border Ruffians"** also rigged elections and recruited friends and family in Missouri to cast illegal ballots. Others voted multiple times or threatened indifferent settlers to vote in favor of slavery. Shocked, Northern abolitionists flocked to the state to establish their own free-soil towns.

The Pottawatomie Massacre

Violence eventually erupted when a group of Border Ruffians burned the free-soil (antislavery) town of Lawrence. In retaliation, a deranged abolitionist named **John Brown**, along with his own band of men, butchered five proslavery settlers in the **Pottawatomie Massacre**. No court ever punished Brown or his followers. Within a few months, Border Ruffians and free-soilers in **"Bleeding Kansas"** had become embroiled in a bloody civil war that foreshadowed the looming greater Civil War.

The Caning of Charles Sumner

The crisis in Kansas deeply shocked and divided Americans, as evidenced by the caning of Massachusetts senator **Charles Sumner** on the Senate floor on May 22, 1856. Incensed over an antislavery speech Sumner had delivered after violence erupted in Kansas, Congressman Preston Brooks from South Carolina mercilessly beat Sumner with his cane on the floor of the Senate. The beating nearly killed the Massachusetts senator, who ultimately left the Senate for several years to receive medical treatment. Southerners hailed Brooks as a hero, while Northerners called him a barbarian. Violence on the floor of the Senate, and the vastly differing reactions to the violence, were more indicators that pro- and antislavery factions had moved beyond debate.

The Election of 1856

Bleeding Kansas dominated the election of 1856, and parties nominated Kansas-neutral candidates in the hope of avoiding sectionalism. The Whig Party had by this time completely dissolved over the slavery and popular sovereignty question, and former Whigs in the North chose to unite with the Free-Soil Party and

unionist Democrats to form the new **Republican Party**. There were three candidates for president in 1856:

- John C. Frémont, the new Republican-nominated adventurer, on a platform against the westward expansion of slavery
- **James Buchanan**, the Democrat-nominated and relatively unknown candidate who championed popular sovereignty (allowing states to decide for themselves whether to enter the Union as slave or free)
- **Millard Fillmore**, ex-president of the nativist **Know-Nothing Party**, on an anti-immigration platform

---

Because most Southern state legislatures threatened to secede from the Union if Frémont became president, Buchanan won easily. Many Northerners, shocked by the violence in Kansas and unprepared for a larger civil war, ultimately voted for the Democrat in order to keep the Union intact, whether they agreed with popular sovereignty or not.

The Lecompton Constitution

Because abolitionist settlers and Border Ruffians couldn't agree on a territorial government in Kansas, they each established their own. The free-soil legislature resided in Topeka and the proslavery government in Lecompton. After free-soilers boycotted a rigged election to choose delegates to draft a state constitution in 1857, proslavery settlers decided to write their own. After drafting the **Lecompton Constitution**, which permitted slavery and placed no restrictions on the importation of slaves into the territory, they then applied for statehood as a slave state.

President Buchanan immediately accepted the constitution and welcomed Kansas into the Union. The Republican-dominated Congress, however, refused to admit Kansas. Senator Douglas declared that Congress would only admit Kansas after honest elections had determined whether the state would be free or slave. The following year, an overwhelming number of Kansas voters flatly rejected the Lecompton Constitution in a referendum, and Kansas entered the Union as a free state in 1861.

PRELUDE TO WAR

North-South relations worsened throughout Buchanan's four years in office. By 1859, civil war appeared inevitable.

The Dred Scott Case

In the 1840s, a Missouri slave named **Dred Scott** sued his master for his family's freedom on the grounds that they had lived with his master for several years in the free states north of the 36° 30' parallel. In fact, his wife and daughter had been born in the North but had become slaves as soon as they accompanied Scott back into the South. In 1857, the case landed in the Supreme Court, where Chief Justice Roger Taney and other conservative justices ruled that only citizens, not slaves, could file lawsuits in federal courts. Moreover, Taney declared the Missouri Compromise of 1820 unconstitutional because the government could not restrict the movement of private property.

Essentially, Taney and the Court argued that slaves had no legal rights because they were property. Taney hoped that the decision in *Dred Scott v. Sanford* would permanently end the sectional debate over slavery.

Northern Backlash to Dred Scott

Instead, the Dred Scott ruling only exacerbated sectional tensions. Southerners praised the ruling while Northerners recoiled in horror. Thousands took to the streets in the North to protest the decision, and many questioned the impartiality of the Southern-dominated Supreme Court. Several state legislatures even nullified the decision and declared that their states would never permit slavery, no matter who ordered them to do so. Many also accused James Buchanan of bias when journalists uncovered that the president had pressured a Northern Supreme Court justice into siding with Taney and the Southerners.

The Lincoln-Douglas Debates

In this atmosphere of national confusion, a relatively unknown former congressman named Abraham Lincoln challenged Stephen Douglas to a series of public debates in their home state of Illinois. Lincoln hoped to steal Douglas's seat in the Senate in the 1858 elections and to be the first to put the question of slavery to the voters. Douglas accepted Lincoln's offer and engaged Lincoln in a total of seven public debates in front of several thousand people. Lincoln denounced slavery as a moral wrong and voiced his desire to see the "peculiar institution" banned entirely in the West. At the same time, however, he also expressed his deep desire to preserve the Union.

Douglas, meanwhile, called Lincoln a radical abolitionist and argued in the **Freeport Doctrine** that only popular sovereignty would provide a democratic solution to resolving the slavery debate in the West. Even though Lincoln lost the Senate seat, the **Lincoln-Douglas Debates** made Lincoln a national figure.

John Brown's Raid

On October 16, 1859, John Brown of Pottawatomie, Kansas, stormed an arsenal at **Harpers Ferry**, Virginia, with twenty other men hoping to spark a slave rebellion in Virginia and throughout the South. Strangely, the insane Brown had

forgotten to inform any slaves of his intentions, and therefore no slaves rose up against their masters. Instead, Brown and his men found themselves trapped inside the arsenal and surrounded by federal troops. Brown eventually surrendered after a long and bloody standoff that killed more than half his men, including his own son.

After a speedy trial, a federal court convicted and hanged Brown. Before his death, the unwavering Brown dramatically announced that he'd gladly die if his death brought the nation closer to justice.

Reactions North and South

Southerners applauded Brown's execution because his raid on Harpers Ferry had touched on the Southerners' deepest fear: that the slaves would one day rise up against them. To them, Brown had been a criminal and a traitor of the worst kind. Northerners, however, mourned his death because they considered him an abolitionist martyr, especially after so boldly denouncing slavery with his final words. He instantly became a national hero and patriot, despite the fact that he'd clearly broken the law. The Northerners' reaction shocked Southerners, driving the two groups further apart.

TIMELINE: 1846–1859

1846	David Wilmot proposes the Wilmot Proviso.
1848	The Mexican War ends.
	The Free-Soil Party forms.
	Zachary Taylor is elected president.
1849	California petitions for admission to the Union.
1850	The Compromise of 1850 includes the passage of the Fugitive Slave Law.
	Taylor dies from cholera.
	Millard Fillmore becomes president.
1852	Franklin Pierce is elected president.
	Harriet Beecher Stowe publishes *Uncle Tom's Cabin*.
1854	Pierce threatens to acquire Cuba in the Ostend Manifesto.
	Stephen Douglas proposes the Kansas-Nebraska Act.
	The Republican Party forms.
1855	William Walker takes Nicaragua.

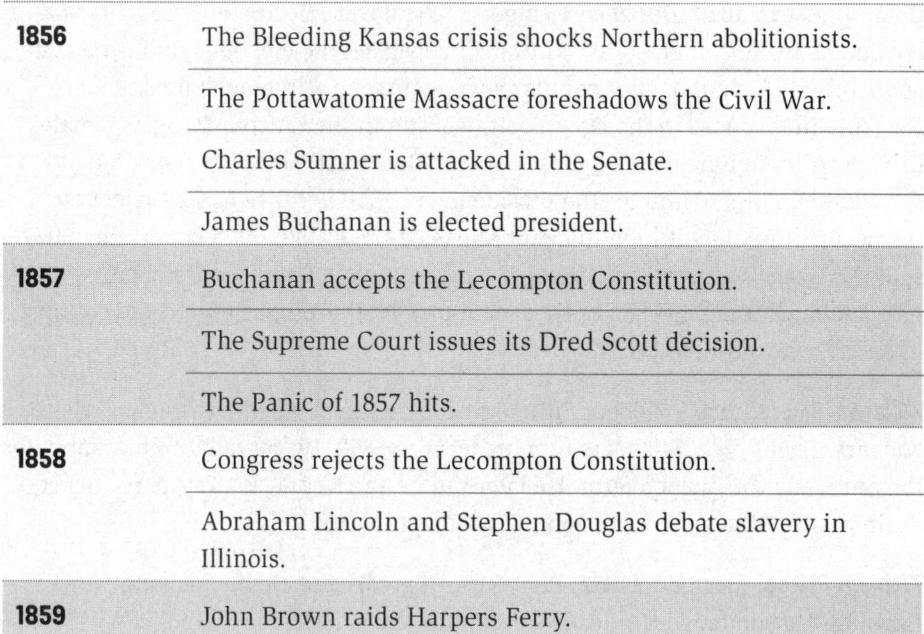

1856	The Bleeding Kansas crisis shocks Northern abolitionists.
	The Pottawatomie Massacre foreshadows the Civil War.
	Charles Sumner is attacked in the Senate.
	James Buchanan is elected president.
1857	Buchanan accepts the Lecompton Constitution.
	The Supreme Court issues its Dred Scott decision.
	The Panic of 1857 hits.
1858	Congress rejects the Lecompton Constitution.
	Abraham Lincoln and Stephen Douglas debate slavery in Illinois.
1859	John Brown raids Harpers Ferry.

MAJOR FIGURES

John Brown. Undoubtedly certifiably insane, Brown was a zealous radical abolitionist from Ohio who violently crusaded against slavery in the 1850s. He moved to Kansas in the mid-1850s with his family to prevent the territory from becoming a slave state. In 1856, he and a band of vigilantes helped spark the Bleeding Kansas crisis when they slaughtered five Border Ruffians at the Pottawatomie Massacre. Three years later, Brown led another group of men in the Harpers Ferry Raid to incite a slave rebellion. He was captured during the raid and hanged shortly before the election of 1860. Though Brown's death was cheered in the South, he was mourned in the North.

James Buchanan. A pro-South Democrat, Buchanan became the fifteenth president of the United States in 1856 after defeating John Frémont of the new Republican party and former president Millard Fillmore of the Know-Nothing party in one of the most hotly contested elections in U.S. history. Buchanan supported the Lecompton Constitution to admit Kansas as a slave state, weathered the Panic of 1857, and did nothing to prevent South Carolina's secession from the Union.

Lewis Cass. As Democratic candidate for the presidency against Zachary Taylor and Martin Van Buren in 1848, Cass was the first to propose allowing Americans in the territories to choose for themselves whether to be free or slave states. The doctrine of popular sovereignty was the hottest election topic in the years leading up to the Civil War.

Stephen Douglas. A Democratic senator from Illinois, Douglas pushed the Kansas-Nebraska Act through Congress in 1854 to entice railroad developers to build a transcontinental railroad line in the North. The act opened Kansas and Nebraska territories to slavery and thus effectively repealed the Missouri

Compromise of 1820. Douglas rejected the proslavery Lecompton Constitution in the Senate in 1857 after Border Ruffians had rigged the elections to draft a state constitution. A champion of popular sovereignty, he announced his Freeport Doctrine in response to the Dred Scott decision in the Lincoln-Douglas debates in 1858. Although he was the most popular Democrat, Southern party members refused to nominate him for the presidency in 1860 because he had rejected the Lecompton Constitution to make Kansas a slave state. As a result, the party split: Northern Democrats nominated Douglas, while Southern Democrats nominated John C. Breckinridge. In the election of 1860, Douglas toured the country in an effort to save the Union.

Millard Fillmore. Vice President Fillmore became the thirteenth president when Zachary Taylor died two years into his term in 1850. He served unremarkably for the remainder of Taylor's term. He later ran on the Know-Nothing party ticket against James Buchanan and John C. Frémont in 1856.

Franklin Pierce. Elected in 1852, Pierce was a proslavery Democrat from New England. He combined his desire for empire and westward expansion with the South's desire to find new slave territories. He tacitly backed William Walker's attempt to seize Nicaragua and threatened Spain in the Ostend Manifesto for Cuba. He also sent Commodore Matthew Perry to forcibly pry open Japan to American trade and authorized the Gadsden Purchase from Mexico in 1853. Pierce's reputation was muddied by his alliance with the South, his aggressive expansionism, and by Bleeding Kansas.

Dred Scott. A slave to a Southern army doctor, Scott had lived with his master in Illinois and the Wisconsin territory in the 1830s. While there, he married a free woman and had a daughter who eventually went back with Scott to the South. Scott sued his master for his and his family's freedom, but Chief Justice Roger Taney and a conservative Supreme Court ruled against Scott, arguing that Congress had no right to restrict the movement of private property. Moreover, he ruled that blacks such as Scott could not file lawsuits in federal courts because they were not citizens. The Dred Scott decision outraged Northerners and drove them further from the South.

Charles Sumner. In 1856, Senator Sumner from Massachusetts delivered an antislavery speech in the wake of the Bleeding Kansas crisis. In response, he was caned nearly to death by South Carolinian congressman Preston Brooks on the Senate floor. The caning demonstrated just how seriously southerners took the popular sovereignty and slavery issue.

Zachary Taylor. A hero of the Mexican War, Taylor became the second and last Whig president in 1848. He campaigned without a solid platform to avoid controversy over the westward expansion of slavery in the Mexican Cession. He died after only two years in office and was replaced by Millard Fillmore.

Harriet Tubman. An illiterate runaway slave from Maryland, Tubman was an active abolitionist as one of the key "conductors" on the Underground Railroad. She led nineteen missions into the South in the years before the war to rescue 300 slaves. She also delivered lectures on the evils of slavery to Northern audiences and served as a Union spy during the Civil War. Many called her "Moses" for her dedication and bravery in leading blacks out of slavery.

William Walker. A proslavery American adventurer from the South, Walker led an expedition to seize control of Nicaragua in 1855. Once in power, he hoped to petition Franklin Pierce for annexation as a new slave state. Unfortunately for him, several Latin American countries sent troops to oust him before he could make the offer. The Nicaraguan adventure was just one example of Pierce's expansionist policies.

Chapter 9

The Civil War: 1860–1865

LINCOLN AND SECESSION

Very little held the United States together in 1860: The political parties had dissolved into sectional parties, and even churches had split over the slavery issue. People in the North simply couldn't understand the South's insistence on expanding the "slavocracy" westward, while Southerners thought that Northerners wanted to completely destroy their way of life. As a result, Americans on both sides of the Mason-Dixon Line wondered and worried about who would become the next president in 1860.

Election of 1860

Four candidates contended for the presidency in the election of 1860:

- **Abraham Lincoln** ran on the Republican ticket in favor of higher protective tariffs and more internal improvements, with promises to maintain the Union at all costs.
- **Stephen A. Douglas** ran for the Northern Democratic Party, also on a pro-Union platform.
- **John C. Breckinridge** ran as a Southern Democrat in strong support of slavery.

- **John Bell** ran with a breakaway group of compromising Republicans on the Constitutional Union Party ticket.

Because none of the slave states even put Lincoln's name on the ballot, the election eventually became two sectional elections, with Lincoln versus Douglas in the North and Breckinridge and Bell in the South. In the end, Lincoln won the presidency with approximately 39 percent of the popular vote, all eighteen free states, and a clear majority of 180 votes in the Electoral College.

Secession

Immediately after the election, South Carolina's legislature convened a special convention and voted unanimously to secede from the Union. South Carolina then issued **"A Declaration of the Causes of Secession,"** which reviewed the threats against slavery and asserted that a sectional party had elected a president hostile to slavery. By February 1861, six other slave states had followed suit, including Mississippi, Florida, Alabama, Georgia, Louisiana, and Texas.

The Crittenden Compromise

Hoping to prevent war, Senator John Crittenden from Kentucky proposed another compromise. He suggested adding an amendment to the Constitution to protect slavery in all territories south of 36° 30'. Popular sovereignty would determine whether the southwestern territories would enter the Union as free or slave states. Conversely, all territories north of 36° 30' would be free. Many Southerners contemplated this **Crittenden Compromise**, but Lincoln rejected it out of the belief that the people had elected him to prevent the westward expansion of slavery.

Lincoln's First Inaugural Address

In his **First Inaugural Address**, Lincoln reaffirmed the North's friendship with the South, stressed national unity, and asked Southerners to abandon secession. Moreover, he declared secession illegal and vowed to maintain the Union at all costs.

Fort Sumter

After declaring their independence, South Carolina authorities demanded the immediate withdrawal of all U.S. troops from **Fort Sumter**, a small island in Charleston Harbor. When Lincoln didn't comply, South Carolina militiamen shelled the fort on April 12, 1861, until the garrison's commander surrendered. Not a single soldier died during the fight, leading many Southerners to conclude that Northerners lacked the will to fight. The fall of Fort Sumter also convinced Arkansas, North Carolina, Tennessee, and Virginia to secede. The Civil War had begun.

Northern and Southern Advantages

In retrospect, Union victory seems to have been inevitable. The Confederate struggle was doomed, lost in the romantic imagery of a lost cause, a small Southern band fighting against a larger Northern force. Large-scale industrialization, an enormous population, more resources, more weaponry, and a better transportation network gave the North a huge advantage. The Union also featured an efficient navy and had the ability to build more ships. The Union quickly used its navy to its advantage and blockaded southern ports.

At the time, however, these northern advantages seemed negligible because the South had superior military leaders, a captive labor force, hope for help from Europe, and the benefit of fighting a defensive war on familiar soil. As a result, both the North and the South naively believed they could defeat the other quickly and easily.

THE NORTH

The Fall of Fort Sumter prompted Lincoln to prepare for war. He called for volunteers to enlist in the army and navy, ordered a naval blockade of Southern ports, and moved troops to protect Washington, D.C. Congress later passed a number of sweeping measures to help industrialists and bolster the national economy.

The Border States

Only ten of the fourteen slave states followed South Carolina and seceded from the Union. The other four—Maryland, Delaware, Kentucky, and Missouri—remained loyal to the United States. West Virginia eventually seceded from Virginia in 1863 and joined the Union as a free state. These five **border states** were crucial to the North because they geographically split the North from the South. Additionally, if the North were able to keep control of the border states, then they would discredit the Confederacy's claim that the Union would emancipate all slaves. Maryland and Delaware also had many factories that could have doubled the South's industrial capabilities, and Maryland's secession would have isolated Washington, D.C., from the rest of the North.

To ensure these states' loyalty, Lincoln sometimes had to resort to force to prevent them from joining the Confederacy. He suspended the **writ of habeas corpus** in Maryland, allowing the government to arrest suspected Confederate sympathizers and hold them without trial, and declared martial law in 1861 after pro-Confederacy protestors attacked U.S. soldiers marching to Washington, D.C.

Bending the Constitution

Lincoln also faced opposition from people in the North. On one side, **Peace Democrats** accused him of starting an unjust war, while **Radical Republicans**

in his own party accused him of being too soft on the Confederacy. Many on both sides also criticized him for usurping unconstitutional powers to achieve his goals. Among other actions, Lincoln suspended the writ of habeas corpus, ordered a naval blockade of all Southern ports without Congress's permission, increased the size of the army without Congress's consent, and authorized illegal voting methods in the border states to ensure they wouldn't secede.

Chief Justice Roger Taney of the Supreme Court deemed these actions unconstitutional, but Lincoln ignored him, believing that desperate times called for drastic measures. Congress and most Northerners generally approved of his decisions anyway.

The 1862 Congress

Congress, for its part, legislated a flurry of progressive new laws as soon as the South seceded from the Union. Without any states-rights advocates, Northern Republicans easily passed the following acts:

- **The Morrill Tariff Act** to help Northern manufacturers by doubling the prewar tariff on imported goods
- **The Legal Tender Act** to create a stable national currency
- **The National Banking Act** to strengthen banks and enforce the Legal Tender Act

---

These acts gave the federal government unprecedented power over the economy and provided stability to the robust industrial economy in the North, both of which ultimately helped the North defeat the South.

The Draft and Draft Riots

In 1863, Congress also passed a conscription law to draft young men into the Union army. The law demanded that men either join the army or make a $300 contribution to the war effort. Although designed to promote support for the war among the rich and poor alike, this "$300 rule" effectively condemned the poorer classes to military service. Thousands of urban poor people staged protests against the law in dozens of northern cities. Protests in New York escalated into a full-scale riot in mid-1863, when racist whites from the poorest neighborhoods burned and looted parts of the city. Protestors also murdered nearly one hundred people in the **New York City Draft Riot** before federal troops arrived.

The Northern Economy

Throughout the war, Northern factories continued to pump out weapons, clothing, and supplies for Union soldiers. Manufacturers increased production of agricultural equipment to help the farmers in the West produce more wheat and corn to feed the troops. The fields in the West benefited from good weather throughout the war, while the South suffered from extreme drought.

Oil production and coal mining became big industries in the North during these years as well. Alternatively, because the South had only a limited number of factories, Confederate troops often fought with antiquated weapons in tattered homespun uniforms and had little to eat.

Northern Women

In the North, women organized the United States Sanitary Commission to provide medical relief and other services to soldiers. Other northern women worked to help starving and homeless freed slaves. Several thousand northern women also worked as nurses.

THE SOUTH

Delegates from the first seven secessionist states (South Carolina, Mississippi, Alabama, Georgia, Florida, Texas, and Louisiana) met in Montgomery, Alabama, in February 1861 to form the government of the new **Confederate States of America**. Using the U.S. Constitution as a template, they drafted a new constitution; chose Richmond, Virginia, to be the new capital; and selected Mississippi planter **Jefferson Davis** as the Confederacy's first president.

President Davis

Although Davis had more political experience than Lincoln (he'd served as secretary of war and as a U.S. senator), he proved to be a poor commander in chief. Unlike Lincoln, he didn't understand the importance of public opinion and as a result didn't connect well with voters. Moreover, his nervousness and refusal to delegate authority alienated many cabinet members, congressmen, and state governors. He often had difficulty controlling his own government.

Federation vs. Confederation

Although the South used the U.S. Constitution as a model, the Confederate government differed radically from that of the United States, primarily because the drafters of the Confederate constitution wanted to protect the rights of the member states. To ensure that individual state governments would remain strong, Southerners refused to give their federal government any real authority. In other words, the Richmond government more closely resembled a loose organization of strongly independent states rather than the tightly knit federation of the United States.

Keeping the Confederacy Together

Because the individual state governments in the South had more power than the central government, Davis had trouble controlling the states and coordinating

the war. Lack of control proved to be the South's greatest weakness in the war for the following reasons:

- State governors refused to send their troops across state lines, even to assist in battle.
- State legislatures generally refused to support the Richmond government financially.
- A nation founded on secession couldn't logically withhold the right of member states to secede.

As a result, the central government in Richmond never had any money, lacked control over the national economy, couldn't maintain a strong national army, and couldn't even prevent states from seceding from the Confederacy during the final weeks of the war.

The Conscription Act

The Richmond government passed the **Conscription Act of 1862** to force young men in all secessionist states into the national army. Like the draft in the North, the Confederate conscription law hurt poor people the most because it exempted wealthy planters and landowners.

Conscription Breeds Class Conflict

Although conscription eventually worked for the North despite the draft riots, it failed miserably in the South. Confederate regiments often suffered extremely heavy losses—and the poor Southerners knew it. Poor soldiers resented the fact that they fought and bled in the war to support the rich whites who had started the war in the first place. They didn't see why they had to fight and their own families had to starve, while the elites in Richmond slept safely and warmly in their beds and ate well every night. Not surprisingly, desertion unfolded as the Southern military's greatest problem during the war.

Courting Great Britain

Davis hoped to end the war quickly by securing international recognition from Europe and possibly even a military alliance with Great Britain. He and most Southerners realized that international recognition would legitimize the Confederacy and justify their cause. Moreover, an alliance with Britain would allow them to break the Union blockade that surrounded Southern ports so that they could supply soldiers with weapons and food.

The Alabama and the Laird Rams

Because Southern planters provided 75 percent of the cotton purchased by British textile manufacturers, Confederate policymakers thought Britain would certainly support them. For a time, Britain did harbor Southern ships and even built Confederate warships, such as the **C.S.S. *Alabama***, which eventually captured or sank more than sixty Union ships on the high seas. British shipbuilders also agreed to build two ironclad warships with **Laird rams** that the Confederate navy could use to pierce the hulls of enemy ships. Despite this assistance from Britain, Davis never managed to secure either official recognition or the alliance he so badly needed. This failure was due mainly to the following:

- British manufacturers had warehouses full of excess cotton shipments and didn't need Southern cotton so urgently.
- British manufacturers had found other sources of cotton in India and Egypt.
- The poorer classes in England opposed slavery and thus opposed helping the South.
- Lincoln threatened to declare war on Britain if Britain helped the Confederacy.

As a result, the Laird rams were eventually scrapped, and Richmond lost all hope for help from Europe.

Collapse of the Southern Economy

Unable to break through the Union blockade around the Southern ports, and thus unable to buy goods or sell cotton, the South witnessed its economy slide into a deep depression in 1862. Worse, inflation skyrocketed when the individual states and private banks printed more cheap paper money to counter the depression. The depression was so bad that many desperate women looted the Confederate capital in the **Richmond Bread Riots** of 1863 in search of food and out of anger at the inept central government.

Southern Women

As the Southern economy collapsed, so too did Southern society. The war's drastic effect on Southern lives tore into the fabric of society. Women, for example, took on traditionally masculine jobs while the men fought on the battlefield. Some women ran farms and plantations, some ran businesses, and some had to supervise slaves. Wealthier women, in particular, were jarred by the harshness of physical labor and rationing. Southern women had to be incredibly innovative and resourceful to feed, clothe, and shelter their families every day.

THE EARLY YEARS OF THE WAR

Both the North and South hurried to create an army and navy after the fall of Fort Sumter, while thousands of men quickly enlisted out of fear they'd miss the fight. The initial enthusiasm and optimism, however, faded as soon as the "ninety-day war" turned into the bloodiest conflict in American history.

The First Battle of Bull Run

The first significant battle of the Civil War occurred at Manassas Junction, thirty miles southwest of Washington, D.C., in 1861. Civilians from both sides attended to watch the show, some even with picnic lunches. The battle proved far bloodier than anyone had expected when the Union soldiers fled and left several thousand dead and wounded behind. Dismayed, Northerners buckled down for a long, bitter war, while Southerners emerged with a false sense of strength.

The Battle of Shiloh

Just as the First Battle of Bull Run had shocked Northerners, the Battle of Shiloh in April 1862 shattered Southerners' hope for a quick and easy victory. Union general **Ulysses S. Grant** engaged Confederate forces at Shiloh, Tennessee, in a battle that killed tens of thousands of men. The eventual victory demonstrated Lincoln's unbending resolve to preserve the Union.

Naval Battles

The Confederate navy tried to break through the U.S. Navy's blockade with their new ironclad ship, the *Virginia*. Formerly an old Union warship named the *Merrimack*, Southerners had salvaged the ship and refitted it with iron armor to make it impervious to cannonballs. The Union eventually developed its own ironclad, the *Monitor*, to destroy the *Virginia*. The two warships engaged in a battle in the Chesapeake Bay in 1862, and though neither ship achieved a clear victory, the so-called **Battle of the Ironclads** marked the beginning of a new era in naval warfare.

The Union navy continued to tighten its grip on the South and eventually freed the lower Mississippi by seizing New Orleans from the Confederates. The navy then began working its way up the Mississippi River to tear the Confederacy in two.

The Battle of Antietam

In September 1862, Union and Confederate forces engaged each other in the **Battle of Antietam**. **Robert E. Lee**, the Confederate general, trying to move the war into the North, had crossed the Potomac with 40,000 men. Union general **George McClellan** moved his troops to meet Lee in western Maryland. Tens of thousands of soldiers died during the single bloodiest day of the entire war. An aide to Union general George McClellan had actually found Lee's battle plan prior to the engagement, but McClellan chose not to make full use of the information. Despite this missed opportunity, Lee was eventually forced to move his tattered army back across the Potomac to Virginia.

Lincoln Fires McClellan

As commander of the Army of the Potomac in Washington, D.C., George McClellan was the highest-ranking general in the Union army even though he had not yet reached forty. Despite his popularity with the troops, the civilian leaders in Washington disliked him because he seemed to avoid fighting battles. Lincoln needed military victories and wanted to end the war as quickly as possible—he knew voters wouldn't support a long and drawn-out war.

To make matters worse, as the war entered its second year, McClellan grew increasingly critical of Lincoln and the Republicans. He made personal jabs against the president in public and privately speculated that only he, personally, could end the war and save the Union. Lincoln eventually fired the disobedient and overly cautious McClellan and filled his post with several other incompetent generals before finally naming Ulysses S. Grant commander of all Union forces.

Antietam's Significance

Lee's failure at Antietam proved incredibly costly for the South because it convinced Britain and France not to support the Confederacy in the Civil War. Without international recognition or military assistance, Davis had little hope of breaking the Union blockade or defeating the Union army. The North's victory at Antietam also gave Lincoln the opportunity to issue the Emancipation Proclamation.

Emancipation

Lincoln decided in 1862 to emancipate the slaves held in areas under Confederate control for three reasons:

- Slave labor helped sustain the Confederacy economically.
- Turning the war into a moral cause would boost support for the war in the North.
- Emancipation would ensure that Britain and France would not enter the war.

Emancipation Proclamation

Although first issued in September 1862, the **Emancipation Proclamation** actually took effect on January 1, 1863. The proclamation did the following:

- Freed all slaves behind Confederate lines
- Did not free any slaves in the border states
- Allowed free blacks to join the U.S. Army and Navy

Slavery had been at the root of every sectional conflict since delegates had made the Three-Fifths Compromise at the Constitutional Convention in 1787. Lincoln needed to cure the disease that had caused the war, not just treat the symptoms. Even though the proclamation didn't emancipate slaves in the border states—Lincoln didn't want any of them to secede in anger—it did mark the beginning of the end for the "peculiar institution" for every state in the Union. Democrats, meanwhile, criticized Lincoln for wedding the goals of emancipation and reunification.

THE TURNING POINT

The year 1863 marked a turning point in the war and the beginning of the end for the Confederacy. Not coincidentally, it was also the year that Lincoln's search for a capable general ended with the selection of Ulysses S. Grant.

Siege of Vicksburg

Ulysses S. Grant was a general in the Union army at the beginning of 1863, in charge of troops trying to gain control of the Mississippi River. Grant turned the tide of the war in the West after laying siege to the port city of Vicksburg, Mississippi, on the Mississippi River. Having been unable to conquer Confederate forces protecting the city, Grant chose instead to merely surround the city and wait until starvation forced the Confederates to surrender, which they did on July 4, 1863, Independence Day.

Many historians agree that the surrender of Vicksburg was the most important Union victory of the war. The surrender gave the Union control of the Mississippi River and split the Confederacy in half. Subsequently, Lincoln promoted the victorious Grant to commander of all Union forces.

Battle of Gettysburg

As fate would have it, the Union achieved not one, but two major victories on Independence Day in 1863. While Grant was accepting Vicksburg's surrender in Mississippi, Union forces were repelling Robert E. Lee's invasion into Pennsylvania at the **Battle of Gettysburg**. After three days of some of the bloodiest fighting in the war, Lee retreated back to Confederate territory, leaving a third of his army among the 50,000 soldiers that lay dead or wounded on the battlefield.

Death Knell for the South

Lee's defeat at Gettysburg crushed the South: Twice the South had invaded the North, and twice it had failed (at Antietam and Gettysburg). The loss of the Mississippi at the Battle of Vicksburg proved more damaging in the long run because it deprived Southerners of their primary mode of transportation in the West.

The Union victories also boosted morale and support for the war in the North and increased Lincoln's popularity. In addition, the Union blockade's chokehold on the South had finally begun to take its toll on the southern economy. By 1863, the Confederacy couldn't trade cotton for war supplies or food. Still, Davis continued to wage war for two more years hoping that chance, providence, or Great Britain would help him.

THE FINAL YEAR

As the fighting dragged on into its fourth year, Lincoln felt increasing pressure to end the war. He knew that even the fieriest abolitionists couldn't tolerate much more bloodshed. As a result, Lincoln put more pressure on his generals to bear down on the Confederacy with as much military might as possible and end the war quickly.

Sherman's March to the Sea

Abraham Lincoln and Ulysses S. Grant knew the South had to be defeated soon if they ever hoped to restore the Union. In 1864, Grant ordered his close friend and fellow general **William Tecumseh Sherman** to take a small force through the heart of the Deep South and destroy everything in his path. Grant hoped that this destruction would bring the South to its knees. Sherman embarked on his famous **March to the Sea** that summer, burning the city of Atlanta and then marching toward Savannah, Georgia. Along the way, he destroyed railroads, burned homes, razed crops, and looted, plundered, and pillaged the entire countryside. Sherman eventually seized Savannah and then marched northward to South Carolina.

Growing Opposition in the North

A growing number of **Peace Democrats** had meanwhile begun to call for an immediate end to the war. More commonly known as **Copperheads**, after the poisonous snake, these Democrats believed that Lincoln and his generals had adequately demonstrated the futility of the war. Many Copperheads in the prosouthern **"Butternut region"** in Ohio, Indiana, and Illinois felt outraged that Lincoln had turned the conflict into a war over slavery. **Radical Republicans** in his own party criticized Lincoln because they thought the Emancipation Proclamation should have freed all slaves, South and North.

The Election of 1864

As a result, bitterness and uncertainty clouded the crucial election of 1864. Democrats who supported the war joined Republicans in giving Lincoln a lukewarm nomination for a second term, despite opposition from the radicals. Lincoln chose War Democrat Andrew Johnson from the conquered state of Tennessee as his running mate in the hope that Johnson would win more votes from Democrats in the North.

Together, Lincoln and Johnson campaigned on a simple platform for continuation of the war until the South surrendered unconditionally. Peace Democrats, on the other hand, nominated former general George McClellan on an equally simple platform calling for immediate peace. In the end, Lincoln won with 55 percent of the popular vote.

A Mandate for Unconditional Surrender

The election of 1864 was in many ways the most crucial event during the entire conflict. The election determined the outcome of the war; if McClellan and the Peace Democrats had won, the war would have ended immediately. The election ruined the Confederacy's last hope for survival. Lincoln's reelection provided a clear mandate from northern voters for unconditional surrender. Surprisingly, many of the soldiers themselves—Democrat as well as Republican—had voted for Lincoln because they wanted to finish what they had begun.

The South Collapses

The South, meanwhile, was on the brink of collapse. The naval blockade, refusals for assistance from Britain, Sherman's March, internal class conflicts, and the complete meltdown of Southern society and the economy had taken their toll. Thousands of men deserted the army daily as thousands more Southern women and children starved at home. Jefferson Davis tried desperately to hold his government together, but none of the states would cooperate. In the final month of the war, the South grew so desperate that they even began offering slaves their freedom if they would enlist in the Confederate army.

The Hampton Roads Conference

In an attempt to save the Confederacy, Davis requested a ceasefire to discuss peace. Lincoln agreed and sent a delegation to the Hampton Roads Conference in February 1865. Negotiations quickly ended, however, because Lincoln refused to settle for anything less than unconditional surrender, which Davis refused to give.

Appomattox

In April 1865, Grant's forces broke through Robert E. Lee's defenses and burned the Confederate capital at Richmond. With his men half starved and heavily outgunned, Lee chose to surrender rather than send his remaining troops to their death. Grant accepted Lee's unconditional surrender at Appomattox Courthouse on April 9, 1865, and provided the Southerners with food for their march home.

Union troops captured Jefferson Davis and other ranking Confederates as they tried to flee Virginia. The Civil War had ended.

The Assassination of Lincoln

Lincoln lived just long enough to see the war's end. **John Wilkes Booth**, a Southern sympathizer, assassinated the president on April 14, 1865, as he sat with his wife in a box at Ford's Theater in Washington, D.C., mere days after Grant accepted Lee's surrender at Appomattox. Booth shot Lincoln and then jumped down to the stage below, shouting, "*sic semper tyrannis*," a Latin phrase meaning "thus always to tyrants."

TIMELINE: 1860–1865

1860	Abraham Lincoln is elected president.
	South Carolina secedes from the Union.
1861	Alabama, Arkansas, Florida, Georgia, Louisiana, Mississippi, North Carolina, Tennessee, Texas, and Virginia secede.
	South Carolina attacks Fort Sumter.
	The first significant battle of the Civil War occurs at the Battle of Bull Run.
1862	Congress passes the Legal Tender Act.
	Confederacy passes the Conscription Act.
	Congress passes the Confiscation Act.
	The Union defeats the Confederacy at the Battle of Antietam.
1863	Lincoln's Emancipation Proclamation takes effect.
	Congress passes the National Bank Act.
	Drafts are initiated in the North.
	Southern women loot the Confederate capital in the Richmond Bread Riots in Richmond, Virginia.
	Nearly 100 people are murdered in the Draft Riots in New York City.
	The Battle of Gettysburg crushes the South.
	The Siege of Vicksburg gives the Union control of the Mississippi River.

1864	Grant takes command of Union troops.
	Lincoln is reelected.
	Sherman begins his March to the Sea.
1865	Davis proposes Hampton Roads peace conference.
	Robert E. Lee surrenders to Grant at Appomattox Courthouse.
	Abraham Lincoln is assassinated.

MAJOR FIGURES

John Bell. The Constitutional Union Party candidate for president, Bell ran against Abraham Lincoln, Stephen Douglas, and John C. Breckinridge in the election of 1860. Bell campaigned for compromise, Union, and slavery. He received wide support in the border states region but carried only Kentucky, Virginia, and Tennessee.

John Wilkes Booth. A famous actor in his day and also a fanatical supporter of the South, Booth shot Abraham Lincoln in the back of the head in Ford's Theater in Washington, D.C., on April 14, 1865.

John C. Breckinridge. When the Democratic Party split after the 1860 nominating convention failed to select a presidential candidate, Southern Democrats met separately in Charleston and nominated Breckinridge. Although Breckinridge claimed to desire unity and compromise, what he really wanted was a Northern concession for the westward expansion of slavery. In the following election of 1860, he carried nine states—all of them in the South.

Jefferson Davis. A former Senator from Mississippi, Davis was selected to be the first president of the Confederacy in 1861. Overworked and underappreciated by his fellow Confederates, Davis struggled throughout the Civil War to unify the Southern states under the central government.

Ulysses S. Grant. Nicknamed "Unconditional Surrender" Grant after his successes as the Union's top general in the Civil War, Grant became a Republican and entered politics during the Reconstruction years. He briefly served as secretary of war after Andrew Johnson fired Edwin M. Stanton but resigned when Stanton was reinstated. In 1868, he defeated Horatio Seymour to become the eighteenth president of the United States. Although he was himself honest, Grant's cabinet was filled with corruption, and his presidency was marred by scandals such as the Fisk-Gould gold scheme, Crédit Mobilier, and the Whiskey Ring. He retired after his second term.

Robert E. Lee. Arguably the most brilliant general in the U.S. Army in 1860, Lee turned down Abraham Lincoln's offer to command the Union forces during the Civil War in favor of commanding the army of northern Virginia for the Confederacy. Although he loved the United States, he felt he had to stand by his native state of Virginia. His defeat at the Battle of Gettysburg was the turning point in the war in favor of the North. He made the Confederacy's unconditional surrender at Appomattox Courthouse to Ulysses S. Grant in April 1865 to end the Civil War.

George McClellan. A young, first-rate U.S. Army general, McClellan commanded roughly 100,000 Union troops in Washington, D.C. Unfortunately for Abraham Lincoln, McClellan proved to be overly cautious and was always reluctant to engage Confederate forces at a time when the president badly needed military victories to satisfy Northern public opinion. He did manage to defeat Robert E. Lee at the Battle of Antietam in 1862, which gave Lincoln the opportunity to issue the Emancipation Proclamation. Lincoln eventually fired McClellan after the general began to publicly criticize the president's ability to command. McClellan ran for president as a Peace Democrat on a platform for peace against Lincoln but was defeated.

William Tecumseh Sherman. A close friend of Ulysses S. Grant, Sherman served as a general in the Union army during the Civil War. Like Grant, he understood that the war would only truly be won when Southerners' will to fight had been broken. He and his expedition force waged a total war on the South during his March to the Sea from Atlanta to Savannah, burning cities and crops, destroying railroad ties, and liberating slaves. His harsh tactic helped break the South and end the war.

[illegible]

[illegible]

[illegible]

[illegible]

Chapter 10

Reconstruction: 1862–1877

WARTIME RECONSTRUCTION

Historians refer to efforts to reunite and reform the nation during the Civil War as a dress rehearsal for Reconstruction. During this phase, President **Abraham Lincoln**, Congress, and military leaders issued a number of proclamations, acts, and field orders related to the ongoing war. Such actions fueled ongoing conflicts over issues including the following:

- Emancipation and the rights of African Americans
- The fate of the Confederacy
- Landownership in the South
- The transformation of the southern labor system and economy

Lincoln's Proclamations

President Lincoln wanted to win the war without annihilating the Old South, whereas Congress wanted to dramatically transform southern society. Still, Lincoln's ultimate goal was to reunite the nation. On the one hand, he wanted to abolish slavery because he knew that this would cripple the southern economy; on the other hand, Lincoln believed emancipation should unfold gradually so as not to alienate the proslavery border states in the Union. Lincoln issued two proclamations during the war addressing reunification and emancipation: the **Emancipation Proclamation** and the **Proclamation of Amnesty and Reconstruction**.

Emancipation Proclamation

Lincoln earned the moniker the "Great Emancipator" for the **Emancipation Proclamation** he issued on January 1, 1863. Despite the nickname, Lincoln's proclamation only liberated slaves in the states at war with the Union. Not surprisingly, months passed before many of those slaves found out they were free. The proclamation did *not* free any slaves in the border states or in areas of the Confederacy occupied by the Union. Nonetheless, Lincoln's proclamation made slavery a central issue of the war.

The proclamation deprived the Confederacy of its labor force and thus crippled the region's economy. It also legalized the enlistment of freedmen, who wanted to fight to keep their freedom. This influx of men reinvigorated the Union military and greatly contributed to the defeat of the Confederate forces.

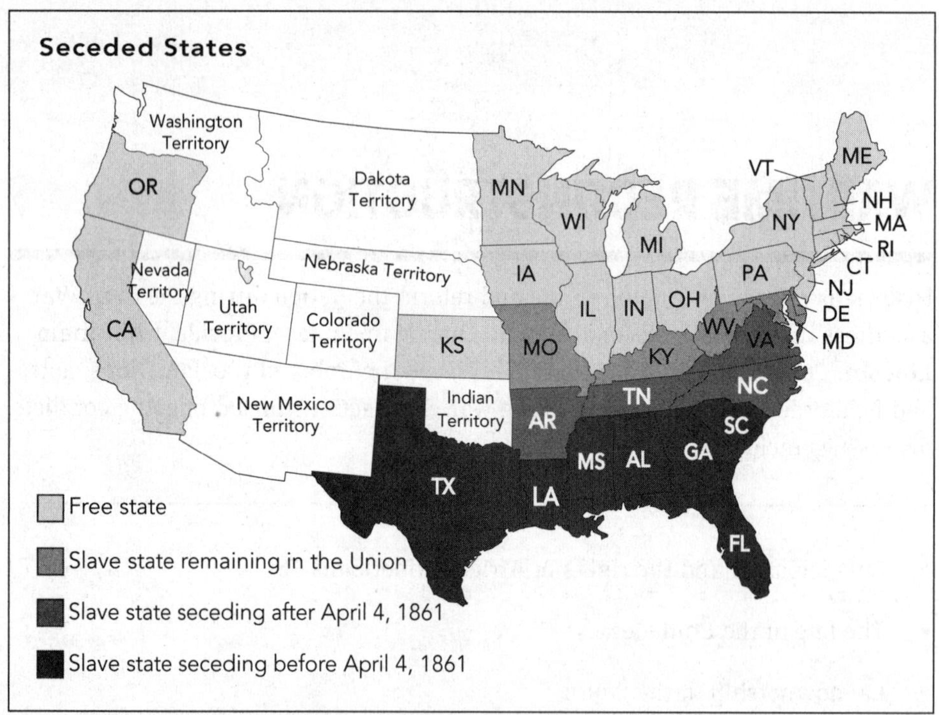

Proclamation of Amnesty

Lincoln outlined his postwar vision for reunification when he issued the **Proclamation of Amnesty and Reconstruction** in December 1863. More commonly known as **Lincoln's Ten-Percent Plan**, the proclamation promised the following:

- The pardoning of all Confederates who signed an oath of allegiance to the United States, excluding government and military leaders.

- The recognition of any Southern state government, provided that 10 percent of the state's voters in the election of 1860 pledged their allegiance to the United States. Arkansas, Louisiana, and Tennessee reorganized under these terms in 1864 but were not recognized by Congress.
- The protection of lower-ranking Confederate officers from trial and execution for treason.
- The return of political rights and land confiscated by the federal government to the Confederates after they received pardons and accepted the emancipation of black people.
- The prosecution of Confederate military and civilian officials and others who left federal positions to join the Confederacy. Ex-Confederates who killed or tortured Union soldiers, both black and white, would also be denied amnesty.

Congress's Acts

Congress favored a more aggressive approach to freeing the slaves than President Lincoln. Even though Republicans in Congress never completely agreed on any issue during Reconstruction, almost all of them wanted to punish the South.

Freeing Slaves in the District of Columbia

In April 1862, Congress passed legislation to free enslaved African Americans in Washington, D.C. Lincoln consented, but only reluctantly, as the **First Confiscation Act** of 1861 guaranteed compensation to the District's slave owners. In July 1862, Congress also passed the **Second Confiscation Act**, which freed all blacks enslaved by government officials in Confederate states. The Confiscation Act of 1862 also freed all southern slaves who sought refuge behind Union lines.

The Wade-Davis Bill

Congressional Republicans, led by **Thaddeus Stevens** and **Benjamin Wade**, opposed Lincoln's Ten-Percent Plan. They wanted to punish the Southerners who had caused the war. Furthermore, they sought to pass additional legislation to protect free blacks. In response to Lincoln's Proclamation of Amnesty and Reconstruction, Wade and Congressman **Henry Winter Davis** of Maryland sponsored the **Wade-Davis Bill** to appoint provisional military governors in the former Confederate states. The bill also required that more than 50 percent of white men in each state take an oath of allegiance to the Union before a new constitution could be drafted. Additionally, this new constitution would have to renounce both slavery and secession and disenfranchise all former Confederate leaders.

Although Congress passed the Wade-Davis Bill in July 1864, Lincoln thought it too radical and refused to sign it. Hoping to avoid the controversy of an outright

veto, he simply **"pocket vetoed"** the bill by withholding his signature until Congress adjourned for the year. Without Lincoln's signature, the Wade-Davis Bill died.

Union Military Leaders' Actions

At the beginning of the Civil War, many Union commanders supported slavery. Some even returned escaped slaves to their Confederate owners, reasoning that they were fighting to preserve the Union, not to free black people. But over time, a number of Northern military officers began to advocate emancipation. Many petitioned for emancipation in order to rid themselves of the responsibility for the thousands of black refugees, or **"contraband of war,"** that flooded Union camps. Consequently, commanders often issued special field orders to help them defeat the Confederacy by depriving the South of its slaves. After the war and the end of slavery, these generals led the way in redefining the status of blacks in the South. Military leaders also made decisions regarding Southern landownership and helped establish a free labor system.

The Port Royal Experiment

In January 1862, **Brigadier General William Sherman** asked the federal government to send teachers to instruct the former slaves on the Sea Islands of South Carolina. This request eventually evolved into the **Port Royal Experiment**, which became a model for educating black people and organizing black communities. Later that year, Lincoln officially emancipated black Sea Islanders, and the U.S. Army began redistributing abandoned plantation lands to the freedmen. In exchange, many blacks on the Sea Islands produced cotton for Union factories and enlisted in the military.

Black and white missionaries from the North also established a string of schools on the islands. These schools educated thousands of former slaves and inspired others to found schools for freed people throughout the South. Unfortunately, federal support for the schools waned after Lincoln's assassination.

General David Hunter and General Order 11

The Union's **General David Hunter** twice defied Lincoln's decree regarding the status of blacks during the war. In March 1862, he ignored the ban on blacks in the military and recruited black men for a special combat unit. In May 1862, he issued **General Order 11** to emancipate slaves in Georgia, Florida, and South Carolina. Lincoln disbanded the combat unit and nullified the order.

General William Sherman and Special Field Order 15

In January 1865, after his infamous **March to the Sea** through Georgia, **General William Sherman** met with twenty black leaders in Savannah to determine the needs of former slaves. The freedmen told Sherman and Secretary of War **Edwin M. Stanton** that black people wanted land. A few days later, Sherman issued **Field Order 15** to redistribute confiscated land in forty-acre parcels to blacks in

Florida and on the Sea Islands off Georgia and South Carolina. Only blacks were allowed to settle these lands.

In less than a month, more than 40,000 freed people received land from the government. The new landowners also received surplus government mules. After the war ended, President Andrew Johnson allowed white planters to reclaim these lands. As a result, thousands of blacks became destitute.

The Freedmen's Bureau

General Oliver O. Howard ran the **Bureau of Freedmen, Refugees, and Abandoned Lands**. More commonly known as the **Freedmen's Bureau**, this agency was created a month before the war ended to provide food, clothing, and medicine to freed people and poor whites. The Bureau also founded the Freedmen's Bank and established more schools. Although the Bureau provided freed people some protection against aggressive whites who tried to take their land and exploit their labor, the organization ultimately undermined blacks.

Essentially, the agency steered freed people into the abusive free-labor systems that replaced slavery. Southern state and local governments supported these systems in order to meet the region's demand for food and jumpstart the agrarian economy. The Freedmen's Bureau was perpetually underfunded by Congress and thus never had the manpower or resources equal to the huge task facing it.

PRESIDENTIAL RECONSTRUCTION

When the Civil War ended in April 1865, President Lincoln asserted that the former Confederate states merely had been "out of their proper practical relation with the Union." In fact, Lincoln firmly believed that these states "had never really left the Union." A few days after Lincoln made this statement, on April 14, 1865, Confederate sympathizer John Wilkes Booth assassinated Lincoln. Lincoln's vice president, **Andrew Johnson**, immediately became president. Surprisingly, Johnson pardoned thousands of Confederate leaders and championed the restoration of white supremacy in the South.

An outraged Congress quickly established the **Committee of Fifteen** to devise progressive new plans for Reconstruction. Republicans fought Johnson's repeated attempts to block constitutional amendments and congressional acts meant to protect freed people and punish ex-Confederates. In the end, Republicans' triumph over the president paved the way for Radical Reconstruction.

Johnson's Plan

A former Tennessee slaveholder, President Johnson did everything in his power to reinstate Southern elites. He implemented a three-pronged strategy to stymie congressional attempts to reform the South:

1. **The Amnesty Proclamation** to pardon former Confederate leaders. This proclamation allowed these elites to reclaim land given to freed people and returned white supremacists to power in the state governments.
2. The vetoing of all legislation designed to grant and protect African Americans' civil liberties.
3. The rallying of conservatives and reactionaries to halt all attempts to change the social order of the South.

Johnson's Amnesty Proclamation

Johnson shrewdly issued and implemented his Amnesty Proclamation during the congressional recess from May to early December 1865. The proclamation resembled Lincoln's Ten-Percent Plan. For example, it required that Southern states approve the **Thirteenth Amendment** to abolish slavery before they could rejoin the Union. But Johnson added a couple of stipulations of his own. He denied amnesty to rich Confederates (i.e., those worth more than $20,000) and required the repudiation of all debts that were owed by the Union to Confederates. Most important, he firmly believed that he should reconstruct the Union without the help of Congress.

President Johnson also accepted Reconstruction governments in Arkansas, Louisiana, and Tennessee created in 1862 during Lincoln's presidency. Moreover, he made governors out of **native Unionists** who had remained loyal during the war. Despite his professed hatred for Confederate leaders, Johnson pardoned 13,000 people, including former Confederate military and civilian officials and allowed the secessionist states to write new constitutions, even if 10 percent of voters had not taken the loyalty oath. As a result, Johnson readmitted all eleven Confederate states into the Union by December 1865 and prematurely declared Reconstruction over.

Johnson's Presidential Vetoes

Johnson repeatedly exercised his right to veto legislation of the Republican Congress. Most of this legislation was passed to elevate the social and political status of black people. Congress overrode the following of Johnson's vetoes:

- **The Civil Rights Act of 1866**, which granted citizenship to blacks and safeguarded their civil liberties
- **The Fourteenth Amendment**, which safeguarded blacks' citizenship rights and reduced congressional representation of states that denied black males voting rights
- **The Freedmen's Bureau Bill**, which extended the life of the agency and increased its authority to help freed people and poor whites

---

Race Riots and "Swing around the Circle"

Many whites in the South responded furiously to the Civil Rights Act of 1866 and the Fourteenth Amendment. Riots erupted in Memphis, Tennessee, and New Orleans, and hundreds of blacks were murdered. The rampant racism and violence shocked Americans in the North who turned an accusing eye toward Johnson for his leniency.

The president in turn blamed the radicals in Congress in his infamous **"Swing around the Circle"** speeches. Traveling throughout the country, he often got carried away lambasting Republicans, prowar Democrats, blacks, and anyone else who challenged him. As a result, he blackened the Democratic Party's already tarnished reputation and inadvertently persuaded many Northerners to vote Republican in the 1866 Congressional elections.

RADICAL RECONSTRUCTION

The race riots and murders combined with Johnson's "Swing around the Circle" campaign convinced Northerners that the president could no longer be trusted to reconstruct the Union. Instead, they turned to Republicans, who consequently swept the 1866 congressional elections. **Radical Republicans** and their moderate allies dominated both the House of Representatives and the Senate and therefore had the ability to override any presidential vetoes. As a result, their ascension to office in early 1867 marked the beginning of **Congressional Reconstruction**, sometimes known as **Radical Reconstruction**.

Military Reconstruction

Congress began the task of reorganizing the South with the **First Reconstruction Act** in March 1867. Also known as the **Military Reconstruction Act** or simply the **Reconstruction Act**, this bill reduced the secessionist states' claim to conquered territories. Congress carved the South into five military districts, which were each governed by a Union general in charge of the Reconstruction process.

Congress also declared martial law and dispatched troops to keep the peace and protect persecuted blacks. All former secessionist states had to once again draft new constitutions, ratify the **Fourteenth Amendment**, and provide suffrage to blacks. To secure black voting rights, Republicans passed the **Second Reconstruction Act**, placing Union troops in charge of voter registration. Congress overrode two presidential vetoes to pass these bills.

The Fifteenth Amendment

Radicals believed that giving blacks the right to vote was the only way to prevent Southern elites from seizing power again. Even though Congress demanded that the Southern states enfranchise blacks, Republicans still feared that whites might one day revoke this right. To prevent this, they decided to incorporate

black suffrage into the Constitution itself: In 1869, they passed the **Fifteenth Amendment** to guarantee that all black males had the right to vote. Furthermore, Republicans made ratification a prerequisite for all Southern states still awaiting readmission. Three-fourths of the states finally ratified the amendment in 1870.

Enfranchising Blacks in the South and North

The Fifteenth Amendment enfranchised not only blacks but also poor Southern white males. Prior to the Civil War, all Southern states had restricted the vote to landowners. This restriction excluded most white males—as well as blacks and women—from political participation. The amendment also forced reluctant Northern states to enfranchise blacks. Even when most state constitutions in the South gave blacks the right to vote, most Northern states still refused to do so. The Fifteenth Amendment changed the political status of blacks throughout the entire United States.

The Quest for Women's Suffrage

The passage of the Fifteenth Amendment in 1869 had an enormous effect on the women's suffrage movement as well. Prior to the Civil War, the quest for women's suffrage and abolition had been closely united, as both groups strove to achieve political and civil rights for those not represented in politics. After the Union victory, many women like **Elizabeth Cady Stanton** and **Susan B. Anthony** thought they had won suffrage for both blacks and women. But radicals in Congress feared that if they granted the right to vote to all men *and* women, they would lose support in both the South and North. Consequently, many women felt betrayed by their exclusion from the Fifteenth Amendment.

Republicanism Takes Root in the South

With their right to vote safeguarded, Southern blacks flocked to register, and by the beginning of 1868, more than 700,000 freedmen had signed up. Not surprisingly, all declared themselves Republicans, as they identified the Democrats with secession and slavery. Almost the same number of landless white males registered, virtually all as Democrats.

Black Political Power

African American civic societies and grassroots political organizations sprouted up everywhere. Most of them were led by prominent blacks who had been freedmen before the war. Black voters quickly dominated the electorate in South Carolina, Alabama, Louisiana, Florida, and Mississippi, giving the Republican Party control over the Reconstruction process in those states. The new voters also elected many black politicians to state legislatures throughout the South. Fourteen black politicians served in the House of Representatives, and Mississippians elected two blacks to the Senate.

Johnson Tried and Acquitted

Congress passed several bills in 1867 to limit President Johnson's power. The **Tenure of Office Act** sought to protect prominent Republicans within the Johnson administration by forbidding their dismissal without congressional authorization. Although the act applied to all office holders approved by Congress, radicals specifically wanted to keep Secretary of War Edwin M. Stanton in office to check Johnson's control over the military. In defiance, Johnson ignored the act, fired Stanton in the summer of 1867 during a congressional recess, and replaced him with Union general **Ulysses S. Grant**. Afraid that Johnson could effectively end military reconstruction in the South, Congress ordered the president to reinstate Stanton when it reconvened in 1868. Johnson refused, Grant subsequently resigned, and Congress put Stanton back in office over the president's objections.

Tired of presidential vetoes and obstruction to Congressional Reconstruction, House Republicans impeached Johnson by a vote of 126 to 47 for violating the Tenure of Office Act and slandering Congress. The Senate tried Johnson in May 1868 in front of a gallery of spectators. Radical Representatives **Thaddeus Stevens** and Benjamin Butler served as prosecutors but couldn't convince a majority of senators to convict the president. The final tally was one vote shy of a conviction.

RECONSTRUCTION IN THE SOUTH

As the Union army advanced deeper into Southern territory during the war's end, more and more slaves enjoyed the fruits of freedom. The army did free some slaves, but most freed themselves by refusing to work and walking away. Tens of thousands of blacks, for example, followed Sherman's troops on his **March to the Sea** in 1864. The end of the war brought jubilation and celebrations. Thousands of blacks left their homes in search of lost family members, while many black couples took the opportunity to marry, knowing no one could ever forcibly separate them again.

Most former slaves faced considerable challenges with their newly acquired freedom. Despite the Radical Republicans' best efforts to protect their civil liberties and voting rights, the freed men and women still faced persecution from racist whites. By the end of Reconstruction, blacks had freedom—but not equality.

Carpetbaggers and Scalawags

Many Northerners jumped at opportunities in the South in the wake of Confederate General Lee's surrender in early April of 1865. These **"carpetbaggers"** (nicknamed for the large carpet bags many of them brought with them) came for a variety of reasons: to promote education, to modernize the South, and to seek their fortunes. White Southern Unionists, or **"scalawags,"** also played roles in achieving the same aims. Both carpetbaggers and scalawags served in legislatures in every reconstructed state.

The Black Codes

White elitist regimes in the Southern states did everything in their power to prevent blacks from gaining too much power. After Republicans in Congress passed the Civil Rights Act of 1866, every Southern legislature passed laws to exert more control on African Americans. These **Black Codes** ranged in severity and outlawed everything from interracial marriage to loitering in public areas.

Southern whites passed these laws partly because they feared a free black population, especially in states where blacks outnumbered whites. Many also worried that freed slaves would terrorize their masters, rape white women, and ruin the economy. Most planter elites passed the codes simply to ensure that they would have a stable and reliable workforce.

Black Codes often dictated that former slaves sign labor contracts for meager wages. Although Congress forced state legislatures to repeal the codes once the radicals took control of Reconstruction, whites still managed to subtly enforce them for years after Reconstruction had ended.

Black Codes differed from state to state but had the following similarities:

- All blacks had to sign labor contracts.
- Blacks could not own land.
- Individuals accused of vagrancy who were unable to pay fines could be sentenced to hard labor on chain gangs.
- States could force orphaned children into apprenticeships that resembled slavery.
- Whites could physically abuse blacks without fear of punishment.

Black Churches and Education

Most freed men and women had a burning desire to educate their children. They recognized that knowledge (especially the previously forbidden ability to read and write) was power and that their futures depended upon it. The Freedmen's Bureau and former abolitionist groups from the North succeeded in founding schools for thousands of blacks. Because white clergymen had often upheld slavery in their sermons prior to the Civil War, many blacks went on to establish their own congregations.

The Sharecropping System

Blacks craved economic independence and resisted white efforts to consign them to chain gangs or wage labor on large plantations. Instead, they preferred the **sharecropping system**, in which former plantation owners divided their lands and rented each plot—or share—to a single black family. The family farmed its own crops in exchange for giving a percentage of the yield to the landowner. In fact, many families sharecropped on their former masters' lands. Landless whites also became sharecroppers for the elites, so that by 1880, almost all farmers in the South sharecropped.

The Ku Klux Klan

Violence also posed a serious threat to African Americans in the South. A secret white-supremacist society called the **Ku Klux Klan** formed in Tennessee in 1866 to terrorize blacks. White-robed Klansmen would harass, beat, and lynch both blacks and white Republicans. They ordered blacks to stay away from voting polls and punished those who didn't obey; in one extreme case, Klansmen butchered several hundred black voters in Louisiana in 1868. Congress eventually passed the **Ku Klux Klan Act** of 1871, which allowed Congress to act against terrorist organizations. Still, racist violence continued to be a serious problem.

GRANT'S PRESIDENCY

As the presidential election of 1868 drew near, Republicans nominated Civil War hero **Ulysses S. Grant**. Grant had proven himself an effective leader in the army and served as a reminder that Republicans had won the war. Democrats nominated former governor of New York **Horatio Seymour**. Seymour hated emancipation, supported states' rights, and wanted to wrest control of Reconstruction out of Congress's hands. In the end, Grant received 214 electoral votes to Seymour's 80 but only 300,000 more popular votes. Republicans also maintained control of Congress. During the Grant years, Congress funded more projects and distributed more money than ever before in U.S. history.

A Multitude of Scandals

Scandal and corruption characterized Grant's two terms in office. Although the president himself was never involved, his lack of political experience hampered his ability to control other politicians.

The Fisk-Gould Gold Scandal

Scandal rocked Washington before Grant had even completed his first year in office. In 1869 the financial tycoons **Jim Fisk** and **Jay Gould** bribed many cabinet officials, including Grant's own brother-in-law, to overlook their attempt to corner the gold market. They even conned Grant himself into agreeing not to release any more of the precious metal into the economy. On September 24, 1869, they succeeded in inflating gold prices. The U.S. Treasury managed to prevent an economic catastrophe by releasing more gold into the economy, in spite of Grant's earlier promise.

The Crédit Mobilier Scandal

Corruption also infected the railroads. In 1872, Union Pacific Railroad executives created a dummy construction company called **Crédit Mobilier**. They then hired Crédit Mobilier at outrageous prices to lay track. To protect their huge profits, the executives bribed several congressmen and even Vice President **Schuyler Colfax** to keep quiet. Colfax ultimately resigned after an exposé revealed his shady dealings. Even though Grant had no involvement in the scandal, it nevertheless damaged his reputation.

The Whiskey Ring Scandal

Yet another scandal broke two years later in 1874, when investigators discovered that several Grant-appointed federal employees had skimmed millions of dollars from excise tax revenue. The president vowed to hunt down and punish all those involved in the **Whiskey Ring** but swallowed his harsh words upon discovering his own secretary's involvement.

The Election of 1872

Fed up with scandals in Grant's administration, a significant number of Republicans broke from the radicals and moderates in Congress just before the 1872 elections. Known as **Liberal Republicans**, these men wanted to end corruption, restore the Union as quickly as possible, and downsize the federal government. They nominated *New York Tribune* editor **Horace Greeley** for the presidency.

Strangely enough, Democrats also nominated Greeley because he opposed the army's presence in the South and wanted to end Reconstruction. Despite the scandals, radicals and moderates again nominated their war hero Grant. On Election Day, Grant easily won with 286 electoral votes to Greeley's 66 and received more than 700,000 more popular votes.

The Liberal Republicans

Led by businessmen, professionals, reformers, and intellectuals, Liberal Republicans helped shape politics in the postwar years. They disliked big government and preferred limited government involvement in the economy. Some historians have argued that the Liberal Republicans even opposed democracy because they detested universal manhood suffrage and didn't want to enfranchise blacks.

The Depression of 1873

Although Grant faced as many problems in his second administration as he had during his first, none were as catastrophic as the **Depression of 1873**. Bad loans and overspeculation in railroads and factories burst the postwar economic boom and forced millions of Americans onto the streets over the next five years. The poor clamored for cheap paper and silver money for relief, but Republicans refused to give in to their demands out of fear that cheap money would exacerbate inflation. Instead, they passed the **Resumption Act of 1875** to remove all paper money from the economy. The act helped end the depression in the long run, but it made the interim years more difficult to bear.

The End of Radical Reconstruction

The Resumption Act proved politically damaging for the Radical and moderate Republicans in Congress. Because they insisted on passing hard-money policies during a time when up to 15 percent of Americans had no work, many Republicans in the North voted with the Democrats in the 1874 congressional elections. Their votes, combined with white votes in the South, ousted many Republicans from Congress and gave the Democrats control of the House of Representatives for the first time since 1856. The remaining radicals in Congress suddenly found themselves commanding the weak minority party. In short, the elections of 1874 marked the end of Radical Reconstruction.

THE END OF RECONSTRUCTION

As the economy plummeted, so too did Northerners' willingness to pursue Radical Reconstruction. Americans had neither the time nor the energy to worry about helping former slaves, punishing Ku Klux Klan terrorism, or readmitting states when so many of them didn't even have jobs. In fact, many in the North had grown tired of Radical Republican zeal altogether.

The Civil Rights Act of 1875

Despite their weakness, Republicans managed to pass one final piece of radical legislation through Congress. The **Civil Rights Act of 1875** aimed to eliminate social discrimination and facilitate true equality for black Americans by stipulating the following:

- Racial discrimination would be outlawed in all public places, such as theaters, hotels, and restaurants.
- Blacks would have the same legal rights as whites.
- Blacks could sue violators in federal courts.

Toothless Legislation

The Civil Rights Act of 1875 proved highly ineffective because Democrats in the House of Representatives made it virtually unenforceable. The law required individual blacks to file their own claims to defend their rights; the federal government wouldn't do it for them. Because lawsuits required money, time, and considerable effort, House Democrats knew that the law would have very little practical impact.

Redemption

The weak Republican foothold in the South had only gotten weaker as Northerners lost interest in Reconstruction. By the mid-1870s, the depression and the Klan had driven off most white Unionists, carpetbaggers, and scalawags, which left African Americans to fend for themselves. Without any support from Southern whites or Congress, Democrats easily seized power once again and "redeemed" the Southern state legislatures one by one. Some Democrats even employed violence to secure power by killing Republicans or terrorizing blacks away from the polls. By 1877, Democrats once again controlled every Southern state.

Court Rulings Against Radical Reconstruction

Several Supreme Court rulings in the 1870s and 1880s also heralded the death of Reconstruction:

- **The Slaughterhouse cases of 1873:** The Fourteenth Amendment did not protect citizens from state infringements on their rights.
- ***United States v. Cruikshank* in 1876:** Only states, not the federal government, could prosecute individuals in violation of the 1871 Ku Klux Klan Act.
- **The Civil Rights cases of 1883:** The Fourteenth Amendment applied only to discrimination by the government (not from individuals).

The Election of 1876

Democrats poured a lot of energy into the 1876 presidential election in order to oust Grant and redeem the White House. The party nominated New York prosecutor **Samuel J. Tilden**, who railed against the corrupt Grant administration. After briefly toying with the idea of choosing Grant again for an unprecedented third term, Republicans finally selected Ohio governor **Rutherford B. Hayes**.

Hayes had served in the war as a Union general, had no overly controversial opinions, and came from the politically important state of Ohio. On Election Day 1876, Hayes won only 165 electoral votes and lost the popular election by roughly 250,000 votes. Tilden, on the other hand, had won the popular vote and had 184 electoral votes, but he lacked the extra electoral vote necessary to become president.

The Compromise of 1877

The election results in South Carolina, Louisiana, and Florida were still in dispute because of confusing ballots. Normally, the president of the Senate would recount the ballots in front of Congress. Because the president of the Senate was a Republican and the Speaker of the House was a Democrat, neither man could trust the other to count the votes honestly.

Instead, Congress passed the **Electoral Count Act** in 1877 to establish a special committee to recount the votes fairly. The committee consisted of fifteen men from the House, the Senate, and the Supreme Court—eight Republicans and seven Democrats. Not surprisingly, the committee concluded by a margin of one vote that Hayes had won the disputed states. Deadlock ensued once again, until both sides agreed to compromise.

In the **Compromise of 1877**, Democrats and Republicans agreed to let Hayes become president in exchange for the complete withdrawal of federal soldiers from the South. Shortly after Hayes took office, he ordered the last remaining troops out of South Carolina and Louisiana. Reconstruction had finally ended.

TIMELINE: 1862–1877

1862	First and Second Confiscation Acts are passed.
1863	Abraham Lincoln issues the Proclamation on Amnesty and Reconstruction.
	Lincoln issues the Emancipation Proclamation.
1864	Lincoln is reelected.
1865	Sherman issues Special Field Order #15.
	Congress establishes the Freedmen's Bureau.
	Robert E. Lee surrenders to Grant.
	John Wilkes Booth assassinates Lincoln.
	Andrew Johnson becomes president.
	Johnson begins Presidential Reconstruction.
	The Thirteenth Amendment is ratified.
1866	Congress passes the Civil Rights Act of 1866.
	The Ku Klux Klan is founded in Tennessee.
	Race riots erupt in Memphis and New Orleans.
	Johnson "Swings around the Circle" in an attempt to gain support from Northern voters.
1867	Radical Reconstruction begins.
	Congress passes the First and Second Reconstruction Acts.
	Congress passes the Tenure of Office Act.

1868	Johnson is impeached by the House of Representatives.
	The Senate acquits Johnson.
	The Fourteenth Amendment is ratified.
	Ulysses S. Grant is elected president.
1869	Jim Fisk and Jay Gould attempt to corner the gold market.
1870	The Fifteenth Amendment is ratified.
1871	Congress passes the Ku Klux Klan Act.
1872	The Republican Party splits.
	The Crédit Mobilier scandal erupts.
	Samuel J. Tilden prosecutes Boss William Tweed.
	Grant is reelected president.
1873	Depression of 1873 begins.
	Supreme Court hears Slaughterhouse cases.
1874	Democrats retake control of the House.
	The Whiskey Ring scandal erupts, futher tarnishing President Grant's record.
1875	Congress passes the Civil Rights Act of 1875.
	Congress passes the Resumption Act.
1876	Democrats and Republicans dispute presidential election results.
1877	Congress passes the Electoral Count Act.
	Democrats and Republicans strike the Compromise of 1877.
	Rutherford B. Hayes becomes president.
	Hayes withdraws all federal troops from the South.

MAJOR FIGURES

Schuyler Colfax. The vice president during Grant's first term, Colfax was passed over for a second term because of his role in the Crédit Mobilier scandal of 1872.

Henry Winter Davis. A Radical Republican Congressman during the Civil War, Davis cosponsored the Wade-Davis Bill with Senator Benjamin Wade.

James "Jim" Fisk. A self-made stockbroker and corporate executive, Fisk joined Jay Gould and others in an attempt to corner the American gold market in 1869.

Jay Gould. A corrupt Erie Railroad executive and speculator, Gould attempted to corner the American gold market. He failed, instead causing a stock-market crisis in September 1869.

Horace Greeley. The nominee of both the Democrats and the Liberal Republicans for the presidency in 1872, Greeley was the choice because both parties wanted limited government, reform, and a swift end to Reconstruction. This political alliance only weakened the Liberal Republicans' cause in the North, where most Americans still did not trust the Democrats. As a result, Ulysses S. Grant easily defeated Greeley.

Rutherford B. Hayes. A nominee for the 1876 presidency, Hayes ran against Democrat Tilden. In the wake of the corruption scandals associated with Ulysses S. Grant, Republicans chose Hayes because he was relatively unknown, had no controversial opinions, and came from the politically important state of Ohio. Even though Hayes received fewer popular and electoral votes than Tilden, he still became president after the Compromise of 1877, when Democrats traded the White House for an end to Reconstruction.

General David Hunter. A Union general during the Civil War, Hunter ignored the ban on blacks in the military and recruited black men for a special combat unit.

Andrew Johnson. A former tailor, governor, and senator from Tennessee, Johnson, a Democrat, was chosen to be Abraham Lincoln's vice-presidential running mate in the 1864 election to persuade middle states to remain in the Union. He became the seventeenth president after John Wilkes Booth assassinated Lincoln. Although he hated the Southern aristocracy, he also had no love for blacks and fought Congress over the Fourteenth Amendment and the Civil Rights Bill of 1866. Johnson believed that only he (not Congress) should be responsible for Reconstruction and recognized new state governments established according to the Ten-Percent Plan. He was impeached by the House of Representatives in 1868, but was acquitted by the Senate.

Horatio Seymour. A former governor of New York, Seymour ran on the Democratic ticket against Republican Ulysses S. Grant in the presidential election of 1868. Seymour campaigned for an end to Reconstruction in the South and repudiation of black civil rights. He lost both the popular vote and the electoral vote.

William Sherman. A brigadier general, Sherman served as the commander of the Union troops in the South Carolina Sea Islands in 1862. During his tenure, Sherman requested that teachers be sent to the islands to educate black refugees. Not to be confused with General William T. Sherman, who was one of the principal Union military commanders.

Edwin M. Stanton. No relation to Elizabeth Cady Stanton, Edwin Stanton served as secretary of war during the Civil War and Reconstruction years under both Abraham Lincoln and Andrew Johnson. Even though he was formerly a Democrat, he supported Radical Reconstruction of the South. Radical Republicans in Congress tried to protect Stanton from Johnson's wrath with the 1867 Tenure of Office Act. This act required Johnson to seek permission from Congress before removing any congressionally appointed administrators. Johnson ignored the

law and fired Stanton anyway. Republicans in the House used this violation as an excuse to impeach Johnson.

Thaddeus Stevens. A staunch Radical Republican, Stevens fought for harsher punishments of former Confederates and for protection of African American rights after the war. He helped draft the Fourteenth Amendment to the Constitution and the Reconstruction Acts of 1867. He also prosecuted Andrew Johnson in the president's 1867 Senate trial.

Samuel J. Tilden. A New York prosecutor, Tilden first became famous in 1871 and 1872 when he brought down the mighty Boss William Tweed on corruption charges. He then ran for president on the Democratic ticket against Rutherford B. Hayes in 1876. Even though he received more popular votes, he fell just one electoral vote shy of becoming president. After much debate, Democrats and Republicans struck the Compromise of 1877, in which Hayes became president in exchange for a complete withdrawal of federal troops from the Southern states.

Harriet Tubman. Nicknamed the "Moses of Her People" for her success and bravery as an Underground Railroad conductor, Tubman served the Union as a spy, a scout, and a nurse during the Civil War. After the war, she continued to fight for African American and women's rights.

Benjamin Wade. A Radical Republican senator both during and after the Civil War, Wade opposed Lincoln's Ten-Percent Plan for Reconstruction. Instead, he cosponsored the harsher 1864 Wade-Davis Bill along with Congressman Henry Winter Davis.

Chapter 11

The Growing Nation: 1877–1901

GILDED AGE POLITICS

The corruption and scandals that plagued President Ulysses S. Grant's administration worsened during the course of the **Gilded Age**, an era of tremendous growth in business and industry. Networks of powerful men and loyal underlings composed political machines in which bribes and pay-offs fueled politicians' quests for power. **Political bosses** embroiled in this **spoils system** (the process by which these bosses paid money to control votes, candidates, and other aspects of the voting system) obtained and maintained control over the political system for many years.

The Stalwarts, Half Breeds, and Mugwumps

Rutherford B. Hayes squeaked into the White House by only one electoral vote after the **Compromise of 1877**, and he remained virtually powerless during his four years in office. The real winners in the election were Republican spoils-seekers who flooded Washington, D.C., in search of civil service jobs. Unfortunately, disputes over the spoils split the Republican party (also known as the Grand Old Party) into three factions:

- **The Stalwarts**—led by New York Senator **Roscoe Conkling**—constituted the conservative faction of the Republican party.
- **The Half-Breeds**—led by Maine Senator **James G. Blaine**—were the moderate faction of the Republican party. The Stalwarts gave the Half-Breeds their disparaging name.
- **The Mugwumps** were a group of liberal Republicans who opposed the spoils system.

None of these groups trusted any of the others, so the Republican party had trouble passing any significant legislation while in office.

The "Forgotten Presidents"

Many historians have dubbed the Gilded Age presidents—Grant, Hayes, Garfield, Arthur, Cleveland, and Harrison—the **"Forgotten Presidents."** Some historians have even suggested that Gilded Age presidents lacked personality precisely because Americans didn't want any bold politicians who might ruin the peace established after the Civil War. Essentially, Americans wanted to focus on other matters like their own prosperity rather than face any more potentially divisive issues.

Garfield and Arthur

Hayes had fallen out of favor with Republicans by the election of 1880, and he only planned to seek one term as president. So the Republicans nominated the relatively unknown **James A. Garfield** and his Stalwart running mate, **Chester A. Arthur**. Democrats nominated Civil War veteran Winfield Scott Hancock, and the pro-labor **Greenback Party** nominated **James B. Weaver**. Garfield received a sizeable majority of electoral votes on Election Day but won only slightly more popular votes than Hancock. Bickering for the spoils dominated Garfield's brief stay in the White House, which ended unexpectedly in 1881 when an insane Stalwart named Charles Guiteau shot and killed him. Guiteau hoped Arthur would become president and give more federal jobs to his loyal Stalwarts.

Although Arthur did replace Garfield, the assassination only convinced policymakers to reform the spoils system by passing the **Pendleton Act** in 1883. The act created the **Civil Service Commission** to hire federal employees based on examinations and merit rather than on political patronage. Over time, these examinations gradually reformed the system.

Grover Cleveland

Despite the Pendleton Act, political spoils continued to dominate politics and the next presidential election in 1884. Republicans nominated the Half-Breed James Blaine while Democrats nominated New York governor **Grover Cleveland**. Democrats accused Blaine of conspiring with wealthy plutocrats to win the White

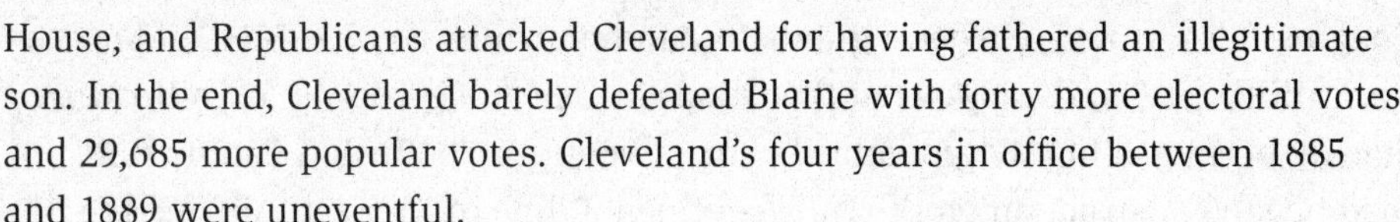

House, and Republicans attacked Cleveland for having fathered an illegitimate son. In the end, Cleveland barely defeated Blaine with forty more electoral votes and 29,685 more popular votes. Cleveland's four years in office between 1885 and 1889 were uneventful.

Benjamin Harrison

Afraid that Democrats would succeed in lowering their precious protective tariffs, Republicans rallied big business in the North and nominated **Benjamin Harrison** for the presidency in 1888. A grandson of former president William Henry Harrison, Benjamin Harrison campaigned for an even higher tariff. Democrats nominated Cleveland again but couldn't garner enough electoral votes to keep the presidency. Harrison slid into office. He worked the Republican majority in Congress and passed the following acts:

- **The Sherman Silver Purchase Act** to purchase more silver for currency
- **The Dependent Pension Act** to distribute more money to aging Civil War veterans and their families
- **The McKinley Tariff**, a controversial tariff that set duties on foreign goods to about 50 percent

INDUSTRIALIZATION

The North emerged from the Civil War as an industrial powerhouse ready to take on the world. Rich with seemingly unlimited natural resources and millions of immigrants ready to work, the United States experienced a flurry of unprecedented growth and industrialization during the Gilded Age. As a result, some historians have referred to this era as America's **second industrial revolution** because it completely transformed American society, politics, and the economy. Mechanization and marketing were the keys to success in this age: Companies that could mass-produce goods and convince people to buy them amassed enormous riches, while those that could not ultimately collapsed.

Transcontinental Railroads

The mass industrialization of the economy during the Gilded Age had its roots in the Civil War. Besides creating a huge demand for a variety of manufactured goods, the war also spurred Congress and the northern states to build more railroads. The rather progressive Congress of 1862 also authorized construction of the first railroad to run from the Pacific to the Atlantic. Because laying track cost so much money, the federal government initially provided subsidies by the mile to the railroad companies in exchange for discounted rates.

Congress also provided federal grants for land on which companies could lay the track. With free land and tens of thousands of free dollars per mile, railroading quickly became a highly profitable business venture. The **Union Pacific Railroad** began construction on the transcontinental line in Nebraska during the Civil War and pushed westward while Leland Stanford's **Central Pacific Railroad** pushed eastward from Sacramento. Tens of thousands of Irish and Chinese laborers laid most of the track. The two lines met near Ogden, Utah, in 1869.

Vanderbilt: Railroad Tycoon

Soon, other railroads—including the Southern Pacific Railroad, the Santa Fe Railroad, and James J. Hill's Great Northern Railway—spanned the western expanse. Federal subsidies and land grants made railroading such a huge business that it bred a new class of "new money" millionaires like Stanford and Hill. **Cornelius Vanderbilt** and his son William H. Vanderbilt were perhaps the most infamous of these railroad tycoons during this era. They bought out and consolidated many of the rail companies in the East and streamlined operations to lower costs. The Vanderbilts also established a standard track gauge and replaced the iron rails with lighter but more durable steel. Their innovation and cutthroat business practices earned them more than $100 million.

Railroad Corruption

Not all railroading profits were earned in a legitimate manner. The industry was filled with dozens of scams and embezzlement schemes to make insiders rich. Besides the infamous **Crédit Mobilier scandal**, railroads also inflated the prices of their own stocks and doled out uncompetitive rebates to favored companies. These practices hurt common people. Some of the states passed new laws to clamp down on the unruly railroads, but the Supreme Court shot all of them down when it ruled that only the federal government could regulate interstate commerce in the 1886 **Wabash Case**.

Captains of Industry

Whereas past generations had sent their best men into public service, young men during the Gilded Age sought their fortunes in the private sector, where a little persistence and ruthlessness could reap enormous profits almost overnight. Unregulated by the government, these so-called **captains of industry** did whatever they pleased to make as much money as possible. In fact, their business practices were quite often so unscrupulous that the term *industrialist* soon became synonymous with the nickname *robber baron*.

Carnegie, Morgan, and U.S. Steel

By the end of the 1900s, **Andrew Carnegie** was the wealthiest and most famous steel magnate in the United States. Carnegie created a veritable steel empire through a business tactic called **"vertical integration."** Instead of relying on expensive middlemen, Carnegie bought out all of the companies needed to produce his steel. He made it, shipped it, and sold it himself. Eventually he sold his company to Wall Street banker **J. P. Morgan**, who in turn used the company as

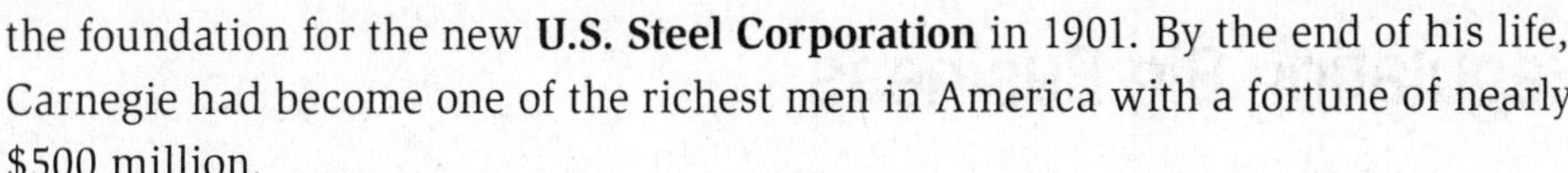

the foundation for the new **U.S. Steel Corporation** in 1901. By the end of his life, Carnegie had become one of the richest men in America with a fortune of nearly $500 million.

Rockefeller's Standard Oil

Oil also became big business during the Gilded Age. Although Americans needed very little oil before the Civil War, demand surged during the machine age in the 1880s, 1890s, and early 1900s. Everything required oil during this era, from factory machines to ships; this demand continued with cars in the 1920s. The oil industry also popularized the use of bright kerosene lamps.

John D. Rockefeller and his **Standard Oil Company** became the biggest names in the oil industry. Whereas Carnegie had employed vertical integration to create his empire, the ruthless Rockefeller used a method called **"horizontal integration"** to make sure he monopolized the industry. He bought out all the other oil companies to make sure he had no competition and in doing so created one of America's first monopolies, or **trusts**, to corner the market on a single commodity.

The Plutocracy

This period in American history witnessed a marked divide between the upper and lower classes. In time, the majority of plutocrats developed the belief that their riches had come not from their good fortune and circumstance but from their own superiority over the poorer classes.

Social Darwinism

In line with Charles Darwin's sensational new theory of natural selection, many of the new rich applied the mantra of "survival of the fittest" to society. In the words of one **Social Darwinist**, "The millionaires are the product of natural selection." Many of the wealthy believed they had become so fabulously rich because they were smarter and had worked harder than everyone else.

The Gospel of Wealth

On the other hand, more religious plutocrats preached the **"Gospel of Wealth,"** believing that God had given them riches for their genius and tenacity. The flip side to Social Darwinism and the Gospel of Wealth was that the poor were in turn considered ungodly and/or biologically inferior.

Philanthropists

Fortunately, not all of the new rich believed the poor should be left to fend for themselves. Many of the new rich demonstrated a keen interest in helping the less fortunate. Andrew Carnegie was by far the most generous of these Gilded Age philanthropists. Having come from a poor family himself, Carnegie firmly believed he would be disgraced if he died wealthy without having helped others. As a result, he donated more than $350 million to dozens of organizations by the time he died.

Regulating Big Business

To rein in the growing number of unwieldy trusts, Congress passed the **Interstate Commerce Act** in 1887, which outlawed railroad rebates and kickbacks. In addition, the act established the **Interstate Commerce Commission** to monitor the railroad companies' compliance with the new laws. To protect consumers by outlawing big trusts, Congress also passed the **Sherman Antitrust Act** in 1890.

Toothless Legislation

Although designed to regulate the corrupt railroad companies, the Interstate Commerce Commission had so many exploitable loopholes that it had almost no effect. Railroads still continued to issue rebates, demand outrageous fares, and charge different customers different prices for the same journey. The act did, however, establish an arena in which the competing railroad corporations could settle disputes without fighting disastrous rate wars. In this sense, the Interstate Commerce Commission helped stabilize the industry rather than control it. The similarly weak Sherman Anti-Trust Act also had very little effect at reining in the trusts.

THE LABOR MOVEMENT

The workforce changed drastically as the economy became more industrialized and mechanized. Competition for jobs grew stiffer as millions of immigrants, blacks, women, and farmers moved to the cities to find work. A mechanized economy also meant that companies required new and different sets of job skills. Unfortunately, organized labor generally floundered without any government regulation.

The National Labor Union

Founded in 1866, the first national labor union was simply called the **National Labor Union (NLU)**. The NLU sought to represent both skilled and unskilled laborers in one large organization. Though it had no ties to either political party, the union generally supported any candidate who would fight for shorter working days, higher wages, and better working conditions. The NLU only existed for six short years, thanks to the Depression of 1873. Union members found it difficult to bargain collectively when companies could easily hire thousands of new immigrant "scabs," or strike breakers, to replace them.

The Knights of Labor

Another union called the **Knights of Labor** survived the depression. Originally begun as a secret society in 1869, the Knights picked up where the NLU had left off. It too united all skilled and unskilled laborers, but unlike the NLU, it allowed blacks and women to join. The Knights won a series of strikes in their fight against long hours and low wages. The Knights of Labor also died

prematurely after Americans falsely associated them with the anarchists responsible for the **Haymarket Square Bombing** in Chicago in 1886. Additionally, the Knights found it difficult to successfully bargain collectively because they represented such a diverse group of workers.

Labor Strikes

Many of the fledgling unions that went on strike during the latter half of the nineteenth century did so to protest poor working conditions, long workdays, and inadequate pay. But most Americans at the time frowned on collective bargaining, which made it difficult for the unions to make any significant gains.

The Railroad Strike of 1877

In 1877, when the railroad companies announced a second 10 percent pay cut in four years, workers met to organize a National Trainmen's Union and plan a general strike. After the railroads fired union organizers, numerous strikes erupted on July 16 throughout the country. President Hayes eventually authorized state governors to use federal troops to suppress the ensuing riots.

The Coeur d'Alene Strike

The **Coeur d'Alene Strike** occurred in Coeur d'Alene, Idaho, in 1892, when several silver-mine owners collectively slashed miners' wages. The silver miners' union protested the wage cuts but had little effect, as eager immigrant scabs quickly replaced the organized laborers. Frustrated, a number of union protestors destroyed one of the mines in the city of Coeur d'Alene with dynamite. President Benjamin Harrison sent more than 1,000 federal troops to end the violence.

The Homestead Strike

Meanwhile, employees of Andrew Carnegie's Homestead Steel Works near Pittsburgh, Pennsylvania, had launched a strike of their own to protest wage cuts. Pittsburgh police refused to end the strike, so Carnegie hired 300 detectives from the renowned Pinkerton Detective Agency to subdue the protestors. Still, the laborers won a surprising victory after a rather bloody standoff. Harrison once again sent troops to break the **Homestead Strike** in 1892.

The Pullman Strike

Grover Cleveland made a similar decision in 1894 to end the **Pullman Strike** at the Pullman Palace Car Company in Chicago. When the company cut employees' wages by 30 percent in the wake of the depression, labor organizer **Eugene V. Debs** organized a massive strike. More than 150,000 American Railroad Union Members refused to work. Some even destroyed Pullman's famed Palace cars and delayed trains as far away as California. Cleveland sent federal troops to break up the strike and had Debs arrested.

The American Federation of Labor

A new labor union called the **American Federation of Labor (AFL)** grew to form an umbrella organization that coordinated the efforts of several dozen smaller, independent unions. Founded by **Samuel Gompers** in 1886, the AFL sought better wages, shorter working days, better working conditions, and the creation of all-union workplaces. Unlike its predecessors, the National Labor Union and Knights of Labor, the AFL only represented skilled white male craftsmen in the cities and exluded farmers, blacks, women, and unskilled immigrants. The AFL survived the rocky Gilded Age and eventually became one of the most powerful labor unions in the twentieth century.

GILDED AGE SOCIETY

The Gilded Age heralded the dawn of a new American society as the nation's base shifted from agriculture to industry. Millions of Americans flocked to the cities in the post–Civil War era. By 1900, nearly 40 percent of Americans lived in urbanized areas, as opposed to 20 percent in 1860. Many young people left their farms in search of the new wonders cities had to offer: skyscrapers, electric trolleys, and department stores, among others. Industrialization and the population swell in urban areas also spawned consumerism and a middle class.

Increased Immigration

A new wave of immigration contributed to a population explosion. Coming mostly from war-torn regions of southern and eastern Europe such as Italy, Greece, Poland, Russia, Croatia, and Czechoslovakia, the majority of these new immigrants had less money and education than the Irish and Germans who had preceded them. By the early twentieth century, a wave of immigrants more than a million strong flooded eastern cities every year. Most barely managed to eke out a living in the New World through low-paying, undesirable, and unskilled jobs in factories or in packinghouses.

Nativist Resurgence

Nativist Americans often despised the new wave of immigrants, claiming they would never assimilate into American society because of their illiteracy, poverty, languages, and inexperience with democracy. Some Protestants also disliked the fact that new immigrants were primarily Catholic, Eastern Orthodox, or Jewish.

Moreover, there was a fear among some Anglo-Saxon Americans that the eastern and southern Europeans would either dilute the race or eventually "outbreed" American whites. In response, the **American Protection Association** formed and lobbied for immigration restriction. Congress eventually conceded and, in 1882, barred criminals and the extremely destitute from entry.

Slums

The sudden influx of nearly a million poor people a year gave rise to slums in the cities. Much of this population inhabited the new **dumbbell tenement** buildings, so named because they resembled giant dumbbells. Entire families usually lived together in tiny, one-room apartments, sharing a single bathroom with other families on the floor. As dumbbell tenements were filthy, poorly ventilated, and poorly lit, they were conducive to disease.

Jane Addams and Hull House

Several reformers tried to fight the increasing poverty and social injustices that were rampant in the cities, including the college-educated **Jane Addams**, who founded **Hull House** in Chicago. Located in one of the city's poorest neighborhoods, Hull House provided counseling, day-care services, and adult-education classes to help local immigrants survive in the United States. The success of Hull House soon prompted **Lillian Wald** to open the **Henry Street Settlement House** in New York.

The successes of Jane Addams and Lillian Wald led other reformers to open similar settlement houses in other eastern cities with large immigrant populations. In time, women like Addams and Wald used their positions to fight for temperance, women's suffrage, civil rights, and improved labor laws.

Faith-Based Reform

Religious communities were another antipoverty force in the slums. Catholic churches and Jewish synagogues led the fight by offering services to the newly arrived immigrants, helping them find their way in the cities. Protestant speeches and lectures became very popular events, as did faith-based social organizations such as the Young Men's Christian Association, or YMCA, and the Young Women's Christian Association, or YWCA.

Christian Science

The post–Civil War period witnessed the birth of several new religions, such as **Christian Science**, which was founded by **Mary Baker Eddy**, who believed that faith could cure all disease. Hundreds of thousands of people converted, as the church spread throughout America.

The Women's Movement

Women achieved significant gains during the latter half of the nineteenth century. Many urban women found jobs, married later, had fewer children, and used various methods of birth control. Feminist **Charlotte Perkins Gilman**'s 1898 book *Women and Economics* demanded that women shirk their traditional roles as homemakers to find independence in the new America. She and other feminists such as **Elizabeth Cady Stanton** also demanded the right to vote. Another leading figure, **Victoria Woodhull**, shocked Americans by advocating

the use of contraceptives in spite of the **Comstock Law** of 1873, which outlawed the use of the U.S. mail to distribute contraceptives and information about contraceptives.

Plessy v. Ferguson and Civil Rights

African Americans did not fare as well as women in the struggle for equality. In 1896, the Supreme Court even upheld the policy of segregation by legalizing "separate but equal" facilities for blacks and whites in the landmark decision ***Plessy v. Ferguson***. In doing so, the court condemned African Americans to more than another half century of second-class citizenship.

Washington v. Du Bois

Black leaders continued to press for equal rights. For example, **Booker T. Washington**, president of the all-black **Tuskegee Institute** in Alabama, encouraged African Americans to become economically self-sufficient so that they could then challenge whites on social issues. The Harvard-educated black historian and sociologist, **W.E.B. Du Bois**, however, ridiculed Washington's beliefs and argued that African Americans should fight for social and economic equality at the same time. Their dispute highlighted the rupture in the Civil Rights movement during the end of the nineteenth century.

THE WEST

Railroads not only transformed industrial cities in the East but also in the West. This transformation happened primarily because travel had become easier, cheaper, and safer. The transcontinental lines moved people, grain, cattle, ore, and equipment across the vast expanses of the Midwest, over the Rocky Mountains and Sierra Nevada, and to the fertile valleys of California and Oregon.

The Homestead Act

Although Americans had continued to move in a steady stream westward, even during the Civil War, this phenomenon picked up steam once the war had ended. Several million Americans surged into the great unknown regions beyond eastern Kansas and Nebraska. Settlers particularly wanted cheap federal land offered by Congress in the **Homestead Act** of 1862. For a small fee, any settler could stake out a 160-acre western claim so long as he and his family improved the land by farming it and living on it for at least five years.

The Native American Wars

In 1881, author **Helen Hunt Jackson** published her book, *A Century of Dishonor*, a book that described the federal government's history of cruelty toward Native Americans over the previous hundred years. The book launched a new debate

about whites' relationship with Native Americans and prompted many people to conclude that assimilation would be the only solution to the problem.

The Sioux Wars

As white settlers pushed farther and farther westward, they repeatedly shoved Native Americans off their lands. Not surprisingly, the two groups frequently clashed. In 1864, for example, Union troops slaughtered several hundred Native American women and children at the **Sand Creek Massacre** in Colorado.

The U.S. Army also fought the Sioux tribes in the Black Hills of Dakota Territory during the 1860s and 1870s. These battles were dubbed the **Sioux Wars**. Lieutenant Colonel **George Armstrong Custer** made his infamous Last Stand during this war at the **Battle of Little Bighorn**, when more than 250 of his troops fell under the hands of Chief **Sitting Bull** and his warriors in 1876. The Sioux's victory was short-lived, and they were defeated a year later.

Chief Joseph, Geronimo, and Wounded Knee

The army also fought the Nez Percé tribe in the Pacific Northwest. United under **Chief Joseph**, the Nez Percé refused to relinquish their lands to white settlers without a fight. They fled all across the Northwest before the army finally defeated them and relocated the tribe to Kansas.

The Apaches in New Mexico Territory, led by **Geronimo**, also fought bravely to protect their homes until their eventual defeat. Hundreds of Native Americans also died at the **Massacre at Wounded Knee** in 1890 during the army's attempt to stamp out the **Ghost Dance Movement**, which called for a return to traditional Native American ways of life and challenged white supremacy.

The Dawes Severalty Act

In order to make room for more whites, the federal government first tried to herd natives onto tribal-owned reservations on the poorest land in the Dakotas, New Mexico, and Oklahoma. Under pressure from reformers who wanted to "acclimatize" Native Americans to white culture, Congress eventually passed the **Dawes Severalty Act** in 1887. The Dawes Act outlawed tribal ownership of land and instead forced 160-acre homesteads into the hands of Indians and their families with the promise of future citizenship. The act tried to forcibly assimilate Native Americans into white culture as quickly as possible.

Transformations in Agriculture

Investors and land speculators followed close behind the rugged homesteaders who had staked their claims in the great unknown and also had a share in transforming the West. Agricultural prices remained relatively high during the good times between the **Depression of 1873** and the **Depression of 1893**, so many farmers with a little capital switched from subsistence farming to growing single cash crops. In the Midwest, growing only wheat or corn or raising cattle to maximize profits in the cities was common for farmers.

The Plight of Small Farmers

The incorporation of farming, high protective tariffs, and the Depression of 1893 ruined subsistence farmers in the Midwest and South. Many of the cash-crop farmers found themselves deep in debt and couldn't afford the unregulated railroad fares to ship their products to cities. More than a million impoverished farmers eventually organized under a social organization called the **National Grange** to fight for their livelihood. They managed to win some key victories in several midwestern legislatures, supported by the Greenback Party in the 1870s and then the **Populist Party** in the 1890s.

THE RISE AND FALL OF POPULISM

Benjamin Harrison's **McKinley Tariff** was one of the highest tariffs in U.S. history—even higher than the 1828 Tariff of Abominations that had nearly split the Union. The tariff particularly hurt farmers in the West and South, who sold their harvests on unprotected markets and bought expensive manufactured goods.

The Populists

In seeking revenge for the McKinley Tariff, the farmers voted Republicans out of the House of Representatives in the 1890 congressional elections. Some of them even formed a pseudo-political party in the late 1880s called the **Farmers' Alliance**. By the time the 1892 elections rolled around, the Alliance had merged with other liberal Democrats to form the **Populist Party**. Populists nominated former Greenback Party candidate **James B. Weaver** and campaigned for the following:

- Unlimited cheap silver money (they wanted a rate of sixteen ounces of silver to one ounce of gold)
- Government ownership of all railroads and telephone companies
- A graduated income tax
- Direct election of U.S. senators
- Single-term limits for presidents
- Immigration restriction
- Shorter workdays

Grover Cleveland Elected Again

The Republicans and Democrats again nominated Benjamin Harrison and Grover Cleveland, respectively, for the presidency in 1892. Weaver and the Populists also entered the race, as did John Bidwell on behalf of the fledgling Prohibition Party. The Populists did surprisingly well and managed to receive more than a million popular votes and twenty-two electoral votes. The McKinley Tariff had ruined Harrison's chance for reelection, so the presidency reverted to Cleveland, who became the only president to serve two inconsecutive terms.

Cleveland's second round in the White House was a lot rockier than his first. The Depression of 1893—the worst depression the country had ever seen—hit just months after he took the oath of office. Additionally, Congress passed the **Wilson-Gorman Tariff** in 1894 in spite of Cleveland's promise to significantly reduce the tariff. This certainly affected his popularity.

Silver, Gold, and J. P. Morgan

Even worse, the federal government had nearly gone bankrupt. Wily investors had traded their silver for gold in a convoluted scheme that ultimately depleted the nation's gold reserves below $100 million. Had this trend continued, the government would not have had enough gold to back the paper currency in circulation or prevent the economic collapse that would have resulted.

Cleveland addressed this situation by repealing the 1890 Sherman Silver Purchase Act to prevent the loss of any more gold. This had no effect, and by the following year, the government had only $41 million in the Treasury. Cleveland and Congress ultimately appealed to Wall Street financier J. P. Morgan to bail them out. For a hefty price, Morgan agreed to loan the government $62 million to put it back on its feet.

Coxey's Army

The Depression of 1893 and Cleveland's repeal of the Sherman Silver Purchase Act only made the Populist movement stronger. More and more disillusioned Democrats flocked to the Populist Party in the hopes of winning free silver and more power for the people. The Depression also encouraged other would-be reformers to cry out for change. The wealthy Ohioan Jacob S. Coxey petitioned the government for cheap money and debt-relief programs. When **"Coxey's Army"** reached the capital in 1894, however, city officials arrested them for marching on the grass.

Islands in the Pacific

After the U.S. Census Bureau declared the continental frontier closed in 1890, Americans began looking overseas to expand. A number of islands in the Pacific Ocean became the first to fall under colonization and the American flag. Hawaii was the plum of the Pacific for its pleasant climate, which was perfect for growing sugar cane. Americans had been settling in Hawaii and living with the native islanders for more than a hundred years. The white American

minority had repeatedly petitioned Congress for annexation and had even overthrown the peaceful Hawaiian **Queen Liliuokalani** to seize control of the government in 1893. Outraged, the anti-expansionist Grover Cleveland rejected annexation and condemned the revolt against the queen.

Cleveland Upholds the Monroe Doctrine

Cleveland also threatened war with Great Britain over a territorial dispute in South America—one that didn't even involve U.S. territory. Both Venezuela and the British colony of Guiana claimed a huge tract of land rich with gold ore along the border. Invoking the Monroe Doctrine (i.e., the principle that mandated that the Americas were no longer open for European colonization), Cleveland threatened the British with war if they didn't back off.

Eventually, Britain acquiesced. They sought arbitration to settle the dispute, not so much because they feared the United States (Britain still had the largest navy in the world) but because they didn't want to alienate a potential ally as European relations grew increasingly chillier. Cleveland's bold stance impressed many Latin American nations, who began to see the United States as a friendly protector.

The Election of 1896

Cleveland had no chance for reelection to a third term. He had failed to correct the Depression of 1893, barely managed to keep the U.S. Treasury full, angered many middle-class constituents by using federal troops to end the Pullman Strike, and neglected to keep his promise to significantly reduce the Wilson-Gorman tariff. These problems proved insurmountable for him.

As the election of 1896 approached, Democrats instead nominated the so-called "Boy Orator" from Nebraska, **William Jennings Bryan**, on a Populist-inspired platform for free silver after he had delivered his rousing **"Cross of Gold" speech**, condemning the gold standard. The Populists threw their support to Bryan and the Democrats to keep the Republicans out of office.

McKinley Kills Free Silver

The Republicans nominated Congressman **William McKinley**, sponsor of the controversial McKinley Tariff, on a pro-business platform. Wealthy Ohioan businessman **Mark Hanna** financed most of the campaign and convinced his colleagues in the East to support McKinley. Despite Bryan's whirlwind speaking tour through the South and Midwest, it was Hanna's politicking that won McKinley the presidency that year.

McKinley appealed to a wide range of Americans. Conservative Americans feared cheap money and inflation so much that they flocked to McKinley and the Republican camp. Wealthy businessmen in the East dumped about $6 million to $12 million into McKinley's campaign, making it the fattest campaign fund of any American candidate ever. Some Democrats quite reasonably claimed that McKinley had purchased the White House. McKinley ultimately killed the

Populists' dream of free silver in 1900 when he signed the **Gold Standard Act** to peg the value of the dollar to an ounce of gold. He also signed the **Dingley Tariff** in 1897 to set overall tariff rates at about 45 percent.

A Key Election

Historians regard the election of 1896 as one of the most important elections of the nineteenth century and certainly the most significant election since the Civil War. First, it represented a victory of urban middle-class Americans over agrarian interests in the West and South. Populism had never really spread into the cities, and Bryan's appeal for free silver and inflation had alienated even the poorest Americans in the cities who depended on a stable dollar for survival. The Bryan campaign thus marked the last attempt to win the presidency through appeals to rural voters. It also marked the death of the Populist movement, which lost steam when it supported the Bryan campaign, essentially merging with the Democratic Party.

THE SPANISH-AMERICAN WAR

William McKinley entered the White House just as the nation was gearing up to its biggest foreign flare-up yet: the Cuban crisis. Spain still controlled the island just ninety miles south of Florida despite repeated American attempts to wrest it away. Depressed sugar prices in the 1890s led Cuban farmers to rebel against their Spanish overlords in a bloody revolution. Spanish forces under General "Butcher" Weyler tried to crack down on the insurrection by herding all suspected revolutionaries—including children—into concentration camps. Americans learned about the situation from the lurid **"yellow press"** of the day as newspaper titans **William Randolph Hearst** and **Joseph Pulitzer** printed sensationalistic stories to outdo each other in a competition for readers.

Remember the *Maine*!

The controversial **de Lôme letter** outraged Americans. Published in newspapers in 1898, the letter from Spanish minister to the United States' Dupuy de Lôme derided McKinley as a dimwitted politician. Shortly thereafter, more than 250 American seamen serving aboard the **U.S.S. *Maine*** died when the ship mysteriously exploded while anchored in Havana Harbor. Although Spanish officials and historians have concluded that a boiler-room accident caused the explosion, Americans at home quickly concluded that Spanish agents had sabotaged the ship. Millions cried, "Remember the *Maine*!" and pressured Congress and McKinley for war.

War Erupts

McKinley didn't want war; however, he eventually requested a war declaration from Congress in April 1898 out of fear that William Jennings Bryan and "free silver" would win the election of 1900. Congress consented on the grounds that

the Cuban people needed to be liberated. To justify the cause, Congress passed the **Teller Amendment**, which promised Cuban independence once they had defeated the Spaniards. Americans won the war quickly and easily, thus causing the Spanish Empire to collapse.

Dewey in the Philippines

Acting outside his orders, Assistant Secretary of the Navy **Theodore Roosevelt** ordered Commodore **George Dewey** to seize the Spanish-controlled Philippine Islands in Asia. Dewey defeated the Spanish fleet in a surprise attack on Manila Bay without losing a single man. Congress then annexed Hawaii on the pretext that the navy needed a refueling station between San Francisco and Asia. While Dewey fought the Spanish on the sea, insurgent **Louis Aguinaldo** led a Filipino revolt on land. Although Britain didn't participate in the fighting, it did help prevent other European powers from defending Spain.

The Rough Riders in Cuba

The U.S. Army, meanwhile, invaded Cuba with more than 20,000 regular and volunteer troops. The most famous of the volunteers were the **Rough Riders**, commanded by the recently commissioned Lt. Colonel Roosevelt, who had left his civilian job to join the "splendid little war." As its name implied, this volunteer company consisted of a sordid lot of ex-convicts and cowboys mixed with some of Roosevelt's adventurous upper-class acquaintances. Roosevelt and the Rough Riders helped lead the charge to take the famous San Juan Hill outside the city of Santiago. Cuba eventually fell, and Spain retreated.

Postwar Legislation

The United States honored the **Teller Amendment of 1898** (which declared that the United States did not have an interest in controlling Cuba after the war) and withdrew from Cuba in 1902, but not before including the **Platt Amendment** in the Cuban constitution to give the United States a permanent military base at Guantanamo Bay. The war gave McKinley more headaches than it cured. First, McKinley had to fight an insurrection led by Filipino rebel Louis Aguinaldo against American forces in the annexed Philippines. It took several years of bloody jungle warfare before U.S. forces defeated him, but even then, Filipinos resisted assimilation into white American culture.

The Supreme Court ruled in the 1901 **Insular Cases** that people in newly acquired foreign lands did not have the same constitutional rights as Americans at home. Congress still upheld the 1900 **Foraker Act** that granted Puerto Ricans limited self-government and eventually full U.S. citizenship in 1917. Finally, McKinley had to contend with the vocal new **Anti-Imperialist League** and its prominent membership, which challenged his expansionist policies and the incorporation of new "unassimilable" peoples into America.

TIMELINE: 1862–1901

1862	Congress passes the Homestead Act.
1866	National Labor Union forms.
1867	The National Grange forms.
1869	The Transcontinental Railroad is completed.
	The Knights of Labor forms.
	Wyoming grants women the right to vote.
1870	Standard Oil Company forms.
1873	Congress passes the Comstock Law.
	Depression of 1873 begins.
1874	Woman's Christian Temperance Union forms.
1875	Sioux Wars occur in Black Hills, Dakota Territory.
1876	Alexander Graham Bell invents the telephone.
	Custer's Last Stand takes place at the Battle of Little Bighorn.
1877	Railroad workers strike across the United States.
	The Nez Percé War occurs.
	Rutherford B. Hayes is elected president.
1879	Thomas Edison invents the light bulb.
	Mary Baker Eddy founds Christian Science.
1880	James A. Garfield is elected president.
1881	Garfield is assassinated.
	Chester A. Arthur becomes president.
	Booker T. Washington becomes president of the Tuskegee Institute.
	Helen Hunt Jackson publishes *A Century of Dishonor*.
1882	Congress passes the Chinese Exclusion Act.
1883	Congress passes the Pendleton Act.
1884	Grover Cleveland is elected president.
	Mark Twain publishes *Huckleberry Finn*.
1885	The Farmers' Alliance forms.

1886	The Haymarket Square Bombing occurs in Chicago.
	The Supreme Court rules that only the federal government can regulate interstate commerce in the *Wabash* case.
	The American Federation of Labor (AFL) forms.
1887	Congress passes the Interstate Commerce Act.
	Congress passes the Dawes Severalty Act.
1888	Benjamin Harrison is elected president.
	Edward Bellamy publishes *Looking Backward*.
1889	Jane Addams founds Hull House in Chicago.
1890	Congress passes the Sherman Silver Purchase Act.
	Congress passes the Sherman Anti-Trust Act.
	Jacob Riis publishes *How the Other Half Lives*.
	Congress passes the McKinley Tariff.
	U.S. Census Bureau declares the continental frontier closed.
	The Sioux Ghost Dance Movement challenges white supremacy.
	The U.S. Army challenges Native American ways of life in the Massacre at Wounded Knee.
	Alfred Thayer Mahan publishes *The Influence of Sea Power upon History*.
1891	The Populist Party forms.
1892	Miners strike in Coeur d'Alene, Idaho.
	Laborers win victory in the Homestead Steel Strike.
	Cleveland is reelected president.
1893	The Depression of 1893 ruins subsistence farming in the Midwest and South.
	Lillian Wald founds the Henry Street Settlement in New York.
	The Anti-Saloon League forms.
	Frederick Jackson Turner publishes *The Significance of the Frontier in American History*.
1894	"Coxey's Army" marches on Washington, D.C.
	Congress passes the Wilson-Gorman Tariff.
	The Pullman Strike occurs.

1895	J. P. Morgan bails out the U.S. government.
1896	The Supreme Court rules on *Plessy v. Ferguson*.
	William Jennings Bryan delivers his "Cross of Gold" speech.
	William McKinley is elected president.
1897	Congress passes the Dingley Tariff.
1898	Eugene V. Debs forms the Social Democratic Party.
	Charlotte Perkins Gilman publishes *Women and Economics*.
	The Anti-Imperialist League forms.
	The U.S.S. *Maine* explodes in Havana Harbor.
	The Spanish-American War begins.
	The United States annexes Hawaii.
	Congress passes the Teller Amendment.
	Admiral Dewey seizes the Philippines at Manila Bay.
1899	Aguinaldo leads the Filipino Insurrection against the United States.
1900	Congress passes the Gold Standard Act.
	Congress passes the Foraker Act.
	McKinley is reelected.
1901	U.S. Steel Corporation forms.
	The Supreme Court rules against equal constitutional rights for Americans on foreign soil in Insular Cases.
	Congress passes the Platt Amendment.

MAJOR FIGURES

Jane Addams. A Nobel Peace Prize–winner, Addams founded Hull House in 1889 to help immigrants make better lives for themselves in Chicago's slums. In doing so, she raised awareness for the plight of the poor while simultaneously opening whole new opportunities for women.

Chester A. Arthur. Elected to the vice presidency as James A. Garfield's running mate in 1880, Arthur became president in September 1881 after a crazed Stalwart assassinated Garfield. While he was president, Arthur refused to award Stalwarts any federal posts and helped legislate civil-service reform by signing the Pendleton Act in 1883.

James G. Blaine. A powerful congressman, senator, and secretary of state from Maine, Blaine was the leader of the Half-Breeds in the Republican Party during the Gilded Age. Like his archrival, Roscoe Conkling of the Stalwarts, Blaine sought to exploit the spoils system by rewarding political supporters with federal civil-service jobs. He ran for president in the vicious campaign of 1884 but lost to Democrat Grover Cleveland.

William Jennings Bryan. A young Democratic congressman from Nebraska, Bryan was the greatest champion of inflationary "free silver" around the turn of the century. Deemed the "Boy Orator," Bryan opposed Grover Cleveland's repeal of the Sherman Silver Purchase Act and won his party's nomination for the presidency in 1896 with his famous "Cross of Gold" speech. Though he never left the Democratic Party, he was closely affiliated with the grassroots populist movement, and the Populist Party chose to back him in the election of 1900. Bryan ran for the presidency three times (in 1896, 1900, and 1904). He died in 1925 after testifying in the infamous Scopes Monkey Trial.

Andrew Carnegie. A Scottish immigrant who came to the United States when he was thirteen, Carnegie built his Pittsburgh steel empire on a foundation of hard work and ruthless business tactics. He used a business method called vertical integration to control all aspects of making, selling, and shipping his steel. He was no friend of labor and sent in 300 Pinkerton Agents to end the 1892 Homestead Strike at one of his steel plants. Carnegie eventually sold his company to Wall Street financier J. P. Morgan, who used it to form the U.S. Steel Corporation trust in 1901. A firm believer that excessive wealth would shame him on his deathbed, Carnegie became one of the nation's first large-scale philanthropists by donating more than $350 million to charities, hospitals, libraries, and universities.

Grover Cleveland. A former Democratic governor of New York, Cleveland was elected president in 1884 after defeating James G. Blaine. His first term was mostly uneventful: His only battle came in his fourth year, when he tried to lower the protective tariff in order to reduce the Treasury surplus. He was defeated by Benjamin Harrison and the Republicans in 1888 but was reelected in 1892. His second term was much rockier: He unsuccessfully battled the Depression of 1893, sent federal troops to break up the Pullman Strike in 1894, and had to ask J. P. Morgan to loan the nearly bankrupt federal government more than $60 million in 1895. He was the only president ever to serve two nonconsecutive terms.

Roscoe Conkling. A powerful U.S. senator from New York, Conkling was the leader of the Stalwarts in the Republican Party during the Gilded Age. Like his bitter rival James G. Blaine of the Half-Breeds, Conkling sought to exploit the spoils system by rewarding political supporters with federal civil-service jobs.

Eugene V. Debs. The pro-labor founder of the Socialist Party, Debs helped to organize the 1894 Pullman Strike at the Pullman Palace Car Company. While serving time for instigating the strike, he began reading radical socialist literature. He ran unsuccessfully for the presidency in 1908 against William Howard

Taft and William Jennings Bryan and again in 1912, when he won roughly 6 percent of the vote. He was again sentenced to prison under the Espionage Act of 1917 after speaking out against America's role in World War I. Debs ran for president again on the Socialist Party ticket in 1920—from prison—and won almost a million popular votes.

W.E.B. Du Bois. A Harvard-educated black historian and sociologist, Du Bois pushed for both equal economic and social rights for African Americans. He disagreed with Booker T. Washington, among others, that economic success was the key to equality.

Mary Baker Eddy. Founder of the Christian Science Church in 1879, Eddy preached that disease could be healed by faith. The new church attracted hundreds of thousands of followers in the growing cities at the end of the nineteenth century and beginning of the twentieth century.

James A. Garfield. Elected president in 1880 on the Republican ticket, Garfield had spent less than a year in office when he was murdered by a crazed Stalwart who wanted Vice President Chester A. Arthur to be president. Garfield's assassination spurred Arthur and Congress to pass the Pendleton Act in 1883 to enact civil-service reform and reduce exploitation of the spoils system.

Geronimo. An Apache leader, Geronimo led his people in a rebellion against white settlement of the Southwest in the 1870s and 1880s. The Apaches were eventually defeated in 1886 and relocated to Oklahoma, Florida, and Alabama, where Geronimo died.

Samuel Gompers. A Jewish immigrant from Great Britain, Gompers founded the American Federation of Labor in 1886 to represent skilled urban craftsmen. He fought to win higher wages, better working conditions, shorter workdays, and all-union workplaces.

Mark Hanna. A wealthy Ohio businessman, Hanna served as William McKinley's campaign manager in the elections of 1896 and 1900. Despite protests from opponent William Jennings Bryan and the Democrats, Hanna convinced other plutocrats to contribute to McKinley's campaign in order to elect a pro-business president. McKinley's election proved that big business and wealth were necessary for twentieth-century politics.

Benjamin Harrison. The grandson of former president William Henry Harrison, the Republican Harrison entered the White House after defeating incumbent Grover Cleveland in 1888. His four years in office were unremarkable, although he did send federal troops to forcibly end the Coeur d'Alene Strike. He also signed the Sherman Silver Purchase Act, Sherman Anti-Trust Act, and McKinley Tariff in 1890. He was ousted from office in 1892 by returnee Grover Cleveland.

Chief Joseph. Leader of the Nez Percé people of the Pacific Northwest, Chief Joseph opposed white expansion westward and relocation to reservations. He led a band of nearly 1,000 warriors on a more than 1,000-mile journey across the Rocky Mountains to escape to Canada but was captured by U.S. forces in 1887. His capture ended the Nez Percé War.

William Kelly. An American small businessman, Kelly discovered the Bessemer process to cheaply make high-quality steel by blowing cold air on hot iron in the 1850s. Unfortunately for him, the process he discovered was named after a British inventor who made the discovery on his own several years later. Kelly's and Bessemer's discovery allowed tycoons such as Andrew Carnegie to make a killing in the steel business.

William McKinley. A powerful congressman from Ohio, McKinley pushed the McKinley Tariff through Congress in 1890, which raised the protective tariff rates on foreign goods to an all-time high. He later ran for president on a pro-Gold Standard platform against Democrat William Jennings Bryan in 1896. He won a resounding victory in the Electoral College, largely thanks to his campaign manager Mark Hanna and donations from wealthy plutocrats. His election marked the beginning of the Fourth Party System, in which Republicans dominated the federal government. Although he was personally against the Spanish-American War and acquiring new territories, his administration has been remembered for its imperialist leanings. McKinley requested that Congress declare war against Spain in 1898, afraid that Democrats would oust him in the next presidential election if he did not. He also annexed the Philippines, though it was against his better judgment. He signed the Gold Standard Act in 1900; that year, he won reelection. In 1901, McKinley was assassinated by an anarchist.

J.P. Morgan. An incredibly wealthy Wall Street banker, Morgan saved the nearly bankrupt federal government in 1895 when he loaned the U.S. Treasury more than $60 million. He later purchased Andrew Carnegie's steel company for nearly $400 million and used it to form the U.S. Steel Corporation in 1901. U.S. Steel was the first $1 billion corporation when Morgan died.

John D. Rockefeller. A wealthy oil baron, Rockefeller dominated the blossoming oil industry when he formed the Standard Oil Company in 1867. Incredibly ruthless, he was the champion of horizontal integration and shaped Standard Oil into one of the nation's first monopolistic trusts by buying out his competition.

Sitting Bull. Chief Sitting Bull, along with the Sioux of South Dakota, defeated General George Custer at the Battle of Little Bighorn in 1876. Sitting Bull eventually retreated to Canada after the U.S. Army retaliated and nearly wiped out the Sioux. He was killed by the police in 1890.

Frederick Jackson Turner. An historian, Turner published *The Significance of the Frontier in American History,* an 1893 essay that argued that western settlement had had an extraordinary impact on the social, political, and economic development of the United States. The essay is regarded as one of the most important works in America history.

William Tweed. More commonly known as "Boss Tweed," this crooked Democrat controlled most of New York City and even much of the state. He preyed on immigrants and the poor, promising improved public works in exchange for votes. Tweed was eventually prosecuted by Samuel J. Tilden in 1872 and died in prison. The Tweed Ring exemplifies the widespread corruption and graft in machine politics in the North during this time.

Cornelius Vanderbilt. A wealthy steamboat tycoon, Vanderbilt moved into the eastern railroad industry in the late nineteenth century. He was one of the first railroaders to replace his tracks' iron rails with steel. He also established a standard gauge for his railroads. Despite these improvements, Vanderbilt and his son were notorious robber barons who issued unfair rebates, hiked rates arbitrarily, and cared little for the American public.

Booker T. Washington. President of the black industrial college Tuskegee Institute in Alabama, Washington pushed African Americans to achieve economic equality with whites. He did not advocate immediate social equality because he believed that economic equality would eventually bring equal rights. Other black leaders, such as W.E.B. Du Bois, sharply disagreed.

James B. Weaver. A former Civil War officer, Weaver ran on the Greenback Party ticket in 1880 against James A. Garfield and Democrat Winfield Scott Hancock. He ran again in 1892 as the Populist Party candidate against Grover Cleveland and Benjamin Harrison and won more than a million popular votes and 22 electoral votes.

Victoria Woodhull. A leading figure of the women's movement, Woodhull shocked Americans when she and her sister began publishing a magazine advocating free love, contraception, and economic independence for women in 1870.

Chapter 12

The Progressive Era and World War I: 1901–1920

BIG STICK DIPLOMACY

An ardent imperialist, Theodore Roosevelt carried out much of William McKinley's foreign policies as well as some aggressive policies of his own. His comfort with forcefully coercing other nations to comply with America's will on a number of occasions prompted anti-imperialists and other critics to dub his foreign policy **"Big Stick" Diplomacy**.

China and the First Open Door Notes

After losing the Sino-Japanese War of 1895, the Chinese could only watch as Japan, Russia, and the Europeans carved their ancient country into separate spheres of influence. Afraid that Americans would be unable to compete for lucrative Chinese markets, McKinley's policymakers scrambled to stop the feeding frenzy. In 1899, President **William McKinley**'s secretary of state, **John Hay**, boldly sent his **First Open Door Notes** to Japan and the European powers requesting that they respect Chinese rights and free trade. The British backed the agreement, but France, Germany, Russia, and Japan agreed only on the condition that other countries adhered to the note, too.

The Boxer Rebellion

Naturally, many Chinese deeply resented Japanese and European conquest, and as a result a new nationalistic movement called the **Boxer Movement** spread across China like wildfire. Hoping to cast out all foreigners, a highly deluded Boxer army invaded Beijing in 1900. The Boxer Army believed they would be divinely protected from enemy bullets. They took a number of foreign diplomats hostage and then barricaded themselves in the city. Nearly 20,000 French, British, German, Russian, Japanese, and American soldiers joined forces to rescue the diplomats. After the coalition had quelled the short-lived **Boxer Rebellion**, Hay then issued his **Second Open Door Note** in 1900 to request the other powers respect China's territorial status in spite of the rebellion.

The Election of 1900

Territorial gains overseas during the Spanish–American War and events unfolding in China made foreign policy and imperialism the dominant issue in the election of 1900.

Republicans nominated the popular McKinley for more prosperity and expansion and chose former Rough Rider Theodore Roosevelt to be his new running mate. Democrats once again selected the old favorite William Jennings Bryan on an anti-imperialism platform.

To most of the Democrats' dismay, Bryan also insisted on pushing for free silver again, even though his free-silver platform had allowed McKinley to win in the previous election. Roosevelt and Bryan traveled throughout the country and played to the crowds on two whirlwind campaigns. In the end, free silver killed Bryan once more, and McKinley won with almost a million more popular votes and twice as many electoral votes. McKinley's tragic death by an anarchist's bullet, just months into his second term, pushed Theodore Roosevelt into the White House in 1901.

The Panama Canal

Roosevelt was not one to shy from responsibility or action, and the boisterous new president immediately went to work, particularly on his pet project to build a canal across Central America. Territorial gains made during the war made it necessary to create a canal in order to ferry merchant and military ships from the American ports in the Atlantic to the Pacific.

The Hay-Pauncefote Treaty

In a display of amity, Britain graciously annulled the 1850 Clayton-Bulwer Treaty that had previously prevented the United States from building such a canal in the past. Instead, they signed the new **Hay-Pauncefote Treaty** in 1901, giving Americans full ownership of any future canal. After purchasing land in the Colombian province of Panama from a French construction company, Roosevelt and Congress then petitioned the Colombian government to sell permanent rights to the land. The Colombians disagreed and demanded more money.

Gunboat Diplomacy

Furious, Roosevelt struck a deal with Panamanian rebels, who were dissatisfied with Colombian rule. He offered independence and American protection in exchange for land to build a canal. The rebels quickly consented and captured the provincial capital in 1903 while U.S. Navy gunboats prevented Colombian troops from marching into Panama. Roosevelt immediately recognized Panama's independence and sent Hay to sign the **Hay-Bunau-Varilla Treaty**, which relinquished ownership of canal lands to the United States. Construction on the canal began the following year, despite Colombian protests. Contractors eventually completed the **Panama Canal** in 1914.

Roosevelt's Corollary to the Monroe Doctrine

Roosevelt further angered Latin Americans when he twisted the Monroe Doctrine by making policy according to his own interpretation. When several South American and Caribbean countries defaulted on their loans, Germany and Britain sent warships to forcibly collect the debts. Afraid that aggressive Europeans would use the debts as an excuse to permanently reinsert their feet into Latin America's doorway, Roosevelt simply slammed the door shut in their faces. In 1904, he announced his own **Roosevelt Corollary to the Monroe Doctrine** by declaring that the United States would collect the debts owed and then pass them on to the European powers. In other words, only the United States could intervene in Latin American affairs. He then sent troops to the Dominican Republic to enforce debt repayment and to Cuba to suppress revolutionary forces in 1906.

Tensions with Japan

Relations between the United States and Japan during the Roosevelt years also soured. In 1905, Roosevelt mediated a dispute between Russia and Japan to end the Russo-Japanese War. Although Roosevelt's efforts won him the Nobel Peace Prize, both powers left the negotiating table unhappy and blamed the American president for their losses.

The Gentlemen's Agreement

Tensions mounted when the San Francisco Board of Education caved to popular anti-Japanese sentiment and banned Japanese students from enrolling in the city's public schools. Japanese diplomats in Washington, D.C., protested loudly and even threatened war. Roosevelt resolved the situation in the 1906 **"Gentlemen's Agreement,"** in which San Francisco promised to retract the racist ban in exchange for Japanese pledges to reduce the number of yearly emigrants to the United States.

The Great White Fleet

Roosevelt sent sixteen new battleships around the world, ostensibly on a goodwill tour. In fact, they were sent to demonstrate American military might to the

Japanese. When the **Great White Fleet** stopped in Tokyo in 1908, Japanese and American officials signed the **Root-Takahira Agreement**, in which both agreed to respect the Open Door policy in China and each other's territorial integrity in the Pacific.

ROOSEVELT AND THE PROGRESSIVES

During his two terms as president, Roosevelt promoted his view of the federal government as an impartial force for the public good, rather than as an advocate for particular interests. For example, he used the power of the government to restrain corporations. In his second term, Roosevelt focused more on enacting social reforms. His progressive policies included engaging in antitrust activities, supporting regulatory legislation, and championing environmental conservation. Roosevelt used his presidency as a **"bully pulpit,"** from which he gave speeches supporting his views on society and government.

The Muckrakers

The term ***muckrakers*** referred to the investigative journalists and crusading writers who sought to expose injustice and corruption and spark social change. During Roosevelt's presidency, several works helped spur the passage of progressive legislation:

- ***Wealth Against Commonwealth*** (1894) by Henry Demarest Lloyd, investigating monopolies such as the Standard Oil Company
- ***History of the Standard Oil Company*** (1904) by Ida Tarbell, also targeting Standard Oil
- ***How the Other Half Lives*** (1890) by Danish immigrant Jacob Riis, relying on photographs as well as text to describe the living conditions of the urban poor
- ***The Shame of the Cities*** (1904) by Lincoln Steffens, exposing municipal corruption
- ***The Jungle*** (1906) by Upton Sinclair, describing unsanitary conditions in the meatpacking plants

Roosevelt's Square Deal

Roosevelt's domestic progressive agenda came to be collectively known as the "Square Deal" and sought to regulate big business, protect consumers, and conserve the nation's natural resources.

Trustbusting

As part of his strategy to regulate big business, Roosevelt revived the 1890 **Sherman Antitrust Act** and prosecuted the giant **Northern Securities Railroad Company** in 1902. The Supreme Court backed the president when it upheld the Sherman Antitrust Act and ordered Northern Securities to dissolve in 1904. Roosevelt then used the Sherman Antitrust Act to prosecute dozens of other trusts.

The Anthracite Coal Strike

In 1902, the **United Mine Workers** went on strike in West Virginia and Pennsylvania to demand shorter workdays and better pay. Months passed with no resolution as mine managers refused to meet the workers' demands. In order to prevent a national coal shortage, Roosevelt finally intervened by threatening to seize the coal mines and use federal troops to run them, forcing management to seek arbitration. The strike eventually ended in October 1902. Soon after, the arbitration awarded miners both shorter workdays and higher wages.

Regulatory Legislation

Roosevelt won the 1904 election with nearly 58 percent of the popular vote—the largest popular majority a presidential candidate had ever garnered. He therefore increased his push for progressive reforms in his second term with the following acts:

- **The Elkins Act** of 1903, which instituted penalties for giving and receiving railroad rebates. Railroads had given rebates to shippers in order to guarantee their continued business.
- **The Hepburn Railroad Regulation Act** of 1906, which gave the Interstate Commerce Commission the power to control railroad rates, inspect company books, and assign a uniform standard of bookkeeping
- **The Meat Inspection Act** of 1906, which required federal inspectors to examine meat
- **The Pure Food and Drug Act** of 1906, which allowed the federal government to regulate the sale of medicine and food

---

Conservation

Roosevelt supported environmental conservation policies as a major tenet of his domestic program. He added millions of acres to the national forest system to conserve forests for future use, and he also increased the size of the National Park System to protect some land from development.

Progressivism on the State Level

Many reformers sought legislative and electoral changes that would give more power to the voters. These progressives succeeded in achieving the following:

- **The direct primary**, which allowed the electorate to elect the nominees for their political party
- **The legislative initiative**, which allowed the electorate to vote directly for specific legislation, rather than going through the state legislature
- **The referendum**, which allowed the electorate to vote on whether to accept or reject government legislation
- **The recall**, which allowed the electorate to vote government officials out of office in special elections

Robert M. La Follette

Governor Robert La Follette of Wisconsin incorporated many progressive policies into his state's government. Under his leadership, progressives in Wisconsin implemented a wide variety of measures:

- Workers' compensation and workplace regulation
- Environmental conservation legislation
- Higher taxes on railroads and other corporations
- The first modern state income tax in the nation

La Follette continued his push for progressive reform as a U.S. senator, representing Wisconsin from 1906 to 1925.

American Socialism

The socialist movement in the United States also reached its height during the Progressive Era. The Socialist Party contained diverse constituents, with its members extending beyond core urban immigrant areas to the rural Midwest and South. Different groups of socialists envisioned different solutions to society's problems, with some advocating radical action, such as the overthrow of capitalism. Other socialists advocated more moderate measures, which would include small private businesses as an alternative to large corporations.

THE TAFT YEARS

With the support of Theodore Roosevelt, **William Howard Taft** ran as the Republican candidate for president in the election of 1908. The Democrats again nominated **William Jennings Bryan**. Taft appealed to members of both parties and thus won the election with 321 electoral votes to Bryan's 162. However, Taft's popularity did not last long, and his presidency consequently lasted only one term. By the end of his presidency, he had alienated progressives and had fallen out of favor with his former friend and ally Roosevelt.

Taft's Dollar Diplomacy

Whereas Roosevelt had employed "big stick" diplomacy to bend weaker nations to his will, Taft preferred to use the buck. He believed he could convince smaller developing nations to support the United States by investing American dollars into their economies. **"Dollar diplomacy,"** as pundits dubbed it, was intended to make allies as well as easy money for American investors.

Dollar Diplomacy Fails

Taft put his new policy to the test in Manchuria. In 1909, he offered to purchase and develop the Manchurian Railway to prevent Russia and Japan from seizing control of it and colonizing north China. Unfortunately, both powers refused to hand over the railway to the United States, and the deal collapsed. The United States went on to dump millions into several unstable Latin American countries, such as Honduras, Nicaragua, Cuba, and the Dominican Republic. Eventually, occupation troops had to be sent to protect those investments. In short, Taft's dollar diplomacy failed miserably.

More Trust-Busting

After the failure of dollar diplomacy, Taft devoted himself instead to domestic matters and made trust-busting his top priority. Amazingly, he filed eighty lawsuits against monopolistic trusts in just four years, more than twice as many as Roosevelt had filed in almost eight years. In 1911, the Supreme Court used the previously neglected Sherman Anti-Trust Act when it dissolved John D. Rockefeller's **Standard Oil Company** for "unreasonably" stifling competition. Taft also famously filed a suit against J. P. Morgan's **U.S. Steel Corporation** later that year, a move that infuriated Theodore Roosevelt, who had helped the company in the past.

The Payne-Aldrich Tariff

Many progressive Republicans hoped Taft would keep his campaign promise and reduce the protective tariff. Taft tried but didn't have enough political clout to prevent conservatives within the party from repeatedly amending the bill for a lower tariff. By the time the **Payne-Aldrich Tariff** reached the president, conservatives had made so many amendments to keep certain tariffs high that the overall tariff rate remained practically unchanged. Taft signed the bill in 1909 anyway and then strangely proclaimed it to be the best bill Republicans had ever passed. Outraged, progressives denounced both the tariff and the "traitor" Taft.

The Ballinger-Pinchot Affair

Taft further alienated supporters when he fired **Gifford Pinchot**. Pinchot was the head of the Forest Service. A progressive, popular conservationist, and personal friend of Roosevelt's, Pinchot had opposed Secretary of the Interior **Richard Ballinger**'s decision to sell public wilderness lands in Alaska and the Rocky Mountains to corporate developers. The president furthermore refused to reinstate Pinchot even after Roosevelt and several prominent Republicans appealed on his behalf. The 1910 **Ballinger-Pinchot Affair** thus blackened Taft's public image and made him many enemies within his own party.

Roosevelt Returns with New Nationalism

Feeling betrayed by his one-time friend turned foe, Roosevelt left retirement in 1910 and dove back into politics to wrest back control of the Republican Party. During the following two years, he denounced Taft in scores of speeches delivered throughout the country. He also took the opportunity to promote his **New Nationalism** program, which entailed the following:

- Greater government regulation of business
- A graduated income tax
- Tariff reform
- A strong central government that acted in defense of the public interest

The former Rough Rider took charge of the fledgling National Progressive Republican League within the Republican Party, trying to win the party's nomination for president in 1912. Divided but still dominated by powerful pro-business conservatives, delegates at the nominating convention eventually chose to stick with Taft.

The Election of 1912

Roosevelt thundered out of the convention still determined to win a third term. He took with him his Progressive allies and founded a new **Progressive (or Bull Moose) Party**. Ultimately, four candidates ran for the White House in 1912:

- **William Howard Taft** for the Republicans
- **Theodore Roosevelt** for the Progressive Republicans
- **Woodrow Wilson** for the Democrats
- **Eugene V. Debs** for the Socialists

In the end, Roosevelt's Bull Moose Party split the Republican Party and allowed Wilson to win an easy victory. Wilson received 435 electoral votes to Roosevelt's eighty-eight and Taft's eight. Surprisingly, Debs managed to win nearly a million popular votes.

WILSON'S FIRST TERM

Even though Woodrow Wilson had promised a new form of progressivism and foreign policy during his campaign in 1912, his policies ultimately resembled those of his predecessors. In other words, he continued to use federal power to regulate big business and protect consumers while exerting American power in Latin America.

New Freedom Progressivism

During the 1912 campaign, Roosevelt and Wilson offered different kinds of progressivism. Wilson countered Roosevelt's New Nationalism with his own **New Freedom** plan. New Freedom championed states' rights, a limited federal government, and support for small businesses. During his two terms in office, however, Wilson compromised and incorporated many elements from New Nationalism into the New Freedom plan.

Economic and Business Changes

Wilson and progressives passed a variety of economic and business reforms:

- **The Underwood-Simmons Tariff** in 1913, which lowered protective tariffs
- **The Glass-Owen Federal Reserve Act**, also in 1913, which established a system of twelve regional Federal Reserve Banks. Each of the Federal Reserve Banks came under the oversight of a **Federal Reserve Board**. This gave the federal government greater control over the U.S. banking system.

- **The Clayton Antitrust Act** in 1914, which outlawed unfair business practices
- **The Federal Trade Commission Act** in 1914, which created the **Federal Trade Commission (FTC)**, a federal regulatory agency with the power to investigate and prosecute businesses engaged in illegal practices. The FTC, with its broader powers, replaced the **Bureau of Corporations** instituted under Roosevelt and served as the foundation of Wilson's antitrust policies.

Wilson's Other Reforms

Other progressive reforms included child labor legislation, aid to farmers, and the institution of an eight-hour workday for railroad employees. In addition, Wilson pleased progressives in 1916 by nominating Louis D. Brandeis to the Supreme Court. A committed progressive, Brandeis was also the Supreme Court's first Jewish member.

Wilsonian Foreign Policy

Wilson envisioned the United States as a moral leader and force for democracy in the world and championed **"missionary diplomacy"** as opposed to Taft's "dollar diplomacy." Despite its strong idealistic underpinnings, Wilson's foreign policy differed very little from Taft's.

U.S. Intervention in Mexico

In 1913, Wilson denounced **Victoriano Huerta**'s revolutionary government in Mexico. This government had seized power and deposed the rightfully elected government of President Francisco Madero. After a year of tense relations, Wilson finally decided to challenge Huerta's regime by sending U.S. troops to invade the Mexican port of **Veracruz**. Another revolutionary named **Venustiano Carranza** capitalized on the American invasion to overthrow Huerta and win the support of the United States. In retaliation, Mexican national hero **Pancho Villa** launched attacks on Americans in New Mexico and Arizona, killing nineteen people; the United States withdrew its forces from Mexico in 1917.

U.S. Presence in the Caribbean

Wilson sent troops to the following locations:

- **Nicaragua** in 1914 to continue Taft's occupation to ensure political and economy stability
- **Haiti** in 1915 to suppress a revolution
- **Dominican Republic** in 1916 to prevent a revolution
- **Danish West Indies** in 1917 after the United States purchased the islands from Denmark and renamed them the U.S. Virgin Islands

WORLD WAR I ERUPTS

Although the United States willingly became involved in disputes and conflicts in the Western Hemisphere, Wilson hoped to avoid involving the United States in the Great War that engulfed Europe in 1914. Several events ultimately forced the United States to enter the war.

The Assassination of Archduke Franz Ferdinand

On June 28, 1914, a Serbian nationalist assassinated **Archduke Franz Ferdinand**, heir to the Austro-Hungarian Empire, in Sarajevo. Austria-Hungary declared war on Serbia following the assassination, prompting every other major European power to choose sides in the largest-scale war the world had ever experienced. Great Britain, France, Russia, Italy, and Japan formed the **Allied Powers** on one side, and Germany, Austria-Hungary, and Turkey formed the Central Powers on the other.

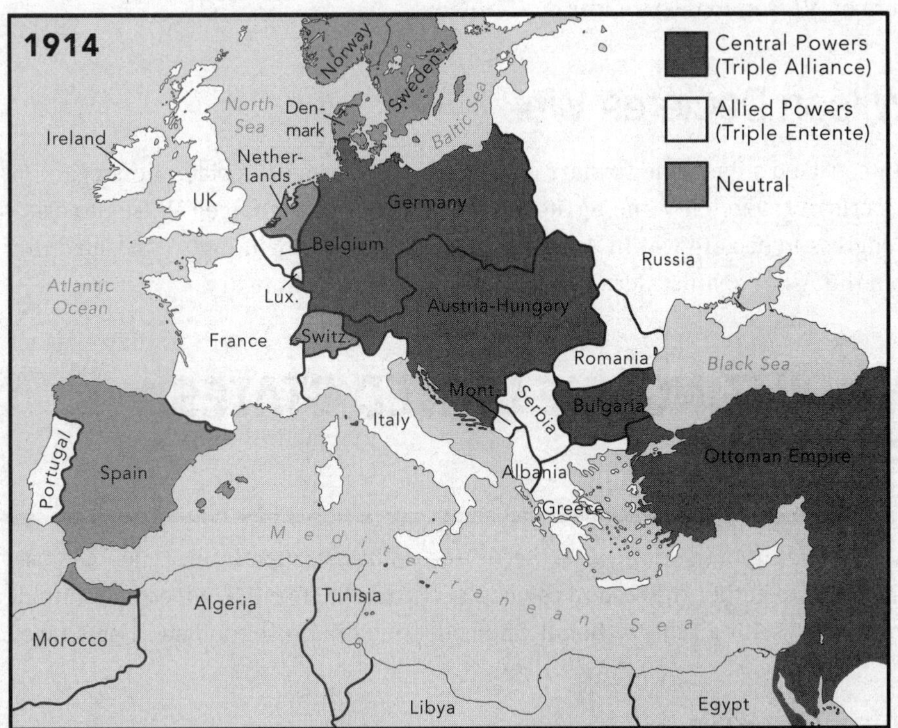

American Neutrality

Wilson tried to keep the United States neutral during the initial years of the war. Even though geography provided a natural buffer, war propaganda eventually crossed the Atlantic and split American public opinion. Moreover, the traditional American policy of neutral trading ultimately collapsed as Britain's blockade of Germany forced the United States to trade mainly with the Allies.

U-Boats, the *Lusitania*, and the *Sussex*

In response to the British blockade, Germany blockaded England with its deadly fleet of submarines, or **U-boats**. While the United States objected to this expansion of the war zone, the situation did not become a crisis until the Germans sank the British passenger ship ***Lusitania*** on May 7, 1915. In the *Lusitania* attack, 1,198 people died, including 128 Americans. Wilson and the German government negotiated to maintain relations after this incident and again after a 1916 attack on the French passenger ship ***Sussex***.

The Zimmerman Note

Despite earlier pledges, the Germans began attacking both neutral and Allied ships in an unrestricted submarine warfare campaign in 1917 to strangle Britain economically. Wilson had no choice but to cut all diplomatic ties with Germany. Then, in February 1917, the British disclosed the contents of an intercepted German telegram promising to expand Mexican territory if Mexico invaded the United States. This **Zimmerman Note** outraged Americans, who put more pressure on Wilson to declare war on Germany.

Wilson Declares War

Unrestricted submarine warfare combined with Germany's blatant disregard for American sovereignty and territorial integrity ultimately forced Wilson to ask Congress to declare war in April 1917. Congress overwhelmingly consented to join the Allies against Germany, Turkey, and Austria-Hungary.

MOBILIZING THE UNITED STATES FOR WAR

After deciding to enter the war, the Wilson administration immediately took several steps to gather the resources necessary to fight. The U.S. government funded the war by selling **Liberty Bonds** and collecting billions of dollars in new taxes.

War Boards

In 1916, the **Army Appropriation Act** established the **Council of National Defense** to oversee production of food, fuel, and railroads during the war. The council, in turn, created the following:

- **The War Industries Board**, headed by **Bernard Baruch**, organized and coordinated military purchases beginning in 1917. The board had extensive powers over U.S. production.
- **The National War Labor Board** settled disputes between labor and industry starting in 1918. Under pressure from the labor-friendly board, industries granted concessions such as an eight-hour workday and the right to bargain collectively.

Committee on Public Information

Journalist George Creel headed the **Committee on Public Information** to produce propaganda in favor of the war effort. In addition to distributing films and printed material, the committee also had considerable control over information about the war that appeared in the popular press.

Espionage and Sedition Acts

The **Espionage Act** of 1917 and the **Sedition Act** of 1918 effectively banned public criticism of governmental policy during the war. More than 1,000 people received convictions under these acts, which the Supreme Court upheld in 1919. Many of those convicted had ties to the growing Socialist party, including antiwar labor leader and presidential candidate Eugene V. Debs.

Domestic Labor

The war also brought changes in the domestic labor force. The flow of millions of working men into the armed forces and a reduction in immigration resulted in a labor shortage. To fill that gap, white women, African Americans, and workers of other races and ethnicities took jobs formerly held by white men.

Women in the Labor Force

During the war, women took jobs previously held by men, such as working on loading docks, operating heavy machinery, and working on the railroads. Some women even joined labor unions, although the American Federation of Labor (AFL) frequently opposed the entry of women into the workforce. Most women only held their new jobs for the duration of the war.

The Nineteenth Amendment

During the war, suffragists increased the intensity of their campaign for the right to vote. Leaders included **Alice Paul**, who led the militant **National**

Woman's Party, and **Carrie Chapman Catt**, who took over the more moderate **National American Woman Suffrage Association** in 1915. Women's roles in the labor force ultimately helped Congress and the states to ratify the **Nineteenth Amendment**, which granted women the right to vote in 1920.

African Americans in the Labor Force

Many African Americans migrated from the South to urban areas in the North during the war years to take advantage of the labor shortage. This influx began the **Great African American Migration**, in which roughly 10 percent of all black southerners relocated to the North. Additionally, cotton-crop destruction by boll weevils and high unemployment rates in the South escalated the migration.

THE UNITED STATES IN WORLD WAR I

World War I had devastating repercussions for many nations. Although the United States had entered the war late, the nation still suffered major casualties. Some 112,000 American soldiers died in World War I, half from influenza and half from the fighting itself. Among all nations involved, some 10 million soldiers died. New military technologies and the use of trench warfare contributed to the high casualty rates.

Effect of U.S. Forces

General John J. Pershing commanded the American Expeditionary Force sent to assist the British and French in Europe in 1917. U.S. forces, however, did not participate in any major fighting until 1918, when they helped achieve an Allied victory at the **Second Battle of the Marne**. Their defensive units defeated, German officials ultimately signed an armistice in November 1918.

The Fourteen Points

On January 8, 1918, Wilson delivered a speech to a joint session of Congress that set forth, in a series of **Fourteen Points**, the aims for which he considered the United States to be fighting. Five of the points called for the following:

- Freedom of the seas
- Armament reduction
- Open diplomacy
- Free trade
- Impartial negotiation regarding colonial claims

Eight other points set forth recommendations for the institution of new national boundaries in the conquered Ottoman and Austro-Hungarian empires. The last point advocated an association of nations, or **League of Nations**, to mediate future disputes and protect countries' "political independence and territorial integrity."

The Paris Peace Conference

In December 1918, the major combatants met at a peace conference in Paris. Wilson, Georges Clemenceau from France, David Lloyd George from Britain, and Vittorio Orlando from Italy made up the so-called **Big Four** that dominated the negotiations. On June 28, 1919, all sides signed the **Treaty of Versailles**, despite Germany's objection that the treaty would destroy its economy. The settlement required the following stipulations of Germany:

- Accept full responsibility for the war
- Pay $33 billion in reparations for the entire cost of the war
- Accept a foreign troop presence for fifteen years
- Cede some of its territory
- Abandon its colonies overseas

The Treaty of Versailles also divided the former Ottoman Empire in the Near and Middle East between Britain and France and established Wilson's League of Nations.

U.S. Controversy over the Treaty

Wilson presented the Treaty of Versailles to the Senate in the summer of 1919 but encountered intense opposition. Republican senator **Henry Cabot Lodge** and his **"reservationist"** allies denounced the treaty primarily because he disliked the League of Nations. Another group of **"irreconcilables"** objected to any American participation in the League. To gather public support, Wilson began a cross-country speaking tour, which was cut short in September 1919 when he fell ill. He later suffered a serious stroke that ruined any chance of the Senate ratifying the treaty. Congress formally declared the war over simply by passing a joint resolution in 1920.

TIMELINE: 1900–1920

1900	Republican president William McKinley is reelected. His vice president is Theodore Roosevelt.
1901	On September 6, an anarchist shoots McKinley during the Pan American Exposition. McKinley dies several days later, and Theodore Roosevelt becomes president.
1902	The Anthracite Coal Strike begins in May. It ends in October after the sides agree to submit to arbitration by a Roosevelt-appointed commission. The resolution of the strike results in Roosevelt's phrase "square deal."
	Roosevelt prosecutes the Northern Securities Company, charging it with violation of antitrust legislation. Two years later, the Supreme Court upholds the Sherman Antitrust Act, ordering Northern Securities to dissolve.
1903	Congress creates the Department of Commerce and Labor, containing a Bureau of Corporations to investigate businesses conducting interstate commerce.
	W.E.B. Du Bois publishes *The Souls of Black Folk*.
1904	Japan attacks the Russian fleet stationed at China's Port Arthur, beginning the Russo-Japanese War.
	Roosevelt wins reelection.
	Roosevelt announces his "Roosevelt Corollary" to the Monroe Doctrine, giving the United States leave to involve itself in the domestic affairs of countries in the Western Hemisphere.
1906	Upton Sinclair publishes *The Jungle*.
	The Hepburn Railroad Regulation Act expands the mandate of the Interstate Commerce Commission.
	The Meat Inspection Act requires federal inspectors to examine meat.
	The Pure Food and Drug Act applies federal regulations to the sale of medicine and foods.
1908	Republican William Howard Taft wins the presidency.
1909	National Association for the Advancement of Colored People (NAACP) is founded.

1910	Congress passes the Mann-Elkins Act, expanding the powers of the Interstate Commerce Commission (ICC).
	Jane Addams publishes *Twenty Years at Hull House*.
1911	A fire breaks out at the Triangle Shirtwaist Company in New York City. The blaze, which kills 146 workers, helps gain support for fire codes, labor laws, and workplace regulation.
	The Taft administration initiates an antitrust suit against U.S. Steel, angering Theodore Roosevelt.
1912	Roosevelt runs for president as head of the "Bull Moose" Party, splitting the Republican vote with Taft, the Republican party's nominee, and allowing for the victory of Democratic challenger Woodrow Wilson.
1913	The ratification of the Sixteenth Amendment to the Constitution allows for a federal income tax.
	The Seventeenth Amendment to the Constitution is ratified, which institutes popular election of U.S. senators.
	Wilson signs the Glass-Owen Federal Reserve Act, establishing a system of regional Federal Reserve Banks under the oversight of a Federal Reserve Board.
1914	A Serbian nationalist assassinates Archduke Franz Ferdinand, the heir to the Austro-Hungarian Empire, leading to the start of World War I in Europe.
	The Panama Canal opens, linking the Atlantic and Pacific Oceans across the Isthmus of Panama.
	The Federal Trade Commission (FTC) is created to regulate businesses practices.
	The Clayton Antitrust Act passes, outlawing practices such as interlocking directorates in large corporations and price discrimination.
	U.S. troops invade the Mexican port of Veracruz.
1915	Germans sink the *Lusitania*, killing 1,198 people, including 128 Americans.

1917	Germany begins unrestricted submarine warfare. Following that development, Wilson breaks diplomatic relations with Germany.
	The British relate the Zimmerman Note to Wilson, soon sparking the United States' entry into World War I.
	The United States declares war on Germany.
	The Selective Service Act establishes a nationwide draft.
	The Espionage Act passes. The Sedition Act passes in 1918. Both acts target public criticism of government policy.
	In Houston, Texas, a deadly clash occurs between black soldiers and the police. The incident results in the execution of nineteen black soldiers.
	The Bolshevik Party overthrows a provisional republican government in Russia. The new government arranges a peace with Germany in March of the following year and exits the war.
1918	Wilson delivers his Fourteen Points to Congress. The speech, which sets forth the aims Wilson considers the United States to be fighting for, includes a proposal for the League of Nations.
	The Sedition Act is passed.
	The Second Battle of the Marne marks a turning point in World War I. In November, German officials sign an armistice.
1919–1920	In the "Red Scare," Attorney General A. Mitchell Palmer and his assistant John Edgar Hoover organize raids in which authorities arrest alleged radicals.
1919	The ratification of the Eighteenth Amendment orders prohibition.
	At the end of the peace conference in Paris, all remaining participants in World War I sign the Treaty of Versailles, despite Germany's objections about the extremely punitive nature of the pact.
	Wilson presents the Treaty of Versailles to the Senate, where the document encounters opposition.
	The "Red Summer" sees race riots in many U.S. cities, including Washington, D.C., and Chicago.
	Steel workers strike for union recognition and an eight-hour day. Workers return to their jobs four months later, without the concessions.
1920	The ratification of the Nineteenth Amendment gives women the right to vote.

MAJOR FIGURES

Bernard Baruch. A Wall Street financier, Baruch headed the War Industries Board during World War I. The Board had extensive powers to oversee all aspects of American war production.

Carrie Chapman Catt. A suffragette who led the National American Woman Suffrage Association in the early twentieth century, Catt helped secure the passage of the Nineteenth Amendment, which enfranchised women.

Eugene V. Debs. Leader of the Socialist Party, Debs ran for president on the Socialist ticket in 1908 and 1912. When Debs criticized the government during World War I, authorities arrested and convicted him under the Espionage and Sedition Acts. Debs ran for president again from prison in 1920.

William Dudley Haywood. As leader of the Industrial Workers of the World, Haywood sought to replace the government with a union comprising all American workers.

Robert M. La Follette. A progressive politician, La Follette served as the governor of Wisconsin from 1901 to 1905 and instituted a number of progressive reforms. He later served as Wisconsin's senator from 1906 to 1925 and ultimately tried to run for president.

Vladimir Lenin. Leader of Russia after the Bolshevik Revolution of November 1917, Lenin negotiated a separate peace settlement with Germany in 1918 to withdraw from World War I.

Henry Cabot Lodge. Republican senator and chair of the Senate Foreign Relations Committee, Lodge led the "reservationist" opposition to the Treaty of Versailles. Concerned that the League of Nations would hinder American foreign policy, Lodge attached numerous amendments to the treaty before passing it to the full Senate. Wilson refused to accept the changes, and therefore the United States never entered the League of Nations.

Alice Paul. A suffragette who led the National Woman's Party, Paul helped secure the ratification of the Nineteenth Amendment to enfranchise women.

John J. Pershing. Commander of the American Expeditionary Force during World War I, Pershing refused to place American troops under Allied command when the United States entered the war, preferring instead to wait until he had enough troops to engage in different tactics. Pershing also pursued Poncho Villa into Mexico before the war but was unable to capture Villa.

Gifford Pinchot. As head of the U.S. Forest Service under William Taft, Pinchot had opposed Secretary of the Interior Richard Ballinger's plans to sell public lands. Taft dismissed Pinchot for insubordination despite Republicans' appeals that he remain. The affair damaged Taft's reputation as a progressive and contributed to the growing rift in the Republican Party.

Theodore Roosevelt. Republican president of the United States from 1901 to 1908, Roosevelt established a reputation for taking on corporate trusts, regulating industry to help consumers, and boldly exerting American dominance in Latin America. After splitting with his successor, William Howard Taft, Roosevelt unsuccessfully ran for president in 1912 on the Progressive Party ticket. Taft and Roosevelt's feud ultimately split the Republican vote and allowed Woodrow Wilson to win.

Upton Sinclair. A muckraker, Sinclair wrote about the deplorable working conditions in the meatpacking industry in his novel *The Jungle* (1906). The book disgusted government officials and Roosevelt so much that Congress passed the Meat Inspection Act, requiring federal inspection of meat.

William Howard Taft. Republican president of the United States from 1909 to 1912, Taft alienated himself from progressive Republicans after mishandling the Payne-Aldrich Tariff and Ballinger-Pinchot Affair. His former ally and boss, Theodore Roosevelt, ran for the presidency on the Progressive Party ticket in 1912, ultimately splitting the Republican vote.

Poncho Villa. A Mexican rebel and hero, Villa helped overthrow Victoriano Huerta's regime and then fought to oust his previous ally, Venustiano Carranza. President Wilson initially backed Villa but then recognized the Carranza government. Feeling betrayed, Villa attacked American interests and subsequently eluded the grasp of American forces in Mexico.

Woodrow Wilson. Democratic president of the United States between 1913 and 1920, Wilson ran on a progressive platform he called the New Freedom to reduce the size of the federal government. Once in office, however, he carried out policies similar to Theodore Roosevelt's. After failing to keep the United States out of World War I, Wilson defined American war aims with his Fourteen Points. He was unable to implement them in full at the Paris Peace conference and failed to convince the Senate to ratify the Treaty of Versailles or enter the League of Nations.

Chapter 13

The Roaring Twenties: 1920–1929

POLITICAL CONSERVATISM AND PROSPERITY

Tired of war and the political squabbling that had characterized the final years of Woodrow Wilson's presidency, Americans craved stable leadership and economic prosperity in the 1920s. Weary voters elected three pro-business conservative Republican presidents in the 1920s: **Warren G. Harding**, **Calvin Coolidge**, and **Herbert Hoover**. As a result, continuity—rather than change—characterized the political climate of the 1920s.

Warren G. Harding and Normalcy

Republican candidate **Warren G. Harding** promised voters a return to **"normalcy"** if elected president in 1920. Disillusioned by the upheaval of World War I, most Americans found Harding's cautious and conservative politics compelling. His popular image as a small-town newspaper editor from the Midwest combined with his consistently neutral policies contributed to his overwhelming victory over Democratic opponent James Cox.

During his three years in office, Harding supported big business, relaxed government control over industry, and promoted high tariffs on imports.

Resistance to the League of Nations

In order to restore stability both at home and abroad, Harding adopted several measures to reduce the country's international commitments. He signed several peace treaties with Germany, Austria, and Hungary soon after taking office and proposed an arms-reduction plan for a new Europe. In doing so, Harding side-stepped the extremely controversial issue concerning American membership in the **League of Nations** that had plagued Woodrow Wilson. Harding's plan allowed the United States to focus more fully on domestic matters while taking a backstage role in the reconstruction of Europe.

Scandal

President Harding gave many of the top cabinet positions and civil-service jobs to his old chums from Ohio. Unfortunately for the president, the **"Ohio Gang"** quickly sullied Harding's name by accepting bribes, defrauding the government, and bootlegging. In fact, grand juries indicted several of Harding's appointees; a few even received prison sentences. The chain of unending scandals prompted many Americans to questions Harding's own integrity and ability to lead.

The **Teapot Dome scandal** shocked Americans most of all. In 1923, journalists discovered that Harding's secretary of the interior, **Albert B. Fall**, had illegally authorized private companies to drill for oil on public lands. Investigators later determined that these companies had bribed the nearly bankrupt Fall to ignore their actions while they drilled. The naïve Harding escaped implication in the scandal only when he died unexpectedly of a heart attack in 1923. Although the nation expressed grief over his death, more scandals continued to surface throughout the decade and tarnish Harding's reputation.

Conservative Calvin Coolidge

The quiet vice president **Calvin Coolidge** entered the White House following Harding's death in 1923. His reserved demeanor, moral uprightness, and distance from the Harding scandals allowed him to win the presidency in his own right the following year in the election of 1924. Although "Silent Cal" Coolidge's personality and public persona differed greatly from Harding's, the two men thought along the same lines politically. Coolidge continued to support big business, propose higher tariffs, and push for deregulation of business and the economy. As a result, his victory in 1924 marked the demise of Progressivism.

The Presidency of Herbert Hoover

Like Harding and Coolidge, **Herbert Hoover** won the presidency on a pro-business, anti-regulation platform. Having grown used to the prosperity associated with previous conservative presidents, Americans in 1928 rejected Democratic candidate Alfred E. Smith and voted for Hoover.

PROHIBITION AND THE RISE OF ORGANIZED CRIME

The **Eighteenth Amendment** took effect in January 1920, banning the manufacture, sale, and transport of all intoxicating liquors. Referred to by supporters as "the noble experiment," Prohibition succeeded at lowering the consumption of alcohol, at least in rural areas. At the same time, the amendment created a lucrative black market for alcohol sales. Illegal, or **bootlegged**, liquor became widely available in cities. Typically, smugglers brought this liquor into the United States from other countries, while other Americans produced it in small homemade stills. **"Speakeasies,"** illegal bars where men and often women drank publicly, opened in most urban areas.

Gangsters and Racketeers

While Prohibition did not necessarily lead to criminal activity and the formation of gangs, both of which existed long before, it did provide criminals with a financially rewarding new business. **"Scarface" Al Capone** emerged as the best-known gangster of the era. He moved to Chicago in 1920 and soon became the city's leading bootlegger and gambling lord, protecting his empire with an army of gunmen. Capone's profits reached approximately $60 million annually by 1927. Although authorities generally tolerated bootleggers and speakeasies at first, they cracked down on the gangsters when a Chicago bootlegging gang disguised as police officers gunned down members of a rival gang in the **St. Valentine's Day Massacre**. Authorities eventually prosecuted Capone in 1931 for federal income tax evasion.

Prohibition Repealed

Because of the widespread availability of black-market liquor, federal authorities had trouble enforcing Prohibition. Still, President Herbert Hoover wanted to continue the morally worthy "experiment" in spite of growing opposition from the general public. Congress eventually passed the **Twenty-First Amendment** in 1933 to repeal Prohibition.

THE CULTURE OF MODERNISM

The expansion of radio broadcasting, the boom of motion pictures, and the spread of consumerism united the nation culturally. At the same time, these changes contributed to the breakdown of America's traditional vision of itself. As a result, a new national identity began to form.

The Impact of Radio

The popularity of radio soared during the 1920s, bringing Americans together and softening regional differences. With the arrival of the first developed radio station in 1920, the format of radio programming changed dramatically, expanding to include news, music, talk shows, sports broadcasts, political speeches, and advertising. The American public eagerly welcomed radios into their homes, signaling their openness to a changing culture. By simply turning on the radio, they received standardized information transmitted through national broadcasts. They also encountered advertising campaigns designed to change their spending habits and lifestyles.

The Rise of Motion Pictures

The American movie industry began in New York City, but when it moved to California in 1915, a true entertainment revolution began. By 1929, nearly every citizen attended the movies weekly, eager to see the latest comedy, thriller, and western. As movie attendance rose, so did the fame of the actors and actresses who performed in them. The "movie star" soon became a figure of glamour and fame.

Mass Production and the Automobile

Mass production allowed **Henry Ford** and his **Ford Motor Company**—the industry leader during the 1920s—to sell cars at prices that the working class could afford. This vastly increased the automaker's market. Cars made on an assembly line could be produced approximately ten times faster than cars assembled using more traditional means. The rapid increase in the supply of new cars combined with dramatically lower prices led to a vast increase in the total number of cars sold. Throughout the course of the decade, the number of cars on American roads tripled to 23 million.

Car ownership changed the way many people experienced American life. Owning cars allowed Americans in rural areas to take advantage of the amenities of nearby cities. Many smaller towns simply disappeared as increased competition closed numerous small businesses.

Aviation

Other modes of transportation also progressed in the 1920s. On May 21, 1927, **Charles Lindbergh** completed the first successful solo flight across the Atlantic. The American public celebrated the flight as a triumph not only of individual heroism but also of technological advancement. This flight foreshadowed the emergence of the commercial airline industry, which would boom in the ensuing decades.

Modernist Literature

Intrigued by what they saw as the fast-paced, fractured, unmoored modern world around them, writers in the 1920s struggled to develop a new type of language for expressing a new type of reality. Poets and fiction writers used new techniques such as **free verse** and **stream of consciousness** to capture the national mood.

The Lost Generation

Some of the most prominent American writers of the 1920s actually lived in Europe. Known collectively as the **Lost Generation**, writers such as Ezra Pound, Ernest Hemingway, Gertrude Stein, and Harold Stearns penned bitter commentaries on postwar America. Cynical about the country's potential for progress and about what they perceived to be misappropriated values, these writers found community abroad and produced some of the most creative literature and poetry in American history.

The Southern Renaissance

In the South, authors dealt with their regions' own transformation from a traditional society to one more influenced by changes in the wider American culture. Bible Belt authors, for example, found abundant material in the struggles of individuals who did not want to relinquish their agrarian lifestyles to modernism. Prominent writers of this movement included Alan Tate, William Faulkner, Thomas Wolfe, and Ellen Glasgow.

RESISTANCE TO MODERNITY

The Red Scare

Americans feared communist and socialist ideas in the wake of the Russian Revolution of 1917. In late 1919, communist fears picked up steam, and in January 1920, police across the nation seized more than 6,000 suspects in a raid to find and expel suspected communists. The government deported many socialists, including several in the New York legislature. Fortunately, the worst of the **Red Scare** had passed by 1921.

The Emergency Immigration Act

Compelled by imagined threats of foreign influences on American values and the rapidly rising rates of postwar immigration in 1920 and 1921, Congress passed the **Emergency Quota Act of 1921**. The act restricted new arrivals of immigrants to 3 percent of foreign-born members of any given nationality. The **Immigration Act of 1924** reduced this number further to 2 percent.

The Sacco and Vanzetti Trial

The trial of two Italian anarchists, **Nicola Sacco** and **Bartolomeo Vanzetti**, illustrated Americans' intolerance for foreign ideas and individuals. Tried and convicted for robbery and murder in Massachusetts in 1920, Sacco and Vanzetti faced an openly bigoted judge who failed to give the defendants a fair trial. Although protesters rallied behind them for six years, Sacco and Vanzetti never received a retrial, and state authorities executed them in 1927.

The Ku Klux Klan

The **Ku Klux Klan** reemerged in the 1920s as a misdirected effort to protect American values. Unlike the Klan of the nineteenth century, which had terrorized blacks in the South, the new KKK of the 1920s had a strong following among white Protestants throughout the country. It targeted blacks, immigrants, Jews, Catholics, and other minority groups that threatened the KKK's homogenous values and identity.

Through the course of the decade, the Klan gained a significant amount of political power, exerting both direct and indirect influence on state politics throughout the country. However, by the end of the 1920s, the Klan attracted considerable negative publicity, which, combined with the diminished threat of immigration, led to its downfall.

The Scopes Trial

In 1925, a Tennessee court tried high school biology teacher **John Scopes** for teaching the theory of evolution in his classroom in spite of a prohibitory state law. Protestant leaders such as William Jennings Bryan (a three-time Democratic candidate for president) spoke out against evolution, while Scopes's famed defense attorney **Clarence Darrow** tried to ridicule Christian fundamentalism. Clarence Darrow hounded and ridiculed William Jennings Bryan on the witness stand so extensively that some blame Darrow for Bryan's death from a stress-related illness several days after the trial concluded.

The so-called **Scopes "Monkey" Trial** captured the nation's interest. Although the court found Scopes guilty of violating the law, it only fined him $100. The high-profile trial illustrated the growing tension between tradition and progress.

IMPACT OF BLACK CULTURE

As Americans became interested in the new musical sounds coming from cities such as New Orleans, New York, St. Louis, and Chicago, jazz music became the rage of the decade, typifying the fluidity and energy of the era. African Americans also captured their culture in literature and art. Many whites became fascinated by the image of the black American that emerged during the 1920s.

Negro Nationalism

Marcus Garvey led the "Negro Nationalism" movement, which celebrated the black experience and culture. As the leader of the **United Negro Improvement Association (UNIA)**, Garvey advocated for the establishment of a Negro republic in Africa for exiled Americans. He argued that racial prejudice ran too deep in white American attitudes to ever be satisfactorily fixed and that black Americans should flee to their ancestral lands. Garvey's influence lessened after he went to prison in 1925 for federal mail fraud. His deportation to Jamaica in 1927 effectively ended his power within the African American community.

The NAACP

The National Association for the Advancement of Colored People (NAACP), established in 1910, remained active in the 1920s. Unlike the UNIA, the NAACP sought to resolve the racial issues in American society. The organization focused specifically on the dissemination of information and the implementation of protective legislation. In 1922, for example, the NAACP succeeded in getting a bill passed that helped end lynching. Although the bill remained mired in the House of Representatives for three years, public attention surrounding the bill helped reduce the number of lynchings in the United States.

The Harlem Renaissance

The **Harlem Renaissance** was one of the major African American cultural and artistic movements during the era. Black authors depicted experiences from urban Manhattan to rural Georgia and included Claude McKay, Langston Hughes, Zora Neale Hurston, and Alain Locke. Their poems and narratives not only captured the diversity of the African American experience but also highlighted the rich culture of black America.

Jazz

The growth of **jazz** music in the 1920s coupled the cultural expression of black Americans with mainstream culture by tapping into the emerging spirit of youth, freedom, and openness. The jazz movement also dissolved many traditional racial barriers in music, allowing young musicians of all races to collaborate and forge individual avenues of expression.

EMERGENCE OF THE "NEW WOMAN"

Women's roles changed at an unprecedented rate. Oppressive taboos such as those against smoking, drinking, and sexually provocative behavior slackened during the decade as women sought more freedom and self-expression. Some women began experimenting with new styles of dress, danced more, and discussed sex openly and freely. However, historians note that most women in the 1920s still adhered to traditional gender roles and customs despite the new freedoms and morality.

Suffrage and the Nineteenth Amendment

After the **Nineteenth Amendment** granted women the right to vote in 1920, former suffragettes formed the **League of Women Voters** to educate American women about candidates, issues, and the political process. Although some Americans feared the political leanings of the new electoral contingency, the addition of women voters had very little impact on voting trends because many women did not exercise their newly earned right to vote.

Many immigrant and southern women, for example, often chose not to vote because they didn't want to challenge their husbands' traditional authority. On the other hand, those who did vote showed little solidarity in their commitment to the advancement of women in society. Activists such as **Alice Paul** of the newly formed Woman's Party lobbied for feminist goals, such as equal rights and greater social justice. The majority of American women, however, still found such radical feminism distasteful and instead chose to fight for moderate and gradual reform through established parties.

Division within the women's movement ultimately led to the defeat of the **Equal Rights Amendment (ERA)**. Proposed in 1923, the ERA would have granted men and women equal legal rights. Female lobbyists did succeed in getting Congress to pass other significant laws to help women. For example, the **Sheppard-Towner Act** passed in 1921 awarding federal funds for health care to women and infants. Unfortunately, such protective legislation and social welfare programs suffered without legislators' vigilant care, and Congress eventually abandoned the Sheppard-Towner program in 1929 to cut costs. Most other legislative efforts concerning women met similar fates.

Flappers

Flapper women became the icon of the 1920s with their short "bobbed" hair, makeup, dangling jewelry, short skirts, and zest for modernity. Unlike the women of previous generations, flappers drank, smoked, danced, flirted, and caroused with men freely and easily. Even though very few women actually became flappers, the image appealed widely to the filmmakers, novelists, and advertisers who made them famous. Thrust into the limelight, flappers helped transform Americans' conservative conceptions of propriety and morality.

THE STOCK MARKET CRASH OF 1929

The prosperity of the 1920s finally ended when the **"bull market"** suddenly showed the strain of overvaluation in the fall of 1929. The value of the stock market had more than quadrupled during the 1920s primarily because Americans had purchased stock **"on margin"** by using the *future* earnings from their investments to buy even more stock. Even though buying stock on margin grossly distorted the real value of the investments, most people naively assumed the market would continue to climb. Therefore, they funded their lavish lifestyles on credit.

When the market buckled and stock prices began to slip, brokers made **"margin calls"** requesting investors to pay off the debts owed on stock purchased on margin. Unfortunately, most people didn't have the cash to pay back the brokers. Instead, they tried to sell all their investments quickly to come up with the extra money. The surge in stock dumping eventually caused the most catastrophic market crash in American history on **Black Tuesday**: October 29, 1929. In spite of attempts by major investors to bolster the rapidly declining market, Black Tuesday marked the beginning of the rapid economic collapse known as the **Great Depression**.

TIMELINE: 1919–1929

1919	The Red Scare begins.
1920	Prohibition begins with the Eighteenth Amendment.
	Women earn equal suffrage in the Nineteenth Amendment.
	Former suffragettes form the League of Women Voters.
	Warren G. Harding is elected president.
1921	Congress passes the Emergency Immigration Act (3 percent quotas).
	Congress passes the Sheppard-Towner Act.
1923	The Teapot Dome scandal shocks Americans.
	Harding dies and Vice President Calvin Coolidge becomes president.
	The Equal Rights Amendment (ERA) is proposed.
1924	Coolidge is elected president.
	Congress passes the Immigration Act of 1924 (2 percent quotas).
1925	Biology teacher John Scopes is tried for teaching evolution.
1927	Charles Lindbergh completes the first solo flight across the Atlantic.
	Nicola Sacco and Bartolomeo Vanzetti are executed.
1928	Herbert Hoover is elected president.
1929	Al Capone is prosecuted for tax evasion.
	The stock market crashes on Black Tuesday.

MAJOR FIGURES

Al Capone. Perhaps the most infamous gangster in American history, "Scarface" Capone led a major bootlegging ring in Chicago during the 1920s. He managed to evade prosecution until a court convicted him of income tax evasion in 1929.

Calvin Coolidge. A superconservative from Massachusetts, Coolidge served as vice president under Warren G. Harding and became president in 1923 after Harding died in office. He then became president in his own right in 1924 but declined the offer to run again in 1928. Like both his predecessor and his successor Herbert Hoover, Coolidge struck down the remnants of Progressive-style legislation in favor of rewarding big business.

Clarence Darrow. Undoubtedly the most famous lawyer in his day, Darrow represented John Scopes during the 1925 Scopes "Monkey" Trial. Although he lost the case, some have said Darrow's relentless badgering of William Jennings Bryan led to Bryan's fatal stress-related illness after the trial concluded.

Albert Fall. Secretary of the interior under Warren G. Harding, Fall accepted bribes from oil companies to look the other way while they illegally drilled for oil on public lands. The Teapot Dome scandal of 1923 rocked Washington and sullied the president's reputation.

Henry Ford. Inventor of the Model T Ford that launched the Ford automobile company, mechanical genius Ford transformed industrial America with his perfected method of assembly-line production that could produce several brand-new cars every minute.

Herbert Hoover. A former engineer and millionaire, Hoover was elected to the presidency in 1928. Even though he had a reputation as a humanitarian for his relief efforts in World War I, Hoover was completely unprepared for the task of guiding the nation out of the Great Depression. After the Crash of 1929, he encouraged Americans not to panic, and promised there would be no recession. Even when millions began losing their jobs and homes, he still refused to act, instead believing that it was not the government's job to interfere in the economy. Many historians believe that he could have curbed the suffering in the Great Depression if only he had chosen to act.

Marcus Garvey. An early civil rights activist, Garvey urged descendants of former slaves to return to their ancestral homes in Africa and take pride in their own culture and achievements.

Warren G. Harding. Harding's election in 1920 not only killed Woodrow Wilson's hopes of joining the League of Nations but also inaugurated a decade of conservatism and benefits for big business. The Teapot Dome scandal erupted in 1923 shortly before his untimely death.

Nicola Sacco. A Massachusetts jury convicted Italian anarchist Sacco and his accomplice Bartolomeo Vanzetti for a bank robbery and murder in 1920. Their speedy and rather unfair trial highlighted Americans' disdain for immigrants.

John Scopes. A high school biology instructor, Scopes brought the debate between Christian fundamentalism and Darwin's theories of natural selection to the fore when he challenged a Tennessee law forbidding the teaching of evolution. A court ultimately found him guilty in the infamous 1925 Scopes "Monkey" Trial and fined him $100.

Bartolomeo Vanzetti. A Massachusetts jury convicted Italian anarchist Vanzetti and his accomplice, Nicola Sacco, for a bank robbery and murder in 1920. Their speedy and rather unfair trial highlighted Americans' disdain for immigrants.

Chapter 14

The Great Depression and the New Deal: 1929–1939

THE DEPRESSION BEGINS

The "Roaring Twenties" came to a crashing halt in 1929. By late October, more and more people had pulled their money out of Wall Street. Consequently, the Dow Jones Industrial Average fell steadily during a ten-day period until it finally crashed completely on October 29, 1929. This day came to be known as **"Black Tuesday."**

On Black Tuesday, investors panicked and dumped an unprecedented 16 million shares. The practice of buying on margin had destroyed Americans' credit and only made the effects of the **Crash of 1929** (or **Great Crash**) worse. Within only one month's time, American investors had lost tens of billions of dollars.

Causes of the Depression

Although the 1929 stock-market crash had acted as the catalyst, a confluence of several factors actually caused the Great Depression.

A Changing Economy

The foundation of the American economy slowly shifted from heavy industrial production to mass manufacturing. In other words, whereas most of America's wealth had come from producing iron, steel, coal, and oil at the end of the nineteenth century, manufacturing consumer goods such as automobiles, radios, and other goods formed the basis of the economy in the twentieth century. As Americans jumped on the consumer bandwagon, more and more people began purchasing goods on credit, promising to pay for items later.

When the 1920s economic bubble burst, creditors had to absorb the cost of millions in bad loans that debtors couldn't repay. Moreover, policymakers found it difficult to end the Depression's vicious circle—Americans couldn't buy goods until they had jobs, but no factories wanted to give people jobs because they couldn't sell goods to a penniless population.

Buying on Margin

Americans had also purchased millions of dollars in stock on credit. Investors could purchase a share of a company's stock, and then use the *projected* earnings of that stock to buy even more. Not surprisingly, many people abused the system to invest huge sums of imaginary money that existed only on paper.

Overproduction in Factories

Overproduction in manufacturing also contributed to the economic collapse. Factories produced more and more popular consumer goods in an effort to match demand during the 1920s. Output soared as more companies utilized new machines to increase production, but workers' wages remained relatively stagnant throughout the decade. Eventually, the price of goods plummeted when factories began producing more goods than people demanded.

Overproduction on Farms

Farmers faced a similar overproduction crisis. Increasing debt forced many of them to plant more and more profitable cash crops such as wheat every year. Unfortunately, wheat depletes the soil's nutrients and renders it unsuitable for planting over time, but impoverished farmers couldn't afford to plant any other crop. Harvesting more wheat only depressed prices and forced them to plant even more the next year, which perpetuated the cycle.

Bad Banking Practices

Poor banking practices didn't help the situation. Many twentieth-century banks were little better than the fly-by-night variety of the previous century, especially in the rural areas of the West and South. The federal government didn't regulate the banks, and Americans had nowhere to turn to lodge complaints against bad banks. In fact, the majority of people had no idea what happened to their money after they handed it over to bankers.

Many bankers capitalized on the bull market to buy stocks on margin with customers' savings. This money simply vanished when the market collapsed, and thousands of families lost their entire savings in a matter of minutes. Hundreds of banks failed during the first months of the Depression, which produced an even greater panic and rush to withdraw private savings.

Income Inequality

Income inequality—the greatest in American history—made the Depression extremely severe. At the end of the 1920s, the top 1 percent of Americans owned more than a third of all the nation's wealth, while the poorest 20 percent of people owned a meager 4 percent of the wealth. The middle class, meanwhile, had essentially shrunk into nonexistence. As a result, only a few Americans had vast amounts of wealth, while the rest lived barely above the poverty level.

Old War Debts

The aftermath of World War I in Europe played a significant role in the downward spiral of the global economy in the late 1920s. According to the Treaty of Versailles, Germany owed France and England impossible sums in war reparations. France and England in turn owed millions of dollars to the United States. Starting in Germany, a wave of Depression spread through Europe as each country became unable to pay off its debts. As a result, the Great Depression affected the rest of the industrialized world.

HOOVER'S RESPONSE

President **Herbert Hoover** and other officials downplayed the crash at first. They claimed that the slump would be temporary and that it would clean up corruption and bad business practices within the system. Wall Street might not boom again, but it would certainly be healthier. The Republican president also believed that the federal government shouldn't interfere with the economy. In fact, he argued, if American families steeled their determination, continued to work hard, and practiced self-reliance, the United States could quickly pull out of the "recession."

The Reconstruction Finance Corporation

Instead of tackling the problem proactively, Hoover took an indirect approach to jump-starting the economy. He created several committees in the early 1930s to assist American farm and industrial corporations. In 1932, he also approved Congress's **Reconstruction Finance Corporation** to provide loans to banks, insurance companies, railroads, and state governments. He hoped that federal dollars dropped into the top of the economic system would help all Americans as the money "trickled down" to the bottom. Individuals were not eligible for RFC loans. Hoover refused to lower the steep tariffs and shot down all "socialistic" relief proposals, such as the **Muscle Shoals Bill** drafted to harness energy from the Tennessee River.

The Dust Bowl

The Depression also hit farmers hard, especially those in Colorado, Oklahoma, New Mexico, Kansas, and the Texas panhandle. Years of farming wheat without alternating crops to replenish the soil had turned the earth into a thick layer of barren dust. Depressed crop prices due to overproduction also forced many farmers off their fields. Unable to grow anything, thousands of families left this **Dust Bowl** region in search of work on the West Coast. Author John Steinbeck immortalized the plight of these farmers in his 1939 novel ***The Grapes of Wrath***.

The Bonus Army

Middle-aged World War I veterans were also among the hardest hit. In 1924, Congress had agreed to pay veterans a bonus stipend to be collected in 1945. As the Depression worsened, many veterans demanded their bonuses early. When Congress refused to pay up, more than 20,000 vets formed the **"Bonus Army"** and marched on Washington, D.C., in the summer of 1932. They set up a giant, filthy Hooverville in front of the Capitol and were determined not to leave until the government paid them. Hoover eventually ordered General Douglas MacArthur (of World War II fame) to forcibly remove the Bonus Army. Federal troops used tear gas and fire to destroy the makeshift camp in what the press dubbed the **Battle of Anacostia Flats**.

The Election of 1932

The brutal treatment of America's war heroes further convinced people that Hoover simply didn't have the gumption or knowledge to resolve the economic crisis. Instead, all eyes focused on the optimistic Democrat, Governor **Franklin Delano Roosevelt (FDR)** of New York. A distant cousin of former president Theodore Roosevelt, FDR promised more direct relief and assistance rather than benefits for big business. Republicans nominated Hoover for a second term in the election of 1932 but couldn't compete with the Democrats. In the end, Roosevelt soundly defeated Hoover, carrying all but six states.

FDR AND THE FIRST NEW DEAL

Roosevelt's policies did much to get Americans back on their feet. The New Deal not only provided **relief**, **recovery**, and **reform** but also drastically changed the federal government's role in politics and society. His successful application of John Maynard Keynes's economic theories transformed Democrats into social-welfare advocates. Even decades after the Great Depression, these politicians would fight for more government intervention in the economy, redistribution of wealth, and aid for the neediest.

The First Hundred Days

Americans had voted for Franklin Delano Roosevelt in the election of 1932 on the assumption that the Democrat would spur Washington to dole out more federal assistance. True to his word, the new president immediately set out to provide relief, recovery, and reform in his bundle of programs, collectively known as the **New Deal**.

Roosevelt drew much of his inspiration for the New Deal from the writings of British economist **John Maynard Keynes**, who believed that government deficit spending could prime the economic pump and jump-start the economy. With the support of a panicked Democratic Congress, Roosevelt created most of the **"alphabet agencies"** of the **First New Deal** within his **First Hundred Days**.

Banking Relief and Reform

On March 6, 1933—just two days after becoming president—Roosevelt declared a five-day national **bank holiday** to temporarily close the banks. Roughly 9,000 banks had closed during each year of the Depression under Hoover, and the new president hoped that a break would give the surviving banks time to reopen on more solid footing. Congress also passed Roosevelt's **Emergency Banking Relief Act**, which gave Roosevelt the power to regulate banking transactions and foreign exchange, and the **Glass-Steagall Banking Reform Act** of 1933, which protected savings deposits. The act created the **Federal Deposit Insurance Corporation** (FDIC) that insured individuals' savings of up to $5,000 (deposits of up to $100,000 are insured today). The act also forbade banks from investing in the stock market and regulated lending policies.

The Civilian Conservation Corps

Congress also created the **Civilian Conservation Corps (CCC)** in March 1933. Commonly known as the CCC, the corps hired unemployed young men to work on environmental conservation projects throughout the country. For $30 a month, the men worked on flood control and reforestation projects, improved national parks, and built many public roads. Approximately 3 million men worked in CCC camps during the program's nine-year existence.

The Federal Emergency Relief Administration

The so-called "Hundred Days Congress" also created the **Federal Emergency Relief Administration (FERA)** in May 1933. During the course of the Depression, FERA doled out $500 million to the states. The administration assigned roughly half of this money to bail out bankrupt state and local governments. States matched the other half (three state dollars for every one federal dollar) and distributed it directly to the people. Over the years, FERA gave more than $3 billion to the states. In addition, FERA created the **Civil Works Administration (CWA)** to create temporary labor jobs to those most in need.

The Agricultural Adjustment Administration

Roosevelt encouraged the creation of the **Agricultural Adjustment Administration (AAA)** to assist farmers. The AAA temporarily reset production quotas for farm commodities, including corn, wheat, rice, milk, cotton, and livestock. The AAA also subsidized farmers to reduce production so that prices would eventually rise again.

Congress also passed the **Farm Credit Act** to provide loans to farmers in danger of bankruptcy.

The Tennessee Valley Authority

May 1933 heralded the creation of the **Tennessee Valley Authority (TVA)** as well. Congress created the TVA to modernize and reduce unemployment in the Tennessee River Valley, one of the poorest regions in the country even before the Depression. The TVA hired local workers to construct a series of dams and hydroelectric power plants that brought cheap electricity to thousands of people. The public corporation also created affordable employee housing, manufactured cheap fertilizer, and drained thousands of acres for farming.

The National Industrial Recovery Act

Roosevelt and Congress attempted to revive the economy as a whole with the **National Industrial Recovery Act** in 1933. The act created two administrations:

- **The National Recovery Administration (NRA)**, which stimulated industrial production and improved competition by drafting corporate codes of conduct. The administration also sought to limit production of consumer goods to drive prices up.
- **The Public Works Administration (PWA)**, which constructed public roads, bridges, and buildings. In accordance with Keynesian economic theories, Roosevelt believed that improving public infrastructure would prime the pump and put more money into the economy.

Restructuring American Finance

Roosevelt spurred Congress to establish new regulations on the financial sector of the economy. After taking office, Roosevelt took the country off the gold standard, which had previously allowed citizens and foreign countries to exchange paper money for gold anytime they wanted. He also ordered Americans to hand over their stockpiles of gold to the U.S. Treasury in exchange for paper dollars. Roosevelt also created the **Securities Exchange Commission (SEC)** to regulate trading on Wall Street and curb the wild speculation that had led to the Crash of 1929.

The Indian Reorganization Act

Native Americans also received federal assistance. In 1934, Congress passed the **Indian Reorganization Act** to promote tribal reorganization and give federal recognition to tribal governments. More important, nearly 100,000 young Native American men participated in relief programs, such as the Civilian Conservation Corps, PWA, and WPA.

The Indian Reorganization Act changed relations between the various tribes and federal government because it reversed the 1887 Dawes Severalty Act. The Dawes Act had weakened tribal affiliations by stipulating that only individual Native Americans—not tribal councils—could own land. Unfortunately, despite Roosevelt's efforts to alleviate Native American suffering, the Indian Reorganization Act accomplished very little. Some tribes had difficulty understanding the terms of the new treaty, for example, while tribes like the Navajo simply rejected it.

First New Deal	Legislation / Policy / Program	How It Helped
March 9, 1933	Emergency Banking Relief Act	Relief
March 31, 1933	Civilian Conservation Corps (CCC)	Relief and Recovery
April 19, 1933	The United States goes off the Gold Standard	Recovery and Reform
May 12, 1933	Federal Emergency Relief Administration (FERA)	Relief
May 12, 1933	Agricultural Adjustment Association (AAA)	Relief and Recovery
May 18, 1933	Tennessee Valley Authority (TVA)	Relief, Recovery, and Reform
June 16, 1933	National Industrial Recovery Act (NIRA)	Relief, Recovery, and Reform
June 16, 1933	Public Works Administration (PWA)	Relief and Recovery
June 16, 1933	Glass-Steagall Banking Reform Act (w/FDIC)	Reform
November 9, 1933	Civil Works Administration (CWA)	Relief
June 6, 1934	Securities Exchange Commission (SEC)	Reform
June 18, 1934	Indian Reorganization Act (IRA)	Reform

Second New Deal	Legislation / Policy / Program	How It Helped
May 6, 1935	Works Progress Administration (WPA)	Relief and Recovery
July 5, 1935	National Labor Relations Act (Wagner Act)	Reform
August 14, 1935	Social Security Act	Reform
February 29, 1936	Soil Conservation and Domestic Allotment Act	Relief and Recovery
September 1, 1937	United States Housing Authority (USHA)	Relief, Recovery, and Reform
February 16, 1938	Second Agricultural Adjustment Association (AAA)	Relief and Recovery
June 25, 1938	Fair Labor Standards Act	Reform

OPPOSITION TO THE NEW DEAL

Roosevelt and the New Deal faced opposition from critics on both ends of the political spectrum. Politicians on the right referred to the New Deal as "Creeping Socialism" because they believed it threatened to subvert capitalism. Others on the far left claimed that Roosevelt and New Dealers had not done enough to help people or stabilize the economy. They regarded capitalism as a dying system and believed that FDR had made misguided and futile attempts to salvage the doomed enterprise.

Critics from the Right

Conservative critics of the New Deal feared that FDR would open the gates to the leftist movements that had already gained footholds throughout the world. In 1934, the **American Liberty League**, led by former Democratic presidential hopeful **Al Smith** and funded by the Du Pont family, claimed that FDR wanted to destroy free-enterprise capitalism and pave the way for communism, fascism, or both in America. Big business generally opposed the New Deal, too, out of fears that the federal government would support organized labor.

Critics from the Far Left

The New Deal faced nearly as much criticism from the progressive left as from the conservative right. Some ultraliberals, for example, thought that FDR's New Deal conceded too much to the wealthy and failed to resolve the problems in the financial sector.

Father Charles Coughlin

A Catholic priest named **Charles Coughlin** became one of the most recognizable opponents of the New Deal when he began broadcasting his criticisms on a weekly radio program. He became so popular that he amassed a following of 40 million listeners within just a few years. He blamed the Depression primarily on crooked Wall Street financiers and Jews and campaigned for the nationalization of the entire American banking system.

Huey P. Long

Senator **Huey P. "Kingfish" Long** of Louisiana also condemned the New Deal. He believed that income inequality had caused the Depression, and he promoted his **"Share Our Wealth"** program, or **"Every Man a King"** program, to levy enormous taxes on the rich so that every American family could earn at least $5,000 a year. He enjoyed enormous popularity during the first few years of Roosevelt's first term but was assassinated in 1935.

Francis E. Townsend

Retired physician **Dr. Francis E. Townsend** also believed he had the solution to drastically reduce poverty. Townsend proposed that the government pay senior citizens approximately $200 every month on the condition that recipients had to spend all their money in order to put money back into the economy. He and Father Caughlin created the **National Union for Social Justice** and even ran as a candidate for the presidency in 1936.

THE SECOND NEW DEAL

FDR responded to many of these critiques with a second bundle of New Deal legislation. Known simply as the **Second New Deal,** Congress passed this follow-up legislation between 1935 and 1938.

The Second New Deal differed drastically from the First New Deal in that its legislation relied more heavily on **Keynesian-style deficit spending**. Keynes strongly believed that the government needed to increase spending during times of economic crisis in order to stimulate the economy. The acceptance of Keynes's ideas was in part due to complaints from critics such as Huey Long but also simply because it was clear by 1935 that more Americans still needed federal relief assistance. Approximately half of the Second New Deal programs and policies were aimed at long-term reform.

The Works Progress Administration

Congress launched the Second New Deal with the **Works Progress Administration (WPA)** in 1935 in an effort to appease those like Senator Long who clamored for more direct assistance from the federal government. Similar to the

Public Works Administration of the First New Deal, the WPA hired nearly 10 million Americans to construct new public buildings, roads, and bridges. Congress dumped more than $10 billion into these projects in just under a decade.

The Social Security Act

Congress also passed the **Social Security Act** in 1935. This act created a federal retirement pension system for many workers that was funded by a double tax on every working American's paycheck. It also created an unemployment insurance plan to assist those temporarily out of work and made funds available to the blind and the physically disabled. Finally, it stipulated that Congress would match with federal dollars every state dollar allocated to workers' compensation funds.

More Help for Farmers

Roosevelt provided more assistance to farmers. After the Supreme Court declared the Agricultural Adjustment Administration unconstitutional in 1936, Democrats immediately responded with the passage of the **Soil Conservation and Domestic Allotment Act** the same year. This act continued to subsidize farmers to curb overproduction and also paid them to plant soil-enriching crops (instead of wheat) or to not grow anything at all so that nutrients would return to the soil. In 1938, Congress created a **Second Agricultural Adjustment Administration** to reduce total crop acreage.

Labor Reform

Much of the Second New Deal legislation promoted organized labor and included these important acts:

- **The National Labor Relations Act**, or **Wagner Act**, passed in 1935, which protected workers' right to organize and strike
- **The Fair Labor Standards Act**, passed in 1938, which established a national minimum wage and forty-hour work week in some sectors of the economy and the outlawing of child labor

---

Like the Social Security Act, these labor reforms also had a lasting effect. The 1935 Wagner Act paved the way for collective bargaining and striking. Within a year, fledgling labor unions had made great headway fighting for better hours and higher wages. For example, assembly-line workers in the General Motors automobile factory used the Wagner Act to initiate a series of sit-down strikes (workers would sit at their stations and refuse to leave, preventing the company from hiring new "scab" workers). By 1937, the company had recognized their right to organize. The Fair Labor and Standards Act also helped promote concepts of minimum wages and child-labor laws.

The Election of 1936

By the time the 1936 elections came around, Republicans barely stood a chance against FDR and the Democrats. The Democratic effort to provide relief, recovery, and reform had by this time become highly visible and had won the support of blacks (who voted Democrat for the first time in large numbers), unskilled laborers, and those in the West and South. Republicans nevertheless nominated moderate Kansas governor **Alfred M. Landon** on an anti-New Deal platform. Not surprisingly, Roosevelt won a landslide victory—523 electoral votes to Landon's eight—and proved that Americans widely supported the New Deal.

THE END OF THE NEW DEAL

In 1938, the New Deal steamroller came to an end. A conservative Supreme Court put the brakes on federal control of the economy and Keynesian-style deficit spending. Roosevelt's own political ambition, as well as the recession in 1937, also turned many Americans against the New Dealers.

Legal Battles

The Republican-dominated Supreme Court had begun to strike down several key pieces of First New Deal legislation in the mid-1930s. For example:

- ***Schecter v. United States*** in 1935 declared that the National Industrial Recovery Act violated the Constitution because it gave too many powers to the president and attempted to control *intra*state commerce rather than *inter*state trade.
- ***Butler v. United States*** in 1936 declared that the Agricultural Adjustment Administration also violated the Constitution because it unconstitutionally tried to exert federal control over agricultural production.

Roosevelt's Court-Packing Scheme

Roosevelt believed the NRA and AAA were crucial to reviving the American economy and feared that any more conservative rulings would cripple or even kill the New Deal entirely. Consequently, he petitioned Congress in 1937 to alter the makeup of the Court; he believed that the justices' old age might affect their ability to concentrate on their work. He also asked for the power to appoint as many as six new justices (to bring the total to fifteen) and for the authority to replace justices over the age of seventy.

FDR's **"court-packing scheme"** backfired. Instead of winning over Democrats and New Dealers in Congress, it had the opposite effect. Even Roosevelt's most ardent fans were shocked by the president's blatant disregard for the cherished tradition of separation of powers. Roosevelt repeatedly denied charges that he wanted to bend the entire federal government to his will and defended his proposal by arguing that aging justices sometimes couldn't perform their duties. The court-packing debate dragged on for several months before Congress and Roosevelt compromised on making minor reforms in the lower courts, while keeping the Supreme Court untouched and intact. Still, the political damage had been done. Roosevelt's plan to "pack" the Supreme Court with pro–New Dealers did more than anything else to turn Americans and other Democrats away from him and the New Deal.

The Roosevelt Recession

Pressured by conservatives in Congress and even by ardent New Dealers in the cabinet, Roosevelt began to scale back deficit spending in 1937, believing that the worst of the Depression had passed. He drastically reduced the size of the Works Progress Administration, for example, and halted paying farmers' federal subsidies.

The early retreat came too soon, and the economy buckled again in the resulting **"Roosevelt Recession."** The stock market crashed again in 1937, and the price of consumer goods dropped significantly. Contrary to conservative beliefs, the economy had not pulled far enough out of the Depression to survive on its own. Roosevelt tried to place the blame on spendthrift business leaders, but Americans didn't believe him. As a result, Democrats lost a significant number of seats in the House and the Senate in the 1938 congressional elections.

The Hatch Act

Republicans in Congress further weakened Roosevelt's power with the **Hatch Act** of 1939, which forbade most civil servants from participating in political campaigns. The act also forbade public office holders (i.e., Roosevelt and New Dealers) from using federal dollars to fund their reelection campaigns. Finally the act made it illegal for Americans who received federal assistance to donate money to politicians.

Conservatives hoped these measures would completely divorce the functions of government from the campaign frenzy and ultimately dislodge entrenched New Dealers who preyed on a desperate public for votes. Blamed for the Roosevelt Recession and for the president's plan to dominate the federal courts, and with their political base kicked out from under them, Democrats and the New Deal met their end in 1938.

TIMELINE: 1929–1939

1929	The stock market crashes.
1930	Congress passes the Hawley-Smoot Tariff.
1932	The Reconstruction Finance Corporation is created.
	The Bonus Army camps in Washington, D.C.
	Franklin D. Roosevelt is elected president.
1933	**First Hundred Days** • Emergency Banking Relief Act • Civilian Conservation Corps • Federal Emergency Relief Administration • Agricultural Adjustment Administration • Tennessee Valley Authority • National Industrial Recovery Act • Public Works Administration
	The Twenty-First Amendment is ratified (repealing the Eighteenth Amendment).
1934	Congress passes the Indian Reorganization Act.
	Roosevelt creates the Security Exchange Commission.
1935	**Second New Deal** • Emergency Relief Appropriations Act • Works Progress Administration • Social Security Act • National Labor Relations Act • Resettlement Administration • National Housing Act
	The Committee for Industrial Organization (CIO) is created.
	The Supreme Court rules on *Schecter v. United States.*
1936	Roosevelt is reelected.
	The Supreme Court rules on *Butler v. United States.*

1937	Roosevelt tries to "pack" the Supreme Court.
	The Roosevelt Recession begins.
1938	The CIO becomes the independent Congress of Industrial Organization.
1939	Congress passes the Hatch Act.

MAJOR FIGURES

Father Charles Coughlin. A Catholic priest in Michigan, Coughlin was also an outspoken critic of the New Deal. He blamed the Crash of 1929 on wealthy financiers and Jews and wanted the federal government to take over the banking system. The Catholic Church eventually cancelled his weekly radio show but not before he had attracted millions of sympathetic listeners.

John Maynard Keynes. A British economist in the early twentieth century, Keynes believed that deficit spending during recessions and depressions could revive national economies. His theories went untested until Franklin Delano Roosevelt applied them in the New Deal to bring the United States out of the Great Depression. The success of the New Deal converted Democrats to Keynesian disciples for the next several decades.

Alfred M. Landon. A Kansas governor, Landon ran against FDR on the anti–New Deal Republican ticket in the presidential election of 1936. Roosevelt beat him in a landslide victory that clearly demonstrated that the American people wanted more relief, recovery, and reform.

Huey P. Long. A senator from Louisiana, Long criticized Franklin Delano Roosevelt and the New Deal for not doing enough to help the American people. He believed that the wealthy should be heavily taxed in order to redistribute income more evenly. He attracted the attention of millions but was assassinated before he could seriously challenge the president. His criticisms played a role in shaping the Second New Deal.

Franklin Delano Roosevelt. A distant cousin of former president Theodore Roosevelt, FDR had served as governor of New York before being elected president in 1932. Roosevelt's New Deal programs and policies to end the Depression focused on immediate relief, long-term recovery, and reform to revive the economy. Despite the fact that he was usually wheelchair-bound (he had suffered from polio as a child), his optimism and charm did much to convince Americans they had "nothing to fear but fear itself." He successfully led the United States through World War II but died while still in office on April 12, 1945.

Chapter 15

World War II: 1939–1945

PRECURSORS TO WAR

World War I planted many of the seeds for World War II. Outstanding war debts in Great Britain and France—combined with the heavy reparations payments forced upon Germany—facilitated the rise of **fascism**. Meanwhile, the strong desire for **isolationism** in the United States prevented the American government from participating in international efforts to check the increasingly aggressive Germany, Italy, and Japan.

War Debts and Reparations

Outstanding debts created lasting problems for the major European powers because the British and French had borrowed much from the United States in the final two years of World War I. Under the terms of the Treaty of Versailles, both countries relied on war reparations from Germany to pay off their debts to the United States. During the 1920s, Germany could no longer keep up its payments, so the United States provided loans to the struggling nation according to the **Dawes Plan**. But the American economic crash in the early 1930s destabilized the already-weak **Weimar Republic** in Germany. These adverse economic conditions encouraged the rise of fascism in Germany.

American Isolationism

The European default on war debts only reinforced American isolationism. By the end of World War I, Americans had grown tired of war and turned their attention away from international affairs. Despite the urgings of President Woodrow Wilson, Congress refused to join the League of Nations. Although American leaders managed to enter a number of international agreements, isolationist sentiments prevailed in the face of a growing international crisis.

1920s Diplomacy

The United States collaborated with the international community on disarmament. Alarmed by the rapid growth of the Japanese navy, the United States government held the Washington Naval Conference in 1921 and cosigned the following treaties:

- **The Five-Power Naval Treaty**, which restricted the size of the American, Japanese, British, French, and Italian navies
- **The Four-Power Treaty**, which required the United States, Japan, Great Britain, and France to maintain the territorial status quo in the Pacific
- **The Nine-Power Treaty**, which bound the United States, Japan, Britain, France, Italy, Belgium, China, the Netherlands, and Portugal to respect the territorial integrity of China and to abide by the Open Door Policy

---

Roosevelt's Foreign Policy

Franklin Delano Roosevelt served as President Woodrow Wilson's secretary of the navy and endorsed an internationalist foreign policy in the late 1920s. Roosevelt supported the League of Nations and wanted to cancel European debts in order to stabilize the European economy. After becoming president in 1932, he promoted international cooperation (through trade) rather than military coercion. In order to accomplish this, he announced the **"Good Neighbor" Policy** in 1933 to reassure Latin American countries that the United States would not intervene in their internal affairs. He also formally recognized the Soviet regime in Russia in 1933.

The Neutrality Acts

Congress also passed several laws designed to prevent American involvement in another European war. The **Johnson Debt Default Act** of 1934 prohibited private loans to all governments that defaulted on their war debts. Congress then passed the **Neutrality Act of 1935** to prohibit the sale of arms and munitions to nations at war.

The following year, Congress renewed these provisions and also forbade American corporations from loaning money to belligerent nations. Congress enforced the **cash-and-carry** policy when it passed the **Neutrality Act of 1937**, which required nations at war to purchase American goods with cash and use their own ships to transport goods back to Europe.

The Rise of Militarism and Fascism Overseas

Events overseas reinforced the American desire to maintain neutrality. By the early 1930s, militaristic and expansionist governments controlled Japan, Italy, and Germany. The League of Nations proved ineffective at stopping these countries as the world inched closer to war.

The Japanese Invasion of Manchuria and China

The first stirrings of war occurred when militarists seized political power in Japan in 1931. Almost immediately, the Japanese invaded Manchuria, an area of China in which Japan had economic interests. Neither the United States nor the League of Nations attempted to intervene. Over the next several years, Japan sought to assert its military power in East Asia with these actions:

- Bombing the Chinese city of Shanghai in 1932
- Withdrawing from the League of Nations in 1933
- Renouncing the Five-Power Naval Treaty in 1934
- Invading China's northern provinces in 1937

Italy and Ethiopia

Meanwhile, the nationalistic **Fascist Party** had maintained control over Italy under the leaders of **Benito Mussolini** since the 1920s. Beginning in the mid-1930s, Mussolini also flexed Italy's military might through these actions:

- Invading Ethiopia in northeastern Africa in 1935
- Withdrawing from the League of Nations in 1937
- Conquering the Kingdom of Albania in 1939

The Rise of Nazism in Germany

Transformations in Germany alarmed European leaders even more. Economic problems facing the country in the aftermath of World War I helped fascist **Adolf Hitler** rise to power as leader of the National Socialists, or **Nazi Party**. The Nazis appealed to many Germans by pointing out the injustices of the Treaty of Versailles and blaming the country's troubles on Jews and other "inferior" races.

After becoming chancellor of Germany in 1933, Hitler recalled the country's representatives to the League of Nations and began to rearm the German military in violation of the Treaty of Versailles. Within a few years, Hitler had used his

military power to expand German territory. In March 1936, for example, German troops had invaded the Rhineland, an area placed under French control at the end of World War I. The French offered no resistance. Two years later, Hitler announced the annexation, or **Anschluss**, of Germany and his native country of Austria.

The Munich Accords

In September 1938, Hitler demanded that Czechoslovakia grant Germany control of the **Sudetenland**, an area where many ethnic Germans lived, but later agreed to meet with French and British envoys in Munich, Germany, to negotiate a peaceful settlement. Adopting a policy of **appeasement**, the British and French agreed to allow the annexation of the Sudetenland in exchange for Hitler's guarantee to halt territorial expansion.

Based on his accomplishments, British Prime Minister **Neville Chamberlain** triumphantly claimed he had secured "peace in our time." But the following March, Hitler broke the **Munich Accords** when he seized control of all of Czechoslovakia. Still, the British and French did nothing in the hope of avoiding another catastrophic war.

The Invasion of Poland

Emboldened by the inaction of France and England, Hitler then looked toward Polish land that had once belonged to Germany before World War I, even though the British and French had promised to assist Poland against German aggression. In August, Hitler signed a nonaggression agreement with Soviet dictator **Joseph Stalin** to ensure that Russia would not assist Poland and then ordered the invasion of Poland on September 1, 1939. France and Great Britain honored their promise to Poland and immediately declared war on Germany.

WAR ERUPTS ABROAD

The first two years of the war went well for Germany, Italy, and Japan. By the end of 1941, Germany and Italy had conquered much of Europe and planned to attack Great Britain and Russia. Japan continued to expand its influence in the Pacific and China, although to a lesser extent. The United States responded to these developments by increasing its aid to the Allies and by arming itself for the possibility of war.

The Escalation of the War

The war in Europe began with Germany's invasion and conquest of Poland, but very little happened the following winter. This **"phony war"** ended in the spring of 1940, when Hitler began his European military campaign in earnest.

The Blitzkrieg

In the spring and summer of 1940, Hitler launched the **Blitzkrieg**, or "lightning war." This rapid series of successful invasions gave him control over much of Western Europe, including Denmark and Norway (in April), Belgium and the Netherlands (in May), and France (in June).

The Nazis established a pro-German regime in southern France called **Vichy France** soon after the invasion. Meanwhile, the British gathered all their ships at **Dunkirk** and used them to return their troops to England.

The Battle of Britain

Hitler next turned his attention to the British Isles. During the summer and fall of 1940, the Germans regularly bombed English cities in preparation for a possible invasion. Inspired by the speeches of their new Prime Minister **Winston Churchill**, Britons deepened their resolve to resist Nazi aggression. The British Royal Air Force took to the skies to counter the German attack and helped win the **Battle of Britain**. Hitler's defeat forced him to put off another invasion until a later date.

German Invasion of Russia

In the summer of 1941, Hitler broke the Nazi-Soviet pact and invaded the Soviet Union. Within four months, Hitler's armies had penetrated deep into Russia. But intense Russian resistance and bitter cold weather stopped the German advance in the winter.

The invasion of Russia proved to be Hitler's greatest blunder during the war. Opening a second front in Russia required the Nazis to divert considerable resources from the fighting in Western Europe for the remainder of the war. Moreover, Germany's invasion of Russia prompted Russia to form an alliance with Britain and later with the United States.

Increasing American Involvement

Despite an official policy of neutrality, the United States became increasingly involved in the war overseas. The American people expressed a strong preference for the Allies, a preference derived partly from the United States' affinity with Great Britain. President Roosevelt also supported the Allies and undertook policies to aid their cause but stopped short of entering the war. In doing so, he slowly unraveled the constraints established by the earlier Neutrality Acts.

Neutrality Act of 1939

After the invasion of Poland, President Roosevelt called a special session of Congress. He asked members to revise the previous neutrality acts that he had come to regard as mistakes. Congress obliged the president and authorized the sale of war goods to belligerent nations on a cash-and-carry basis in the **Neutrality Act of 1939**, though American ships still could not enter war zones or the ports of belligerents. Soon after, Roosevelt secretly circumvented the cash-and-carry

policy when he provided the British with fifty destroyers in exchange for long-term leases on bases in British colonies in the Western Hemisphere.

War Preparedness

Concerned that the United States would be unprepared if it had to go to war, Roosevelt and Congress bolstered American defenses by increasing military spending almost tenfold in 1940. Additionally, they passed the **Burke-Wadsworth Conscription Act**, the first peacetime draft in United States history. All men aged 21 to 35 had to register for a year's worth of military service.

The Election of 1940

Roosevelt ran for an unprecedented third term against Republican challenger **Wendell Willkie** in 1940. When Willkie fell behind in the race, he accused Roosevelt of leading the country into war. Roosevelt responded by telling the American people, "Your boys are not going to be sent into any foreign wars." Roosevelt won the election by a landslide.

Lend-Lease

In March 1941, Congress enacted the **Lend-Lease** policy, which permitted the president to loan or lease arms to any nation considered vital to American defense. Britain and China received arms first, followed by the Soviet Union after Hitler's invasion.

Shipping in the Atlantic

The United States also increased its shipping activities in the Atlantic Ocean, where German **U-Boat** submarines had proven adept at sinking British ships. In order to help deliver aid to the Allies, President Roosevelt claimed the western Atlantic neutral territory and then extended American patrols as far as Iceland in July 1941.

In September, a German U-Boat fired on an American destroyer, prompting Roosevelt to order American ships encountering German submarines to "shoot on sight." When another U-Boat sunk an American destroyer the following month, Congress quickly authorized the arming of all merchant vessels and began permitting American ships to enter combat zones and the ports of nations at war.

The Atlantic Charter

In August 1941, Roosevelt met with Churchill off the coast of Newfoundland, where the pair signed a set of "common principles" known as the **Atlantic Charter**. In addition to calling for the "final destruction of Nazi tyranny," the charter sought to establish the following:

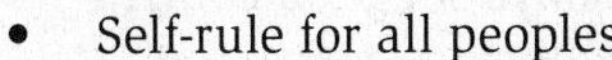

- Self-rule for all peoples
- International economic cooperation
- Disarmament and a system of collective international security
- Freedom of the seas

Growing Tensions Between the United States and Japan

The United States also inched away from strict neutrality in Asia. When Japan invaded China in 1937, Roosevelt responded by calling for a "quarantine" of aggressor nations. In 1940, Japan began working with its allies to secure a foothold in Southeast Asia and the Pacific in order to secure important war materials, including rubber and oil. Japan widened the scope of its war through measures such as the following:

- Securing the right to build airfields in Indochina from the Vichy government
- Occupying French Indochina
- Signing the **Tripartite Pact** with Germany and Italy to form the **Axis** alliance
- Signing a nonaggression pact with the Russians in order to ensure the safety of its northern front in China

The American Response to Japanese Expansion

The United States responded to these actions by voicing its disapproval and pursuing economic policies meant to discourage Japan from further aggression, such as the following:

- Granted loans to China
- Refused to export arms to Japan
- Froze all Japanese assets in the United States
- Stopped exporting oil to Japan—a significant punishment, considering 80 percent of Japanese oil came from the United States

Roosevelt refused to lift the embargo until Japanese troops withdrew from China and Indochina. In Japan, Prime Minister Fumimaro Konoye sought a compromise, but militants led by War Minister **Hideki Tojo** pushed Konoye out of office. Japanese diplomats continued to negotiate with the United States while the military planned a strike on Allied bases in the Pacific. American intelligence learned of a forthcoming attack but did not know the target.

Pearl Harbor

On the morning of **December 7, 1941**, Japanese planes took off from aircraft carriers and attacked the American naval base at **Pearl Harbor**. Within two hours, the Japanese had sunk or damaged nineteen ships, destroyed scores of planes, and killed more than 2,400 service members and civilians. The next day, President Roosevelt and Congress condemned the attack and declared war on Japan. Because of the Tripartite Pact, Italy and Germany then declared war on the United States on December 11, 1941. This prompted Congress to respond in kind.

THE UNITED STATES ENTERS THE WAR

The Japanese had coordinated a campaign to cripple the Allied presence in the Pacific, so U.S. forces immediately went on the defensive upon entering the war. Within months, however, the Japanese had nevertheless succeeded in capturing several important Allied territories.

By the end of 1942, U.S. forces stopped the Japanese advance at several decisive battles and then went on the offensive. In battles on the Atlantic and in North Africa, the Americans helped the Allies stop the Germans as well, making Atlantic and Mediterranean waters safe for Allied ships. By early 1943, the tide had finally begun to turn in the Allies' favor.

War in the Pacific

Following the attack on Pearl Harbor, the Japanese quickly conquered Allied territory in the Pacific and East Asia. Japanese **Admiral Isoruku Yamamoto** believed that only quick victories would allow Japan to beat the Allies. The attack on Pearl Harbor had damaged—but not crippled—the American navy. This was because all of the American aircraft carriers in the Pacific Fleet had left Hawaii several days before the attack.

The Japanese Offensive

Japan followed up its attack on Pearl Harbor by capturing a succession of Allied outposts in the Pacific and in Asia. The Japanese quickly conquered the following regions:

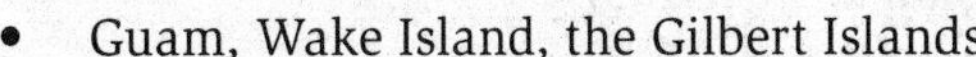

- Guam, Wake Island, the Gilbert Islands
- Hong Kong and Singapore
- The Dutch East Indies (Indonesia)
- Burma

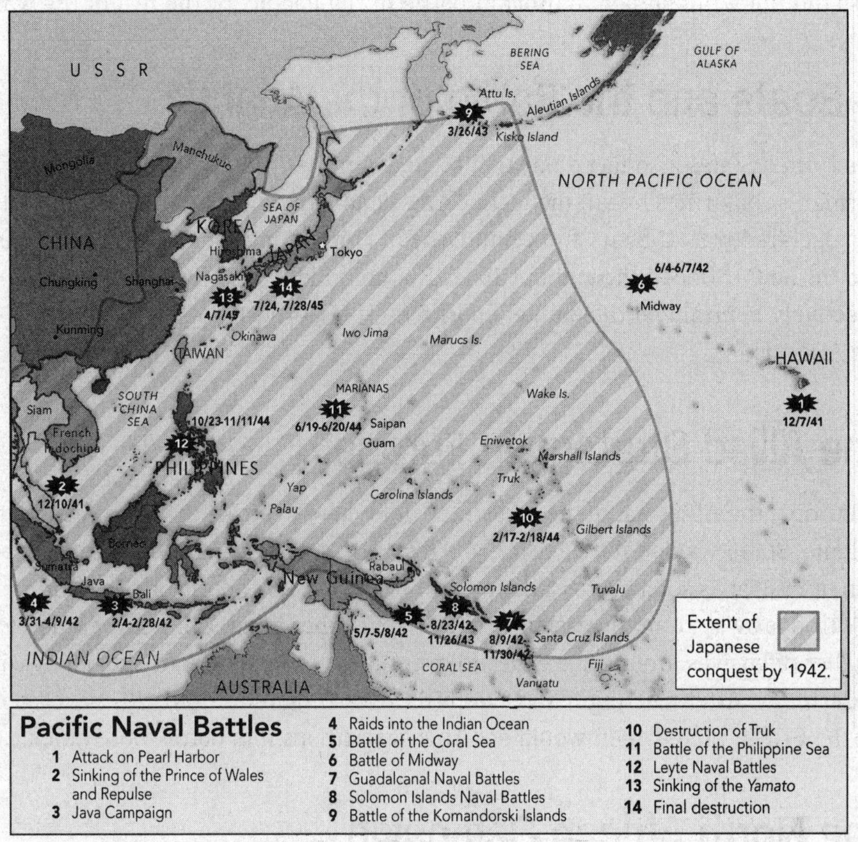

The Philippines

Within hours of the attack on Pearl Harbor, Japanese planes also bombed U.S. airfields in the Philippines. Later that month, American forces under the command of **General Douglas A. MacArthur** abandoned Manila and retreated to the Bataan Peninsula. In March 1942, MacArthur escaped to Australia under orders from his superiors. The following month, American troops retreated to the island of **Corregidor**. The remaining American forces at Corregidor surrendered on May 6.

The Battle of the Coral Sea

The United States finally managed to halt Japanese advances at the **Battle of the Coral Sea** in early May 1942. The battle began when American forces encountered Japanese ships bound for New Guinea. The United States successfully

turned the ships back. This victory prevented the deployment of Japanese troops sent to participate in an eventual invasion of Australia.

The Battle of Midway

The United States achieved another major victory over the Japanese at the **Battle of Midway** in June 1942. After American cryptologists had uncovered a secret Japanese plan to invade Hawaii, U.S. Navy commanders decided to intercept the Japanese fleet before it could attack. The Japanese lost all four of the aircraft carriers they brought to Midway, while the United States lost only one. The Japanese did not win another significant battle in the Pacific for the rest of the war.

U-Boats and the Battle of the Atlantic

The United States also faced naval challenges in the Atlantic. "Wolf packs" of German submarines began menacing American shipping after the United States had declared war. U-boats sunk hundreds of ships along the U.S. Atlantic coast and in the Caribbean throughout 1942. By the middle of 1943, the Allies had effectively neutralized the dangers posed by U-boats and won the Battle of the Atlantic.

The Allied Strategy in Europe

In Europe, the Allies had to decide when and where to strike the Germans and Italians. Stalin wanted the British and Americans to stage a cross-channel invasion of France as soon as possible in order to open a second major front and pull troops away from the eastern front. On the other hand, Churchill argued for smaller offensives around the edges to eventually build up to a full-scale invasion of Germany. After meeting with Churchill in Washington in 1942, Roosevelt opted for the British plan, which would get American troops into battle more quickly.

The North African Campaign

American ground forces faced their first real test in the deserts of North Africa. German forces under **General Erwin Rommel** had penetrated British-controlled Egypt in the hope of capturing the Suez Canal. In October 1942, the British halted Rommel's advance at **el-Alamein** in Egypt. They then began pushing the Germans back across Libya. On November 8, 1942, **General Dwight D. Eisenhower** landed American troops in French Morocco to join the British forces attacking Rommel. By May 1943, the Allies had forced the Germans out of North Africa and cleared the way for the invasion of Italy.

Casablanca

In January 1943, Roosevelt and Churchill met again in **Casablanca**, Morocco, to further discuss war plans. Both the Americans and British ultimately decided they needed more time to prepare for an invasion of France. However, they did agree to invade Italy via Sicily and accept only unconditional surrender from the Axis powers. They also agreed to launch major offensives in the Pacific.

WAR ON THE HOME FRONT

World War II had a significant impact on the lives of all Americans. More than 15 million men and women served in the armed forces. Even though the fighting never directly affected civilians at home, it nonetheless transformed their lives. The demands of war production brought about a return to prosperity after a decade-long depression, increased membership in labor unions, ended many of the reform programs of the New Deal, and provided new opportunities for women and minorities.

War Production and the Economy

Most historians agree that World War II effectively ended the Great Depression. The demand for war materials drove up production, which in turn created jobs and put money in the hands of American workers. At the same time, the draft removed millions of men from the workforce. To meet the needs of the growing economy and conserve resources, the U.S. government poured money into war production, as well as established agencies to manage the **economic conversion** of industry. Additionally, the government established **price and wage controls** to prevent runaway inflation, rationed vital resources, and worked with **labor unions** to prevent slowdowns in production.

Government Spending During the War

By funneling money into war industries, the American government played an important role in the economic boom. The federal budget rose from $9 billion in 1939 to $100 billion in 1945. Roosevelt wanted to fund the war solely with tax increases, but conservatives in Congress would not comply. They reached a compromise by agreeing to pay for half of the war with revenue raised from increased taxes and the remainder by borrowing from the public. The federal government did this by issuing **War Bonds** throughout the war, and Americans purchased more than $150 billion worth of bonds. Additional money came from banks and other financial institutions.

Economic Conversion

In order to manage the economic conversion, the United States moved quickly to organize and direct the national economy. In 1942, the government created the **War Production Board** to manage the conversion of private industry to war production. **"Dollar-a-year men,"** businessmen who moved to Washington, D.C., to work without pay, led a multitude of new agencies designed to oversee war production. As a result of these efforts, larger companies grew stronger because they could better handle mass production.

Price and Wage Controls

Americans had more money in their pockets, but the industrial commitment to war production meant that people could not spend their money on new housing, automobiles, or appliances. Because officials feared that scarcity of goods would create inflation, Congress created the **Office of Price Administration (OPA)** to set caps on prices, wages, and rents in 1942. By the end of the war, prices had risen 31 percent—only half as much as they had risen during World War I.

Rationing and Shortages

Consumer items such as sugar, gasoline, and meat also came in short supply. The government addressed these shortages by instituting a rationing program. Officials also encouraged the public to conserve precious resources for the good of the war effort. Some Americans, for example, planted "victory gardens," in which they grew their own food. Others gathered old rubber and scrap metal to be recycled and reused as war materials.

Labor Unions

The government ensured that all new workers would automatically join unions. In exchange, labor leaders agreed to accept limits on wage increases and made a **"no-strike" pledge** for the duration of the war. As a result, membership in labor unions rose from about 10.5 million in 1941 to 15 million just four years later.

Cooperation between the government and labor occasionally broke down. Sometimes workers would strike without the approval of their unions. In 1943, a United Mine Workers strike led by **John L. Lewis** prompted Congress to pass the **Smith-Connally Act**. The law required a thirty-day cooling-off period before unions could strike and gave the president authority to seize war plants if necessary. States also passed additional laws to curtail the power of unions.

Politics During Wartime

The federal government gradually became more and more conservative as the American economy improved. With the Great Depression over, New Deal reforms seemed less pressing and less necessary, and as a result, the 1942 elections led to the repeal of some Depression-era programs.

The End of Reform

Soldiers and war workers who had moved away from home could not cast their traditionally Democratic votes in 1942. This, plus general annoyance with wartime shortages and controls, helped Republicans in congressional elections. Conservatives grabbed the opportunity to end or cut back popular New Deal programs, including the following:

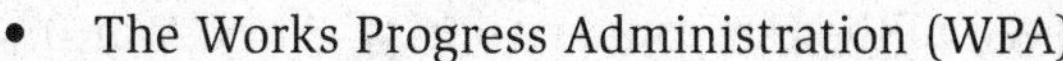

- The Works Progress Administration (WPA)
- The Farm Security Administration
- The National Planning Resources Board

By the end of 1943, Roosevelt had acknowledged the changing priorities of Americans and announced that winning the war would take precedence over the New Deal.

The Election of 1944

Roosevelt sought reelection once again in 1944 and ran against Republican Thomas E. Dewey from New York. Bowing to pressure from Democratic leaders, Roosevelt agreed to drop his vice president, Henry Wallace, and ran with the more moderate **Harry S Truman**, who had chaired a Senate committee to investigate fraud and waste in war production. Roosevelt won with 432 electoral votes to Dewey's ninety-nine.

Women and the War

The war emergency produced new opportunities for women in the workplace and the military. Women experienced unprecedented economic and social freedom as a result.

Women in War Industries

During the Great Depression, women had been discouraged from seeking work for fear that they would steal jobs from men. But the new demand for labor during the war prompted the government and industries to recruit women to increase war production. The government's publicity campaign encouraged women to enter traditionally male manufacturing positions by producing famous images of **Rosie the Riveter**.

Their campaign was successful, and about 6 million women entered the workforce during the war, an overall increase of more than 50 percent. The number of women working in manufacturing increased 110 percent, and the percentage of married women in the workforce rose from 15 percent in 1940 to 24 percent in 1945.

African Americans and the War

The war also had a profound social impact on African Americans. Many joined the military and saw other parts of the country and the world for the first time. The demand for labor in northern and western industrial cities also prompted more than 5 million blacks to move out of the agricultural South and to the cities during the 1940s.

African Americans in the Military

One million African Americans served in the U.S. military during World War II. Most served in segregated units due to a military policy that remained largely intact throughout the war. The Red Cross even maintained separate blood supplies for whites and blacks. In 1940, however, the government ended segregation in all officer candidate schools except for those training air cadets. About 600 black pilots received their training at a special military flight school established at Tuskegee, Alabama. Many of these **Tuskegee Airmen** went on to serve in decorated combat units.

African American Employment

In 1941, **A. Philip Randolph**, the head of the Brotherhood of Sleeping Car Porters, announced plans for a massive **March on Washington**. This march was to demand that the government require defense contractors to integrate their workforce and open more skilled-labor jobs to African Americans. Afraid of racial violence, Roosevelt convinced Randolph to cancel the march in exchange for creating the **Fair Employment Practices Commission**. During the war, the commission helped reduce black unemployment by 80 percent.

The Double-V Campaign

Because the war against fascism implicitly criticized the racial theories of Nazi Germany, African Americans seized the opportunity to fight all forms of prejudice at home. The NAACP started launched the "victory at home, victory abroad" campaign, also known as the **Double-V Campaign**. As a result, NAACP membership during the war increased from 50,000 members to roughly 450,000. A new civil rights group founded in 1942, the **Congress of Racial Equality (CORE)**, also campaigned for desegregation by staging demonstrations and sit-ins around the country.

Race Riots

The influx of African Americans into the workforce and cities, combined with growing demands for equal rights, created serious tensions with white Americans. During 1943, 242 separate incidents of racial violence occurred in forty-seven different American cities, the most serious being the **Detroit Race Riots**, in which twenty-five African Americans and nine whites died.

Native Americans and the War

More than 25,000 Native Americans served in uniform during World War II, often in integrated units. Some of the most famous were the Native American **"Code-talkers"** who used their native languages to encode important military messages. Many Native Americans also worked as laborers alongside whites in various war industries. Those who left their reservations for military service or war work acquired new skills, came into close contact with whites for the first time, and discovered new opportunities in American society.

Internment of Japanese Americans

After Pearl Harbor, Americans grew deeply distrustful of Japanese Americans, many of whom lived on the West Coast. Although no Japanese American ever committed treason during the war, Roosevelt authorized the **internment** of all Americans of Japanese descent in "relocation centers" in early 1942.

Internment camps in the western interior of the United States eventually housed about 100,000 Japanese Americans, two-thirds of whom were American citizens. Prisoners had little time to make arrangements for their property before being deported to the camps, so many people lost homes and businesses. The Supreme Court upheld the order in 1944 in *Korematsu v. United States*.

VICTORY IN EUROPE

In 1943, the Allies began their campaign to roll back the Axis in earnest. Churchill and Roosevelt ignored Stalin's request to engage the Germans on a second front and instead followed up on their success in North Africa by invading Italy. But a year later, the United States and Great Britain attacked in the West when they invaded France. The Allies pressed in on Germany from both sides, meeting in the spring of 1945 and forcing Germany's surrender.

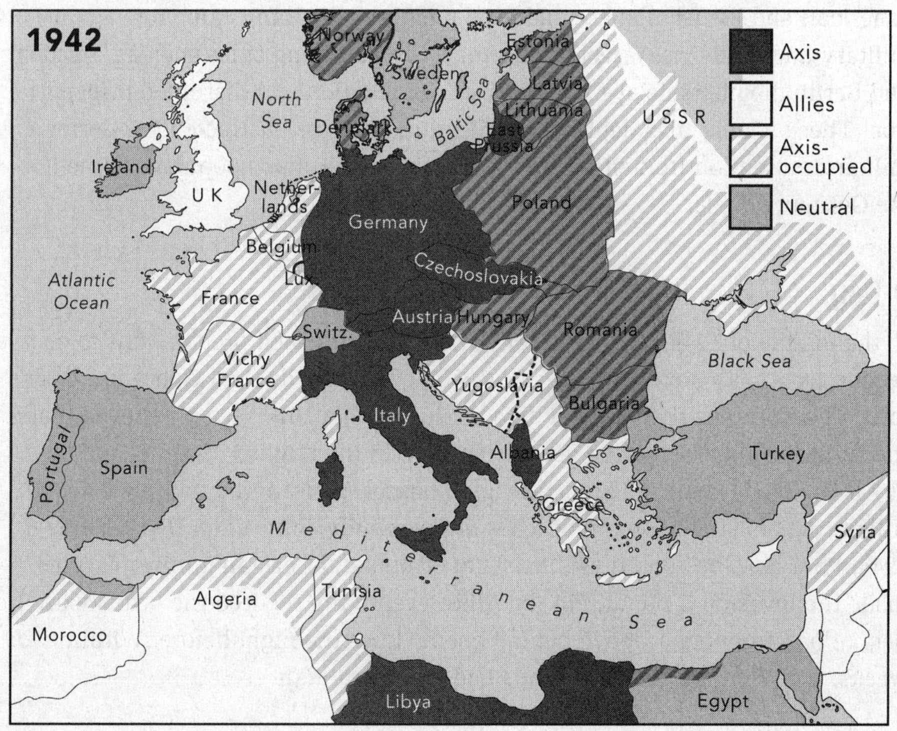

The Italian Campaign

In July 1943, roughly 160,000 American and British troops invaded the island of Sicily. Unprepared to fight, the Italians quickly retreated to the Italian mainland.

By the end of the month, the fascist regime had collapsed and Mussolini had fled to northern Italy. The Italian government soon surrendered unconditionally and even joined the Allies. Despite Hitler's eleventh-hour campaign to restore Mussolini to power, the Allies finally captured Rome in June 1944.

Cairo and Tehran

In November 1943, Roosevelt, Churchill, and Stalin met face to face for the first time. After conferring with Chinese leader **Chiang Kai-shek** in Cairo, Egypt, the Allies issued the **Declaration of Cairo**, which reaffirmed the demand for Japan's unconditional surrender, promised to return all Chinese territory occupied by Japan to China, and declared that the Korean peninsula would become an independent state free from outside control.

The **"Big Three"** leaders then proceeded to **Tehran**, Iran, to plan their final assault on the Axis powers. In Tehran, they agreed that the United States and Great Britain would invade France the following May, that the Soviet Union would begin fighting Japan once Germany had surrendered, and that all three countries would occupy Germany at the end of the war and establish a postwar security organization.

Strategic Bombing over Europe

American and British planes conducted a lengthy bombing campaign against military and industrial targets in Germany. By targeting cities such as Dresden and Berlin, bombers delayed German war production and disrupted transportation. These attacks also depleted the German air force, distracted the German military's attention from other fronts, and reduced Hitler's popularity amongst the German people.

D-Day

In the middle of 1944, the Americans and British finished preparations to open a second front with a cross-channel invasion of France, dubbed **Operation Overlord**. The Germans prepared for an assault, but they mistakenly believed that the Allies would cross at the narrowest point in the English Channel and land at Pas de Calais, near the French-Belgian border. Instead, the roughly 150,000 Allied soldiers landed on the beaches of **Normandy**, France, on **D-Day**: June 6, 1944. Poor landing conditions, logistical errors, and German gun emplacements made the invasion difficult, but the Allies eventually secured the beach with the help of paratroopers dropped behind enemy lines the night before. Within two weeks, a million more Allied troops had landed in France.

The Allied Advance from the West

The Allies pushed through France and toward Germany during the summer of 1944. The most serious resistance posed by the Germans occurred at the **Battle of the Bulge**. By the end of the year, the Americans, British, and French in the West and the Russians in the East had effectively surrounded the Germans.

The Surrender of Germany

After successfully breaking through German lines at the Battle of the Bulge, American **General Omar Bradley** led his troops toward Berlin through central Germany, while the British swept through the North and the Russians moved from the East. Meanwhile, Adolph Hitler retreated to his underground bunker in Berlin and committed suicide on April 30. On May 2, Berlin fell to the Soviets, and within a few days, the Germans had unconditionally surrendered.

The Death of President Roosevelt

Though he conducted the war through an unprecedented three presidential terms and part of a fourth, Franklin Roosevelt did not live to see Germany defeated. After a lengthy illness, he died of a massive stroke on April 12, 1945. The nation's grief for the beloved president cast a shadow over the otherwise jubilant celebration for the victory in Europe. Roosevelt's vice president, Harry S Truman, immediately assumed office.

The Holocaust

The defeat of Germany also uncovered disturbing revelations about Hitler's **"final solution."** Even though the Nazis had announced their belief in the racial inferiority of Jews to "pure" Germans, American anti-Semitism and isolationism during the 1930s had prevented Roosevelt from changing immigration policies to welcome European refugees. As early as 1942, the U.S. government had received reports that Germany had detained Jews and other "impure" peoples in concentration camps, with the intention of systematically exterminating them. But many officials had dismissed such reports as preposterous. When the Allies liberated the camps in 1945, they found incontrovertible proof of genocide. As many as 10 million Jews and other minorities died in the **Holocaust**.

VICTORY IN THE PACIFIC

The Americans finally went on the offensive against the Japanese in the Pacific in mid-1942. The victories at Coral Sea and Midway had damaged the Japanese fleet and marked the start of an American campaign to roll back Japanese gains. U.S. forces succeeded every step of the way, despite intense and extremely bloody opposition from the Japanese at Guadalcanal, Iwo Jima, and Okinawa. The anticipation of a costly invasion of Japan inspired support for President Truman's decision to ultimately end the war by dropping two **atomic bombs**.

Guadalcanal

The first major American offensive in the Pacific occurred in the Solomon Islands, east of New Guinea. On August 7, 1942, the First Marine Division attacked a Japanese installation building on an airfield on the island of **Guadalcanal**. It

took American forces six months of brutal fighting to push the Japanese off the island and prevent them from building air bases from which to attack Australia and New Zealand.

The American Offensive in the Pacific

After Guadalcanal, the American military leaders put into action a two-pronged strategy that combined the recommendations of General MacArthur and **Admiral Chester Nimitz**. American troops in the South Pacific would move northward through New Guinea and retake the Philippines, while naval forces would simultaneously sweep westward through the Pacific from Hawaii toward Japanese island outposts. The two would eventually meet and prepare for an invasion of Japan.

MacArthur in the South Pacific

American forces in Australia and New Guinea approached the Philippines by attacking Japanese-controlled territory in the South Pacific. In the **Battle of the Bismarck Sea**, which lasted from March 2 to March 3, 1943, U.S. forces sank eighteen enemy ships and discouraged the Japanese from shipping future reinforcements to besieged islands. The victory allowed MacArthur's forces to reclaim the western Solomon Islands and the northern coast of New Guinea with the help of Australian troops.

Nimitz in the Central Pacific

Meanwhile, the Navy moved westward from the central Pacific. In November 1943, Admiral Nimitz began his **island-hopping campaign** by attacking Japanese bases in the Gilbert Islands. Over the next year, Nimitz moved westward across the Pacific. In 1944, he conquered the Marshall Islands in February, the Mariana Islands in June, and the western Caroline Islands in September.

Battle of Leyte Gulf

MacArthur met with Nimitz in October of 1944 at Leyte Gulf near the Philippines. In the **Battle of Leyte Gulf**, the largest naval battle in history, American forces effectively decimated what remained of Japan's navy. Japanese pilots in **"kamikaze"** units attacked U.S. battleships and aircraft carriers in suicide attacks.

Iwo Jima and Okinawa

Fighting grew more intense and more costly as American forces inched closer toward Japan. On February 19, 1945, U.S. Marines landed on the island of **Iwo Jima** only 750 miles from Tokyo. In roughly six weeks, U.S. troops secured the island at a cost of 7,000 dead and nearly twice that number wounded. On April 1, 1945, the Americans landed on the island of **Okinawa**, 370 miles from Tokyo. For nearly three months, 300,000 U.S. servicemen fought to secure the island.

Once again, kamikaze pilots flew their planes into American ships. In the end, more than 100,000 Japanese soldiers and about a third as many Okinawans died in the fighting. American troops suffered 50,000 casualties.

The Atomic Bomb

The dropping of the terrifying atomic bomb marked the end of the war in the Pacific. President Truman's decision to drop two atomic bombs hastened an inevitable Japanese defeat and arguably saved thousands of American lives. His decision also ushered in the atomic age and changed the nature of modern warfare.

The Manhattan Project

The United States worked on developing an atomic bomb throughout the war. In 1939, famous physicist **Albert Einstein** warned Roosevelt that the Germans had experimented with nuclear fission in the hope of creating their own atomic bomb. Roosevelt therefore diverted military funds into a secret nuclear research program called the **Manhattan Project** in order to develop the weapon first.

More than 100,000 people worked on the secret project in thirty-seven locations throughout the United States. **Dr. J. Robert Oppenheimer** led the theoretical research team based in Los Alamos, New Mexico. On July 16, 1945, scientists witnessed the first explosion of an atomic bomb in the desert near Alamogordo, New Mexico.

Truman's Ultimatum

After becoming president, Harry Truman had little time to contemplate the ramifications of using a nuclear weapon to end the war, because he and military commanders feared that as many as 250,000 Allied troops would die in the invasion of Japan. Upon hearing of the successful test at Alamogordo, Truman issued an ultimatum to the Japanese by demanding that the Japanese surrender unconditionally before August 3, 1945, or face "utter devastation."

Hiroshima and Nagasaki

When the Japanese still failed to surrender, Truman authorized dropping the bomb. On August 6, 1945, the B-39 bomber ***Enola Gay*** dropped an atomic bomb on **Hiroshima**, Japan. The explosion flattened the city and killed 78,000 people instantly. By the end of the year, 70,000 more had died from radiation exposure. On August 9, the United States dropped a second atomic bomb on **Nagasaki**, Japan, killing more than 100,000 civilians.

Japanese Surrender

Truman's decision to use the bomb succeeded in averting an Allied invasion. After the bombing of Nagasaki, a peace faction assumed control of the Japanese government and surrendered unconditionally. On September 2, 1945, Japan signed a formal surrender on the deck of the battleship ***Missouri*** in Tokyo Bay.

TIMELINE: 1921–1945

1921	Congress collaborates with the international community on disarmament with the Five-Power Naval Treaty, the Four-Power Naval Treaty, and the Nine-Power Naval Treaty.
1924	The United States provides loans to Germany through the Dawes Plan.
1931	Japan invades Manchuria.
1933	Roosevelt announces the Good Neighbor Policy.
1935	Italy invades Ethiopia.
	Congress passes the Neutrality Act of 1935.
1936	Congress passes the Neutrality Act of 1936.
	Spanish Civil War begins.
	Roosevelt is reelected.
1937	Congress passes the Neutrality Act of 1937.
	Japan invades China.
1938	Germany invades Austria.
	The Munich Conference is held in Germany.
1939	Germany invades Czechoslovakia.
	Hitler signs Nazi-Soviet Pact, a nonaggression agreement.
	Germany invades Poland to begin World War II.
	Congress passes the Neutrality Act of 1939.
1940	Germany invades France, Denmark, Norway, the Netherlands, and Belgium.
	The British Royal Air Force counters the German attack in the Battle of Britain.
	The United States makes the Bases-for-Destroyers Deal with Great Britain.
	Roosevelt is reelected.

1941	Congress passes the Lend-Lease Act.
	Germany invades the Soviet Union.
	Roosevelt and Churchill sign the Atlantic Charter.
	Japan attacks Pearl Harbor.
	The United States enters the war.
	Randolph prepares the March on Washington.
	Roosevelt establishes Fair Employment Practices Commission.
1942	Japanese-Americans are forced into internment camps.
	Japan invades the Philippines.
	The Battle of the Coral Sea occurs.
	The Battle of Midway occurs.
	The United States invades North Africa.
	Congress of Racial Equality is founded.
	The first major American offense in the Pacific occurs at the Battle for Guadalcanal.
1943	Roosevelt and Churchill hold the Casablanca Conference.
	Allies invade Italy.
	The United States achieves victory at the Battle of Bismarck Sea.
	The "Big Three" plan their final assault on the Axis powers at the Tehran Conference.
1944	Allies invade Normandy on D-Day.
	Roosevelt is reelected.
	The Battle of the Bulge begins.
1945	Roosevelt dies.
	Truman becomes president.
	Germany surrenders.
	U.S. Marines invade Iwo Jima.
	Thousands die in the battle at Okinawa.
	The United States drops atomic bombs on Hiroshima and Nagasaki.
	Japan signs a formal surrender on the Missouri in Tokyo Bay.

MAJOR FIGURES

Winston Churchill. As prime minister of Great Britain between 1940 and 1945, Churchill helped Franklin Roosevelt conduct the war for the Allies against Nazi Germany.

Albert Einstein. The most prominent physicist of his time, Einstein proposed the Theory of Relativity, changing the way scientists conceived of the relationship between space and time.

Dwight D. Eisenhower. Commander in chief of Allied forces in Western Europe during World War II, Eisenhower led the massive D-Day invasion of Normandy in 1944 and directed the conquest of Nazi Germany. He later served as president from 1953 until 1961. President Eisenhower's restrained style of leadership helped create nearly a decade of economic growth but was slow to support social change. In foreign policy, Eisenhower showed a willingness to coexist with the Soviet Union, while simultaneously building up the U.S. nuclear arsenal.

Adolph Hitler. Chancellor of Germany and leader of the fascist Nazi Party, Hitler tried to conquer all of Europe during World War II. He also ordered the execution of as many as 10 million Jews and other minorities in the Holocaust. He committed suicide in 1945 as Allied forces entered Berlin.

Douglas A. MacArthur. American general McArthur served as Allied supreme commander in the Southwest Pacific and supervised the conquest of Japan during World War II. He later directed American forces against communist North Korean and Chinese forces in the Korean War until President Harry S Truman fired him for insubordination.

Benito Mussolini. As leader of the Italian fascist party, Mussolini fought alongside Germany in the early years of the war to conquer Europe, North Africa, and much of the Near East.

Dr. J. Robert Oppenheimer. The directory of the team of scientists under the Manhattan Project, Oppenheimer helped devise the atomic bomb.

A. Philip Randolph. An African American labor leader, Randolph convinced Roosevelt to eliminate racial discrimination in defense industries and federal bureaus during the war.

Joseph Stalin. The Soviet leader, Stalin, had initially signed a nonaggression treaty with Adolph Hitler at the beginning of the war, but he quickly joined the Allies after the Germans invade Russia.

Harry S Truman. President after Roosevelt's death in 1945, Truman made the decision to drop the atomic bomb on Japan to end World War II. Truman earned admiration for his strong stand against the Soviet Union at the start of the Cold War. His initiatives in Europe bolstered democratic governments and restrained communist aggression. However, Truman faced high opposition at home as he attempted a smooth transition from war to peace.

Chapter 16

The Cold War: 1945–1963

THE YALTA CONFERENCE

As the Allies prepared for victory in Europe and Japan, they also laid plans for the postwar world. In separate conferences at **Yalta** and **Potsdam**, the United States, Great Britain, and Soviet Russia sought to avoid the mistakes of the post–World War I negotiations and prevent another world war in the future. These powers created a new organization more powerful than the League of Nations: the United Nations. Still, disagreements among the three produced mixed results over the postwar fates of both Germany and Poland.

Planning the Postwar World

In February 1945, Roosevelt, Churchill, and Stalin met in the Russian town of Yalta to discuss the postwar world. Stalin agreed to side against Japan in exchange for authority over areas controlled by China and Japan. At the end of the **Yalta Conference**, the three leaders released the **Yalta Declaration of Liberated Europe**, which affirmed the promises in the Atlantic Charter to ensure free democratic systems in postwar Europe. In addition, there were three points of discussion:

1. The establishment of a new international organization
2. The plans for occupied Germany
3. The fate of a liberated Poland

The United Nations

Roosevelt, Churchill, and Stalin endorsed a plan for the establishment of a new world body called the **United Nations (UN)**. Every nation would have a seat in the organization's General Assembly, but real power would reside with the smaller **UN Security Council**. The United States, the Soviet Union, Great Britain, France, and China would each have a permanent seat on the Security Council as well as veto power. In April 1945, fifty nations met at the **UN Conference in San Francisco** to draft the charter for the United Nations. The U.S. Senate ratified the charter in July 1945.

The Partition of Germany

Discussions at Yalta also determined the fate of occupied Germany. Roosevelt, Churchill, and Stalin agreed to temporarily divide occupied Germany into four zones to be controlled by the United States, the Soviet Union, Great Britain, and France. The city of Berlin, located in the Soviet zone, would consist of four similar zones. The agreement, which anticipated the eventual reunification of Germany, provided no specific plan or timeline. Stalin requested that Germany pay $20 billion in reparations to the Allies, half of which would go to the Soviets, although the Reparations Committee never resolved the issue.

Poland

The Allies also discussed the future of Poland. At the Tehran Conference, Roosevelt and Churchill had agreed to let the Soviet Union annex sections of eastern Poland but refused Stalin's proposal to install a procommunist government. Instead, the pair wished to return the Polish government-in-exile that had operated out of London since Hitler's invasion in 1939. At Yalta, they agreed to allow both the old government and communists to form a new provisional government for the duration of the war. Stalin promised free elections in Poland, but he set no specific deadline. Poles ultimately waited forty-five years before they could vote in free democratic elections.

Potsdam

Shortly after Roosevelt's death, President Truman attempted to revisit the open issues of the Yalta Conference. In April 1945, he met with the Soviets and accused them of breaking the agreements set at Yalta. That July, he met with Churchill and Stalin in Potsdam, Germany, in Russian-controlled territory. There, Truman accepted Stalin's proposed borders for Poland but refused to agree to reparations from the other Allied zones of Germany. In 1949, the Russian zone became the republic of East Germany, and the three remaining zones joined together to form the separate state of West Germany.

Not long after the war, Europe grew divided between democracy and communism. President Franklin D. Roosevelt had anticipated that rivalries between nations would lead to conflict. To compensate, he developed a plan for the UN that would force nations to cooperate and maintain peace. Both the United

States and the Soviet Union agreed to join the UN. But, as members of the UN Security Council, both countries held a veto over UN actions. Thus, the Cold War held the UN hostage and rendered the organization relatively powerless.

THE COLD WAR BEGINS

As soon as World War II ended, soldiers and their families anticipated a quick return to normality. Instead, the United States found itself in a new kind of war: the **Cold War**. In the aftermath of World War II, the United States and the Soviet Union stood alone as the two great world powers. While the United States sought to defend democracy, the Soviet Union appeared eager to spread communism across the globe.

United States–Soviet Union Rivalry

President Franklin D. Roosevelt hoped to work with Soviet leader Joseph Stalin, but Roosevelt's death prevented such a partnership. When Truman succeeded Roosevelt as president, he brought with him a reluctance to deal with Stalin, and soon Cold War tensions cooled relations between the United States and Soviet Union. The Truman administration drastically expanded its role in the postwar world order. With the atomic bomb and a country relatively undamaged by World War II, American leaders created a new foreign policy based strictly on anticommunism.

The Berlin Airlift

Stalin's actions in Poland led many U.S. policymakers to believe that the Soviet Union would also try to expand into Western Europe. Therefore, the Truman administration took immediate steps to confront the Soviet empire. Truman authorized the creation of an intelligence organization called the **National Security Agency** as well as the **National Security Council** to advise him. When Stalin cut off western access to Berlin, Truman refused to back down. He ordered the Air Force to drop thousands of pounds of food, clothing, and other goods to West Berlin in the **Berlin Airlift** in 1948.

Containment

Truman built his foreign policy around U.S. diplomat **George Kennan**'s containment theory. Kennan believed that the Soviet Union wanted to expand and that if the United States kept the Soviets within their current borders, communism would eventually collapse. Kennan argued that a patient policy of containment would allow the United States to defeat the Soviet Union without having to suffer any loss of life on the battlefield. The Truman administration quickly applied the containment theory as follows:

- Pledging to assist other countries fighting communist armies or revolutionaries in the **Truman Doctrine** in 1947. The first aid payments supported democratic governments in Greece and Turkey.
- Giving billions of dollars in aid to Western Europe according to the **Marshall Plan** in 1948. This aid improved the tattered economies of Western Europe and quieted communist movements. The plan also ensured that Western Europe would spend much of its aid money buying American goods.
- Forming the **North Atlantic Treaty Organization (NATO)**. NATO allied the United States with Canada, France, Great Britain, and other countries in Western Europe. Each NATO member pledged to support the others in the event of a Soviet invasion.

When Germany joined NATO in 1954, the Soviet Union formed its own treaty with the nations of Eastern Europe known as the **Warsaw Pact**.

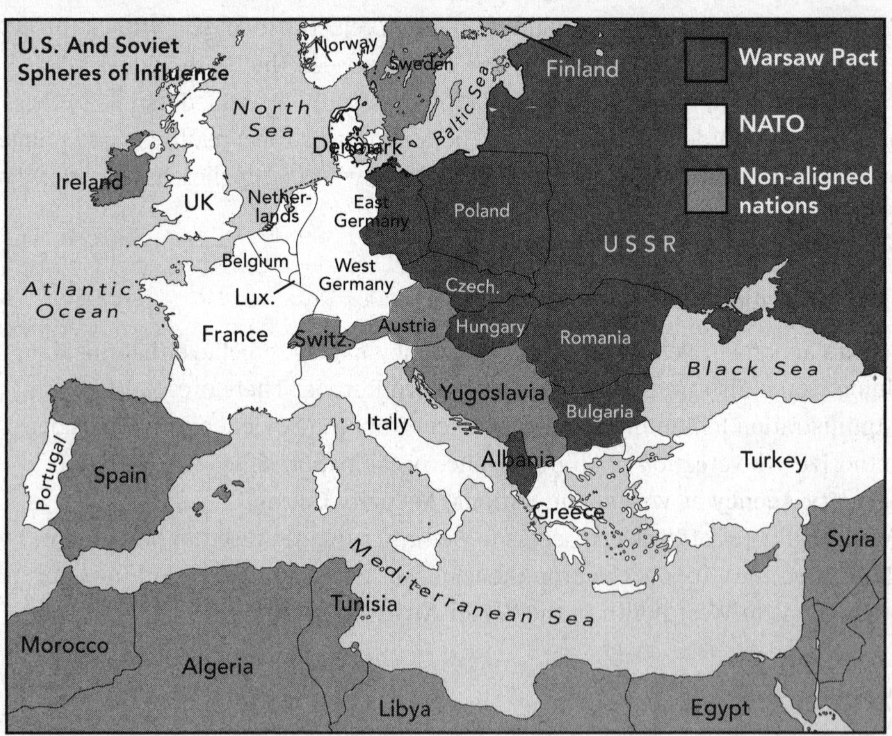

The Founding of Israel

Jews across the world had long sought their own independent state. In the twentieth century, they focused their effort on creating a state in British-controlled Palestine, their spiritual home. After the Holocaust, world sentiment began to increase in favor of a Jewish state in Palestine. Eventually, Palestinian Jews founded the independent Jewish state of Israel in 1948, and Truman offered diplomatic recognition. Despite some criticism, Truman believed in the Jewish right to a home state and also knew that the decision would prove popular during the upcoming presidential election.

THE KOREAN WAR

Even though the Truman administration applied its containment strategy primarily in Europe, the first major battle in the Cold War occurred in East Asia as the Soviet Union and the United States backed different factions in the Korean civil war.

The War Begins

After World War II, the United States and the Soviet Union had their own areas of influence on the Korean peninsula. Stalin installed a Soviet-friendly government in the north, while the American-backed **Syngman Rhee** controlled the southern half below the **Thirty-eighth Parallel**.

North Koreans Invade the South

In June 1950, North Korea launched an attack on the South. In accordance with containment and the Truman Doctrine, Truman immediately sent troops to protect South Koreans and managed to garner UN support for the mission. The initial fighting proved disastrous for the U.S. military, and by mid-September, the North Korean army had nearly conquered the entire peninsula.

MacArthur's Inchon Landing

On September 15, 1950, General **Douglas A. MacArthur** launched a daring amphibious assault at Inchon near Seoul and then proceeded to drive back communist forces north of the Thirty-eighth Parallel. When U.S. troops reached the border between North and South, Truman ordered MacArthur to invade the North, hoping to wipe out communism in Korea altogether. In early October, MacArthur's troops entered North Korea and quickly trounced the communist forces.

Disaster on the Yalu River

As the U.S. Army approached the Yalu River, which separated North Korea from China, Chinese troops swarmed into North Korea and quickly drove the U.S. soldiers back southward well into the territory MacArthur had just regained. U.S. General Matthew Ridgway eventually halted the U.S. retreat and pushed the Chinese forces back to the Thirty-eighth Parallel. By 1951, it was apparent both sides had stalemated each other, even though fighting continued for another two years.

Truman Fires MacArthur

After Ridgeway and American forces drove the Chinese north of the Thirty-eighth parallel, Truman decided to negotiate a peace settlement. But MacArthur couldn't stand the idea of cutting a deal with communists after so many men had died for so little gain. The general therefore ignored Truman's orders and demanded that China surrender or face a United States invasion.

Moreover, General MacArthur publicly criticized the president's decisions in the American press, especially because Truman refused to use nuclear weapons in Korea or China. MacArthur's threats ended the peace negotiations and forced the stalemated war to drag on for almost two more years. Truman fired MacArthur for his insubordination.

The Aftermath of Korea

The Korean War finally ended after Eisenhower negotiated an armistice. After almost four years of war, North and South Korea had the same boundaries as before the war. Even though historians have dubbed the conflict America's "forgotten war," the Korean War killed roughly 33,000 Americans and injured more than 100,000. North Korea and China had more than 1.5 million casualties.

The Korean War prompted the United States to implement **NSC-68**, a National Security Council report that called for a massive military buildup to wage the Cold War. NSC-68 tripled defense spending and fueled anticommunism both at home and abroad.

THE COLD WAR AT HOME

Truman had to balance his attention between the Cold War overseas and demobilization at home. However, just as life began to return to normal, fears of communist infiltration in the United States gripped American society.

Demobilization

Demobilization from war to peace proved to be an uneasy process, as millions of G.I.s returned home hoping to find work. They wanted the millions of women who had joined the workforce during World War II to give up their jobs. Business leaders meanwhile pressured Truman to remove the government regulations Congress had enacted during the war, such as price controls and pro-labor laws. Workers, on the other hand, refused to give up their rights. A series of strikes broke out in the years following the war, including a railroad strike that almost completely paralyzed the nation.

The postwar turmoil eventually settled down. The Truman administration gradually ended price controls, and Americans began to spend the money they had saved during the war. The **GI Bill** provided veterans with money for education, housing, and job training. However, organized labor suffered when

Congress passed the **Taft-Hartley Act** in 1947, which placed harsh restrictions on unions and limited the right to strike. Truman vehemently opposed the law, but Congress passed it over his veto.

Truman's Fair Deal

Truman's support of organized labor made up just one part of his domestic agenda that sought to expand Franklin Roosevelt's New Deal. His support was dubbed the **"Fair Deal"** and included the following stipulations:

- Stronger civil rights laws, including a ban on racial discrimination in the hiring of federal employees
- A higher minimum wage
- Extension of Social Security benefits
- Funding of low-income housing projects

The Republican-dominated Congress rejected other more radical aspects of Truman's Fair Deal. Several Democrats, mostly from southern states, disagreed with Truman over his stance on civil rights. When Truman ran for reelection in 1948, a group of southern Democrats broke from the party. Calling themselves **Dixiecrats**, they nominated Senator **Strom Thurmond** for president. Although Truman won the election, he continued to face opposition from the Republican Congress and the southern wing of his own party.

The Second Red Scare

The fear of communism also spawned a **Second Red Scare** in the mid-1950s. Ordinary people began to believe that communist insurgents had infiltrated American institutions and suspected Hollywood actors, government officials, and even their own neighbors of being communist spies. Politicians capitalized on these fears and used anticommunism in their favor as a political tool to purge their enemies from office. Americans had grown more afraid of communism since the end of World War II for the following reasons:

- Communist forces under **Mao Zedong** had taken control of China in 1949. The so-called **Fall of China** meant that communists ruled the two largest nations on earth.
- Espionage trials had concluded that **Klaus Fuchs** and **Julius and Ethel Rosenberg** had given secret information about the atomic bomb to the Soviet Union.
- The Soviet Union had developed nuclear weapons.

- Communist forces had nearly overwhelmed American troops in Korea.
- U.S. officials had convicted former State Department official **Alger Hiss** of perjury.

Growing Suspicion

Although only a few hundred people belonged to the American Communist Party, government authorities began a comprehensive campaign against socialist influences in the United States. The **Federal Bureau of Investigation (FBI)** under the direction of J. Edgar Hoover, for example, began spying on people suspected of being communists. In Congress, the **House Un-American Activities Committee (HUAC)** also held widely publicized investigations of labor unions and other organizations suspected of harboring communist sympathizers.

Government Action

Upon realizing that anticommunism played well with the American people, the Republican party criticized the Truman administration for being "soft on communism." As a result, Republicans in Congress passed two acts:

- **The Loyalty Acts**, which required federal employees to remove any worker who had any connection to a communist organization
- **The McCarran Act**, which forced communist groups to register their names with the attorney general and restricted immigration of potential subversives. Truman vetoed this, but Congress overruled him.

McCarthyism

Senator **Joseph McCarthy** from Wisconsin took anticommunism to new heights by holding public hearings in which he badgered witnesses and accused people of being communists. He rarely proffered any evidence and branded anyone who disagreed with him a communist. Despite this, his tactics made him extremely popular and won him national fame and reelection to the Senate.

McCarthy finally overstepped his reach in 1954 when he accused the U.S. Army of harboring communists. Aired on national television, the **Army-McCarthy Hearings** revealed McCarthy's vindictive behavior to millions of Americans across the country. The Senate censured McCarthy for his misconduct shortly after the hearings and effectively ended his career.

PROSPERITY AND CONSUMERISM

Domestic politics settled into a tame routine after the tumult of the Second Red Scare. An economic boom muted political divisions, and American society embraced an exploding consumer economy.

Eisenhower's Domestic Agenda

President **Dwight D. Eisenhower** loomed over the 1950s as the central political figure of the age. The economy soared, creating a level of affluence not seen before in American history. Additionally, Eisenhower worked to maintain the essential elements of the New Deal.

Dynamic Conservatism

In the 1952 election, Eisenhower defeated Democrat Adlai Stevenson. A moderate conservative, Eisenhower appealed to members of both parties, and partisan tensions decreased during his two terms in office. "Ike" Eisenhower championed **dynamic conservatism**, a philosophy that combined conservative fiscal policies with the social reforms of the New Deal. Policies included the following:

- Closer ties between government and business
- Reduction of federal spending, balancing the budget, ending wage and price controls, and lowering farm subsidies
- Expansion of Social Security benefits and raising the minimum wage
- Funding of public works programs, including the **St. Lawrence Seaway** and **Interstate Highway system**

Economic Boom

The **Gross National Product (GNP)** more than doubled between 1945 and 1960 as the economy grew stronger and stronger in the postwar years. Inflation stayed low, and the income of the average American household rose, allowing more people to buy expensive consumer goods. The economy thrived, for the following reasons:

- Government spending encouraged economic growth. Federal funding of schools, housing, highways, and military expenditures created jobs.
- Europe offered little competition to American levels of production. As the rest of the world recovered from World War II, the United States exported goods across the globe.

- New technologies such as computers boosted productivity in many areas, including heavy industry and agriculture.
- Consumption increased. After the lean years of the Great Depression and World War II, Americans bought goods they couldn't previously afford. The **baby boom** also increased consumer needs.

The rising level of affluence in America left some people behind. Small farmers and residents of rural areas, for example, suffered hardship. The total number of farmers fell as prices steadily dropped. Many city dwellers, including African Americans and other minorities, often lived in poverty. Many industries cut jobs for unskilled workers, and racial discrimination often kept minorities out of other jobs.

Consumer Culture

Although rural and urban areas suffered during the 1950s, the suburbs boomed. Meanwhile, the postwar prosperity gave birth to a new consumer culture.

The Growth of Suburbs

As middle-class Americans grew wealthier, every family wanted a home of their own. Americans began spreading out of the cities and into the suburbs. Builders rapidly constructed suburbs such as New York's Levittown, which consisted of nearly identical houses. Levittown and other suburban developments often excluded African Americans.

The Consumer Culture

During the 1950s, industrial jobs began to disappear, while white-collar jobs in industries like advertising and finance increased. The newly expanded industry of advertising encouraged Americans to buy new goods such as televisions, cosmetics, and frozen TV dinners. The consumption of consumer goods soon became one of the driving forces behind the American economy. Shopping malls consequently sprouted in suburbs across the United States. When Americans could not afford a purchase, they relied on credit, a psychology that differed greatly from the thrift and financial conservatism of the previous generation that had come of age during the Great Depression.

Critics of the Postwar Culture

Not everyone approved of the changing American culture. Some artists and writers began to challenge the culture of suburbs, nonindustrial jobs, and interstates. For example, William H. Whyte's *The Organization Man* argued that American business had lost its enterprising spirit. Whyte believed that instead of encouraging innovation, white-collar jobs stifled creativity by forcing workers to conform to company norms. Many Americans extended this argument to apply to the suburbs. Critics argued that the suburbs lacked the cultural institutions and ethnic diversity of the cities; rather, suburbanites focused on matching the consumption of their neighbors.

A literary group known as the **Beats** challenged the conformity of the times. The Beats rejected mainstream culture and embraced spontaneity and individuality in personal behavior. "Beatnik" Jack Kerouac and his 1957 novel *On the Road* typified the movement.

THE CIVIL RIGHTS MOVEMENT BEGINS

Although many Americans prospered during the 1950s, African Americans experienced few benefits from the economic boom. **Jim Crow laws**—laws that enforced segregation throughout the South—continued to exist, while the Eisenhower administration expressed little interest in civil rights. A landmark Supreme Court decision in the mid-1950s, however, sparked a massive **civil rights movement** that ultimately reshaped American society. Historians identify several factors that led to the rise of African American protest during the 1950s and 1960s:

- Experiences in World War II had offended many African Americans' sense of justice. The United States had fought a war for freedom abroad but had ignored civil rights at home.
- A black middle class began to emerge. This class consisted of doctors, ministers, lawyers, and teachers, who also acted as community leaders. The civil rights movement relied heavily on these men and women.
- University enrollment began to increase after World War II. African American college students formed networks of activism that eventually helped end segregation.

Brown v. Board of Education

For decades, the **National Association for the Advancement of Colored People (NAACP)** had issued court challenges against segregated schooling. In 1954, the Supreme Court, under the stewardship of Chief Justice **Earl Warren**, unanimously struck down segregated education with its landmark decision in ***Brown v. Board of Education of Topeka, Kansas***. The decision overturned the notion of "separate but equal" previously established by ***Plessy v. Ferguson*** in 1896.

Unfortunately, very little changed after the ruling. The predominantly black schools still lacked the resources and money of white schools. President Eisenhower refused to voice support for the *Brown* v. *Board of Education* decision.

School Desegregation

Across the South, racist whites campaigned vigorously against the Court's decision. Many school districts desegregated as slowly as possible, and some whites even shut down their schools rather than admit black students. A showdown over school integration occurred in Little Rock, Arkansas, in 1957, when an angry mob of whites prevented a group of nine African Americans from entering Little Rock's Central High School. Arkansas governor Orval Faubus supported the mob but eventually backed down after Eisenhower reluctantly sent army troops to escort the **"Little Rock Nine"** to class. Eisenhower's decision demonstrated that the federal government supported desegregation.

The Montgomery Bus Boycott

Having won desegregation in schools, African American activists began to challenge other Jim Crow laws as well. The first major burst of activism occurred in Montgomery, Alabama, after police had arrested black resident **Rosa Parks** for refusing to give up her seat on a city bus to a white man in December 1955. NAACP attorneys immediately filed a lawsuit against the city, while the African American community boycotted the bus service.

The Rise of Martin Luther King, Jr.

A young, charismatic preacher named **Martin Luther King, Jr.**, who empowered the civil rights movement with powerful rhetoric and skillful, nonviolent tactics, mobilized Montgomery's religious community behind the bus boycott. King's eloquence eventually won the movement national support. Within a year, Montgomery city officials agreed to desegregate its bus system.

THE COLD WAR IN THE FIFTIES

The Cold War moved in two directions during the 1950s. On the one hand, the United States and the Soviet Union moved closer together. After Stalin died in 1953, Eisenhower reached out to the new, more moderate Soviet leader **Nikita Khrushchev**. Eisenhower and Khrushchev began a dialogue about ending the arms race and reducing nuclear weapons. In other ways, however, Cold War tensions increased. The development of new technologies and weapons threatened the peace with new methods of destruction. As a result, Eisenhower's administration adopted a newer and more aggressive foreign policy.

The New Look and Massive Retaliation

Eisenhower and his secretary of state, **John Foster Dulles**, promised a new type of foreign policy. They sought to contain the Soviet Union, but they also wanted to "roll back" communism and liberate Eastern Europe. The new foreign policy also relied on covert **Central Intelligence Agency (CIA)** operations to prevent communist groups from taking power in strategic countries. Additionally,

Eisenhower sought to reduce spending on conventional weapons and increase spending on nuclear weapons, believing that nuclear weapons provided "more bang for the buck," a policy known as the **New Look**. Dulles promised that the United States would respond to Soviet aggression with **massive retaliation**, i.e., a devastating nuclear attack.

The Cold War in the Third World

The Eisenhower administration devoted much attention to preventing communism in the third world, or areas outside of American or Soviet spheres of influence. In fact, Eisenhower and Dulles often used the CIA to topple unfriendly governments or combat communist revolutionaries. The CIA prevented a coup from deposing the corrupt shah, or king, of Iran in 1953; engineered a coup against a popularly elected socialist government in Guatemala in 1954; and invaded Cuba in 1961 after communist Fidel Castro seized power, for example.

The Suez Crisis

In 1956, Dulles froze American aid in Egypt when Egyptian president **Gamal Abdel Nasser** voiced his intention to accept aid from communist countries. Nasser responded to Dulles's actions by seizing the **Suez Canal**, jointly owned by Great Britain and France. When Great Britain, France, and Israel attacked Egypt in order to take back the Suez Canal, an outraged Eisenhower refused to sell them the oil they needed to maintain their economies. Unable to risk angering the United States and thus endanger their oil supply, they withdrew and allowed UN peacekeeping forces to stabilize the region.

Vietnam Troubles

Eisenhower also faced a growing crisis in Southeast Asia, where France had struggled to maintain control of its colonies since the end of World War II. In Vietnam, for example, rebels led by procommunist **Ho Chi Minh** declared their independence from France in 1954 after seizing the strategic French army garrison at **Dien Bien Phu**. Although the United States provided France with plenty of aid to support its war in Indochina, Eisenhower refused to commit U.S. troops to the conflict.

The Arms Race

The arms race continued to escalate during the 1950s. In 1957, advances in rocketry allowed the Soviet Union to launch an artificial satellite called ***Sputnik*** into orbit around the earth. This event sparked fears in the United States that Soviet science and technology had surpassed America. *Sputnik*'s flight also meant that the Soviets might soon be able to launch **intercontinental ballistic missiles (ICBMs)** that could travel from silos in the Soviet Union to destroy targets in the United States. Suddenly, the threat of nuclear attack became a real possibility for Americans.

The Space Race

In response, the Eisenhower administration accelerated its own space program. Soon, the United States had ICBMs of its own, while the **National Aeronautics and Space Administration (NASA)** blazed a trail in the exploration of space. Eisenhower soon became concerned about the increased militarization of American life. In his 1961 farewell address, he warned Americans to defend against the influence of the **military-industrial complex**. He feared that a powerful military linked to wealthy defense industries would negatively influence "every city, every state house, every office of the federal government."

KENNEDY AND THE RISE OF LIBERALISM

Americans in the 1960s anticipated that the new decade would bring a sharp break with the past. A new generation came of age and attempted to distance itself from what it regarded as a stagnant 1950s. Instead of merely accumulating wealth, Americans began to envision using their wealth for something meaningful. During the 1960s, President John F. Kennedy established a powerful liberal state that extended some of the vast resources of the United States to people who needed them. At the same time, Kennedy promised a new approach to the Cold War.

The Election of 1960

The election of 1960 featured many remarkable twists and turns. At first, many observers predicted Republican vice president **Richard Nixon** would win because his Democratic opponent, **John F. Kennedy**, lacked Nixon's experience and national exposure. But Kennedy overcame these obstacles and narrowly won by just more than 100,000 votes. Rather than challenge the results, Nixon gracefully accepted his surprising defeat.

The New Frontier

In his inaugural address, Kennedy challenged the American people to accept the nation's role as a world power and outlined his **New Frontier** program for the United States. "Ask not what your country can do for you," he stated. "Ask what you can do for your country." During his campaign, Kennedy promised changes toward economic equality and civil rights. With time, he grew increasingly frustrated as Republicans and southern Democrats joined together to defeat most of his domestic programs. As a result, Kennedy abandoned the New Frontier at home and refocused his attention on foreign policy.

Many of the liberal reforms of the 1960s originated from the Supreme Court, still led by Chief Justice Earl Warren. For example, the Warren Court did the following:

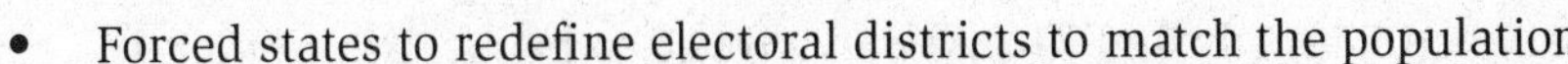

- Forced states to redefine electoral districts to match the population
- Provided the right to counsel for accused criminals who could not afford lawyers
- Required law enforcement officials to read suspected criminals their rights
- Worked to limit religion in schools

Kennedy and "Flexible Response"

At first, Kennedy's foreign policy appeared to share the same idealism as his domestic agenda. He founded the **Peace Corps**, which sent volunteers on humanitarian missions in underdeveloped countries. But the centerpiece of Kennedy's foreign policy was on anticommunism.

Whereas Truman had fought communism by giving money to fight communist insurgents and Eisenhower had threatened the U.S.S.R. with "massive retaliation," the Kennedy administration devised the doctrine of **"flexible response."** Developed by Defense and State Department officials such as Robert S. McNamara, the containment doctrine of "flexible response" gave Kennedy a variety of military and political options to use depending on the situation.

The Bay of Pigs Invasion

Kennedy chose to fight **Fidel Castro**'s revolutionary army in Cuba by allowing the CIA to train an anticommunist invasion force comprising 1,500 Cuban expatriates. The small invasion army landed at the Bay of Pigs in Cuba in spring 1961 only to find the Cuban revolutionaries waiting for them. The failed **Bay of Pigs Invasion** evolved into a major political embarrassment for the United States, and it ruined American-Cuban relations.

Commitment in Southeast Asia

Kennedy also sent approximately 30,000 troops to South Vietnam in 1961 as "military advisors" to prevent South Vietnamese from toppling **Ngo Dinh Diem**'s corrupt regime in Saigon. These troops served as the first American ground forces in Vietnam and thus marked the beginning of American military commitment in the region that would plague future administrations.

The Berlin Crisis

Relations between Kennedy and Khrushchev proved to be just as difficult. In 1961, Khrushchev erected the **Berlin Wall** between the eastern and western sections of Berlin. The wall quickly became a symbol of Cold War divisions.

The Cuban Missile Crisis

The most intense confrontation between the two leaders occurred in October 1962 when Kennedy learned that Khrushchev had sent nuclear missiles to Cuba. The drama of the **Cuban Missile Crisis** played out as follows over thirteen days:

- U.S. intelligence photos showed Soviet workers constructing nuclear missile silos in Cuba on October 14, 1962.
- Kennedy then announced a blockade of Cuba on October 22. He stated that U.S. forces would fire on any ships that attempted to pass through the blockade.
- Soviet ships approached the blockade but stopped just short of entering Cuban waters on October 24.
- Kennedy and Khrushchev finally reached an agreement on October 28 in which Khrushchev agreed to remove the missiles in exchange for Kennedy's promise not to invade Cuba.

Never before had the Cold War powers come so close to nuclear war. In 1963, the United States and the Soviet Union agreed to the first arms control measure of the Cold War, when they signed the **Nuclear Test Ban Treaty**, limiting the testing of nuclear weapons.

JFK's Assassination

On November 22, 1963, a gunman shot and killed President Kennedy in Dallas, Texas, as he was riding in an open car. The Kennedy assassination continues to puzzle Americans to this day. Soon after the assassination in November 1963, authorities arrested **Lee Harvey Oswald** for the murder. Days later, during transport between jails, Dallas nightclub owner **Jack Ruby** murdered Oswald. An investigation headed by Supreme Court Chief Justice Earl Warren concluded that Oswald had acted alone, but the mysterious circumstances surrounding his death have left some questions unanswered. Books, films, and other media have kept different conspiracy theories alive.

TIMELINE: 1945–1963

1945	Roosevelt, Churchill, and Stalin discuss the postwar world at the Yalta Conference.
	The Potsdam Conference ends with an ultimatum for Japan to unconditionally surrender.
	The United Nations is formed.
1947	Truman announces his Truman Doctrine.
	Congress sends $400 million to Greece and Turkey.
	The United States gives Europe aid under the Marshall Plan.
	Congress passes the Taft-Hartley Act.
	Congress passes the National Security Act.
	House Un-American Committee hunts for communists.
1948	Israel is founded.
	Truman orders the Berlin Airlift.
	Truman is elected.
1949	North Atlantic Treaty Organization is created.
1950	Senator McCarthy begins hunting for communists.
	NSC-68 is put into effect.
	The Korean War begins.
	Congress passes the McCarran Act.
1951	Truman fires General MacArthur.
1952	Dwight D. Eisenhower is elected president.
1953	Julius and Ethel Rosenberg are executed.
1954	The Army-McCarthy Hearings are aired on national television.
	Segregated education is struck down in *Brown v. Board of Education*.
1955	The Warsaw Pact is created.
	Montgomery Bus Boycott begins.
1956	Eisenhower is reelected.

1957	U.S.S.R. launches *Sputnik*.
	Southern Christian Leadership Coalition (SCLC) forms.
1960	The U-2 Incident angers the Soviets.
	John F. Kennedy is elected president.
	Student Nonviolent Coordinating Committee (SNCC) forms.
1961	Bay of Pigs Invasion tranishes Kennedy's image.
	Freedom Rides occur throughout the South.
1962	The Cuban Missile Crisis brings the Cold War powers close to war.
1963	The Nuclear Test Ban Treaty is signed.
	Martin Luther King, Jr., leads the March on Washington.
	Kennedy is assassinated.

MAJOR FIGURES

John Foster Dulles. As secretary of state under President Dwight D. Eisenhower, Dulles's strong anticommunism and reliance on nuclear deterrence drastically altered U.S. foreign policy during the 1950s.

George Kennan. An American diplomat who served in the Soviet Union during the 1940s, Kennan outlined the strategy of containment that called for the United States to thwart communist advances abroad in order to prevent more countries from falling under the influence of the U.S.S.R.

John F. Kennedy. President John F. Kennedy's exuberance and charisma energized the nation after the conformity of the 1950s. While Congress stalled his domestic initiatives, Kennedy's foreign policy proved to be risky and dramatic. Under his leadership, the Cold War intensified in underdeveloped countries.

Martin Luther King, Jr. As a civil rights leader, King's passionate oratory and skillful civil disobedience tactics helped end legal racial segregation in the United States. His assassination in 1968 sparked riots across the country and caused a rift in the civil rights movement.

Douglas A. MacArthur. General of the U.S. Army during World War II and the Korean War, MacArthur's masterful landing at Inchon reversed a series of dramatic U.S. defeats. His later departure from President Truman's conduct of the war led to his controversial dismissal.

Joseph McCarthy. A Wisconsin senator made famous by his controversial anticommunism, McCarthy accused people of being communists with little or no evidence and labeled any political opponent as procommunist. His combative tactics proved popular and successful during the Red Scare of the 1950s.

Richard Nixon. A former communist-hunter and vice president under Dwight D. Eisenhower, Nixon defeated Hubert Humphrey and George Wallace for the presidency in 1968. Despite his policy of Vietnamization to withdraw American troops from Vietnam, Nixon nevertheless intensified the Vietnam War by bombing Cambodia and North Vietnam. By opening relations with China, he and Henry Kissinger forced the Soviet Union into negotiating a new era of eased tensions known as détente. Surprisingly, he expanded and improved Lyndon Johnson's Great Society social welfare programs and helped eliminate racial discrimination in the federal government. After defeating George McGovern in a landslide victory in 1972, Nixon increased bombing raids in Vietnam and forced a peace settlement out of North Vietnam. The Watergate scandal and his unwillingness to hand over several incriminating audio tapes eventually forced him to resign in 1974 rather than face unfavorable impeachment proceedings and trial in Congress.

Rosa Parks. Parks's 1954 arrest sparked a grassroots protest in Montgomery, Alabama. The subsequent victory for Parks's supporters helped launch the civil rights movement.

Earl Warren. As chief justice of the Supreme Court from 1953 to 1969, Warren helped decide one of the most dramatic Supreme Court rulings in U.S. history when he orchestrated the unanimous verdict in *Brown v. Board of Education* (1954) that ended school segregation in the United States. During the 1960s, Warren presided over a Supreme Court that dramatically expanded civil liberties in the United States.

Chapter 17

Civil Rights and Vietnam: 1963–1975

THE CIVIL RIGHTS MOVEMENT

Across the South, African Americans waged campaigns of civil disobedience that often proved effective enough to bring about social change. As the movement gained momentum, however, white racists increased their efforts to stop it. The conflict between social change and hatred drew national attention to civil rights.

Student Activism

Students, including the **Student Nonviolent Coordinating Committee (SNCC)**, waged some of the more powerful campaigns of the civil rights movement. The SNCC organized a number of events that had far-reaching consequences. In 1960, African American college students and other activists seated themselves at white-only lunch counters, refusing to leave until served. The demonstrators frequently suffered abuse from white onlookers and ended up in jail. Additionally, members of the SNCC and the **Congress of Racial Equality** embarked on a series of bus rides across the South in 1961. The rides aimed to integrate traveling facilities across the South. White mobs greeted the riders with violence in Alabama. Finally, in 1964, northern college students went to Mississippi to register African Americans to vote. By the end of the summer, many activists had been severely beaten by the police, and a few lost their lives.

Major Civil Rights Organizations		
Acronym	**Name**	**Major Accomplishments**
CORE	Congress of Racial Equality	Freedom Rides
NAACP	National Association for the Advancement of Colored People	*Brown v. Board of Education*
SCLC	Southern Christian Leadership Conference	Birmingham, Alabama, civil rights campaign; March on Washington
SNCC	Student Nonviolent Coordinating Committee	Freedom Summer

The King Campaigns

In 1963, **Martin Luther King, Jr.**, began a civil rights campaign in Birmingham, Alabama, to pressure the municipal government to end segregation in the city. King and his fellow activists staged sit-ins and marches. When authorities arrested demonstrators, including King himself, more demonstrators took their places. The city jail soon filled up and the city's bureaucracy became overwhelmed. A series of economic boycotts of downtown businesses also brought the city's economy to a halt.

As demonstrations grew in number and power, white resistance to the movement increased. Vigilante bombers attempted to kill King and his family, and city police attacked demonstrators with fierce dogs and fire hoses. Pictures of the violence ended up in newspapers across the country, turning public opinion in favor of the civil rights activists. Eventually, city officials capitulated and ended segregation.

The March on Washington

Months after the successful Birmingham campaign, King led more than 200,000 civil rights activists in a **March on Washington, D.C.** Standing in front of the Lincoln Memorial, King gave his **"I Have a Dream"** speech, one of the key speeches of his career.

Selma

The next major civil rights campaign occurred in Selma, Alabama, in 1965. Civil rights activists planned a march from Selma to Montgomery to publicize whites' disenfranchisement of Alabama blacks. But Alabama state troopers attacked the activists as soon as they began their march. When the protestors demonstrated their determination to march again a few days later, President **Lyndon Johnson** sent the Alabama National Guard to protect them.

Government Action

Johnson supported the civil rights movement and succeeded in getting Congress to pass the **Civil Rights Act of 1964**. The act effectively ended legal segregation and discrimination. Racial discrimination in all public places, including hotels, restaurants, and schools, was outlawed. The Equal Employment Opportunity Commission was also created, which prevented racial and gender discrimination in the workplace.

After the Selma campaign demonstrated the degree of disenfranchisement among southern blacks, Johnson and Congress also passed the **Voting Rights Act of 1965**, which allowed African Americans to register to vote quickly and easily, without fear of violence.

The Movement Splits

Most civil rights activism during the 1950s and 1960s occurred in the South. Racism existed in the North, of course, but ghettoes and urban poverty made civil disobedience far less effective there. Pent-up rage over black poverty and racial injustice eventually exploded across northern cities in the mid- to late-1960s.

Riots

For some African Americans, social change occurred too slowly. Outside the South, certain black Americans concerned themselves more with fighting poverty than with voting rights or desegregation. Beginning in 1964, riots erupted across major U.S. cities, the largest occurring in Watts, Detroit, and Washington, D.C. Rioters often had no specific goals other than expressing rage and frustration over the racial and economic inequality in American society.

Malcolm X

For decades, the **Nation of Islam** advocated black independence in the United States and drew a large African American following in many northern cities. In the 1960s, **Malcolm X**, who promoted black pride and self-reliance, became one of the most eloquent and widely followed black Muslims. At times, he called for active self-defense against white violence. He was assassinated in 1965.

Black Power

Some African American activists concluded that laws and speeches would not change the deep-rooted causes of racism and oppression. In the mid-1960s, these activists embraced a more radical approach to civil rights. SNCC leader **Stokely Carmichael** began to use the term **Black Power** to describe his cause. Black Power expressed many of the themes advocated by Malcolm X, and its supporters encouraged African Americans to become independent of white society.

Advocates of the movement formed all-black schools, organizations, and political groups such as the **Black Panthers**. Above all, Black Power expressed pride

in African American culture. Mainstream press coverage of Black Power often emphasized its aggressive side, leading to a severe backlash among whites.

JOHNSON IN THE 1960s

After taking office in 1963, **Lyndon Johnson** pledged himself to righting the nation's social wrongs. In his State of the Union Address in January 1964, he informed Congress of his plans to build a **Great Society** by waging a **War on Poverty**.

The Great Society

Author **Michael Harrington**'s 1962 national bestselling book, *The Other America*, exposed middle-class suburbanites to the hunger, poverty, homelessness, and disease that afflicted as many as 50 million Americans. In response, Johnson and Democrats in the House and Senate passed the **Economic Opportunity Act** in the summer of 1964 to help the poorest Americans, especially urban blacks. Johnson and the Democrats promised a revolution with more than $2 billion in social-welfare reform and hailed the Great Society as the beginning of a new tomorrow.

The War on Poverty

The Economic Opportunity Act created the Office of Economic Opportunities to spearhead the various projects aimed at creating jobs, improving education and housing, and providing medical care to those who could not afford it. OEO Programs included the following:

- **The Job Corps**, which offered vocational training to thousands of young inner-city black men
- **Project Head Start**, which educated more than 2 million of the poorest preschool-age children
- **Medicaid**, which offered federally funded health benefits to the poor
- **Medicare**, which offered health benefits to the elderly

Johnson also helped immigrants by passing the **Immigration and Nationality Act of 1965** to eliminate the national quota system. As a result, the number of yearly immigrants, especially from East Asia, skyrocketed.

The War on Poverty had only limited success in helping the poor. This was primarily because none of the new government programs tackled the root problem of enormous income inequality. Although the government did redistribute roughly $1 billion, most of this money went to Americans who already earned middle-class incomes—not those in poverty. Blacks in particular saw very little of this money, even though they had been among the first to demand more social-welfare spending. The Job Corps, for example, taught obsolete skills and provided only temporary unskilled work that offered no future. The war in Vietnam also siphoned the most money away from the War on Poverty, because Congress simply couldn't afford to fund both an antipoverty campaign and a major war abroad. Johnson's semiutopian vision of a Great Society had all but died by the mid-1970s.

Tonkin Gulf

As the War on Poverty moved forward, Johnson pledged to honor John F. Kennedy's limited troop commitments in Vietnam. More specifically, he promised not to send any more "American boys nine or ten thousand miles away from home to do what Asian boys ought to be doing for themselves." The president's policy changed dramatically, though, just a few months later when several **North Vietnamese Army (NVA)** gunboats allegedly attacked two U.S. Navy destroyers in the **Gulf of Tonkin** off the coast of North Vietnam.

In response, Johnson requested from Congress the authority to take "all necessary steps" to protect U.S. servicemen in South Vietnam. Congress complied and passed the **Tonkin Gulf Resolution** in August 1964. Out of the 535 total members of Congress, only two voted against this resolution. Many policymakers considered this to be a de facto declaration of war.

The Election of 1964

Johnson easily won the support of the Democratic nominating convention on a Great Society platform. The attack in the Gulf of Tonkin and the congressional resolution only helped him in his election bid. Johnson's Republican opponent **Barry M. Goldwater** argued that much more needed to be done in Vietnam to contain communism; he even advocated using nuclear weapons. A self-proclaimed extremist, he also denounced the Great Society, War on Poverty, and civil rights movement in favor of near-radical conservatism. Not surprisingly, Johnson won the presidency that year with more than 60 percent of the popular vote and with 486 electoral votes to Goldwater's 52.

Escalation in Vietnam

In February 1965, procommunist **Viet Cong** guerillas in South Vietnam attacked Marine barracks on an American base in the hamlet of Pleiku. Eight soldiers died, and more than a hundred more suffered casualties. Newly endowed with a blank check from Congress, Johnson capitalized on the **Pleiku Raid** and immediately ordered the air force and navy to begin an intense series of air strikes called **Operation Rolling Thunder**. He hoped that the bombing campaign would demonstrate his commitment to the South Vietnamese and his resolve to halt the spread of communism. Ironically, the air raids seemed only to increase the number of NVA and Viet Cong attacks.

Operation Rolling Thunder

Operation Rolling Thunder set the gears in motion for a major escalation of the war. Johnson believed that he could convince the NVA to withdraw by slowly increasing the number of American troops in Vietnam. He ordered more and more troops to South Vietnam in the next two years, bringing the total to a staggering 400,000 men by the end of 1966. By 1968, the total number of troops had further jumped to more than 500,000. Sadly, as the number of in-country troops increased, so, too, did the number of casualties. More than 100,000 American men were killed or wounded by 1968.

The Destruction of South Vietnam

Although Johnson hoped the 500,000 American troops would save South Vietnam, his policy of escalation effectively destroyed the country. By 1968 alone, the military had used 3 million tons' worth of bombs on Vietnam, more than all the bombs dropped in Europe during World War II. The United States also used **napalm**, a slow-burning chemical agent dropped with bombs to maximize destruction. The military also used 20 million gallons of another chemical weapon called **Agent Orange** to kill forestlands and drive out the Viet Cong.

College Student Activism

By 1968, the war had drastically divided society. College students made up one of the more vocal segments of the antiwar movement. On campuses across the nation, students held teach-ins, marches, and other forms of civil disobedience in protest of the war. Some of the more radical activists initiated student strikes and violently occupied campus administration buildings. At the same time, many Americans continued to support the war. These **"hawks"** opposed the peace-advocating **"doves"** and tried to brand their antiwar activities as un-American.

The Tet Offensive

In 1968, the Vietnamese communists launched a major offensive against the South's major cities on the Vietnamese New Year, or Tet. Nightly news broadcasts showed the increasing violence and seemingly endless numbers of dead U.S. soldiers. Although American forces repelled the attackers and inflicted serious damage on the Viet Cong, most Americans at home interpreted the **Tet Offensive** as evidence that America was losing.

Consequently, criticism of the war increased sharply, and massive demonstrations occurred on college campuses and in Washington, D.C., while Johnson's popularity plummeted. With the situation in Vietnam becoming ever more hopeless, Johnson announced a bombing halt in March 1968. He then added that he would not seek reelection in the upcoming presidential election.

The Assassinations of King and Robert F. Kennedy

As the war raged, tumultuous events continued to upset the nation. In April 1968, an assassin gunned down Martin Luther King, Jr., in Memphis, Tennessee. Riots broke out across America, an expression of tremendous rage and grief over the loss. Later that summer, an assassin killed **Robert F. Kennedy** at a California campaign rally. The younger brother of John F. Kennedy, Robert Kennedy had been running for president on a platform of opposition to the Vietnam War and support for civil rights.

The Election of 1968

In the summer of 1968, thousands of protestors traveled to Chicago for the Democratic National Convention. As the convention proceeded, massive demonstrations took place around the city. While most of the demonstrations remained peaceful, certain radical factions made more provocative statements. Chicago police forces started to attack the demonstrators, and a full-scale riot broke out.

The divisions in society caused by the war played out in the 1968 presidential election. Democrats nominated Vice President **Hubert Humphrey**, but his refusal to denounce the Vietnam War divided the party. Republicans meanwhile nominated **Richard Nixon**, who campaigned on a platform of "law and order." **George Wallace** also ran on the third-party American Independent ticket. Nixon's campaign appealed to many Americans who believed in the war or thought that the antiwar and Black Power movements had gotten out of hand. Nixon won with 301 electoral votes to Humphrey's 191 and Wallace's 46.

NIXON ABROAD

Soon after entering the White House, Nixon announced his new policy of **"Vietnamization"**—a slow withdrawal of the more than 500,000 American soldiers from Vietnam and a simultaneous return of control of the war to the South Vietnamese. He still intended to fund and train the South Vietnamese Army, but hoped that slow troop withdrawals would appease voters at home and reduce casualties in the field. He also announced the **Nixon Doctrine**: America would honor its current defense commitments but would not commit troops anywhere else to fight communism.

The Secret Invasion of Cambodia

Nixon sought instead to defeat the North Vietnamese by destroying their supply lines and base camps in neighboring Cambodia. Although Cambodia officially remained neutral during the war, the NVA ran weapons and troops through the country to circumvent American bombers and raiding parties. In the spring of 1970, Nixon authorized the invasion of Cambodia. The order shocked Congress and the American public. Renewed public outcry and waves of protests convinced Nixon to renege the order later that summer.

My Lai and the Pentagon Papers

Other scandals sparked protest against the military and the president. In 1971, the U.S. Army court-martialed Lieutenant William Calley for ordering the rape, torture, and murder of more than 350 women and children in the 1968 **My Lai Massacre**. Other soldiers anonymously confessed that dozens of similar incidents had taken place during the course of the war. The military came under fire again that year when the *New York Times* published a series of leaked documents called the **Pentagon Papers**, which accused the army, John F. Kennedy, and Lyndon Johnson of deceiving the public during the war.

Congress Checks Unlimited Power

Outraged by the unauthorized invasion of Cambodia and by the double scandal of the My Lai Massacre and the Pentagon Papers, many in Congress took steps to exert more control over the war and appease an equally angry public. For example, the Senate (but not the House of Representatives) voted to repeal the Tonkin Gulf Resolution to reduce the military's unchecked spending power. Congress reduced the number of years drafted soldiers needed to serve in the army, and they also ratified the **Twenty-Sixth Amendment** in 1971 to lower the voting age from twenty-one to eighteen on the grounds that young soldiers in Vietnam should help elect the politicians who sent them to fight.

Dētente

Nixon decided the only solution rested on improving relations with the Soviet Union; this policy came to be known as **détente**. He believed détente would divert attention from the growing failures in Vietnam and allow the United States to eventually withdraw on more graceful terms. Nixon's national security advisor **Henry Kissinger** supported the plan.

Nixon Goes to China

The president chose to approach Russia by opening relations with China in 1972. Although both were communist countries, Maoist China and the Soviet Union were deeply suspicious of each other. Consequently, they had one of the most heavily fortified borders in the world. Nixon hoped dialogues with China would spark fear in Russia over a possible American-Chinese alliance. After visiting Beijing in 1972, Nixon and Kissinger then flew to Moscow, where they played their so-called **"China card"** to bring the Soviets to the negotiating table.

ABM and SALT I

Even though the tactic outraged liberals and conservatives alike back in the United States, Nixon's ploy worked. While in the U.S.S.R., Nixon managed to smooth tensions with Soviet leader **Leonid Brezhnev** and usher in a new era of "cooler" American-Soviet relations called détente. He agreed to sell the Soviets $1 billion worth of badly needed American grain. This arrangement both helped Brezhnev feed his starving people and boosted Nixon's popularity with farmers in the Midwest.

In 1972, Nixon signed the **Anti-Ballistic Missile (ABM) Treaty** to limit the missile defense system, and the **Strategic Arms Limitation Talks Treaty (SALT Treaty)** to prevent both sides from developing any more nuclear weapons for the next five years. Washington enjoyed improved relations with Beijing as an added benefit.

Nixon's Landslide in 1972

Nixon's successful trip to China and Russia gave him the advantage he needed in Vietnam. When the NVA crossed the demilitarized zone and invaded South Vietnam in 1972, Nixon authorized an intense bombing campaign of Hanoi without fear of retaliation from Moscow or Beijing. Nixon also secretly sent Kissinger to meet with North Vietnamese diplomats in Paris that year to discuss peace.

As the presidential elections of 1972 approached, Nixon clearly had the upper hand: He had initiated détente, reduced the number of American troops in Vietnam from 500,000 to 30,000, and halted a major NVA advance. As a result, he easily defeated peace Democrat **George McGovern** in a landslide victory with 520 to 13 electoral votes and nearly 20 million more popular votes.

The Christmas Day Bombing and Cease-Fire

Nixon authorized the **Christmas Day Bombing**, an intense two-week bombing campaign of North Vietnam that he hoped would end the war. Kissinger and North Vietnamese officials finally announced a cease-fire in January 1973. Nixon accepted and agreed to withdraw the remaining American troops, despite the fact that the NVA controlled only a quarter of South Vietnamese territory. In exchange, the North Vietnamese promised that an election in Saigon would determine the fate of the country.

NIXON AT HOME

Although Nixon focused most of his attention on Vietnam and détente, he could not avoid contending with domestic issues, particularly the stagnant economy at home. Beginning in the early 1970s, both inflation and the cost of living crept skyward, while wages remained the same. Worker productivity was declining for the first time since before World War II. To make matters worse, cheaper and better foreign products from Japan started entering the market. On top of all this, Congress paid roughly $22 billion a year to fund Lyndon Johnson's social-welfare programs and the war in Vietnam.

The New Left

The war in Vietnam and continuing racial strife in the United States spurred the radicalization of American youth during the 1960s and 1970s. In the early 1960s, idealistic young white Americans involved in the civil rights movement and other liberal endeavors expanded their efforts to other issues, forming what collectively became known as the **New Left**.

Counterculture

Students and other radical young people created a new **counterculture** in America. This counterculture flouted the values and conventions of middle-class society and embraced a new style that defied traditional standards. Many young Americans grew their hair long, wore shabby clothing, and exhibited rebellious disregard for the old manners and rules. Rock, folk music, and drugs, such as marijuana and LSD, came into vogue, as did new attitudes about sexuality. The ascendancy of the counterculture reflected wider currents in American society at large as growing numbers of Americans became distrustful of the American government and official rhetoric during the Vietnam era.

Nixon and Race Relations

Even in 1969, fifteen years after the Supreme Court ruled in favor of mandatory desegregation in *Brown v. Board of Education,* the majority of southern schools were not racially integrated. Backed by a supportive Supreme Court, civil rights advocates pushed through a number of policies that fostered integration in schools across the entire country. The Nixon administration placed severe limits on the methods schools used to achieve integration goals. One of the most controversial integration measures involved busing students across cities and school districts in order to achieve desegregation.

Some of Nixon's policies furthered the goals of the civil rights movement. He enacted several initiatives intended to motivate contractors and unions to hire more minorities, offered incentives to minority businesses, and expanded the power of the Equal Employment Opportunity Commission. While Nixon never supported racial quotas in hiring or education, his administration did support certain forms of affirmative action.

Women's Liberation

The women's liberation movement gained new momentum in the 1970s. Engaging in peaceful protests for equality, these activists voiced their dissatisfaction with women's rights in the United States. Although women gained the right to vote in the 1920s, structural and cultural factors maintained inequality. The **National Organization for Women (NOW)** emerged as the primary group voicing the concerns of mainstream feminists. NOW initiated strikes and protests to demand equality in employment, education, child care, and reproductive

control. Many smaller groups also fought for the passage of the **Equal Rights Amendment (ERA)** to the Constitution.

The ERA

The proposed Equal Rights Amendment to the Constitution would have required equal treatment of men and women in all domains. Although the amendment passed Congress and was ratified in a number of states, it failed to receive the three-fifths majority required to make it part of the Constitution. As a result, women continued to generally receive lower wages for comparable work in the ensuing decades.

Nixon and the Environment

Although the Nixon administration generally prioritized economic interests over environmental concerns, Congress passed several protective acts in the 1970s. The administration supported the **Occupational Safety and Health Act (OSHA)**, the **Clean Air Act**, and the **Endangered Species Act**. At the same time, Nixon also created the **Environmental Protection Agency (EPA)** to protect air and water quality and monitor the use of pesticides.

Nixon's Social Welfare Programs

Nixon publicly advocated decreased government participation in social welfare. He cut key programs, such as Medicare, Head Start, and legal services, as part of his commitment to "Middle America." In spite of these cuts, Nixon also increased Social Security benefits, subsidized low-income housing, expanded the food stamp program, and established a government assistance program for low-income students.

Economic Policy

The Arab **oil embargo of 1973** combined with inflation at home created the nation's first energy crisis. Inflation rose steadily, as did the unemployment rate. The United States gradually lost its predominant place in the world economy as foreign countries such as Japan and Germany finally rebounded from post–World War II depressions. Nixon temporarily improved the economy by increasing exports while freezing wages and prices. Yet by 1974, the United States faced a severe economic crisis.

WATERGATE, RESIGNATION, AND FORD

On June 17, 1972, local police officers apprehended five men during an early-morning break-in at the national Democratic Party headquarters in the **Watergate** apartment and office complex. Police soon discovered that the men worked for the **Committee to Reelect the President (CREEP)**. The burglars had attempted to repair a bugging device that they had installed during a previous forced entry.

During the next two years, the investigation brought the Nixon administration's worst secrets to light.

The Nixon Tapes

In April 1973, Nixon appeared on television to publicly accept responsibility for the Watergate events. He adamantly denied any direct knowledge of the break-in and cover-up and announced the resignations of several of his subordinates. The Senate investigative committee uncovered more incriminating evidence against the president and added charges concerning the misuse of federal funds and tax evasion. The committee subpoenaed some of the president's audiotapes of White House conversations, but Nixon refused to relinquish them.

Nixon's Resignation

In July 1974, the Supreme Court unanimously decided that the president had to present his White House tapes to congressional investigators. These tapes clearly established Nixon's guilt in the Watergate cover-up. Armed with damning evidence, the House Judiciary Committee gained majority support on three charges of impeachment against Nixon:

- Obstruction of justice
- Abuse of power
- Contempt of Congress

Faced with imminent impeachment, Nixon chose instead to resign. In a dramatic, nationally televised speech on August 8, 1974, he accepted responsibility for his poor judgment in the Watergate scandal but continued to defend his good intentions.

Ford: the Unelected President

Following Nixon's resignation, Nixon's vice president, **Gerald Ford**, became president of the United States. Congress had recently appointed Ford to office after Vice President Agnew had resigned in the wake of a corruption scandal in 1973. As a result, Ford became the nation's first and only unelected president. Highlights of the Ford presidency include the following:

- **Nixon's presidential pardon**. Only a month into his presidency, Ford granted a formal pardon to Nixon for all his purported crimes, sparing the ex-president and the nation the embarrassment of a trial and likely conviction. The decision angered many Americans and ruined Ford's political and public credibility.

- **Evacuating Vietnam**. Ford pulled the last remaining troops out of Vietnam in 1975, which marked the end of American involvement in the Vietnam War. U.S. forces helped approximately 150,000 South Vietnamese flee the country.
- **The Continuing Economic Crisis**. Ford faced a number of liabilities during his brief term in office that proved insurmountable. He lacked the resources, knowledge, and political clout to tackle the stagnant economy. He also vetoed thirty-nine bills Congress had passed to improve domestic affairs and reduce taxes, and at the same time, he increased government spending. As a result, Americans faced the deepest recession since the Great Depression by the end of his two years in office.

TIMELINE: 1963–1975

1963	Lyndon Johnson becomes president.
1964	Tonkin Gulf Resolution authorizes military action in Southeast Asia.
	Johnson launches War on Poverty.
	Freedom Summer marks the climax of intensive voter-registration activities in the South.
	Congress passes the Civil Rights Act of 1964.
1965	Johnson begins "escalation" in Vietnam.
	The Pleiku Raid sparks off an intense series of airstrikes called Operation Rolling Thunder.
	Peace protestors march on Washington, D.C.
	Congress passes the Voting Rights Act.
1967	Rallies, riots, and protests erupt throughout the United States.
1968	The Tet Offensive incites massive demonstrations on college campuses throughout the United States.
	Paris peace talks begin.
	Robert Kennedy is assassinated.
	Martin Luther King, Jr., is assassinated.
	Riots erupt outside the Democratic convention in Chicago.
	Richard Nixon is elected president.

1969	The Woodstock Music and Art Fair attracts 400,000 people.
	Nixon begins "Vietnamization" withdrawal of U.S. troops.
1970	The United States bombs Cambodia.
	Student protests turn violent throughout the country.
1971	The *New York Times* publishes the Pentagon Papers.
	The Twenty-Sixth Amendment is ratified.
	Lieutenant William Calley is court-martialed for the My Lai Massacre.
1972	Nixon and Henry Kissinger visit China and the Soviet Union.
	Nixon signs the SALT and ABM treaties to reduce nuclear weapons.
	Nixon is reelected.
	Nixon authorizes the Christmas Day Bombing in North Vietnam.
1973	Congress passes the War Powers Act.
	The Watergate scandal erupts.
	Roe v. Wade gives women the right to an abortion.
	Arab oil embargo begins an oil/energy crisis.
1974	The House of Representatives prepares to impeach Nixon.
	Vice President Spiro T. Agnew resigns.
	Nixon resigns.
	Gerald Ford becomes president.
	Ford pardons Nixon.
1975	The Helsinki Accords reduce tension between Soviet and western blocs.
	Communists declare victory in South Vietnam.

MAJOR FIGURES

Spiro Agnew. Elected vice president under Richard Nixon in 1968, Agnew resigned in 1973 after journalists discovered he had accepted several bribes while in office. Congress selected Congressman Gerald Ford to be the new vice president later that year. Agnew's resignation was merely one of the many scandals that soured public opinion against Nixon and politics in the 1970s.

Stokeley Carmichael. Radical civil rights leader in the mid-1960s, Carmichael coined the phrase "black power." He served as chairman of the Student Nonviolent Coordinating Committee (SNCC) and was a leading member of the Black Panthers. He took the name Kwame Ture in 1968 and died in 1998.

Gerald Ford. Congress selected Ford from the House of Representatives in 1973 to replace Richard Nixon's vice president Spiro Agnew after Agnew had resigned in the wake of a bribery scandal. Ford became the first "unelected" president the next year after Nixon himself resigned. He unfortunately ruined his squeaky-clean image after he pardoned Nixon within days of taking office. Ford continued the policy of détente by signing the Helsinki Accords in 1975. That year he also withdrew the final remaining troops from South Vietnam. Hoping to win the presidency in his own right, he ran on the Republican ticket in 1976 but lost to Democrat James "Jimmy" Carter. Ford died in 2006.

Barry M. Goldwater. An ultraconservative senator from Arizona, Goldwater ran against Democrat Lyndon Johnson in the election of 1964. He hated Johnson's vision of a Great Society and the War on Poverty, despised the notion of equal rights for blacks, and advocated the use of nuclear weapons in Vietnam. He received 40 percent of the popular vote but lost with only fifty-two electoral votes to Johnson's 486.

Michael Harrington. Author of the widely read *The Outer America*, Harrington was a prominent socialist during the 1960s. He served as a member of the League for Industrial Democracy and became an advisor to Martin Luther King, Jr., in 1965. *The Outer America* revealed that in spite of the postwar economic boom, many Americans remained trapped in poverty. President Kennedy used the book to help shape his War on Poverty.

Hubert Humphrey. Vice president under Lyndon Johnson, Humphrey ran for president against George Wallace and Richard Nixon in 1968 on a platform to continue the War on Poverty and the war in Vietnam. The split in the Democratic party between Humphrey and Wallace and the Chicago riots at the nominating convention, however, gave Nixon an easy victory.

Lyndon Johnson. Vice president under John F. Kennedy, Johnson became president after JFK's assassination in 1963. In January 1964, he launched several new social-welfare programs, such as Head Start, Medicare, and Medicaid, as part of his War on Poverty to create a Great Society. A nearly unanimous vote in Congress passed the Tonkin Gulf Resolution that gave Johnson a free hand to escalate the war in Vietnam. After defeating Republican Barry M. Goldwater in the election of 1964, he authorized Operation Rolling Thunder in February 1965, hoping to bomb North Vietnam into peace. When this failed, Johnson sent more than 500,000 troops to South Vietnam and ultimately converted the conflict into a protracted and bitter war.

Robert Kennedy. A former attorney general and younger brother to President John F. Kennedy, Democrat "Bobby" Kennedy campaigned in the 1968 presidential primary on a pro–civil rights and antiwar platform. He posed a serious threat to candidate Hubert Humphrey until a deranged Islamic American named Sirhan Sirhan assassinated him that summer.

Henry Kissinger. A former political science and history professor from Harvard, German-born Kissinger first served as Richard Nixon's national security advisor and then as Nixon's and Ford's secretary of state. Many historians believe he first proposed making a trip to China to scare the Soviets into détente. Although he has since retired from politics, his essays and works on diplomatic history and foreign policy are still highly regarded.

George McGovern. A Democratic senator from South Dakota, McGovern ran against incumbent Richard Nixon for the presidency in 1972 on an anti–Vietnam War platform. Nixon defeated him in a landslide victory with 520 electoral votes to McGovern's seventeen and with almost 20 million more popular votes.

George Wallace. Wallace ran for president on the American Independent Party ticket against Democrat Hubert Humphrey and Republican Richard Nixon in 1968. A former governor from Alabama, he had vehemently opposed the civil rights movement and desegregation. In his bid for the presidency, Wallace campaigned for segregation and intensified bombing in Vietnam. He carried only five states in the Deep South on Election Day.

Malcom X. Malcolm X's powerful rhetoric and calls for black self-reliance drew many supporters from urban areas. His ideas of black pride signaled a split with the mainstream civil rights movement. He was murdered in 1965.

Chapter 18

Carter and Reagan: 1976–1988

THE PRESIDENCY OF JIMMY CARTER

After defeating **Gerald Ford** in 1976, **Jimmy Carter** assumed the presidency with promises to improve the economy, strengthen education, and provide assistance to the aging and the poor. Carter began his term in office with confidence and enthusiasm. A variety of obstacles and unexpected events prevented the new president from achieving many of his goals.

The Election of 1976

Gerald Ford received the Republican party's official nomination in the summer of 1976 and was desperate to win the presidency in his own right. Unfortunately for him, Americans had a tainted image of Washington politics, the White House, and anything even remotely tied to Richard Nixon. Instead, they turned to a surprise presidential contender, James "Jimmy" Carter. A Democrat, peanut farmer, and former governor of Georgia, Carter had almost no political experience in Washington, D.C., and was therefore "clean" in the eyes of many Americans. His down-to-earth demeanor and truthfulness only made him more likeable and refreshing to American voters.

During the campaign, Carter vowed to clean up Washington, cut taxes, and end the energy crisis. Thanks largely to enormous support from southern and black voters, Carter received slightly more than 50 percent of the popular vote and 297 electoral votes to Ford's 240.

Domestic Policy

Unlike most of his Democrat predecessors, Carter increased taxes for the lower and middle classes and cut taxes for wealthier individuals. In the face of soaring inflation, slow economic growth, and high levels of unemployment, Carter also made minimizing federal spending and preserving Social Security two of his top priorities. Additionally, he protected struggling big businesses by reducing capital gains taxes and deregulating the banking, airline, trucking, and railroad industries.

The Energy Crisis

Carter tried to reduce domestic oil consumption and American dependence on foreign crude oil, but he lacked the necessary support from consumers and Congress. As a result, none of the initiatives that Carter successfully launched had any real effect.

"Stagflation"

The president's inability to tackle the **energy crisis** damaged his reputation, especially considering that voters had elected him to do just that. Americans were forced to wait in long lines or buy gasoline only on certain days, just as they had under Nixon and Ford. Moreover, soaring gas prices made it more expensive to transport goods across the country. Manufacturers and retailers compensated for the increased transportation costs by raising retail prices so that, on average, inflation increased by 10 percent *per year* between 1974 and 1980 without any economic growth or change in wages. In other words, a product that cost $100 in 1974 cost more than $180 in 1980. It thus became more expensive to drive, buy a house, buy consumer goods, and even buy groceries.

Carter's Foreign Policy

Carter made the protection of human rights through diplomacy his highest foreign policy priority. He slapped economic sanctions on countries such as Argentina, Chile, and South Africa, which were infamous for rampant human rights violations. Critics argued that the president's human-rights policies displayed inconsistencies. In strategically important countries, such as China, Iran, and South Korea, for example, he overlooked human rights violations. Others charged that Carter's human-rights-centered foreign policy distracted the United States from facing Cold War concerns, such as the communist revolution in Nicaragua. Outside of America, many leaders around the world lauded his morally grounded foreign policy.

Carter attempted to extend his moral principles to amend some of America's past imperialist actions. In 1977, Carter signed a new treaty with Panama regarding the control and use of the **Panama Canal**. Until this point, the United States enjoyed sole control of the isthmian canal, but the new treaty granted Panama joint control until the year 2000 (at which point Panama would assume complete control). Many Americans perceived this action as compensation for the "big

stick" tactics the United States had utilized to secure the land to build the canal in the first place. At the same time, critics became concerned with Carter's willingness to forgo control of such an economically and strategically vital waterway.

Peace in the Middle East

Carter's successful leadership during negotiations between Egyptian president **Anwar el-Sadat** and Israeli prime minister **Menachem Begin** proved to be one of his greatest international achievements. After inviting the two men to the presidential retreat at Camp David, Maryland, Carter spent days guiding the discussion between the bitter rivals, who often refused even to meet face to face. Largely thanks to Carter, both men signed the **Camp David Accords** in 1978 to agree to end several decades of war. As a result, Egypt also became the first Arab nation to formally recognize Israel, and Israel agreed to withdraw from the Sinai Peninsula.

SALT II

Carter hoped to end his first term on a high note before the 1980 elections by reducing the threat of Soviet aggression and nuclear holocaust. In 1979, he met with Soviet premier Leonid Brezhnev to sign the **Second Strategic Arms Limitation Talks (SALT II Treaty)**, which aimed to reduce the number of both countries' nuclear warheads.

Although a treaty would have significantly eased American-Soviet relations, conservatives in the Senate bitterly opposed it out of fear that the treaty would leave Americans vulnerable to attack. They pointed to Russia's support of the Cuban interventions in Ethiopia and Angola and the Soviet invasion of Afghanistan in December 1979. Carter denounced the invasion and stopped all grain shipments to the U.S.S.R., but party leaders in Moscow refused to withdraw.

The Iran Hostage Crisis

Carter's greatest international policy challenge came from Iran. Although the shah of Iran, **Mohammad Reza Pahlavi**, had long been a U.S. ally, Carter criticized the shah's autocratic rule and refused to provide military aid to support him against an armed insurrection. In 1979, Carter allowed the shah to flee to the United States for medical treatment and political asylum. Iranian militants—who were enraged by American support of the ousted leader—broke into the U.S. embassy in Tehran and took fifty-three hostages.

The militants demanded that the United States return the shah for trial and possible execution in return for the release of the hostages. The new Iranian government, headed by the Shi'ite cleric **Ayatollah Khomeini**, actively participated in the hostage situation. Khomeini established a Shi'ite theocracy in Iran that remains in power.

Carter's attempts to deal with the hostage crisis were ineffective. After a year of failed negotiations, he authorized a military rescue operation. The rescue turned out to be a complete disaster, however, when eight American soldiers died in a

helicopter crash in the Iranian desert. Khomeini refused to sign an agreement for the release of the hostages. Carter's inability to resolve the **Iran hostage crisis** weakened American confidence in the administration and contributed to his defeat in the election of 1980.

THE REAGAN REVOLUTION

Americans elected **Ronald Reagan**, a former movie actor and governor of California, to the presidency in 1980. Reagan swept into the White House in 1981 on a mission to reduce the size of the federal government and shift the balance of political power back to the individual states. A diehard conservative Republican, he abhorred most social-welfare programs, hated affirmative action, and felt that policymakers in Washington had overstepped their mandate by exerting too much control over the lives of average Americans.

Reagan managed to overcome opposition and pass most items on his agenda by cajoling southern conservative Democrats in Congress to vote with his Republican allies. He also received support from the so-called **Religious Right**, a prominent group of conservative Protestant ministers who opposed homosexuality and abortion, among other things. More important, he had the support of the vast majority of Americans.

"Reaganomics"

Reagan immediately set out to balance the budget and curb the growing deficit that had plagued Jimmy Carter's administration. He proposed to slash social-welfare programs in order to reduce the budget deficit to just less than $40 billion a year. Then he slashed tax rates across the board by nearly 25 percent. Corporations received even more benefits from Washington, D.C., in the hopes that their prosperity would "trickle down" to the average American worker. Although most conservatives praised Reagan's **"supply-side economics,"** a few Republicans dissented, including Vice President **George H. W. Bush**, who had previously denounced Reagan's fiscal agenda as **"voodoo economics"** because it simply made no sense.

The Recession of 1982

By 1982, "**Reaganomics**" had taken its toll as several banks failed, the stock market plummeted, and unemployment soared in the worst economic recession since the Great Depression. Eventually the economy pulled out of the pit, thanks in part to sound policies from the Federal Reserve Board. Prosperity eventually came, but at a steep price, as the gap between the very rich and the very poor widened considerably. With reduced government welfare programs to alleviate the hunger and homelessness, the poor had nowhere to turn for help. The recession hit women, children, and blacks especially hard.

Deficits and Debt

Although Reagan entered the White House promising to reduce government spending and return more power to the states, he ironically became the biggest spender in American history. Not even Roosevelt's New Deal during the Depression or Johnson's Great Society had dumped so much money into the economy as Reaganomics. Between 1980 and 1988, Congress overspent its budget by more than $200 billion every year, while the national debt soared from roughly $1 trillion to $2.5 trillion.

Moreover, almost all of Reagan's spending went into the military and defense; very little actually "trickled down" to the average American. Still, Americans continued to support the president. For many citizens, his charisma and unwavering stance against Soviet aggression abroad translated to a sense of safety. In the wake of Vietnam, social unrest, the energy crisis, and the Iran hostage crisis, Americans sought strength and protection above all else.

The Savings and Loan Crisis

Reagan also deregulated many aspects of the banking industry, which allowed the traditionally local, financially conservative **savings and loan** institutions to enter the arena of high-yield, high-risk corporate investments. As a result, hundreds of savings and loans across the country had gone bankrupt by the late 1980s. Congress's decision to rescue failing institutions not only saved many families from financial ruin but also further increased the federal budget deficit.

The Stock Market Crash of 1987

Though a bull market ruled for much of the decade, Americans indulged in several imprudent financial practices that ultimately caused a stock market crash. Following the cue of the federal government's increased deficit spending, both consumers and businesses ran up huge debts. The United States also had a very high trade deficit, importing much more than it exported. Again, borrowed money often paid for these imports.

A shaky stock market finally buckled on October 19, 1987, or **Black Monday**, when the Dow Jones Industrial Average lost nearly 23 percent of its value in a single day. Paper assets disappeared in the amount of $560 billion. Reagan reassured the nation that the economy would remain stable and tried to help the economy by reducing some deficit spending and increasing some taxes. These measures could not prevent stock markets around the world from buckling.

Conservatism in the Court

Reagan's long presidency altered the composition of the federal courts. Reagan tended to appoint judges and justices who held politically conservative views and focused less on protecting individual rights. Reagan's most high-profile appointment was **Sandra Day O'Connor**, a middle-of-the-road conservative who became the first female Supreme Court justice.

While many critics expected Reagan's appointments to signal a profound change in the federal court system, the new conservative judges tended to maintain the status quo. Even when given the opportunity, they rarely overturned long-standing decisions on controversial issues (e.g., abortion). Instead, the justices began to defer to state government decisions regarding rights issues.

Landslide Reelection in '84

Democrats prayed that the recession would ruin Reagan's chances for reelection in 1984. But the president's popularity held steady. Democrats nominated Jimmy Carter's former vice president **Walter Mondale**, who surprised everyone by choosing a woman, **Geraldine Ferraro**, as his vice-presidential running mate. In the end, Reagan and Bush easily defeated Mondale and Ferraro with approximately 17 million more popular votes and 525 electoral votes to the latter's 13.

REAGAN ABROAD

A former "red" hunter in Hollywood during the McCarthy era, Reagan also took a hard stance against the "evil empire" of the Soviet Union. He believed that a **"window of vulnerability"** had temporarily weakened the United States.

Star Wars

Tired of détente and outraged by Soviet aggression in Afghanistan, Reagan proposed to dramatically boost defense spending based on the belief that a crippled Russian economy wouldn't be able to keep up with American military development. His plan culminated with the proposal of a futuristic orbital laser defense system called the **Strategic Defense Initiative (SDI)**. Most scientists agreed that **"Star Wars,"** as pundits called it, would never work. Still, Reagan hoped the proposal would strong-arm the Soviet Union to the bargaining table on American terms.

The Reagan Doctrine

The **Reagan Doctrine** stated that the United States had to combat any Marxist revolutions abroad in order to counter Soviet advances. The president employed this doctrine in several developing Latin American countries. For example, Reagan denounced the communist **Sandinista** revolutionaries in Nicaragua and gave tens of millions of dollars to the pro-American **"contra"** rebels to take back the country. He dumped even more money into neighboring El Salvador and sent military advisors to prevent a revolution there too. On top of this, Reagan then ordered the invasion of the tiny island nation of Grenada in the Caribbean in 1983 to oust communist usurpers.

The Iran-Contra Affair

Even though the vast majority of Americans supported Reagan's tough stance against communism, Congress did not. This was primarily because upholding the Reagan Doctrine simply cost too much money. The United States had poured hundreds of millions of dollars into fighting communist revolutions abroad—most notably in Nicaragua, to help the contras fight the Marxist Sandinistas. Finally, the invasion of Grenada had proven that Reagan would not hesitate to use troops to fight these insurgents.

The Boland Amendment

Hoping to avert a Vietnamesque war in Nicaragua, Congress passed the **Boland Amendment** in 1983, which forbade the federal government from further assisting the contras with either troops or money.

Illegal Arms Sales

Scandal erupted when journalists discovered that the White House had ignored the amendment and funneled secret money raised from arms sales in Iran and other Middle Eastern countries into Nicaragua. After a lengthy investigation, a congressional committee indicted several officials on the president's National Security Council, including Admiral Poindexter and Marine Corps colonel **Oliver North**. Both Poindexter and North claimed they acted in the interests of national security. Essentially, they argued that the ends justified the illegal means. The investigation implicated Reagan and Bush, but their involvement was never proven.

Reform in Russia

Although Reagan had taken an incredibly harsh stance against the Soviet Union, he actually played a key role in ending the Cold War. In 1985, reform-minded **Mikhail Gorbachev** came to power in the Soviet Union with some radical new ideas about politics, the economy, and society as a whole. Soon after taking office, he initiated ***glasnost***, or "openness," to relax some political controls, including restrictions on the press, and ***perestroika***, or "restructuring," to slowly convert the Soviet Union into a more capitalist economy.

In order to transition to capitalism, Gorbachev drastically reduced the amount the U.S.S.R. spent on its military, which effectively meant a reduction in Cold War tensions. He met with Reagan at four different summit meetings between 1985 and 1988 and signed the **INF Treaty** at the final summit in Washington, D.C., to remove all nuclear weapons aimed at Europe and begin the end of the Cold War.

TIMELINE: 1976–1988

1976	James "Jimmy" Carter is elected president.
1978	Anwar Sadat and Menachem Begin agree to end hostility and sign the Camp David Accords.
1979	Carter delivers his Malaise Speech.
	Carter meets with Lenoid Brezhnev to sign the SALT II Treaty (never signed by the Senate).
	The Iran hostage crisis begins.
	The Soviet Union invades Afghanistan.
1980	Ronald Reagan is elected president.
1981	The Iran hostage crisis ends.
	Reagan slashes taxes but increases government spending.
1982	Recession hits.
1983	Reagan announces SDI, or "Star Wars."
	Two hundred forty-one American troops are killed in Lebanon.
	The United States invades Grenada.
1984	Reagan is reelected.
1985	Mikhail Gorbachev initiates reform in the U.S.S.R.
	Nuclear disarmament is discussed at the first Reagan-Gorbachev summit meeting.
1986	The Iran-Contra Affair erupts.
	Congress passes the Immigration Reform and Control Act.
	The second Reagan-Gorbachev summit meeting is held.
1987	The third Reagan-Gorbachev summit meeting is held.
	Reagan signs the INF Treaty at the fourth Reagan-Gorbachev summit meeting in Washington, D.C., to remove all nuclear weapons.
1988	George H. W. Bush is elected president.

MAJOR FIGURES

George H. W. Bush. A former director of the CIA and ambassador to China and the UN, Bush attacked Ronald Reagan's supply-side economic policies during the 1980s. He even referred to "Reaganomics" as "voodoo economics" during the 1980 presidential primaries. Ironically, however, he accepted Reagan's invitation to be his running mate. He served as vice president throughout Reagan's two terms and defeated Michael Dukakis for the presidency in 1988.

James "Jimmy" Carter. A former peanut farmer and Georgia governor, Carter beat incumbent President Gerald Ford for the presidency in 1976 with promises to clean up Washington, D.C. He revised the tax system and gave Americans $18 billion in tax cuts but failed to curb rising inflation or resolve the energy crisis. Public opinion of the president soured after he blamed the crises on over-consumption and the degradation of society in his infamous Malaise Speech in 1979. Although he successfully negotiated a lasting peace between Israel and Egypt with the Camp David Accords, the rest of his humanitarian-oriented foreign policy floundered, especially after he bungled the Iran hostage crisis. He ran for reelection in 1980 but lost to Republican Ronald Reagan.

Geraldine Ferraro. A New York congresswoman, Ferraro was the first woman nominated for the vice presidency by a major political party. She unsuccessfully ran with Walter Mondale on the Democratic ticket against Ronald Reagan and George H. W. Bush in 1984.

Mikhail Gorbachev. Selected to lead the Soviet Union in 1985, Gorbachev initiated sweeping reforms that drastically changed the U.S.S.R. His policy of *glasnost*, or "openness," for example, introduced free speech and a degree of political liberty to the country. Gorbachev also initiated *perestroika*, or "restructuring," to revive the stagnant Soviet economy with capitalist market principles. He met with Ronald Reagan at four summits between 1985 and 1988 to discuss improved Soviet-American relations and signed the INF Treaty with Reagan to remove nuclear warheads from Europe. Gorbachev's reforms shook the U.S.S.R. to its core and contributed both to the collapse of the Soviet Union in 1991 and the end of the Cold War.

Ayatollah Ruholla Khomeini. A fundamentalist Muslim cleric, Khomeini led the radical revolutionary forces that overthrew the American-backed shah of Iran in 1979. As the new religious ruler of Iran, he cut off all oil exports to the West, which sent the United States into a second oil crisis. In November 1979, his forces took several Americans hostage at the U.S. embassy in Tehran and demanded the return of the escaped shah. President Jimmy Carter refused to negotiate and instead ordered an unsuccessful military rescue operation. His failure to end the Iran hostage crisis helped lead to his defeat in the 1980 presidential election. Khomeini released the hostages on Ronald Reagan's inauguration day in 1981 after holding them for 444 days.

Walter Mondale. A Democrat, Mondale ran against incumbent Ronald Reagan for the presidency in 1984. Even though he lost badly, with only thirteen electoral votes to Reagan's 525 and with 20 million fewer popular votes, he nevertheless

distinguished himself as the first presidential candidate to choose a woman, Geraldine Ferraro, as his vice-presidential running mate.

Oliver North. A lieutenant colonel in the Marine Corps and staffer on the National Security Council, North testified at a congressional hearing in 1987 about his role in the Iran-contra Affair. He freely admitted that he and his superiors on the council had destroyed evidence of their illegal actions, arguing that he had acted honorably, in the best interests of the United States. A court convicted him for blatantly defying the Boland Amendment, but North was eventually acquitted. Still, his actions cast a pall on Ronald Reagan's presidency and integrity.

Ronald Reagan. A former movie star from the 1930s, '40s, and '50s and governor of California, Reagan defeated incumbent Democrat Jimmy Carter for the presidency in 1980 with promises to drastically downsize the federal government. His election ushered in a new era of political conservatism. Reagan cut almost all federally funded social-welfare programs in an effort to shift the balance of power back to the individual states. Ironically, he spent more than all previous twentieth-century presidents combined in an effort to bolster national defense against Soviet attack. Reagan declared the Soviet Union an "evil empire" and proposed the Strategic Defense Initiative, also known as SDI or Star Wars, to build a laser defense shield. He spent millions of dollars funding the anti-communist contras in Nicaragua and El Salvador and sent troops to Grenada, though the Iran-contra Affair proved that he didn't always have control over his foreign policy advisors. Reagan's supply-side economic theories, dubbed "Reaganomics" or "voodoo economics," meanwhile made wealthy Americans wealthier and poor Americans poorer. He participated in four debates with Soviet leader Mikhail Gorbachev, cosigned the INF Treaty, and thus helped end the Cold War.

Chapter 19

The End of the Cold War and the War on Terror: 1989–2007

THE PRESIDENCY OF GEORGE H. W. BUSH

As president, George H. W. Bush led America through the end of the Cold War after the Soviet empire collapsed. New challenges arose with an economic recession and new instability in the Middle East.

The Election of George Bush and Economic Troubles

President Reagan's vice president, George H. W. Bush, easily defeated Democrat and Massachusetts governor Michael Dukakis in the election of 1988. Bush promised voters that he would not institute new taxes. While Bush and his running mate, Dan Quayle, had little difficulty overcoming their Democratic opponents and carried forty states, the Republicans were unable to gain seats in Congress.

Soon after his inauguration, Bush was forced to support the savings and loan industry by signing legislation that created the **Resolution Trust Corporation**.

More than $300 billion of federal funds were needed to cover the bad debts. In addition, a recession beginning in 1990 resulted in unemployment, corporate downsizing, and a rising federal budget deficit. Determining that maintaining the deficit (more than $450 billion in 1991) was riskier than increasing taxes, Bush proposed raising taxes and disallowed certain deductions. He raised excise taxes in 1992 and therefore violated his 1988 campaign pledge.

Rise of Global Democracy

Global democracy emerged as a powerful force during the Bush administration as a number of formerly totalitarian governments (governments that regulate nearly every aspect of their citizens' behavior) collapsed. Eastern European nations opened their borders, allowed free elections, and removed themselves from the Soviet sphere of influence following Soviet premier Mikhail Gorbachev's announcement of *perestroika* and *glasnost*. The announcement resulted in a reduction in economic restraints and media censorship. The most visible sign of the collapse of the Soviet Empire was the **destruction of the Berlin Wall** by the citizens of East and West Berlin in November 1989. The wall had been the chief symbol of the Cold War since its construction in 1961.

Collapse of Soviet Union and the Cold War's End

The Soviet Union's breakup began in 1990 when Lithuania declared itself independent. Other republics followed, and President Bush and Premier Gorbachev both deactivated land-based intercontinental ballistic missiles and removed weapons from ships and submarines. A group of political and military leaders tried to seize power from Gorbachev on August 18, 1991, but the coup collapsed as foreign leaders, including Bush, voiced support for **Boris Yeltsin**, president of the Russian Republic. Foreign leaders refused to recognize the coup leaders as a legitimate government. By the end of 1991, the Soviet Union dissolved into a loose association of eleven autonomous republics renamed the Commonwealth of Independent States, and Yeltsin replaced Gorbachev as president.

Panama and Noriega

Panamanian dictator **Manuel Noriega**, who had formerly been supported by the United States, became a concern for the White House when he became a key link in the drug trade between Latin America and the United States. When economic sanctions, diplomacy, and an October 1989 coup all failed to topple the Noriega regime, Bush sent 12,000 troops, installed a new government, and captured Noriega, bringing him to the United States to face drug-trafficking charges. Noriega was convicted and sentenced to forty years' imprisonment in 1992.

Crisis in the Persian Gulf

Iraq's **Saddam Hussein** invaded the neighboring nation of Kuwait in August 1990, triggering the UN's condemnations and a massing of 400,000 American forces in the region by the end of 1990. When Iraq did not meet the UN deadline of January 15, 1991, for withdrawal from Kuwait, an international force led by the United States bombed Iraq, occupied Kuwait, and began a land invasion of Iraq in a campaign named **Operation Desert Storm**. Four days after the invasion on February 23, Iraq surrendered and withdrew from Kuwait. More than 100,000 Iraqi civilians and soldiers were killed with a loss of 115 American lives.

THE PRESIDENCY OF WILLIAM J. CLINTON

Arkansas governor **William Jefferson Clinton**, the successful Democratic candidate for president in 1992, strove to move his party closer to the mainstream of the American electorate. A self-proclaimed moderate, he projected an image of energy and enthusiasm and accomplished some domestic and foreign successes. His two terms were marred by personal scandal, however, and he became the first president impeached since the Reconstruction.

The Election of 1992

Despite a high approval rating following his successes in Iraq and the end of the Cold War, President Bush's economic policies and the longest recession since the Great Depression provided strong challenges for both Democratic opponent Bill Clinton and Reform Party candidate H. Ross Perot. Clinton won 370 electoral votes, but only 43 percent of the popular vote compared with Bush's 38 percent; Perot won 19 percent but no states.

Clinton's First Term

The Clinton presidency began with a rocky start as both a proposed ending of a ban on gays in the military and a comprehensive reform of the nation's health care system were defeated. As a compromise, the "Don't ask, don't tell" policy was established for gays in the military. Republicans won both houses of Congress in the 1994 fall elections in a repudiation of Clinton's attempts to increase the reach of the federal government.

Clinton had some success with the passage of the **Family and Medical Leave Act**, which required large companies to provide twelve weeks' unpaid leave for family emergencies, and a **welfare reform bill** that was finally passed in 1996.

In foreign affairs, Clinton brought together Itzhak Rabin, prime minister of Israel, and Yasir Arafat, chairman of the Palestine Liberation Organization, for a White House summit that resulted in Palestinian self-rule in the Gaza Strip in 1994. In addition, the **North American Free Trade Agreement (NAFTA)** was signed in January and removed trade barriers and tariffs between the United States, Canada, and Mexico.

The Election of 1996

Clinton's popularity and a resurgent economy provided him with a victory in the 1996 presidential election over Republican Bob Dole. Although Clinton received 49 percent of the popular vote along with 379 electoral votes, Republicans retained control of both houses of Congress.

Scandals and Impeachment

Some of President Clinton's private affairs became public during his second term. The affairs included his involvement in a complicated real estate deal called **Whitewater**, the suicide of Deputy White House Counsel Vince Foster, and a series of allegations of sexual impropriety, leading to the appointment of independent counsel Kenneth Starr to investigate wrongdoings.

While looking into charges of sexual harassment of state employee Paula Jones during Clinton's term as governor of Arkansas, Starr learned of another Clinton affair: with White House intern **Monica Lewinsky**. Starr's 445-page report led to a vote supporting **impeachment of Clinton** by the House of Representatives on December 19, 1998. The resulting impeachment trial by the Senate fell short of the two-thirds vote needed for conviction on the charges of perjury and obstruction of justice, but it was the first impeachment trial of a president since 1868.

Unrest in the Balkans

During the second Clinton term, civil war erupted on the Balkan Peninsula as Yugoslavia President Slobodan Milosevic asserted Serbian control in 1999 over the mostly Muslim ethnic Albanians residing in the province of **Kosovo**. Widespread ethnic cleansing led to the burning of villages, mass murders, rapes, and the forced displacement of thousands of people. NATO forces, with the United States providing most of the air attacks, bombed Yugoslavia for seventy-two consecutive days, forcing a troop withdrawal and the signing of a peace agreement on June 3, 1999.

THE PRESIDENCY OF GEORGE W. BUSH

President George H. W. Bush's son, **George W. Bush**, won the White House following a contested 2000 election. Terrorist attacks and the newly created Bush Doctrine led the United States into two wars during Bush's first two years in office.

The Election of 2000

The **election of 2000** revealed an almost exactly evenly divided nation. Democratic vice president Al Gore and Republican governor George W. Bush of Texas held radically different views of the role of government. Gore favored an activist federal government that would support a continued Social Security system and strong environmental controls, and Bush advocated for tax cuts and increased state responsibility in the areas of the environment and education. Bush also questioned the U.S. role in the Balkans and other global military commitments.

Early election results indicated Gore was the narrow winner in the Electoral College with a 540,000-vote lead in the popular vote, but Florida's balloting proved to be too close, and a recount was demanded. For five weeks, the results of the election were in doubt. Finally, on December 12, 2000, the U.S. Supreme Court ruled 5–4 in ***Bush v. Gore*** that a recount was illegal, and Bush was declared the winner of the decisive 25 electoral votes by a margin of 537 Florida voters.

Bush's First Term

Despite the disputed election and a balanced Congress, President Bush pushed for major domestic changes, including a massive $1.6 trillion tax cut to stimulate the economy and a **No Child Left Behind** plan that would significantly raise standards for teachers and students in public elementary and secondary schools by 2014. If test scores did not improve, sanctions and eventually state takeovers of schools would result. In international affairs, Bush refused to sign the **Kyoto Protocol** in 2001, an international agreement setting limits on carbon dioxide emissions, because he felt it would harm the American economy.

September 11th and Its Aftermath

Two major symbols of American military and economic strength—the Pentagon just outside Washington, D.C., and the twin World Trade Center towers in New York City—were attacked on **September 11, 2001**, when hijackers, trained in the Al Qaeda network of Islamic extremists headed by **Osama bin Laden**, crashed three planes into the buildings, killing themselves, passengers, and thousands of individuals. A fourth plane crash-landed in rural Pennsylvania. The final death toll was more than 3,000, with many firefighters and police officers in New York City among those killed.

Using remote bases in Afghanistan, bin Laden had earlier declared holy war on the United States and Israel and recruited as many as 20,000 Muslim militants to carry out attacks and prepare for war. The Bush administration immediately formed a coalition of nations and launched **Operation Enduring Freedom** to locate the terrorists and overthrow the **Taliban** regime in Afghanistan that sheltered them. Less than two months later, the Taliban government collapsed, but coalition forces had yet to find bin Laden.

Antiterrorism at Home

As the military campaign progressed in Afghanistan, concern that terrorists would launch further attacks on American soil led to significant federal action. President Bush created a new federal agency, the **Office of Homeland Security**, along with another agency within the office called the Transportation Security Administration, which assumed responsibility for screening airline passengers. The controversial **USA Patriot Act** was passed by Congress. Its goals were to strengthen the authority of U.S. law enforcement agencies and to fight terrorist acts at home and in foreign nations. The act stated the following:

- Suspected terrorists could be tried in military tribunals with a much lower standard for a burden of proof than in a civilian court.
- FBI agents could obtain warrants to review library or bookstore records of individuals.
- Wiretaps could be authorized more easily for use on suspected terrorists.

While civil liberties advocates expressed concern about potential abuses and racial profiling, most Americans initially supported these agencies and the Patriot Act.

The Bush Doctrine

President Bush announced a new national security doctrine in September 2002 that specifically addressed terrorism. While containment and deterrence had been the chief doctrines of the Cold War, Bush proposed that preemptive military action against terrorists and those that harbor terrorists should be the focus of American foreign policy.

Iraq quickly emerged as the focus of the **Bush Doctrine** in the Middle East after Saddam Hussein resisted UN attempts to search for biological and chemical weapons and flouted numerous UN sanctions and resolutions. Bush warned that if the UN did not respond, the United States would act alone. On March 19, 2003, after announcing that diplomatic efforts had failed and that evidence of the existence of weapons of mass destruction had been found, the United States and Great Britain launched **Operation Iraqi Freedom**, an air and ground assault of more than 300,000 troops across the Saudi border into Iraq. Six weeks after the initial bombing, allied troops had occupied Baghdad and most of the country and defeated the Iraqi army, and Bush declared that the mission had been accomplished.

Iraqi Insurgency

U.S. forces captured Saddam Hussein on December 13, 2003. After being turned over to the Iraqi government in June 2004, Saddam faced trial and on November 5, 2006, was found guilty of crimes against humanity and sentenced to death by hanging. On December 30, 2006, Saddam was hanged.

Securing the peace in Iraq needed more time. Early attempts at establishing a democratic government were difficult because Shi'ite and Sunni Muslim Iraqis disagreed on power sharing, as did the ethnic Kurds in the north of the country. No weapons of mass destruction—a primary reason for going to war—were found. Iraqi insurgents, angered by the American presence, launched almost daily suicide car bombings and roadside ambushes of U.S. soldiers and the newly trained Iraqi military and police forces. By May 2007, more than 3,500 American troops had been killed. The federal budget and military resources were strained by the continuing campaign to defeat the insurgency, and many Americans called for a complete withdrawal from Iraq.

The Election of 2004

While concern about American involvement in Iraq caused President Bush's approval rating to decline, the Democratic presidential nominee, Senator John Kerry of Massachusetts, a Vietnam veteran who had helped organize Vietnam Veterans Against the War in the 1970s, proved to be an ineffective campaigner as the Republicans retained the White House by the narrowest margin won by any incumbent president.

Hurricane Katrina

In August 2005, **Hurricane Katrina** slammed into the Gulf Coast, flooding large sections of low-lying cities and towns. More than 500,000 New Orleans residents were displaced, and widespread looting forced officials to declare martial law. The Federal Emergency Management Administration (FEMA) proved unable to deal with providing basic services to the Gulf Coast. The Bush administration was criticized heavily for its lack of response and coordination of relief efforts, and the FEMA director resigned. One of the worst natural disasters in American history, Katrina caused at least 1,800 deaths and more than $80 billion in damages.

TIMELINE: 1989–2005

1989	Students begin pro-democracy demonstrations in China.
	Berlin Wall falls.
	Panamanian dictator Manuel Noriega is arrested by U.S. troops.

1990	Saddam Hussein of Iraq invades Kuwait.
1991	Operation Desert Storm ends Iraq's occupation of Kuwait.
	Soviet Union breaks up as the Cold War ends.
1992	William J. Clinton is elected president, defeating George H. W. Bush and Ross Perot.
1994	North American Free Trade Agreement (NAFTA) is approved.
1995	U.S. and NATO forces enforce peace in Bosnia.
1996	Clinton defeats Bob Dole for the presidency.
1999	Clinton is acquitted following impeachment.
2000	George W. Bush defeats Al Gore in disputed election.
2001	Al Qaeda hijackers crash planes into World Trade Center towers and the Pentagon.
	The United States invades Afghanistan to overthrow Taliban government.
	Patriot Act gives the United States broad powers to investigate terrorism.
2003	The United States invades Iraq following Saddam Hussein's defiance of UN resolutions.
2004	Bush defeats John Kerry for the presidency.
2005	Hurricane Katrina devastates Gulf Coast areas of Mississippi and Louisiana.

MAJOR FIGURES

George W. Bush. The forty-third president of the United States, Bush took power following the disputed election of 2000. He achieved a 271–266 victory in the Electoral College, despite losing the popular vote to Democrat Al Gore. The suicide attacks on the Pentagon and the World Trade Center on September 11, 2001, changed the course of Bush's presidency, as he focused on attempting to defeat the Islamic extremist group Al Qaeda, capture its leader Osama bin Laden, and overthrow the Taliban leaders in Afghanistan. Following Iraqi dictator Saddam Hussein's repeated refusals to allow UN weapons inspectors to search sites in Iraq, American and British troops bombed and invaded Iraq in March 2003. Although defeating Saddam's forces proved to be relatively easy, securing peace in Iraq proved to be extremely difficult as sectarian fighting and insurgent attacks prevented political and economic recovery. Bush defeated John Kerry in 2004 but faced increasing opposition from inside and outside his party during his second term over the deteriorating situation in Iraq.

William Jefferson (Bill) Clinton. Elected president in 1992 and then again in 1996, Clinton achieved several domestic and foreign successes even as personal scandals marred his presidency and eventually lead to his impeachment trial for perjury and obstruction of justice in 1999. Clinton pushed through legislative initiatives that approved a major welfare bill and the North America Free Trade Agreement (NAFTA) and presided over a long period of economic growth that provided a balanced budget and government surpluses. His second term was tarnished with several financial and sexual scandals, although he left the White House with an approval rating of 65 percent, the highest of any post–World War II president.

Al Gore. U.S. vice president from 1993 to 2001 and unsuccessful Democratic candidate for president in 2000, Gore defeated George W. Bush by 540,000 popular votes but lost the state of Florida by 537 votes, thus giving Bush the Electoral College victory. A 5–4 Supreme Court decision (*Bush v. Gore*) ruled that any further recounts of Florida ballots would violate state law, and Bush was declared the official winner of the presidential race in December 2000.

Saddam Hussein. Iraqi dictator Saddam Hussein fought the United States in two Persian Gulf Wars, in 1991 and 2003. The first conflict, which resulted in the American-led Desert Storm, followed Saddam's invasion of neighboring Kuwait. Air strikes and a land invasion by coalition troops forced an Iraqi surrender four days after the invasion in February 1991. Saddam remained in power until 2003 when U.S. forces again invaded Iraq to search for weapons of mass destruction. Saddam's forces were overrun, and he was eventually captured, tried, and convicted for war crimes by an Iraqi court. He was executed in 2006.

Osama bin Laden. Saudi leader of the Al Qaeda Islamic extremist group, bin Laden claimed responsibility for the attacks of September 11, 2001, which resulted in the deaths of more than 3,000 Americans. In return for providing financial support for the Taliban leaders of Afghanistan, bin Laden was given sanctuary and was allowed to establish training camps. Repeated U.S. military attempts to capture him have proven unsuccessful.

Monica Lewinsky. A former White House intern in the Clinton administration, Lewinsky admitted to having several sexual encounters with the president. Her revelations of the affair contributed to Clinton's impeachment because his testimony under oath contradicted her sworn testimony to special investigator Kenneth Starr.

Slobodan Milosevic. The president of Serbia and later Yugoslavia, Milosevic helped negotiate the Dayton Accords, which settled the Croatian War in 1995. He later approved the invasion of Kosovo by Serbian troops to ethnically cleanse the region of Muslim Albanians, which led to mass murders, rapes, and the forced resettlement of thousands. Following NATO air strikes in 1999, Milosevic withdrew Serbian troops. He was later forced from power, arrested, and then tried for war crimes and genocide at an international tribunal in The Hague. He died in prison in 2006 before completion of the trial.

Manuel Noriega. A Panamanian dictator who ruled with support from the United States from 1983 to 1989, Noriega was ousted from his position by U.S. forces after rigging a presidential election in 1989. Following a standoff between Panamanian and American troops, President Bush ordered an invasion of Panama and the capture of Noriega. Noriega eventually surrendered in 1990 and was tried and convicted in an American court for drug trafficking and racketeering. In 1992, he was sentenced to forty years in federal prison.

Boris Yeltsin. The first president of the newly formed Russian Federation, Yeltsin took power in 1991 after a struggle in the Kremlin. As the Soviet Union disintegrated over the next few months, Yeltsin replaced Gorbachev, who officially resigned as president on December 25, 1991.

PART II

AP U.S. HISTORY PRACTICE EXAMS

AP U. S. HISTORY ANSWER SHEET — PRACTICE EXAM 1

1. Ⓐ Ⓑ Ⓒ Ⓓ Ⓔ Ⓕ
2. Ⓐ Ⓑ Ⓒ Ⓓ Ⓔ Ⓕ
3. Ⓐ Ⓑ Ⓒ Ⓓ Ⓔ Ⓕ
4. Ⓐ Ⓑ Ⓒ Ⓓ Ⓔ Ⓕ
5. Ⓐ Ⓑ Ⓒ Ⓓ Ⓔ Ⓕ
6. Ⓐ Ⓑ Ⓒ Ⓓ Ⓔ Ⓕ
7. Ⓐ Ⓑ Ⓒ Ⓓ Ⓔ Ⓕ
8. Ⓐ Ⓑ Ⓒ Ⓓ Ⓔ Ⓕ
9. Ⓐ Ⓑ Ⓒ Ⓓ Ⓔ Ⓕ
10. Ⓐ Ⓑ Ⓒ Ⓓ Ⓔ Ⓕ
11. Ⓐ Ⓑ Ⓒ Ⓓ Ⓔ Ⓕ
12. Ⓐ Ⓑ Ⓒ Ⓓ Ⓔ Ⓕ
13. Ⓐ Ⓑ Ⓒ Ⓓ Ⓔ Ⓕ
14. Ⓐ Ⓑ Ⓒ Ⓓ Ⓔ Ⓕ
15. Ⓐ Ⓑ Ⓒ Ⓓ Ⓔ Ⓕ
16. Ⓐ Ⓑ Ⓒ Ⓓ Ⓔ Ⓕ
17. Ⓐ Ⓑ Ⓒ Ⓓ Ⓔ Ⓕ
18. Ⓐ Ⓑ Ⓒ Ⓓ Ⓔ Ⓕ
19. Ⓐ Ⓑ Ⓒ Ⓓ Ⓔ Ⓕ
20. Ⓐ Ⓑ Ⓒ Ⓓ Ⓔ Ⓕ
21. Ⓐ Ⓑ Ⓒ Ⓓ Ⓔ Ⓕ
22. Ⓐ Ⓑ Ⓒ Ⓓ Ⓔ Ⓕ
23. Ⓐ Ⓑ Ⓒ Ⓓ Ⓔ Ⓕ
24. Ⓐ Ⓑ Ⓒ Ⓓ Ⓔ Ⓕ
25. Ⓐ Ⓑ Ⓒ Ⓓ Ⓔ Ⓕ
26. Ⓐ Ⓑ Ⓒ Ⓓ Ⓔ Ⓕ
27. Ⓐ Ⓑ Ⓒ Ⓓ Ⓔ Ⓕ
28. Ⓐ Ⓑ Ⓒ Ⓓ Ⓔ Ⓕ
29. Ⓐ Ⓑ Ⓒ Ⓓ Ⓔ Ⓕ
30. Ⓐ Ⓑ Ⓒ Ⓓ Ⓔ Ⓕ
31. Ⓐ Ⓑ Ⓒ Ⓓ Ⓔ Ⓕ
32. Ⓐ Ⓑ Ⓒ Ⓓ Ⓔ Ⓕ
33. Ⓐ Ⓑ Ⓒ Ⓓ Ⓔ Ⓕ
34. Ⓐ Ⓑ Ⓒ Ⓓ Ⓔ Ⓕ
35. Ⓐ Ⓑ Ⓒ Ⓓ Ⓔ Ⓕ
36. Ⓐ Ⓑ Ⓒ Ⓓ Ⓔ Ⓕ
37. Ⓐ Ⓑ Ⓒ Ⓓ Ⓔ Ⓕ
38. Ⓐ Ⓑ Ⓒ Ⓓ Ⓔ Ⓕ
39. Ⓐ Ⓑ Ⓒ Ⓓ Ⓔ Ⓕ
40. Ⓐ Ⓑ Ⓒ Ⓓ Ⓔ Ⓕ
41. Ⓐ Ⓑ Ⓒ Ⓓ Ⓔ Ⓕ
42. Ⓐ Ⓑ Ⓒ Ⓓ Ⓔ Ⓕ
43. Ⓐ Ⓑ Ⓒ Ⓓ Ⓔ Ⓕ
44. Ⓐ Ⓑ Ⓒ Ⓓ Ⓔ Ⓕ
45. Ⓐ Ⓑ Ⓒ Ⓓ Ⓔ Ⓕ
46. Ⓐ Ⓑ Ⓒ Ⓓ Ⓔ Ⓕ
47. Ⓐ Ⓑ Ⓒ Ⓓ Ⓔ Ⓕ
48. Ⓐ Ⓑ Ⓒ Ⓓ Ⓔ Ⓕ
49. Ⓐ Ⓑ Ⓒ Ⓓ Ⓔ Ⓕ
50. Ⓐ Ⓑ Ⓒ Ⓓ Ⓔ Ⓕ
51. Ⓐ Ⓑ Ⓒ Ⓓ Ⓔ Ⓕ
52. Ⓐ Ⓑ Ⓒ Ⓓ Ⓔ Ⓕ
53. Ⓐ Ⓑ Ⓒ Ⓓ Ⓔ Ⓕ
54. Ⓐ Ⓑ Ⓒ Ⓓ Ⓔ Ⓕ
55. Ⓐ Ⓑ Ⓒ Ⓓ Ⓔ Ⓕ
56. Ⓐ Ⓑ Ⓒ Ⓓ Ⓔ Ⓕ
57. Ⓐ Ⓑ Ⓒ Ⓓ Ⓔ Ⓕ
58. Ⓐ Ⓑ Ⓒ Ⓓ Ⓔ Ⓕ
59. Ⓐ Ⓑ Ⓒ Ⓓ Ⓔ Ⓕ
60. Ⓐ Ⓑ Ⓒ Ⓓ Ⓔ Ⓕ
61. Ⓐ Ⓑ Ⓒ Ⓓ Ⓔ Ⓕ
62. Ⓐ Ⓑ Ⓒ Ⓓ Ⓔ Ⓕ
63. Ⓐ Ⓑ Ⓒ Ⓓ Ⓔ Ⓕ
64. Ⓐ Ⓑ Ⓒ Ⓓ Ⓔ Ⓕ
65. Ⓐ Ⓑ Ⓒ Ⓓ Ⓔ Ⓕ
66. Ⓐ Ⓑ Ⓒ Ⓓ Ⓔ Ⓕ
67. Ⓐ Ⓑ Ⓒ Ⓓ Ⓔ Ⓕ
68. Ⓐ Ⓑ Ⓒ Ⓓ Ⓔ Ⓕ
69. Ⓐ Ⓑ Ⓒ Ⓓ Ⓔ Ⓕ
70. Ⓐ Ⓑ Ⓒ Ⓓ Ⓔ Ⓕ
71. Ⓐ Ⓑ Ⓒ Ⓓ Ⓔ Ⓕ
72. Ⓐ Ⓑ Ⓒ Ⓓ Ⓔ Ⓕ
73. Ⓐ Ⓑ Ⓒ Ⓓ Ⓔ Ⓕ
74. Ⓐ Ⓑ Ⓒ Ⓓ Ⓔ Ⓕ
75. Ⓐ Ⓑ Ⓒ Ⓓ Ⓔ Ⓕ
76. Ⓐ Ⓑ Ⓒ Ⓓ Ⓔ Ⓕ
77. Ⓐ Ⓑ Ⓒ Ⓓ Ⓔ Ⓕ
78. Ⓐ Ⓑ Ⓒ Ⓓ Ⓔ Ⓕ
79. Ⓐ Ⓑ Ⓒ Ⓓ Ⓔ Ⓕ
80. Ⓐ Ⓑ Ⓒ Ⓓ Ⓔ Ⓕ

PRACTICE EXAM 1

AP* U.S. HISTORY
SECTION I: MULTIPLE-CHOICE QUESTIONS

Time—55 minutes
80 Questions

Directions: The questions or incomplete statements below are followed by five possible answers or completions. After selecting the one that is best in each case, fill in the corresponding oval on the answer sheet.

1. Before 1763, the policy of salutary neglect practiced by Great Britain toward the colonies had the express purpose of

(A) establishing a favorable balance of trade between Great Britain and the colonies and stopping trade on the black market
(B) paying off debt incurred from supplying British troops during the French and Indian War
(C) raising funds to support colonial expansion westward across the Appalachian Mountains
(D) preventing a colonial independence movement
(E) letting many of the British laws slide while attempting to keep the colonies economically and politically subordinate to Great Britain

2. Bacon's Rebellion occurred primarily as a result of

(A) tidewater dissatisfaction with Governor Berkeley and his enforcement of the Navigation Acts
(B) tidewater discontent with Governor Berkeley's repressive administrative policies
(C) backcountry fears that Governor Berkeley's uncompromising Indian policy would lead to an Indian attack on settlers
(D) backcountry discontent with Governor Berkeley's Indian policy
(E) the failure of Governor Berkeley's administration to seat any backcountry settlers on the ruling council

3. All of the following accurately describe the emergence of political parties in the United States EXCEPT:

(A) The origin of the two parties can be traced to the debate between strict constructionists and loose constructionists
(B) Federalists and Antifederalists differed mostly in their views about whether power should rest in state governments or in a strong central power
(C) Geographically, Federalists were generally centered in the Northeast, while the Antifederalists were centered in the more agrarian South
(D) George Washington's administration actually favored the creation of political parties because Washington vowed to uphold the political ideals of the original framers of the Constitution
(E) The opposition political party during Washington's presidency effectively used the media to draw supporters to its cause

4. Andrew Jackson opposed the recharter of the Second Bank of the United States for all of the following reasons EXCEPT:

(A) He felt the bank was unconstitutional
(B) He felt that the bank actually hurt western interests and was monopolistic
(C) He realized the Whigs were using the bank as a political tool against him
(D) He personally disliked the bank's president, Nicholas Biddle
(E) He felt that the bank was no longer popular

GO ON TO THE NEXT PAGE.

*AP is a registered trademark of the College Board, which was not involved in the production of, and does not endorse, this product.

5. A muckraker would most likely be interested in
   (A) the founding of settlements similar to Hull House
   (B) a meatpacking plant with serious labor and production problems
   (C) farmers' economic interests
   (D) a labor shortage caused by strikes
   (E) the free coinage of silver

6. Despite the passage of the Thirteenth, Fourteenth, and Fifteenth Amendments after the Civil War, many Southern governments hindered the rights of freedmen by passing laws known as
   (A) sharecropper regulations
   (B) carpetbagger laws
   (C) Jim Crow laws
   (D) scalawag laws
   (E) former slave laws

7. In 1899, U.S. Secretary of State John Hay proposed a major initiative with the Open Door policy by stating the
   (A) desire to increase Latin American trade with the United States
   (B) desire to promote more open trade with Mexico after the annexation of Texas and the Mexican-American War
   (C) desire to overthrow the Spanish government in Cuba and in the Philippines
   (D) desire to open ports in China for American businesses competing with other nations in an effort to create a sphere of influence for everyone involved
   (E) desire to lower tariffs on imports

8. Richard Nixon resigned from the presidency in August 1974 primarily due to
   (A) the unpopularity of his Vietnam War policies
   (B) his role in planning and overseeing the original Watergate break-in in June 1972
   (C) his role in the coverup of the expanding Watergate crisis
   (D) criticism of his firing of Special Prosecutor Archibald Cox during the Saturday Night Massacre
   (E) the publication of the Pentagon Papers by the *New York Times*

9. Literature written during the Great Depression tended to focus on the themes of
   (A) fear and anxiety prevalent in society
   (B) excitement and optimism that "happy days" indeed were here again
   (C) disillusionment and cynicism about society in general
   (D) anger and hatred toward the government
   (E) faith and prayer as promoted by Father Charles Coughlin's weekly inspirational messages

10. The phenomenon of the baby boom was a result of all of the following EXCEPT
   (A) a sexual revolution in the 1950s
   (B) a decline in the infant mortality rate
   (C) a rise in general prosperity following the end of World War II
   (D) an increase in the fertility rate in the 1950s
   (E) the promotion of conservative views of women and their role in the family

11. After the House of Burgesses was established in Jamestown in 1619, what event occurred in the colony within the next few months?
   (A) The Pilgrims set sail to the New World.
   (B) Jamestown was founded.
   (C) Tobacco was first cultivated.
   (D) African slaves first arrived in the colonies.
   (E) A rebellion erupted between indentured servants and the elite landowners in the tidewater region.

GO ON TO THE NEXT PAGE.

12. The basic difference between the Constitution and the Articles of Confederation was that the Constitution
    (A) created a much stronger national government
    (B) reserved powers explicit to the states
    (C) created a "loose confederation of states"
    (D) protected civil liberties with written guarantees
    (E) retained the single-house legislature system already in use

13. After the phrase "manifest destiny" was coined, it was ultimately used to justify
    (A) state and federal government subsidies of canal construction
    (B) regulation of railroad companies in interstate trade disputes
    (C) extension of the doctrine of popular sovereignty to newly admitted territories and states in the land acquired in the Mexican cession
    (D) forced removal of Native American populations to western lands in what would become the Oklahoma Territory
    (E) the Free-Soil Party platform of territorial settlement without restrictions

14. The 1848 Seneca Falls Convention included discussion about all of the following EXCEPT
    (A) the sanctioning of a woman's right to hold political office
    (B) the involvement of women in the antislavery movement
    (C) the liberalization of divorce laws
    (D) the need to reform laws affecting the property rights of women
    (E) universal suffrage

15. The Treaty of Tordesillas (1494)
    (A) sought to prevent conflict between French and English colonization efforts in the Western Hemisphere
    (B) was an agreement that divided the newly discovered New World between Spain and Portugal
    (C) gave most of the Western Hemisphere to Portugal
    (D) ended all disputes between European nations concerning colonies in the Western Hemisphere
    (E) was issued by Pope Alexander VI

16. Frederick Douglass spoke in favor of all of the following EXCEPT
    (A) sending freed slaves back to Africa
    (B) women's suffrage
    (C) ending slavery once and for all
    (D) supporting civil rights for Black people
    (E) his work on the publication of *The North Star*

17. The Platt Amendment in 1901
    (A) provided support for the civil war in the Philippines
    (B) opened up trade relations with China
    (C) established diplomatic relations with Japan
    (D) restricted Cuban sovereignty by giving the United States the right to intervene in Cuban foreign affairs
    (E) secured land for the construction of the Panama Canal

18. The Ku Klux Klan (KKK) of the 1920s differed from the earlier Klan of the Reconstruction era because
    (A) it banned lynching
    (B) it was now a secret society dedicated to White supremacy
    (C) it concentrated its practices solely in the South
    (D) it banned the use of white robes and hoods
    (E) in addition to increased hostilities toward Black people, it also targeted Catholic and Jewish immigrants from southern and eastern Europe

GO ON TO THE NEXT PAGE.

19. Winston Churchill created the term "iron curtain" to address
    (A) the repression of democratic freedoms in Eastern Europe
    (B) impending elections in Poland
    (C) Stalin's non-negotiable demands at Potsdam
    (D) the Soviet-imposed dividing line separating Eastern Europe from the West
    (E) the U.S. monopoly on nuclear technology at the end of World War II

20. In 1964, the alleged attack by the North Vietnamese against U.S. naval ships in the Gulf of Tonkin resulted in
    (A) President Johnson asking Congress for a formal declaration of war against North Vietnam
    (B) Congress requesting that the president immediately withdraw all American troops from the region
    (C) the United States launching secret bombing raids against Cambodia and North Vietnam
    (D) Congress passing a resolution granting the president the necessary authority to escalate military involvement in Vietnam as needed
    (E) plans for a nuclear strike against North Vietnam

21. John Winthrop's description of the Massachusetts Bay Colony as being like a "city on a hill" is related to the Puritan founder's idea that the colony should be
    (A) a refuge for all religious dissenters
    (B) located on a healthful site
    (C) a model for the world as a "holy commonwealth"
    (D) located in an easily defensible area
    (E) a religious community with a unique work ethic

22. Colonists began to use the rallying cry of "no taxation without representation" in an effort to openly protest against all of the following legislative acts of Parliament EXCEPT
    (A) the Stamp Act
    (B) the Sugar Act
    (C) the Declaratory Act
    (D) the Townshend Duties
    (E) the Intolerable Acts

23. Secretary of the Treasury Alexander Hamilton's proposed financial policy for the new government was designed to
    (A) increase the amount and types of currency in circulation
    (B) protect the infant southern cotton industry from unfair competition from Great Britain
    (C) establish a credible credit policy for the country and stimulate the economic growth of new manufacturing in the states
    (D) create new opportunities for northern manufacturers to export their goods to England
    (E) generate higher revenue from duties

24. Andrew Jackson's response to the Supreme Court ruling about the forced removal of the Cherokee people from their tribal lands demonstrated that
    (A) even the president of the United States was bound to enforce the rulings of the Supreme Court
    (B) the Supreme Court didn't have the authority to declare the Cherokee an "independent nation"
    (C) Jackson believed the Supreme Court was the ultimate authority in enforcing its rulings
    (D) the rulings of the Supreme Court rely on enforcement by the president
    (E) Jackson didn't believe that the Supreme Court had the final authority to interpret the constitutionality of laws in the country

GO ON TO THE NEXT PAGE.

25. In the presidential election of 2000,

(A) Republican George W. Bush won the popular vote by more than 500,000 votes
(B) Democrat Al Gore won a narrow victory in the Electoral College
(C) the Supreme Court decided 5–4 that Florida's ballots should not be recounted, thus assuring the election of Bush
(D) third-party candidate Ralph Nader had no significant impact on the election
(E) the House of Representatives elected Bush, as no candidate had a majority of electoral votes

26. Between 1880 and 1920, the United States experienced a dramatic wave of immigration that was encouraged by all of the following EXCEPT

(A) intense population and socioeconomic pressures in Europe
(B) the spread of pogroms and discrimination against Jews in eastern Europe
(C) the efforts of "political machines" that encouraged immigrants to remain in the large cities
(D) the hopes of European peasants from southern and eastern Europe, who were eager to begin a new life with opportunities in America
(E) the great Oklahoma land rush of 1889

27. The significance of the *Plessy v. Fergusson* Supreme Court case in 1898 was that it

(A) abolished the Jim Crow laws in the South
(B) upheld only a portion of the Jim Crow laws
(C) allowed for the policy of "separate but equal" to be used to discriminate against Black people
(D) ruled that separate was "not equal"
(E) allowed segregation for a limited time in the South

28. During the 1920s, all of the following items were important issues to the general public in the United States EXCEPT

(A) the corruption scandals of the Harding administration
(B) the halting of German reparations payments to France and Great Britain
(C) prohibition of alcohol and enforcement of regulations
(D) limits on immigration
(E) the possibility of Al Smith becoming the first Catholic president

29. The Marshall Plan was a significant piece of Cold War strategy by the United States designed to

(A) use massive economic assistance to rebuild European countries after World War II, in order to promote political stability
(B) provide funds for scientific research for the H-bomb
(C) aggressively promote democratic reforms in Latin America and the Middle East
(D) control nuclear technology and place it under the control of the United Nations energy commission
(E) provide military assistance to countries fighting Communist uprisings

30. The 1963 publication of Betty Friedan's *Feminine Mystique* called for women to

(A) work hard to continue to live up to their popular image as wives, mothers, and homemakers
(B) pursue other interests and opportunities in life and not be bound to their domestic roles
(C) denounce the passage of the Equal Rights Amendment (ERA)
(D) use their newfound status in society to work for social reform and to run for political office
(E) enter the work force in large numbers

GO ON TO THE NEXT PAGE.

31. When the Albany Congress convened in 1754, Benjamin Franklin took the opportunity to propose
    (A) a common postal system for the colonies
    (B) a new alliance with France
    (C) a trade system to connect the colonies
    (D) a defensive plan of union for the colonies
    (E) a taxation system to counter British taxation policies

32. All of the following are true about the colonial policy of nonimportation of British goods EXCEPT:
    (A) The Daughters of Liberty used it as an important step in their resistance movement
    (B) It appealed to a growing community of people involved in the resistance movement
    (C) It was mostly symbolic rather than a successful tool against British policies
    (D) It added to the growing independence movement
    (E) It added to the growing discontent with "virtual representation"

33. All of the following are true about the outcomes of the Second Great Awakening EXCEPT:
    (A) It fueled social activism among its followers
    (B) It urged followers to reach a personal, emotional understanding of God
    (C) It had a broad appeal to a wide range of people
    (D) It emphasized gradual spiritual growth as promoted by trained preachers
    (E) It increased the growth and popularity of Protestant groups, including Methodists and Baptists

34. The major focus of the Monroe Doctrine was
    (A) reinforcing the fact that the United States wouldn't get directly involved in European conflicts
    (B) protecting Latin America from additional conquests by European powers
    (C) opening up the ports of Asia to trade with the United States
    (D) laying the initial groundwork for a transcontinental railroad
    (E) warning the British away from their Canadian holdings in the Oregon country

35. John Brown's abolitionist activities in the years leading up to the Civil War can best be described as
    (A) ways to promote the capture and return of escaped slaves
    (B) evidence that the debate over slavery could turn explosive and violent
    (C) the focal point of the Lincoln-Douglas debates in 1858
    (D) a model of the type of civil disobedience encouraged by Henry David Thoreau
    (E) representative of the antislavery opinions favored by many Northerners at the time

36. All of the following were results of the Spanish-American War in 1898 EXCEPT
    (A) the addition of the Roosevelt Corollary to the Monroe Doctrine
    (B) the Supreme Court ruling that unincorporated possessions, such as Puerto Rico, didn't have to be considered for statehood
    (C) Spain was no longer in control of Cuba
    (D) renewed interest in building a canal in the Panama region
    (E) interest in establishing a very strong naval presence in the Pacific and Atlantic Ocean regions

GO ON TO THE NEXT PAGE.

37. The most obvious motivation behind the request by Americans in Hawaii for annexation to the United States was

(A) economic self-interest
(B) patriotic nationalism
(C) protection from European powers
(D) protection from hostile native Hawaiians
(E) the Hawaiian queen Liliuokalani's support

38. How would you compare the Progressive Movement of the early 1900s with the Reform Movement in the mid-1800s?

(A) The progressives were still largely unsuccessful in achieving a measure of success with their reform efforts.
(B) Since the Progressive Movement sprang from the American reform tradition, its assumptions and goals were identical to those of earlier movements.
(C) Progressive reformers were much more individualistic than earlier reformers.
(D) Earlier movements had been limited to political reform, while the progressives concentrated on social and economic reforms.
(E) Unlike earlier reformers, progressives thought of the government as a major ally.

39. When President Wilson was lobbying for ratification of the Treaty of Versailles, he firmly believed the most important element to be

(A) the redistribution of German territory
(B) the establishment of the new country of Poland to serve as a buffer state between Germany and Russia
(C) the plan for a League of Nations
(D) the scheduled plan for German war reparations payments
(E) German disarmament and Allied occupation

40. "I believe that it must be the policy of the United States to support free peoples who are resisting attempted subjugation by armed minorities or by outside pressures. I believe that we must assist free people to work out their own destinies in their own way. I believe that our help should be primarily through economic and financial aid which is essential to economic stability and orderly political processes."

The statement above is taken from

(A) Wilson's request for a declaration of war against Germany in 1917
(B) Hoover's statement on Japanese aggression in China in 1931
(C) a joint statement by the United States, Great Britain, and France about the Spanish Civil War in 1936
(D) Franklin Roosevelt's request for a declaration of war against Japan in 1941
(E) Truman's request for funds to support Greece and Turkey against communism in 1947

41. The First Great Awakening in the 1730s resulted in

(A) the separation of colonial Protestants from the Anglican Church
(B) the appeal of religious revival to a broader group of people including women, African Americans, and Native Americans
(C) the exclusion of women from revival meetings
(D) increased training of clergy members
(E) increased intolerance of religious dissent

42. Which of the following countries allied itself with the United States' fight against Great Britain in 1778, providing the Americans with much-needed military assistance?

(A) Prussia
(B) France
(C) Spain
(D) the Dutch Republic
(E) Italy

GO ON TO THE NEXT PAGE.

43. The earliest human visitors to North America came from

(A) Africa
(B) South Pacific Islands
(C) Asia
(D) Scandinavia
(E) Palestine

44. In *Marbury v. Madison*, Chief Justice Marshall of the Supreme Court established the principle that

(A) Native Americans can have redress in the federal courts
(B) a president can exercise executive privilege in foreign policy
(C) interstate commerce can be regulated only by the national government
(D) only the federal judiciary can decide what is constitutional
(E) judicial review was limited to this particular case

45. The War of 1812 is considered a significant turning point in American foreign policy because

(A) the United States began its policy of manifest destiny
(B) the War Hawks in the South and West were able to gain wide support for the war
(C) the United States entered a new period in which European events no longer shaped American domestic and foreign policies
(D) the European nations agreed to a newfound cooperation with the United States
(E) the United States pursued a more aggressive foreign policy stance

46. The Populist Party promoted the silver standard in its party platform in 1896 for all of the following reasons EXCEPT:

(A) The issue was the focus of William Jennings Bryan and his "Cross of Gold" speech
(B) The issue appealed to prominent industrialists and bankers, securing even broader support for the party
(C) The party hoped to gain the support of silver-mine owners
(D) Farmers widely supported the idea, hoping to generate mild inflation to help in the credit crisis
(E) The Populist supporters wanted to win, and they thought the silver issue would help elect the first Populist presidential candidate

47. The declaration from the Federal Census Office about the census report from 1890, along with Frederick Jackson Turner's frontier thesis in 1893, were significant because

(A) most Americans lived in big cities
(B) northern Europeans had again begun to exceed the number of immigrants from southern and eastern Europe
(C) the reservation policy had completely resettled all Native Americans to a productive life on reservations
(D) America continued to be a country dominated by the overwhelming majority of its population who resided in rural and small urban settings
(E) the frontier line no longer existed in the West, symbolizing the closing of the frontier

48. The presidents of the Progressive Era (Roosevelt, Taft, and Wilson) promoted ideas about the role of the federal government that brought back which old philosophical beliefs from earlier administrations?

(A) States' rights
(B) A strong centralized government to control operations
(C) A decentralized central government
(D) The Bank of the United States
(E) Strict interpretation of the Constitution

GO ON TO THE NEXT PAGE.

49. Many of the New Deal programs that Franklin Roosevelt favored were based on economic policies originating with John Maynard Keynes' theories that stated
   (A) government spending could help revive a failing economy
   (B) a government should encourage consumers to spend money in order to "prime the pump" in a slumping economy
   (C) the government should encourage consumers to save their money by investing it in the banks
   (D) a failing economy would eventually revive if the government simply stood by and waited long enough for the system to work itself out
   (E) the government should be cautious about spending too much money on economic programs that haven't been tested

50. After the unanimous Supreme Court ruling in the *Brown v. Board of Education* case, which required schools to desegregate with "all deliberate speed," southern states reacted by denying funding to school districts working to desegregate and by
   (A) boycotting public buses throughout the South
   (B) having the ruling overturned on an appeal two years later
   (C) not allowing Black people into all-White schools
   (D) calling in National Guard troops to assist various schools in their desegregation efforts
   (E) immediately complying with the Court's ruling

51. Someone involved in the Halfway Covenant in a Puritan church would
   (A) become a limited member by being baptized without a conversion experience
   (B) go from being an Old Light to a New Light
   (C) no longer have alien residence status in the community
   (D) not have to attend church every Sunday
   (E) be allowed to participate in colonial politics to a limited degree

52. The pre-Columbian mound-building culture of Cahokia was located near the present-day city of
   (A) Seattle
   (B) Phoenix
   (C) Mexico City
   (D) Houston
   (E) St. Louis

53. Henry Clay's American System promoted
   (A) sectionalism
   (B) nationalism
   (C) individualism
   (D) international trade
   (E) rivalries between the North and South

54. The 1973 Supreme Court decision in *Roe v. Wade*
   (A) concluded there is no right to privacy protected in the Constitution
   (B) assumed that life begins at conception
   (C) declared that the rights of the mother supercede those of the fetus during the first three months of pregnancy
   (D) was opposed by Presidents Nixon, Ford, and Reagan
   (E) approved most state laws restricting abortions

55. The impeachment of Andrew Johnson was motivated mainly by the fact that
   (A) he had committed gross "high crimes and misdemeanors" as president
   (B) he was at odds with the radical Republicans in Congress over the plans for Reconstruction
   (C) the Republicans were trying to force him to resign rather than removing him by the Senate trial
   (D) he had failed to appoint a Republican vice president
   (E) Johnson failed to fully investigate the assassination of Abraham Lincoln

GO ON TO THE NEXT PAGE.

56. A major difference between W. E. B. Du Bois' message and that of Booker T. Washington centered on

(A) the use of White politicians to gain support for Black causes in the struggle for equality
(B) the focus on economic equality alone
(C) the reliance on education alone to combat racial injustice
(D) the appeal to the Talented Tenth
(E) the focus on voting rights for Black people

57. The Supreme Court ruling in the case of *Schechter Poultry Corporation v. U.S.* was significant because

(A) it reversed an earlier decision in the *U.S. v. Butler* case
(B) it found the National Industrial Recovery Act (NIRA) unconstitutional because it involved a dispute over the right of the federal government to control a business exclusively engaged in intrastate commerce
(C) it upheld the government's action in trade control in both interstate and intrastate trade
(D) it upheld the constitutionality of the Agricultural Adjustment Association (AAA)
(E) it supported the 1906 Pure Food and Drug Act

58. The United Nations was created in 1945 in order to

(A) rebuild the economies of European nations and Japan after the end of World War II
(B) prosecute war crimes from World War II
(C) halt Communist expansion in Eastern Europe
(D) collect war reparations from the World War II Axis powers
(E) maintain global peace through collective security

59. Students for a Democratic Society was primarily founded as

(A) a group of college students who supported Richard Nixon and the so-called silent majority in the 1968 election
(B) an organization that promoted leftist politics in America, openly opposing the war in Vietnam and favoring racial equality in the United States
(C) a group working for the reelection campaign of President Johnson early in 1968
(D) an organization of students in Eastern Europe promoting democratic reforms
(E) a group of students openly opposed to Richard Nixon and Lyndon Johnson

60. During Jimmy Carter's term as president, all of the following events occurred EXCEPT

(A) Iranians holding Americans from the U.S. Embassy in Tehran hostage for 444 days
(B) an increase in the promotion of human rights issues in U.S. foreign policy
(C) double-digit inflation, a rise in interest rates, and a general slowdown in the economy
(D) growing popular confidence in the ideals of limitless economic opportunities for Americans and democratic freedom in the world
(E) improved relations between Israel and Egypt

61. Indentured servants in the British colonies of North America

(A) often became plantation owners after they earned their freedom
(B) moved to the New England colonies after serving their labor terms
(C) were mostly Africans
(D) bound themselves to work on a plantation for a set number of years
(E) were mostly orphaned adolescents and criminals

GO ON TO THE NEXT PAGE.

62. The impact of the panic of 1837
    (A) worked against the Whig Party's chances in the 1840 election
    (B) was traceable to Jackson's actions as president but was blamed on President Van Buren (Martin Van "Ruin")
    (C) had little effect on the working class
    (D) was ended by the specie circular
    (E) was not affected by economic conditions in Europe

63. The Republican agenda in Congress in 1862–1863 included passage of all of the following EXCEPT
    (A) the Homestead Act
    (B) the Morrill Land Grant Act
    (C) the Pacific Railroad Act
    (D) the National Bank Act
    (E) the Military Provision Act

64. Compared with the North, what was the rate of industrialization in the South after the end of the Civil War?
    (A) Industry began to gradually develop in the South, but it lagged far behind industrial growth in the North well into the twentieth century.
    (B) Southerners generally feared its potentially adversarial effects on agriculture.
    (C) The South failed to industrialize after the Civil War.
    (D) Infant industries in the South quickly developed into advanced manufacturing plants that within twenty years surpassed those in the North.
    (E) The South quickly became the industrial leader in the country because of the rapid increase in trade and the accessibility to ports in the South for shipping.

65. The political cartoon is titled "Every Dog (No Distinction Of Color) Has His Day, Red Gentleman to Yellow Gentleman—Pale face 'fraid you crowd him out, as he did me."

    This cartoon most likely would be used to support
    (A) Chinese labor in California only
    (B) the Gentleman's Agreement
    (C) the influx of immigrants to the United States who had been exiled from China and used as forced labor to work on the transcontinental railroad
    (D) the establishment of Chinatown as a place for Chinese immigrants to live and work separately from other people in San Francisco
    (E) the Chinese Exclusion Act

GO ON TO THE NEXT PAGE.

66. A progressive politician's aims would have dealt with all of the following items EXCEPT

(A) the implementation of direct primaries
(B) the establishment of a graduated income tax
(C) the promotion of unregulated big businesses
(D) the conservation of the nation's natural resources
(E) the regulation of interstate railroad rates

67. The political cartoon above illustrates Herbert Hoover's position on the question of relief for people hurt by the effects of the depression by claiming that

(A) it was the responsibility of the federal government to provide economic security for U.S. citizens
(B) citizens should look to local and state governments for assistance because the federal government was too busy with other matters
(C) the unemployed should be drafted into the military
(D) the federal government would appoint a commission to study possibilities for assistance
(E) businesses were encouraged to assist those in need by providing more jobs for the unemployed

68. Which of the following became the foundation for the affirmative action programs that established quotas and favorable policies for minorities and women?

(A) The Voting Rights Act of 1965
(B) The decision in the *Roe v. Wade* court case in 1972
(C) The Civil Rights Act of 1964
(D) The *Brown v. Board of Education* ruling in 1954
(E) The Nineteenth Amendment to the Constitution, ratified in 1920

69. All of the following events sparked further fear that the Cold War was spreading EXCEPT

(A) the launching of Sputnik by the USSR in 1957
(B) the development of an ICBM by the Russians
(C) the United States' entry into the space race
(D) the development and testing of the hydrogen bomb by the United States and the USSR
(E) the U.S. troops' victory at the Bay of Pigs invasion in Cuba

70. Reagan's economic program, nicknamed "Reaganomics," generated criticism that

(A) claimed tax increases would stifle economic recovery
(B) supply-side economics had run its course
(C) a huge federal deficit would only be passed on to future generations
(D) a huge tax cut was necessary to kick-start the economy
(E) Reagan was following the same economic programs started by Jimmy Carter and Gerald Ford

71. The colonial legislatures' "power of the purse" was negated by passage of the

(A) Townshend Duties
(B) Stamp Act
(C) Tea Act
(D) Currency Act
(E) Sugar Act

GO ON TO THE NEXT PAGE.

72. One of the major issues between the United States and England in the early 1800s was impressment. This meant that the British were

(A) imposing outrageous tariffs on American products
(B) keeping posts in the Great Lakes in violation of the 1783 Treaty of Paris
(C) seizing American ships and cargo going to France and keeping them in port
(D) removing men from American ships and putting them into British naval service
(E) drafting Americans for a two-year period of service aboard British ships

73. Under the terms of the Treaty of Guadalupe Hidalgo in 1848, the United States

(A) promised to respect Mexican sovereignty in the future
(B) gained Texas and Oregon
(C) agreed to continue Mexico's ban on slavery in the Southwest
(D) gained the New Mexico and upper California regions of the Southwest
(E) firmly established the boundaries of the state of Texas

74. All of the following were elements of the Progressive Reform Movement EXCEPT

(A) immigration limits
(B) limits on labor unions' power
(C) muckraker exposés
(D) regulation of medicines and foods
(E) breaking up monopolies

75. The Iran-contra scandal of the Reagan administration

(A) involved selling weapons to Iran and using the profits to aid the pro-American contras in Nicaragua
(B) was a secret U.S. military attempt to invade Iran
(C) was an effort to assist Iraq in its war with Iran
(D) sent cash donations from the CIA directly to the contras
(E) ended the Iranian hostage crisis that began in 1979

76. Black men drafted by the U.S. military for service in World War I were typically

(A) trained but not called up for active duty; they were held as reservists
(B) treated with respect by civilian society in the United States
(C) placed on the front lines in the trenches
(D) fully integrated with White troops for the first time in U.S. military history
(E) placed in segregated units, usually commanded by White soldiers

77. The passage of the Sheppard-Towner Act in 1921 was significant because

(A) it was the first bill aimed at reducing childbirth mortality rates and infant mortality rates
(B) it provided federal funding of highway construction
(C) it was one of many bills aimed at limiting the actions of labor unions in response to the Red Scare
(D) it provided for management and regulation of the stock market
(E) it began the process of immigrant restriction during the decade of the 1920s

78. The first talking motion picture was

(A) Snow White
(B) Gone with the Wind
(C) Birth of a Nation
(D) The Jazz Singer
(E) Steamboat Willie

GO ON TO THE NEXT PAGE.

79. Executive Order 9066 issued by President Franklin Roosevelt in February 1942

(A) established German POW camps in the United States
(B) established a new nuclear policy after World War II
(C) established Japanese relocation camps
(D) established the policy to rebuild Germany after World War II
(E) established the guidelines of the Atlantic Charter

80. During the 1970s, the two major oil news stories were the OPEC oil embargo, resulting in a sharp increase in oil prices, and

(A) a legislative battle between conservatives and liberals over drilling rights on the continental shelf
(B) the construction of the Alaska pipeline
(C) the U.S. dependence on Mexican oil reserves
(D) the Teapot Dome scandal involving the sale of naval oil reserves
(E) the oil drilling crisis in the Gulf of Mexico

END OF SECTION 1

AP* U.S. HISTORY
SECTION II
Time—2 hours and 10 minutes

Percent of total grade—50

General Instructions

Reading Period—15 minutes: All students should read and plan their answer to Part A, Question 1, the document-based essay question. If time permits, they may also read the essay questions in Part B and Part C.

Part A Suggested writing time—45 minutes: All students must answer Question 1.
Part B Suggested planning and writing time—35 minutes: Answer ONE question from Part B.
Part C Suggested planning and writing time—35 minutes: Answer ONE question from Part C.

Section II of this examination requires answers in essay form. The supervisor will announce the time for starting and ending the Reading Period. To help you use your time efficiently, the supervisor will also announce the time at which the writing for Part A should be completed. Be careful not to exceed the writing time suggested for Part A. If you do, you may endanger your grade on the whole examination. If you finish writing Part A before time is announced, you may go on to plan and write Part B. If you finish the examination in less than the time allotted, you may go back and work on either Part A, Part B, or Part C. Keep in mind that in an essay you should pay attention to the organization of your material, the validity and clarity of your general statements, and the intelligent and appropriate use of facts to support your generalizations.

You should write your answers with a pen, preferably one with black or dark blue ink. Be sure to write CLEARLY and LEGIBLY. Cross out any errors you make.

GO ON TO THE NEXT PAGE.

AP U.S. HISTORY
SECTION II
PART A
(Suggested planning and writing time—45 minutes)

Percent of Section II score—45

Directions: The following question is based on the accompanying Documents A–J. (Some of the documents have been edited for the purpose of this excercise.) Write your answer on the lined pages of the essay booklet.

This question is designed to test your ability to work with historical documents. As you analyze the documents, take into account both the sources of the documents and the authors' points of view. Write an essay on the following topic that integrates your analysis of the documents. Do not simply summarize the documents individually. You may refer to relevant historical facts and developments not mentioned in the documents.

1. "From 1820 to 1860, the concept of manifest destiny played a major role not only in the imagination of Americans but also in American politics."

   Evaluate the main arguments for American territorial expansion from 1820 to 1860 and the impact they had on the nation leading up to the Civil War.

Document A

Source: Walt Whitman, editorial, *Brooklyn Daily Eagle*, July 7, 1846

We love to indulge in thoughts of the future extent and power of this Republic—because with its increase is the increase of human happiness and liberty . . . What has miserable, inefficient Mexico—with her superstition, her burlesque upon freedom, her actual tyranny by the few over the many—what has she to do with the great mission of peopling the New World with a noble race? Be it ours, to achieve that mission! Be it ours to roll down all of the upstart leaven of old despotism, that comes our way!

GO ON TO THE NEXT PAGE.

Document B

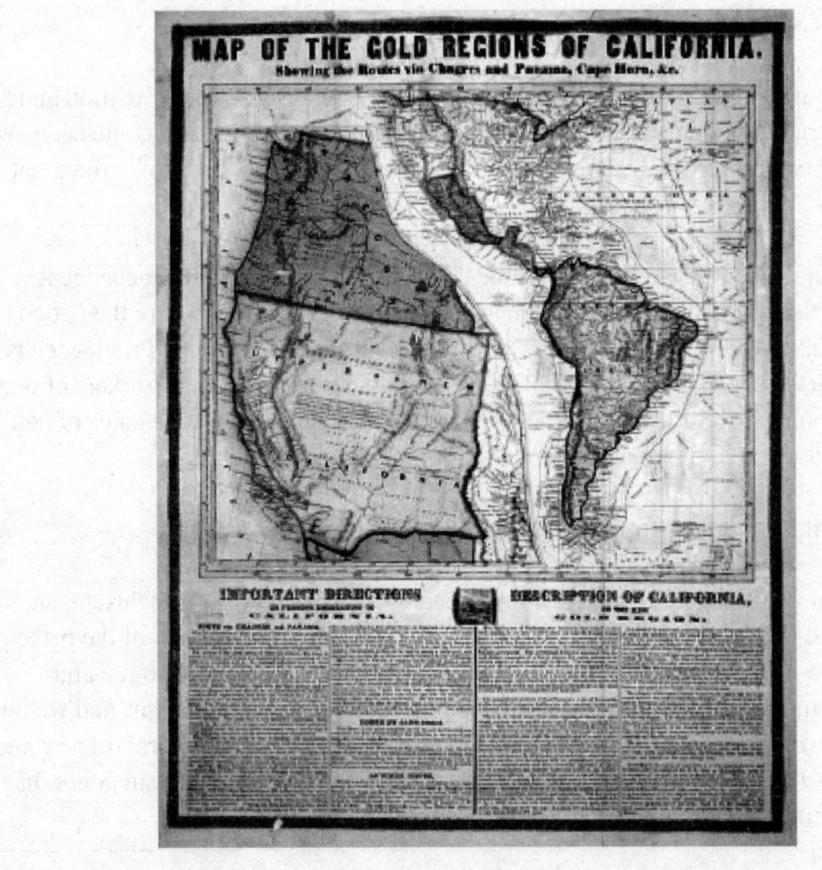

Document C

Source: The Wilmot Proviso, 1846

Provided, territory from That, as an express and fundamental condition to the acquisition of any the Republic of Mexico by the United States, by virtue of any treaty which may be negotiated between them, and to the use by the Executive of the moneys herein appropriated, neither slavery nor involuntary servitude shall ever exist in any part of said territory, except for crime, whereof the party shall first be duly convicted . . .

GO ON TO THE NEXT PAGE.

Document D

Source: John L. O'Sullivan on *Manifest Destiny*, 1839

On the contrary, our national birth was the beginning of a new history, the formation and progress of an untried political system, which separates us from the past and connects us with the future only . . . we may confidently assume that our country is destined to be the great nation of futurity.

We are entering on its untrodden space, with the truths of God in our minds, beneficent objects in our hearts, and with a clear conscience unsullied by the past. We are the nation of human progress, and who will, what can, set limits to our onward march? Providence is with us, and no earthly power can. We point to the everlasting truth on the first page of our national declaration, and we proclaim to the millions of other lands, that "the gates of hell"—the powers of aristocracy and monarchy—"shall not prevail against it."

The far-reaching, the boundless future will be the era of American greatness . . .

Yes, we are the nation of progress, of individual freedom, of universal Enfranchisement. . . . We must onward to the fulfillment of our mission—to the entire development of the principle of our organization—freedom of conscience, freedom of person, freedom of trade and business pursuits, universality of freedom and equality. This is our high destiny, and we must accomplish it. All this will be our future history, to establish on earth the moral dignity and salvation of man—the immutable truth and beneficence of God. Who, then, can doubt that our country is destined to be *the great nation* of futurity?

Document E

Source: Abraham Lincoln's "Spot Resolution," 1848

Let the President answer the interrogations I proposed, as before mentioned, or some other similar ones. Let him answer fully, fairly and candidly. Let him answer with facts and not with arguments . . . And, if, so answering, he can show us that the soil was ours where the first blood of the war was shed . . .

GO ON TO THE NEXT PAGE.

Document F

Source: United States Congress. Joint Resolution for the Admission of the State of Texas into the Union

[No. 1.]—Joint Resolution for the Admission of the State of Texas into the Union.

WHEREAS the Congress of the United States, by a joint resolution approved March the first, eighteen hundred and forty-five, did consent that the territory properly included within, and rightfully belonging to, the Republic of Texas, might be erected into a new State, to be called The State of Texas, with a republican form of government, to be adopted by the people of said republic, by deputies in convention assembled, with the consent of the existing government, in order that the same might be admitted as one of the States of the Union; which consent of Congress was given upon certain conditions specified in the first and second sections of said joint resolution; and whereas the people of the said Republic of Texas, by deputies in convention assembled, with the consent of the existing government, did adopt a constitution, and erect a new State with a republican form of government, and, in the name of the people of Texas, and by their authority, did ordain and declare that they assented to and accepted the proposals, conditions, and guaranties contained in said first and second sections of said resolution; and whereas the said constitution, with the proper evidence of its adoption by the people of the Republic of Texas, has been transmitted to the President of the United States and laid before Congress, in conformity to the provisions of said joint resolution:

Therefore—

Resolved by the Senate and House of Representatives of the United States of America in Congress assembled, That the State of Texas shall be one, and is hereby declared to be one, of the United States of America, and admitted into the Union on an equal footing with the original States in all respects whatever.

SEC. 2. And it be it further resolved, That until the representatives in Congress shall be apportioned according to an actual enumeration of the inhabitants of the United States, the State of Texas shall be entitled to choose two representatives.

APPROVED, December 29, 1845.

GO ON TO THE NEXT PAGE.

Document G

Source: Free-Soil party platform, 1848

"We inscribe on our banner, 'Free Soil, Free Speech, Free Labor, and Free Men,' and under it we will fight on, and fight ever until a triumphant victory shall reward our exertions."

Resolved, That we accept the issue which the slave power has forced upon us; and to their demand for more slave states and more slave territory, our calm but final answer is: No more slave states and no more slave territory. Let the soil of our extensive domain be kept free for the hardy pioneers of our own land and the oppressed and banished of other lands seeking homes of comfort and fields of enterprise in the new world.

Resolved, That it is the duty of the federal government to relieve itself from all responsibility for the existence or continuance of slavery wherever the government possesses constitutional power to legislate on that subject, and is thus responsible for its existence.

Resolved, That the true and, in the judgment of this convention, the only safe means of preventing the extension of slavery into territory now free is to prohibit its extension in all such territory by an act of Congress.

Document H

Source: "The Elephant"—http://www.goldrush.com/~joann/elephant.htm

I think that I may without vanity affirm that I have "seen the elephant."—Louisa Clapp

To forty-niners and those following, no expression characterized the California gold rush more than the words "seeing the elephant." Those planning to travel west announced they were "going to see the elephant." Those turning back claimed they had seen the "elephant's tracks" or the "elephant's tail," and confessed they'd seen more than enough of the animal.

The expression predated the gold rush, arising from a tale current when circus parades first featured elephants. A farmer, so the story went, hearing that a circus was in town, loaded his wagon with vegetables for the market there. He had never seen an elephant and very much wished to. On the way to town, he encountered the circus parade, led by an elephant. The farmer was thrilled. His horses, however, were terrified. Bolting, they overturned the wagon and ruined the vegetables. "I don't give a hang," the farmer said, "for I have seen the elephant."

For gold rushers, the elephant symbolized both the high cost of their endeavor—the myriad possibilities for misfortune on the journey or in California--and, like the farmer's circus elephant, an exotic sight, and unequaled experience, the adventure of a lifetime.

GO ON TO THE NEXT PAGE.

Document I

Source: Polk's Request for War with Mexico, 1846

Washington, May 11, 1846

To the Senate and House of Representatives: The existing state of the relations between the United States and Mexico renders it proper that I should bring the subject to the consideration of Congress. In my message at the commencement of your present session the estate of these relations, the causes which led to the suspension of diplomatic intercourse between the two countries in March, 1845, and the long-continued and unredressed wrongs and injuries committed by the Mexican Government on the citizens of the United States in their persons and property were briefly set forth.

The strong desire to establish peace with Mexico on liberal and honorable terms, and the readiness of this Government to regulate and adjust our boundary and other causes of difference with that power on such fair and equitable principles as would lead to permanent relations of the most friendly nature, induced me in September last to seek the reopening of diplomatic relations between the two countries. Every measure adopted on our part had for its object the furtherance of the desired results. In communicating to Congress a succinct statement of the injuries which we had suffered from Mexico, and which have been accumulating during a period of more than twenty years, every expression that could tend to inflame the people of Mexico or defeat or delay a pacific result was carefully avoided. An envoy of the United States repaired to Mexico with full powers to adjust every existing difference. But though present on the Mexican soil by agreement between the two governments, invested with full powers, and bearing evidence of the most friendly dispositions, his mission has been unavailing. The Mexican government not only refused to receive him or listen to his propositions, but after a long-continued series of menaces have at last invaded our territory and shed the blood of our fellow-citizens on our own soil.

GO ON TO THE NEXT PAGE.

Document J

Source: John Gast, *American Progress*, 1872.

END OF DOCUMENTS FOR QUESTION 1

GO ON TO THE NEXT PAGE.

AP U.S. HISTORY
SECTION II
Part B and Part C
(Suggested planning and writing time—70 minutes)

Percent of Section II score—55

Part B

Directions: Choose ONE question from this section. The suggested writing time for this question is 30 minutes. You are advised to spend 5 minutes planning your answer in the area below. Reference historical evidence in support of your generalizations and make sure you present your arguments clearly and logically.

2. Social and political tension illustrated growing problems in colonial America. Choose *three* of the following and discuss the impact each one had on colonial society from the mid-1630s to the 1770s.

   Halfway Covenant

   Bacon's Rebellion

   Salem witchcraft trials

   Albany Plan of Union

   Boston Massacre

3. John Marshall served as chief justice of the Supreme Court for thirty-five years, from 1801 to 1836. In what ways did his rulings in the following court cases help establish the power of the Supreme Court? Choose *three* of the following court cases to illustrate your answer.

   Marbury v. Madison (1803)

   Dartmouth College v. Woodward (1819)

   McCulloch v. Maryland (1819)

   Gibbons v. Ogden (1824)

   Cherokee Nation v. Georgia (1831) and *Worcester v. Georgia* (1832)

GO ON TO THE NEXT PAGE.

Part C

Directions: Choose ONE question from this section. The suggested writing time for this question is 30 minutes. You are advised to spend 5 minutes planning your answer in the area below. Reference historical evidence in support of your generalizations and make sure you present your arguments clearly and logically.

4. To what extent did life in the Roaring Twenties create a national culture? Use examples from the decade of the 1920s to illustrate your answer.

5. Some people have claimed that impeachment has been used as a political tool of one political party against the political party in power. Assess the validity of this statement with respect to the impeachment of Andrew Johnson and the impeachment proceedings against Richard Nixon.

STOP

END OF EXAM

PRACTICE EXAM 1: ANSWER KEY

No.	Answer	Right	Wrong	No.	Answer	Right	Wrong	No.	Answer	Right	Wrong
1	E	__	__	27	C	__	__	54	D	__	__
2	D	__	__	28	B	__	__	55	B	__	__
3	D	__	__	29	A	__	__	56	D	__	__
4	E	__	__	30	B	__	__	57	B	__	__
5	B	__	__	31	D	__	__	58	E	__	__
6	C	__	__	32	C	__	__	59	B	__	__
7	D	__	__	33	D	__	__	60	D	__	__
8	C	__	__	34	A	__	__	61	D	__	__
9	C	__	__	35	B	__	__	62	B	__	__
10	A	__	__	36	A	__	__	63	E	__	__
11	D	__	__	37	A	__	__	64	A	__	__
12	A	__	__	38	E	__	__	65	E	__	__
13	C	__	__	39	C	__	__	66	C	__	__
14	A	__	__	40	E	__	__	67	B	__	__
15	B	__	__	41	B	__	__	68	C	__	__
16	A	__	__	42	B	__	__	69	E	__	__
17	D	__	__	43	C	__	__	70	C	__	__
18	E	__	__	44	D	__	__	71	A	__	__
19	D	__	__	45	C	__	__	72	D	__	__
20	D	__	__	46	B	__	__	73	D	__	__
21	C	__	__	47	E	__	__	74	B	__	__
22	E	__	__	48	B	__	__	75	A	__	__
23	C	__	__	49	A	__	__	76	E	__	__
24	D	__	__	50	C	__	__	77	A	__	__
25	C	__	__	51	A	__	__	78	D	__	__
26	C	__	__	52	E	__	__	79	C	__	__
				53	B	__	__	80	B	__	__

HOW TO CALCULATE YOUR SCORE

Section I: Muliple Choce

[________ - ¼ × ________] × 1.125 = ________

Number Correct (out of 80)	Number Wrong	Multiple-Choice Score	Weighted Section I Score (Do not round.)

Section II: Free Response

4.50 × ________ = ________

Question 1 (0-9 ponts) — Question 1 Weighted Score

2.75 × ________ = ________

Question 2 (0-9 ponts) — Question 2 Weighted Score

2.75 × ________ = ________

Question 3 (0-9 ponts) — Question 3 Weighted Score

________ + ________ + ________ = ________

Question 1 Weighted Score	Question 2 Weighted Score	Question 3 Weighted Score	Weighted Section II Score (Do not round)

Composite Score

________ + ________ = ________

Weighted Section I Score	Weighted Section II Score	Composite Score (Round to the nearest whole #.)

Composite Score*	AP Grade	Interpretation
114-180	5	extremely well qualified
91-113	4	well qualified
70-94	3	qualified
49-73	2	possibly qualified
0-48	1	no recommendation

*Each year the Development Committee determines the formulas used to calculate the raw composite scores. The Chief Faculty Consultant determines how the composite scores fit into the 5-point AP scale.

SECTION I: MULTIPLE CHOICE

1. **E** Political Institutions, Behavior & Public Policy: Pre-Columbian–1789 *Fact*
Salutary neglect was the lax enforcement of British trade laws in the colonies. For nearly a century, Great Britain used this trade policy with the colonies while it dealt with problems in Europe. This all changed with King George in 1763.

2. **D** Social Change, Cultural & Intellectual Developments: Pre-Columbian–1789 *Fact*
Governor Berkeley wanted to avoid dealing with problem with Native Americans on the frontier, and he sought to limit the fur trade to keep skirmishes with Native Americans to a minimum. This upset the settlers along the frontier, or backcountry.

3. **D** Political Institutions, Behavior & Public Policy: 1790–1914 *Except*
George Washington felt that political parties were divisive factions. During his first term in office, disagreements over strict and loose interpretations of the Constitution led to the formation of the Federalists and the Antifederalists.

4. **E** Political Institutions, Behavior & Public Policy: 1790–1914 *Except*
Jackson was a farmer and also a Westerner. He felt that the bank practices were hurting western farmers, and he vowed to destroy the bank because it was "killing him." Some felt that the bank served a purpose, but Jackson was out to destroy it regardless of what others thought.

5. **B** Social Change, Cultural & Intellectual Developments: 1790–1914 *Fact*
Muckrakers were journalists who wrote about abuses during the Progressive Era. This is a reference to Upton Sinclair and his novel *The Jungle.*

6. **C** Social Change, Cultural & Intellectual Developments: 1790–1914 *Fact*
As the North retreated from the South and from Reconstruction, Southerners were free to write new laws restricting freedmen in the South. These new Jim Crow laws began a nearly century-long rise of segregation throughout the South.

7. **D** Diplomacy and International Relations: 1790–1914 *Fact*
The Open Door policy sought to give the United States an opportunity to open up markets for trade in China. Many European nations, along with Japan, had already claimed spheres of influence in trade in China.

8. **C** Political Institutions, Behavior & Public Policy: 1915–Present *Fact*
Richard Nixon became the first president to resign the office as a result of his participation in a coverup of the break-in of the Watergate complex. He resigned before the Senate could begin impeachment hearings.

9. **C** Social Change, Cultural & Intellectual Developments: 1915–Present *Trend*
Literature written during the 1930s, such as *The Grapes of Wrath*, tended to portray disillusionment and cynicism about conditions in society. A general feeling of hopelessness and despair was prevalent in many sectors of society.

10. **A** Social Change, Cultural & Intellectual Developments: 1915–Present *Except*
The sexual revolution didn't occur until a decade later in the 1960s. This change stemmed from altered relationships between women and men. The women's liberation movement and an increase in reproductive choices and sexual expression influenced women in the 1960s.

11. **D** Social Change, Cultural & Intellectual Developments: Pre-Columbian–1789 *Fact*
The first slaves arrived in Jamestown in 1619.

12. **A** Political Institutions, Behavior & Public Policy: Pre-Columbian–1789 *Fact*
The Constitution created a strong federal government with power divided among three branches of government, attempting to address the failure of the weak central government under the Articles of Confederation.

13. **C** Social Change, Cultural & Intellectual Developments: 1790–1914 *Fact*
During the decade of the 1850s, as people moved westward into the new lands acquired in the Mexican cession and the Kansas-Nebraska territories, popular sovereignty became the major political element surrounding the issue of slavery expansion. Popular sovereignty would allow for the people living in an area to decide on the issue of slavery.

14. **A** Social Change, Cultural & Intellectual Developments: 1790–1914 *Except*
Women weren't allowed to participate in politics. The Declaration of Sentiments stated women's desire for equal treatment in a male-dominated society. It also included the idea of universal suffrage.

15. **B** Diplomacy and International Relations: Pre-Columbian–1789 *Fact*
The Treaty of Tordesillas followed the Papal Decree of Demarcation (1493) issued by Pope Alexander VI and essentially divided the undiscovered world between Spain and Portugal.

16. **A** Social Change, Cultural & Intellectual Developments: 1790–1914 *Except*
Frederick Douglass was one of the most outspoken abolitionists of his time. He wanted freedom for all Black people and felt that America was their home now. He was publisher of *The North Star* as well as a speaker for abolition.

17. **D** Political Institutions, Behavior & Public Policy: 1790–1914 *Except*
The United States was successful in getting Spain out of Cuba in 1898 and in guaranteeing Cuban independence. The United States retained its right to "intervene" in Cuban foreign affairs when it felt a need to "protect" Cuba and Cuban interests. The United States also established a naval base at Guantanamo Bay, which is still operational today.

18. **E** Social Change, Cultural & Intellectual Developments: 1915–Present *Fact*
The Ku Klux Klan (KKK) extended its White supremacist movement to target not only Black people but also Catholics and Jewish immigrants as "unAmerican."

19. **D** Diplomacy and International Relations: 1915–Present *Fact*
The iron curtain became the dividing line between Communist Eastern Europe and the free West following the end of World War II.

20. **D** Diplomacy and International Relations: 1915–Present *Fact*
War was never actually declared in Vietnam. The Gulf of Tonkin Resolution allowed the president to escalate U.S. military action in the region as needed. As a result of President Johnson's actions in Vietnam, the War Powers Act was passed in 1973, dramatically curtailing the power of a president when ordering military intervention.

21. **C** Social Change, Cultural & Intellectual Developments: Pre-Columbian–1789 *Fact*
John Winthrop, founder of the Massachusetts Bay Colony, intended it to be a "city on a hill" as a model of Christian living for the rest of the world.

22. **E** Social Change, Cultural & Intellectual Developments: Pre-Columbian–1789 *Except*
The Intolerable Acts closed the port of Boston in retaliation for the colonists' actions in the Boston Tea Party.

23. **C** Economic Developments: 1790–1914 *Fact*
Alexander Hamilton was concerned about getting the young United States on a sound economic standing, especially with foreign countries. His economic policies included repaying debt, establishing a favorable credit standing with foreign nations, and founding the Bank of the United States to control the financial actions of the federal government.

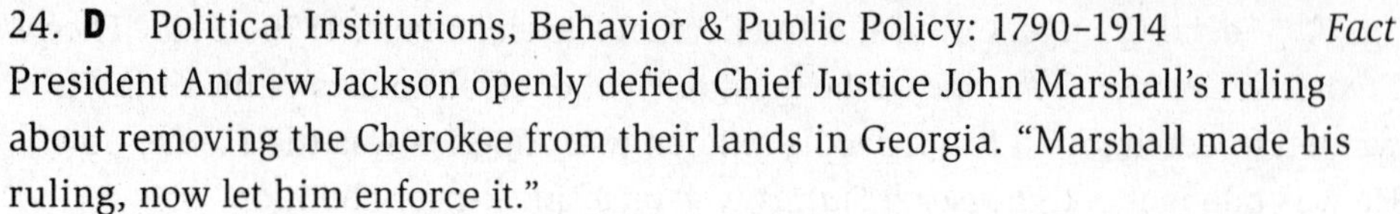

24. **D** Political Institutions, Behavior & Public Policy: 1790–1914 *Fact*
President Andrew Jackson openly defied Chief Justice John Marshall's ruling about removing the Cherokee from their lands in Georgia. "Marshall made his ruling, now let him enforce it."

25. **C** Social Change, Cultural & Intellectual Developments: 1915–Present *Fact*
The presidential election of 2000 marked the fourth time a candidate who received the most popular votes was not made president (Andrew Jackson in 1824, Samuel Tilden in 1876, and Grover Cleveland in 1888).

26. **C** Social Change, Cultural & Intellectual Developments: 1790–1914 *Except*
There was no political effort to keep recent immigrants in the large cities. Political machines took advantage of large immigrant populations who had settled in cities to work in factories for big businesses, but many immigrants also settled out West.

27. **C** Social Change, Cultural & Intellectual Developments: 1790–1914 *Fact*
This court case allowed for segregation according to the doctrine of "separate but equal." Facilities could segregate as long as there were facilities provided for both White and Black people. The case allowed for a policy of segregation in the South until it was overturned by the 1954 *Brown v. Board of Education* case.

28. **B** Diplomacy and International Relations: 1915–Present *Except*
Although the government endorsed the Dawes Plan—devised by American banker Charles G. Dawes in 1924—to scale back U.S. demands for debt payments and reparations, the general public seemed more concerned about domestic issues than foreign affairs. People were extremely disillusioned about war and sought to isolate themselves from it.

29. **A** Diplomacy and International Relations: 1915–Present *Fact*
In an effort to keep communism from expanding its influence on a weakened Western Europe after World War II, the United States developed a multibillion-dollar aid package, known as the Marshall Plan, to rebuild the economies of Western Europe.

30. **B** Social Change, Cultural & Intellectual Developments: 1915–Present *Fact*
The book urged women not to be bound by society's traditional roles. It literally urged liberation for women by encouraging them to pursue other interests and opportunities.

31. **D** Political Institutions, Behavior & Public Policy: Pre-Columbian–1789 *Fact*
Benjamin Franklin proposed the Albany Plan of Union in 1754 for colonial defense, but the colonists weren't interested or ready to unite because they saw no purpose in working together at this time. Franklin's proposal is important, however, as it signified the beginning thoughts of the colonies unifying under one central government. In 1754, though, the colonies were wary of any federal influence that would seem to limit the freedom they currently enjoyed.

32. **C** Social Change, Cultural & Intellectual Developments: Pre-Columbian–1789 *Except*
The colonial boycotts arranged by the colonists proved to be a very successful tool against Great Britain, as colonists pledged to each other not to purchase goods with duties on them. It also united the colonists against a common enemy. All other answer choices are correct.

33. **D** Social Change, Cultural & Intellectual Developments: 1790–1914 *Fact*
The Second Great Awakening in the 1820s and 1830s encouraged immediate spiritual growth through a personal relationship with God. People were free to come to God on their own and experience salvation.

34. **A** Diplomacy and International Relations: 1790–1914 *Fact*
The United States would stay out of European conflicts, and Europe would no longer involve itself in political conflicts in the Western Hemisphere. The United States wouldn't intervene in any European conflicts until World War I, when America entered the war in 1917 on the side of the Allies.

35. **B** Social Change, Cultural & Intellectual Developments: 1790–1914 *Fact*
Events in Kansas, the Pottawatomie massacre, and the raid at Harpers Ferry proved that the debate over slavery could turn explosive and violent.

36. **A** Diplomacy and International Relations: 1790–1914 *Except*
Roosevelt developed his "Big Stick" policy to deal with affairs in the Caribbean and in Latin America in 1904, a few years after the Spanish-American War.

37. **A** Political Institutions, Behavior & Public Policy: 1915–Present *Fact*
Economic self-interest in the sugar and pineapple trade in Hawaii motivated U.S. actions to make it a territory.

38. **E** Social Change, Cultural & Intellectual Developments: 1790–1914 *Fact*
Progressive reformers looked to local, state, and federal government as a major ally in using legislation to change society.

39. **C** Diplomacy and International Relations: 1915–Present *Fact*
President Wilson was firmly convinced of the need for a League of Nations to secure the future peace of the world and to prevent another world war from occurring.

40. **E** Diplomacy and International Relations: 1915–Present *Fact*
President Truman began his policy of containment by trying to prevent any further spread of communism. He did this with massive economic aid to assist countries in resisting communism.

41. **B** Social Change, Cultural & Intellectual Developments: Pre-Columbian–1789 *Fact*
The religious revival during the First Great Awakening appealed to many people, especially women, African Americans, and Native Americans.

42. **B** Diplomacy and International Relations: Pre-Columbian–1789 *Fact*
The alliance with France during the American Revolution was a major turning point in the war for the Americans.

43. **C** Social Change, Cultural & Intellectual Developments: Pre-Columbian–1789 *Fact*
Virtually all scholars agree the first humans came to the Americas in several migrations via the land bridge in the Bering Sea between Siberia and Alaska.

44. **D** Political Institutions, Behavior & Public Policy: 1790–1914 *Fact*
This court case established the precedent of judicial review—that the Supreme Court could rule a law unconstitutional. John Marshall was significant in this case as well because he was one of the midnight judge appointments made by outgoing President John Adams. Adams appointed Marshall, a Federalist, as chief justice of the Supreme Court.

45. **C** Diplomacy and International Relations: 1790–1914 *Fact*
After the War of 1812, which some historians call the Second Revolutionary War, the United States proved to itself that it could stand up to foreign intervention. After this war, the United States began to focus primarily on internal affairs and generally remained out of European conflicts until World War I.

46. **B** Economic Developments: 1790–1914 *Except*
Business leaders favored a single gold standard. They opposed the silver standard because of the inflationary and economically destabilizing effects a silver standard would have on the country.

47. **E** Social Change, Cultural & Intellectual Developments: 1790–1914 *Fact*
Both the 1890 census and Turner's foreign thesis were significant in symbolizing the closing of the frontier in American history. Since early colonial times, America had always been defined by having a frontier—land out west—that spurred exploration and settlement.

48. **B** Political Institutions, Behavior & Public Policy: 1790–1914 *Fact*
The presidents during the Progressive Era were strong leaders who thought the federal government should increase its role in the lives of Americans. Roosevelt developed the Square Deal program, Taft developed Dollar Diplomacy, and Wilson developed the New Freedom program.

49. **A** Economic Developments: 1915–Present *Fact*
Keynes believed that to "prime the pump" during an economic downturn, a government should spend money on programs that would get the economy on the right track of recovery and growth.

50. **C** Social Change, Cultural & Intellectual Developments: 1915–Present *Fact*
Many states in the South resisted the Supreme Court's unanimous ruling to integrate "with all deliberate speed." Many schools stalled or took steps to prevent Black people from integrating the schools. Violence over this issue erupted in Little Rock, Arkansas, in 1957.

51. **A** Social Change, Cultural & Intellectual Developments: Pre-Columbian–1789 *Fact*
Because of declining church membership, Puritans sought to allow more people to be baptized and to join the church while they awaited a conversion experience in what was known as the Halfway Covenant, attempted to bring the unconverted halfway to a conversion experience and to the protection in the church.

52. **E** Social Change, Cultural & Intellectual Developments: Pre-Columbian–1789 *Fact*
The Cahokia settlement was established by the Mississippi mound-building culture near the present-day city of St. Louis, Missouri.

53. **B** Social Change, Cultural & Intellectual Developments: 1790–1914 *Fact*
Henry Clay sought to promote nationalism with his proposal for the American System of internal improvements in 1816. It ushered in the "Era of Good Feelings," a postwar euphoria that swept the nation. After the victory at the Battle of New Orleans and at the end of the War of 1812, people were ready to focus on the growth of the United States.

54. **D** Political Institutions, Behavior & Public Policy: 1915–present *Fact*
Republican presidents Nixon, Ford, and Reagan all opposed the 1973 *Roe v. Wade* decision that permitted states to approve abortions in many instances.

55. **B** Political Institutions, Behavior & Public Policy: 1790–1914 *Fact*
President Andrew Johnson was at odds with the radical Republicans in Congress over the terms of Reconstruction. Johnson felt the president should dictate the terms of Reconstruction, while Congress felt it should do so.

56. **D** Social Change, Cultural & Intellectual Developments: 1915–Present *Fact*
Washington argued that Black people should concentrate all their energies on industrial education in proving their worth to society. Du Bois promoted the concept of higher education for a Talented Tenth of Blacks who, through their knowledge of modern culture, could guide other Black people into a higher standard of living in a White society.

57. **B** Political Institutions, Behavior & Public Policy: 1915–Present *Fact*
This court case was significant because it ruled the NIRA New Deal program unconstitutional on the grounds that the government had overstepped its bounds in regulating business actions. The federal government wasn't allowed to regulate intrastate trade, only interstate trade.

58. **E** Diplomacy and International Relations: 1915–Present *Fact*
The United Nations was forced to maintain global peace through actions of collective security—nations working together to prevent war and to promote peace.

59. **B** Social Change, Cultural & Intellectual Developments: 1915–Present *Fact*
Students for a Democratic Society (SDS) focused on peaceful efforts to promote the civil rights movement and became known for its leading role in student opposition to the Vietnam War. SDS formed the core of the New Left countercultural movement in the 1960s.

60. **D** Political Institutions, Behavior & Public Policy: 1915–Present *Except*
Consumer confidence in the U.S. economy in the late 1970s was not high. Inflation, rising prices for goods, and spiraling interest rates cost Jimmy Carter his reelection bid in 1980.

61. **D** Social Change, Cultural & Intellectual Developments: Pre-Columbian–1789 *Trend*
Indentured servants were bound to work for a set number of years—generally five to seven—on a plantation in return for their passage to the New World.

62. **B** Economic Developments: 1790–1914 *Fact*
President Martin Van Buren received the blame for the panic of 1837, and his party lost the 1840 election to the Whigs because of that panic.

63. **E** Political Institutions, Behavior & Public Policy: 1790–1914 *Except*
The Military Provision Act was not part of the Republican agenda. The other answer choices were major parts of Republican legislation in 1862 and 1863. The Homestead Act made land grants of 160 acres available in the West for settlement; the Morrill Land Grant Act set aside land in each state for land grant colleges; the Pacific Railroad Act helped provide funding for construction of the transcontinental railroad; and the National Bank Act created a national banking system and stabilized the national currency by reducing the number of conflicting state bank policies.

64. **A** Economic Developments: 1790–1914 *Except*
The South gradually began to industrialize, but the North, bolstered by pre-Civil War levels of industrialization, became the industrial leader in the country following the economic boom after the Civil War.

65. **E** Political Institutions, Behavior & Public Policy: 1790–1914 *Trend*
The Chinese Exclusion Act of 1882 was the first legislation to target a specific group of people for nonimmigration purposes. It barred Chinese immigration into the United States.

66. **C** Political Institutions, Behavior & Public Policy: 1790–1914 *Except*
Businesses began to be targeted as unfair monopolies by Progressive Era presidents Roosevelt, Taft, and Wilson. The Sherman Antitrust Act and the Clayton Antitrust Act were used against businesses that were deemed to be in "constraint of trade."

67. **B** Political Institutions, Behavior & Public Policy: 1915–Present *Trend*
President Hoover didn't believe it was the federal government's role to directly assist people in distress. He believed local and state governments should provide this kind of economic assistance. Hoover would later be criticized for his lack of support for people affected by the Great Depression. He lost his reelection bid for the presidency in 1932 to Franklin Roosevelt.

68. **C** Social Change, Cultural & Intellectual Developments: 1915–Present *Except*
The Civil Rights Act of 1964 barred discrimination on the basis of race and gender, giving more rights to minorities and women.

69. **E** Social Change, Cultural & Intellectual Developments: 1915–Present *Except*
The United States trained troops that invaded Cuba during the Bay of Pigs invasion in 1961 and then faced a humiliating defeat at the hands of Castro's troops. All of the other answer choices were major parts of the escalating Cold War crisis in the 1950s.

70. **C** Economic Developments: 1915–Present *Except*
Critics claimed "Reaganomics" created huge deficits that would only be passed on to future generations to pay back.

71. **A** Political Institutions, Behavior & Public Policy: Pre-Columbian–1789 *Except*
The money raised from the Townshend Duties was to be used to pay for royal officials in the colonies.

72. **D** Diplomacy and International Relations: 1790–1914 *Except*
British sailors were in essence "kidnapping" U.S. sailors and putting them to work on British ships. This became one of the major conflicts leading up to the War of 1812.

73. **D** Diplomacy and International Relations: 1790–1914 *Except*
In the terms of the Treaty of Guadalupe Hidalgo in 1848, the United States received the Mexican cession containing the territory of New Mexico and upper California.

74. **B** Social Change, Cultural & Intellectual Developments: 1790–1914 *Except*
Progressive reformers favored the use of labor unions to secure rights for employees. Labor unions often worked to support better hours, better wages, and better working conditions.

75. **A** Diplomacy and International Relations: 1915–Present *Fact*
Beginning in 1985, the CIA sold arms to Iranians, hoping they would assist in obtaining the release of American hostages in Lebanon. The profits from the sale were given to the contras in Nicaragua in an attempt to bypass congressional restrictions on funding them directly.

76. **E** Social Change, Cultural & Intellectual Developments: 1915–Present *Trend*
Black men serving in World War I were kept in segregated units commanded by White officers.

77. **A** Social Change, Cultural & Intellectual Developments: 1915–Present *Fact*
The Sheppard-Towner Act was the first legislation aimed at providing financial assistance to pregnant mothers and young infants.

78. **D** Social Change, Cultural & Intellectual Developments: 1915–Present *Trend*
Made in 1927, *The Jazz Singer* was the first talking motion picture ("talkie"). *Birth of a Nation* was a silent movie produced in 1915. *Steamboat Willie* was the first talking cartoon and was made in 1928. *Snow White* and *Gone with the Wind* were produced in the 1930s.

79. **C** Social Change, Cultural & Intellectual Developments: 1915–Present *Fact*
Executive Order 9066 established Japanese internment camps across the West in the United States.

80. **B** Economic Developments: 1915–Present *Trend*
The Alaska pipeline was constructed to help decrease U.S. dependence on foreign oil imports. It opened in 1977.

SECTION II: SAMPLE DBQ AND FREE-RESPONSE QUESTIONS

A note about the sample essays: We've included sample answers to each of the questions included in the Free-Response section. These essays would receive a top score from graders. It is possible to receive an equally high score without mentioning all of the facts and themes included here. If your essay is well-crafted and supported but all of the points and themes below aren't included, a top score may still be given. Since the DBQ and Free-Response essays are graded by humans instead of machines, and these humans usually have somewhere between 2–4 minutes to read and grade your essay, it is hard to pin down what will constitute a high-scoring response.

Question 1

John L. O'Sullivan's concept of manifest destiny represented the idea that America was ready to embrace its fate as "the great nation of futurity" (Doc D). Given the humble beginnings and relative "progress of an untried political system" (Doc D), Americans increasingly believed that the United States was justified in expanding its borders. However, successful gains in the West and South raised new political issues about the spread of slavery. While the country began to divide along sectional lines, attempts to maintain balance resulted in the Compromise of 1850. The compromise introduced the idea of popular sovereignty, which in turn led to the admittance of the Kansas and Nebraska territories in 1854. Kansas soon became the site of volatility as proslavery and antislavery sides fiercely sought to influence the decision about slavery. Ultimately, despite popular support for manifest destiny, the resulting expansion had disastrous ramifications that steadily divided the country until the final outbreak of the Civil War.

The imagination of the American people was captivated by the idea of manifest destiny. The possibility for expansion was appealing for both practical and romantic reasons. The population had grown exponentially in the first half of the nineteenth century, which literally meant that more land and resources would be needed. But more significantly, many Americans believed that the progress of the country, as mentioned by John L. O'Sullivan (Doc D), also included a moral slant. Walt Whitman wrote that the United States needed to "increase human happiness and liberty" (Doc A). He believed this to be "the great mission" of the United States (Doc A). Expansion into Oregon and Texas strengthened the American resolve that such a mission was accomplishable. This mentality became so accepted that even individuals were inspired to go "see the elephant" (Doc H). This was an expression popularized by the pioneers of the California gold rush of 1849. They were willing to take great personal risks in pursuit of "the adventure of a lifetime" (Doc H), and embodied the faith that Americans and America were not only able, but also destined to accomplish great things.

One of the first areas of contention and success was Oregon. The United States was able to solidify its claims to the Oregon territory after Spain and Russia each surrendered separate claims around 1820. While Oregon briefly fell under joint British and American occupation, James K. Polk eventually forced the British to give up their claims by threatening war. The success of Polk's bold strategy reflected the popular American attitude of entitlement. Using the momentum from Oregon, Polk set his sites on Mexico. He built a case justifying the declaration of war against Mexico, arguing that Mexico had "at last invaded our territory and shed the blood of our fellow-citizens on our own soil" (Doc I). Although there were some doubts such as those voiced by Abraham Lincoln (Doc E), Congress granted the declaration of war.

The appeal of expansion created an appearance of unity throughout the country, but there were traces of friction beneath the surface. Reminiscent of the Missouri Compromise, the underlying issue behind expansion was the balance between slave states and free states. The annexation of Texas in 1845 (Doc F) highlighted those very concerns. Following the onset of the Mexican War, the Wilmot Proviso urged that "neither slavery nor involuntary servitude" should exist in any of the territory gained from Mexico (Doc C). This suggestion inspired fierce sectional debate and raised further constitutional issues. The debate eventually led to the formation of the Free-Soil Party. Martin Van Buren ran as the Free Soil candidate during the Presidential election of 1848, with a platform that advocated "Free Soil, Free Speech, Free Labor, and Free Men" (Doc G). The issue of morality was once again at the forefront, with each side claiming to hold the higher ground. Van Buren did not win the election, but split votes with the Democrats, and the Whig candidate, Zachary Taylor prevailed.

By the end of the Mexican War, the balance between free states and slave states had been restored, but questions about the land gained from Mexico threatened to upset that balance. Ultimately, the Compromise of 1850 provided answers. It proposed the admission California as a free state, and introduced the idea of popular sovereignty for the territories of Utah and New Mexico. Southerners were happy with popular sovereignty because of its nullifying effect upon the Wilmot Proviso, but the Free-Soil Party continued to be a threat. The seeds of secession began in the early 1850s, indicating the determination of the South to preserve the institution of slavery, which it felt was increasingly under attack from the North.

The admittance of Kansas and Nebraska to the Union brought the debate about slavery to new heights. The Kansas-Nebraska Act of 1854 was able to pass through Congress because of its endorsement of popular sovereignty. Northerners were outraged by the implicit annulment of the Missouri Compromise, which had prohibited slavery that far north, but willing to do what they could do to make the new territories free states. Kansas quickly became the site of intense conflict, as both proslavery and antislavery activists squared off. The conflict quickly turned violent, and John Brown's retaliatory raid helped inspire the nickname "bleeding Kansas." The violence in Kansas served as an unfortunate prelude to the Civil War. The emotions surrounding slavery had become too adamant to be reconciled politically. The fervor that fueled manifest destiny had spiraled beyond control, and the United States was finally forced to confront the repercussions of rampant expansion.

Question 2

As was the case throughout Europe, the motivation for English colonization revolved around religious and economic incentives. By the end of the seventeenth century, two distinctive English colonies had emerged in America. The Puritans established the Massachusetts Bay Colony in pursuit of religious purity and John Winthrop's vision of a "city on a hill." Virginia was chartered as a joint-stock company, which attracted entrepreneurs willing to venture stakes in tobacco. During the colonial period, both regions experienced hardships that slowly pulled each colony away from its founding principles. The Halfway Covenant and Bacon's Rebellion reflected the underlying social and political tension, yet helped to create a new understanding of community. The Albany Plan of Union extended the concept of community and indicated that the colonies were ready to cooperate with one another in the decades prior to the Revolutionary War.

The Halfway Covenant was an indirect concession that the Puritan way of life was in jeopardy. Second and third generation Puritans had strayed from the strict ways of the founders and were looking for an easing of church standards. As originally conceived, the elect Puritans were the only ones entitled to the rite of Baptism. In order to become a "saint," an individual had to endure the process of public conversion. This process involved an intense scrutiny of one's life and offered no guarantees for selection. Facing the unsettling prospect of unbaptized grandchildren, the original saints were willing to compromise. The Halfway Covenant enabled the children of saints to be baptized but denied

them the privileges of Communion and voting in church affairs. Increasing numbers of Puritans accepted "halfway" status, which eventually left the saints in the minority. The Halfway Covenant responded to the demands of contemporary Puritans and signaled an erosion of the community's founding principles. In the process, the Puritans moved towards a more inclusive and secular society.

The tension in New England was not isolated and could also be seen in the growing discontent in the Chesapeake Bay. Bacon's Rebellion in Virginia was the pinnacle of the unrest. Since the colony's inception, Virginia's prosperity was dependent on tobacco farming. The profits yielded from tobacco led to a polarized division of wealth. A powerful merchant class relied upon a large work force, which was initially supplied by indentured servants. The division continued to widen as indentured servants who had fulfilled their servitude were forced to move further inland (since the most profitable land was already owned by the wealthy). The new land was less productive and forced more interaction with the Native Americans. After years of tension along the frontier, a series of attacks against the colonists sparked Bacon's Rebellion. Bacon organized a few hundred men who were frustrated by financial strains—especially after the Tobacco Depression—and the Governor's costly proposal to establish a line of forts along the frontier. After a couple of successful raids, Bacon looked to wage an all out war on the Native Americans, and his support swelled to more than one-thousand men. The Governor was forced to give his support to Bacon, but he soon renounced it. Angered at being called back, Bacon set off for Jamestown, and his men proceeded to burn it to the ground. The rebellion came to a quick end after Bacon fell ill and died. Although his supporters went their separate ways, their frustration actually fostered a new sense of community. The previous division of class dissolved as colonists banded together along racial lines.

Safety continued to be an issue along all parts of the frontier. Another source of concern for colonists was the escalation of clashes between the English and the French. The failure of King George's War to solve the territorial dispute eventually led to the French-Indian War. In an effort to combat French aggression against frontier settlements, delegates from seven colonies met in Albany. The result was the Albany Plan of Union in 1754. Benjamin Franklin was among the delegates who proposed a plan for a colonial confederation. The confederation was to be led by an executive officer appointed by the crown and was also empowered to collect funding for military defense and Indian affairs. Collecting funds proved to be divisive, and the Albany Plan faltered. However, the precedent had been set for American unity and the self-sufficiency of Black people.

The conflicts of the colonial period have a pivotal place in early American history. The circumstances that resulted in the Halfway Covenant and Bacon's Rebellion were unique to each region but helped forge common social grounds. The relaxing of Puritan strictness and the increased appreciation of community in Virginia enabled the colonists to begin the unifying process demonstrated by the Albany Plan of Union. The social and political tension and the desire to relieve it would continue to move America on its course toward revolution.

Question 3

John Marshall was appointed to the Supreme Court by President John Adams in 1801. Adams was a Federalist but had recently been defeated in the presidential election of 1800 by the Republican Thomas Jefferson. Shortly before leaving office, Adams issued a series of judicial appointments, which were aimed at extending Federalist influence in the judiciary. His appointments have become known as the midnight judges. Despite the quickness of Marshall's appointment, he served on the Supreme Court for thirty-five years, a span of six presidents. Marshall's Federalist convictions were shaped by his service to the Continental Army during the Revolutionary War. His sympathy toward federal power is illustrated in three early court cases: *Marbury v. Madison, Dartmouth College v. Woodward,* and *McCulloch v. Maryland.* The results of his pivotal rulings in each of these three cases helped to establish the power of the Supreme Court and the authority of the federal government.

William Marbury was to be the last of the midnight judges. On his last day in office, Adams appointed Marbury to serve as the Justice of the Peace in the District of Columbia; however, Adams failed to submit the commission before midnight. With the change of administrations, the new Secretary of State, James Madison, refused to accept Marbury's commission. Marbury petitioned the Supreme Court for a writ of mandamus, which would force Madison to honor his commission. Despite the circumstances of his own appointment, Marshall did not rule in favor of Marbury. Rather, he boldly declared that the Constitution did not bestow such power on the Supreme Court. He reasoned that the power to issue a writ of mandamus was actually established by the Judiciary Act of 1789, and that in effect, that part of the Judiciary Act was unconstitutional. Marshall's ruling became monumental because it was the first time that the Supreme Court declared a congressional act unconstitutional. Likewise, Marshall's decision represented a crucial step in the establishment of the Supreme Court's authority.

Sixteen years later, Marshall issued another defining decision in the case of *Dartmouth College v. Woodward*. The controversy arose when New Hampshire's government attempted to transform Dartmouth into a public institution. New Hampshirer wanted to replace Dartmouth's Federalists Board of Trustees with a state-created Republican governing board. Daniel Webster represented Dartmouth College when the case was taken up in the Supreme Court. On the grounds that Dartmouth's founding charter, issued by the King of England, was essentially a contract and that the Constitution prohibited state governments from interfering with contracts, Marshall eventually sided in favor of Dartmouth. Marshall's ruling severely limited the regulatory power of the state government and affirmed his Federalist tendencies.

In the case immediately following *Dartmouth College v. Woodward*, the boundaries of state government were again called into question, but Marshall's ruling in *McCulloch v. Maryland* was even more monumental. President Madison had reintroduced the Bank of the United States, which established a local branch in Baltimore. Maryland maintained its ability to tax the bank, which outraged the bank's cashier, McCulloch, who refused to pay. The first question considered by the Court was whether Congress had the ability to charter a national bank. Using a loose interpretation of the Constitution, Marshall decided that it did. The next question was whether a sate could tax an agency of the federal government. Marshall eventually overruled Maryland on the grounds that states did not have such authority. He maintained that constitutional law was more fundamental than individual state laws since it was created to govern the states collectively. His ruling angered Republicans but left no doubt about the court's position that states were subordinate to the federal government.

Marshall's presence on the Supreme Court for thirty-five years significantly shaped the power of the Court during its formative years. His rulings established boundaries for state government, and he set the important precedent for overturning congressional laws deemed unconstitutional. Through his loose and strict interpretations of the Constitution, he upheld its authority as the foundation of law in America, and in doing so he validated the very authority of the Supreme Court.

Question 4

The Roaring Twenties are one of the most distinguished decades in American history. Sandwiched between the end of World War I and the beginning stages of the Great Depression, the twenties were a tumultuous time of social and cultural change. Urbanization and mass production characterized the general trend of modernization. Society embraced new forms of media, and national heroes gained widespread notoriety. Despite these superficial emblems of popular culture, backlash, including Fundamentalism, followed and was often motivated by a desire for purity and simplicity; these larger concerns about the direction society was moving in ultimately revealed a period of profound conflict.

Cities factored prominently in the social and cultural changes during the 1920s. For the first time in American history, more people lived in cities than in rural areas. This process of urbanization was caused in part by the steady migration of Black people and immigrants to large cities. One appeal of city-life was that cities were the primary site of industry and technology. New inventions such as the refrigerator, vacuum cleaner, and electric washing machine revolutionized daily life. The efficiency of mass production enabled the average citizen to afford and enjoy these conveniences. Other modern advances included the creation of department stores and supermarkets. Neighborhood grocery stores were replaced by the spread of supermarkets from the Atlantic to the Pacific, which was made possible by motor transportation.

Automobiles themselves were the single most significant invention of the twenties. Enormous corporations like Ford and General Motors utilized the urban supply of labor to man assembly lines. The definitive cultural transformation occurring in cities steadily expanded throughout America.

The concept behind mass production extended to the realm of media as well. Magazines such as *Reader's Digest* and the *Saturday Evening Post* played an important role in the mass-circulation of ideas. Similarly, the invention of the radio and the creation of national corporations (like the National Broadcasting Company and Columbia Broadcasting System) enabled news, sports, music, and various other programs to be transmitted across the country. The film industry originated during the twenties, and movies also reached beyond local communities. The popularity of movies created celebrities like Charlie Chaplin, Gary Cooper, and Gretta Garbo. The celebrity status of actors also led to the emergence of national heroes. Babe Ruth and Red Grange were idolized for their athletic prowess. Perhaps the biggest hero was Charles Lindburgh. His solo transatlantic flight captivated imaginations and was celebrated nationally. His popularity suggested the existence of mass-culture facilitated by the media.

Despite the superficial indications of a national culture, there were many who actively resisted the social and cultural transformation. The backlash was fueled by a desire for purity and simplicity and was justified on ethnic, racial, religious, and moral grounds. The process of urbanization was also caused by a continued surge of unwelcome immigration. In the early twenties, Congress took steps to limit immigration, and in 1924 it approved a strict system of quotas designed to drastically reduce it; Asians were excluded completely, for example. There was also backlash against immigrants already living in America. The Sacco-Vanzetti trial, which sentenced two Italian immigrants to death with little conclusive evidence, exemplified the sentiment of ethnic mistrust. Backlash against racial and religious diversification was also initiated by the resurgence of the Ku Klux Klan. The Klan was extremely active during the twenties and was able to make legitimate political gains before succumbing to internal moral corruption. Sensing a trend of loosened morality, religious fundamentalists were also on the offensive. The issue of evolution and subsequent Scopes trial brought the fundamentalist crusade to the forefront. The temperance movement successfully lobbied for Prohibition, which represented a fundamental desire for moral rigidity. Finally, there was even backlash inspired by the backlash. Marcus Garvey founded the Universal Negro Improvement Association aimed at fighting poverty and racism by glorifying the self-sufficiency of Black people.

The Roaring Twenties were truly a time of transformation. The spread of mass culture produced common goods, popular ideas, and national heroes. These signs of unity existed only on the surface, though. Uncertainty about the products and progress of modernization fueled widespread backlash and undermined a true national culture.

Question 5

The second Article of the Constitution establishes the precedent of impeachment. It specifies that, upon being convicted of high crimes and misdemeanors, the president will be removed from office. Impeachment proceedings formally

begin in the House of Representatives. If charges are approved by the majority, the matter passes to the Senate. In order for the president to be convicted, a two-thirds majority vote to convict must carry in the Senate. The first impeachment proceedings occurred in 1868 during Andrew Johnson's presidency. Nearly one century later, Richard Nixon faced the country's second impeachment proceedings. While these instances have been exceptionally rare, some people have claimed that impeachment has been used as a political tool. These claims seem to be legitimate in the case of Johnson, as the origins of the impeachment were motivated by Republican frustration. However, the overwhelming circumstances incriminating Nixon negate claims of political motivation. In spite of the varying motives behind each case, the outcome in both proceedings has been a triumph for constitutional process and nonpartisan politics.

Ironically, party affiliation had been the very appeal of Andrew Johnson for the Republicans. In an attempt to broaden support, Republicans created the temporary National Unity Party and selected Andrew Johnson as Lincoln's running mate in the election of 1864. After Lincoln's assassination, Johnson welcomed the responsibilities of Reconstruction. From the outset, he had a rocky relationship with the Republican-dominated Congress. While Congress was out of session, Johnson initiated his plan of Reconstruction, which Republicans felt was too lenient. The tension between Johnson and Congress escalated after he vetoed the Freedmen's Bureau bill and the Civil Rights bill. These measures alienated Republicans and forged an alliance between the moderate and radical Republicans in Congress. The newfound Republican unity enabled Congress to override Johnson's vetoes. Congress then looked to find ways to limit presidential authority and passed the Tenure of Office Act. In an act of defiance, Johnson suspended the Secretary of War without seeking the necessary approval from the Senate. Republicans accused Johnson of violating the Tenure of Office Act and used this opportunity to bring up impeachment proceedings against him.

The premise for President Nixon's impeachment was the Watergate scandal, which seemed to suggest the worst conceivable partisan corruption. Burglars were caught breaking into the Democratic Party headquarters with the intent of tapping phone lines. Nixon immediately distanced himself and denied any White House involvement. Despite the potential for disaster, Nixon was able to win his re-election campaign. Only afterwards did information leak out, including a blockbuster story appearing in the *Washington Post*. Nixon continued to maintain his innocence, but the Senate was suspicious enough to launch an investigation. More incriminating evidence steadily turned up, but the absolute proof that would connect Nixon remained elusive. The break in the investigation came with the discovery that Nixon had installed a secret taping system that recorded all conversations in the Oval Office. Nixon adamantly refused to surrender the tapes until the Supreme Court legally forced him to do so. The investigation finally produced the necessary evidence proving Nixon's complicity and that he had ordered the cover-up. Amidst the overwhelming evidence, the House of Representatives began the process of impeachment on the grounds of obstruction of justice and two other counts.

While Nixon's corruption was politically motivated, his impeachment proceedings were not biased by party affiliation. Even the most stubborn of Republican allies were forced to surrender allegiance in the end. The absolute certainty of impeachment led Republican leaders advised Nixon to resign. Rather than facing the Senate trial, he complied and became the first president in history to resign from office. In many ways the outcome of Nixon's impeachment proceedings were made possible by the precedent set in the impeachment of Johnson. Unlike Nixon, the House technically impeached Johnson. However, the Senate acquitted him. The Senate missed the necessary two-thirds majority by a single vote, which meant that several Republicans had crossed over party lines to vote alongside the Democrats. They were motivated by a fear that impeaching the president would disrupt the fundamental system of checks and balances. The constitutional process requiring a two-thirds majority vote to convict had succeeded in preventing a politically motivated impeachment. Despite the partisan context surrounding the impeachment proceedings of Johnson and Nixon, the final outcome of both cases transcended partisan politics.

AP U. S. HISTORY ANSWER SHEET — PRACTICE EXAM 2

1. Ⓐ Ⓑ Ⓒ Ⓓ Ⓔ Ⓕ	28. Ⓐ Ⓑ Ⓒ Ⓓ Ⓔ Ⓕ	55. Ⓐ Ⓑ Ⓒ Ⓓ Ⓔ Ⓕ
2. Ⓐ Ⓑ Ⓒ Ⓓ Ⓔ Ⓕ	29. Ⓐ Ⓑ Ⓒ Ⓓ Ⓔ Ⓕ	56. Ⓐ Ⓑ Ⓒ Ⓓ Ⓔ Ⓕ
3. Ⓐ Ⓑ Ⓒ Ⓓ Ⓔ Ⓕ	30. Ⓐ Ⓑ Ⓒ Ⓓ Ⓔ Ⓕ	57. Ⓐ Ⓑ Ⓒ Ⓓ Ⓔ Ⓕ
4. Ⓐ Ⓑ Ⓒ Ⓓ Ⓔ Ⓕ	31. Ⓐ Ⓑ Ⓒ Ⓓ Ⓔ Ⓕ	58. Ⓐ Ⓑ Ⓒ Ⓓ Ⓔ Ⓕ
5. Ⓐ Ⓑ Ⓒ Ⓓ Ⓔ Ⓕ	32. Ⓐ Ⓑ Ⓒ Ⓓ Ⓔ Ⓕ	59. Ⓐ Ⓑ Ⓒ Ⓓ Ⓔ Ⓕ
6. Ⓐ Ⓑ Ⓒ Ⓓ Ⓔ Ⓕ	33. Ⓐ Ⓑ Ⓒ Ⓓ Ⓔ Ⓕ	60. Ⓐ Ⓑ Ⓒ Ⓓ Ⓔ Ⓕ
7. Ⓐ Ⓑ Ⓒ Ⓓ Ⓔ Ⓕ	34. Ⓐ Ⓑ Ⓒ Ⓓ Ⓔ Ⓕ	61. Ⓐ Ⓑ Ⓒ Ⓓ Ⓔ Ⓕ
8. Ⓐ Ⓑ Ⓒ Ⓓ Ⓔ Ⓕ	35. Ⓐ Ⓑ Ⓒ Ⓓ Ⓔ Ⓕ	62. Ⓐ Ⓑ Ⓒ Ⓓ Ⓔ Ⓕ
9. Ⓐ Ⓑ Ⓒ Ⓓ Ⓔ Ⓕ	36. Ⓐ Ⓑ Ⓒ Ⓓ Ⓔ Ⓕ	63. Ⓐ Ⓑ Ⓒ Ⓓ Ⓔ Ⓕ
10. Ⓐ Ⓑ Ⓒ Ⓓ Ⓔ Ⓕ	37. Ⓐ Ⓑ Ⓒ Ⓓ Ⓔ Ⓕ	64. Ⓐ Ⓑ Ⓒ Ⓓ Ⓔ Ⓕ
11. Ⓐ Ⓑ Ⓒ Ⓓ Ⓔ Ⓕ	38. Ⓐ Ⓑ Ⓒ Ⓓ Ⓔ Ⓕ	65. Ⓐ Ⓑ Ⓒ Ⓓ Ⓔ Ⓕ
12. Ⓐ Ⓑ Ⓒ Ⓓ Ⓔ Ⓕ	39. Ⓐ Ⓑ Ⓒ Ⓓ Ⓔ Ⓕ	66. Ⓐ Ⓑ Ⓒ Ⓓ Ⓔ Ⓕ
13. Ⓐ Ⓑ Ⓒ Ⓓ Ⓔ Ⓕ	40. Ⓐ Ⓑ Ⓒ Ⓓ Ⓔ Ⓕ	67. Ⓐ Ⓑ Ⓒ Ⓓ Ⓔ Ⓕ
14. Ⓐ Ⓑ Ⓒ Ⓓ Ⓔ Ⓕ	41. Ⓐ Ⓑ Ⓒ Ⓓ Ⓔ Ⓕ	68. Ⓐ Ⓑ Ⓒ Ⓓ Ⓔ Ⓕ
15. Ⓐ Ⓑ Ⓒ Ⓓ Ⓔ Ⓕ	42. Ⓐ Ⓑ Ⓒ Ⓓ Ⓔ Ⓕ	69. Ⓐ Ⓑ Ⓒ Ⓓ Ⓔ Ⓕ
16. Ⓐ Ⓑ Ⓒ Ⓓ Ⓔ Ⓕ	43. Ⓐ Ⓑ Ⓒ Ⓓ Ⓔ Ⓕ	70. Ⓐ Ⓑ Ⓒ Ⓓ Ⓔ Ⓕ
17. Ⓐ Ⓑ Ⓒ Ⓓ Ⓔ Ⓕ	44. Ⓐ Ⓑ Ⓒ Ⓓ Ⓔ Ⓕ	71. Ⓐ Ⓑ Ⓒ Ⓓ Ⓔ Ⓕ
18. Ⓐ Ⓑ Ⓒ Ⓓ Ⓔ Ⓕ	45. Ⓐ Ⓑ Ⓒ Ⓓ Ⓔ Ⓕ	72. Ⓐ Ⓑ Ⓒ Ⓓ Ⓔ Ⓕ
19. Ⓐ Ⓑ Ⓒ Ⓓ Ⓔ Ⓕ	46. Ⓐ Ⓑ Ⓒ Ⓓ Ⓔ Ⓕ	73. Ⓐ Ⓑ Ⓒ Ⓓ Ⓔ Ⓕ
20. Ⓐ Ⓑ Ⓒ Ⓓ Ⓔ Ⓕ	47. Ⓐ Ⓑ Ⓒ Ⓓ Ⓔ Ⓕ	74. Ⓐ Ⓑ Ⓒ Ⓓ Ⓔ Ⓕ
21. Ⓐ Ⓑ Ⓒ Ⓓ Ⓔ Ⓕ	48. Ⓐ Ⓑ Ⓒ Ⓓ Ⓔ Ⓕ	75. Ⓐ Ⓑ Ⓒ Ⓓ Ⓔ Ⓕ
22. Ⓐ Ⓑ Ⓒ Ⓓ Ⓔ Ⓕ	49. Ⓐ Ⓑ Ⓒ Ⓓ Ⓔ Ⓕ	76. Ⓐ Ⓑ Ⓒ Ⓓ Ⓔ Ⓕ
23. Ⓐ Ⓑ Ⓒ Ⓓ Ⓔ Ⓕ	50. Ⓐ Ⓑ Ⓒ Ⓓ Ⓔ Ⓕ	77. Ⓐ Ⓑ Ⓒ Ⓓ Ⓔ Ⓕ
24. Ⓐ Ⓑ Ⓒ Ⓓ Ⓔ Ⓕ	51. Ⓐ Ⓑ Ⓒ Ⓓ Ⓔ Ⓕ	78. Ⓐ Ⓑ Ⓒ Ⓓ Ⓔ Ⓕ
25. Ⓐ Ⓑ Ⓒ Ⓓ Ⓔ Ⓕ	52. Ⓐ Ⓑ Ⓒ Ⓓ Ⓔ Ⓕ	79. Ⓐ Ⓑ Ⓒ Ⓓ Ⓔ Ⓕ
26. Ⓐ Ⓑ Ⓒ Ⓓ Ⓔ Ⓕ	53. Ⓐ Ⓑ Ⓒ Ⓓ Ⓔ Ⓕ	80. Ⓐ Ⓑ Ⓒ Ⓓ Ⓔ Ⓕ
27. Ⓐ Ⓑ Ⓒ Ⓓ Ⓔ Ⓕ	54. Ⓐ Ⓑ Ⓒ Ⓓ Ⓔ Ⓕ	

PRACTICE EXAM 2

AP* U.S. HISTORY
SECTION I: MULTIPLE-CHOICE QUESTIONS
Time—55 minutes
80 Questions

Directions: The questions or incomplete statements below are followed by five possible answers or completions. After selecting the one that is best in each case, fill in the corresponding oval on the answer sheet.

1. “You have stepped out of your place, you have rather bine a Husband than a Wife and a preacher than a hearer.” This quote supports the idea that the Puritan authorities
   (A) believed Anne Hutchinson to be a threat because she owned her own business
   (B) saw Anne Hutchinson as a threat because she challenged traditional gender roles
   (C) believed Anne Hutchinson to be a valuable asset to the community
   (D) allowed divorce even when it couldn’t be proven that the wife had not been submissive to her husband
   (E) believed that after this reprimand, Anne Hutchinson would no longer challenge male-dominated rule in the society

2. The First Continental Congress
   (A) denied that Parliament had any authority in America
   (B) renounced any allegiance to King George III
   (C) approved acts of civil protest in retaliation for the recent Coercive Acts but didn’t approve a measure to strengthen the colonial militia
   (D) approved of Parliament’s actions in the colonies
   (E) agreed that the meeting had been successful and that there was no need for further meetings

3. The Missouri Compromise of 1820 was developed to
   (A) prevent the entry of more slave states into the Union
   (B) prevent the entry of more free states into the Union
   (C) preserve the delicate balance between free states and slave states in the Union
   (D) prevent Maine from seceding from the Union
   (E) prohibit the expansion of slavery in the Louisiana Purchase territory

4. The Wilmot Proviso of 1846 and the Compromise of 1850 addressed which of the following issues?
   (A) The acquisition of western territories from Great Britain and Russia
   (B) The proposed statehood of Kansas
   (C) The abolition of slavery in all American states
   (D) The establishment of popular sovereignty in newly acquired territories
   (E) The extension of slavery into the territories acquired from Mexico

GO ON TO THE NEXT PAGE.

5. The Crédit Mobilier scandal focused on
   (A) whiskey farmers planning another rebellion if they didn't receive tax relief
   (B) lucrative construction contracts for the builders of the Union Pacific Railroad, who in turn inflated prices and gave kickbacks to members of Congress
   (C) the infamous Tweed Ring and corruption in New York City politics
   (D) the political scandal involving the sale of stock and the construction of the Erie Canal
   (E) kickbacks to owners of the steamboat *Effie Afton*, which crashed into the Rock Island Bridge spanning the Mississippi River, and their claims that the bridge hindered steamboat business

6. The National Origins Act in 1924 was intended to
   (A) restrict Chinese and Japanese immigration with quotas
   (B) open up Asia to immigration to the United States
   (C) restrict immigration from southern and eastern Europe with quotas
   (D) restrict Catholic immigration
   (E) use only Angel Island and Ellis Island as the two ports of entry for immigrants coming into the United States

7. Senator Joseph McCarthy gained popularity in the country in 1950 when he
   (A) served as a member of the HUAC
   (B) had Richard Nixon censured in Congress
   (C) claimed to have a list of 206 "card carrying Communists" in the U.S.
   (D) voted against U.N. actions in Korea
   (E) aided in the convictions of Alger Hiss and Ethel and Julius Rosenburg

8. Puritan life in 17th century America fundamentally revolved around
   (A) elaborate church rituals
   (B) the family
   (C) a social hierarchy based on wealth
   (D) a social hierarchy based on education
   (E) the individual

The Sherman Anti-Trust Law Returns from the Dead
(Bartholomew in the Minneapolis Journal.)

9. Even though it had not been used effectively in the previous administration, President Teddy Roosevelt began to use the Sherman Antitrust Act to
   (A) establish laissez-faire policies for big businesses
   (B) regulate the clothing sweatshops
   (C) add enforcement to the Pure Food and Drug Act of 1906
   (D) regulate monopolies found to be "in constraint of trade"
   (E) outlaw union activity

10. The biggest accomplishment women gained during the Progressive Era was
   (A) the right to vote
   (B) the right to an abortion
   (C) the passage of the ERA
   (D) mandatory eight-hour work days
   (E) equal pay in the workplace

GO ON TO THE NEXT PAGE.

11. The Boston Massacre in March 1770 marked the peak of colonial resistance to

(A) the Stamp Act
(B) the Sugar Act
(C) the Townshend Duties
(D) the Intolerable Acts
(E) the Declaratory Act

12. Shays' Rebellion, a revolt by farmers seeking debt relief in 1787, persuaded many in the country that

(A) stronger regulation of indentured servants was necessary
(B) a stronger, more stable federal government was necessary
(C) personal wealth should be regulated
(D) if the rebellion were left alone, a similar crisis wouldn't occur in the future
(E) it concerned only veterans from the recent Revolutionary War seeking additional pensions

13. The Lowell system relied on a work force consisting primarily of

(A) indentured servants
(B) slaves
(C) young girls from surrounding rural areas
(D) Irish immigrants
(E) young boys and girls

14. Settlement houses in the late 1800s and early 1900s

(A) were boarding houses in which middle-class women lived together
(B) were government-sponsored homes for the poor
(C) provided a myriad of social services to neighborhood dwellers
(D) served primarily as social clubs
(E) were used as half-way houses for juveniles convicted of minor crimes

15. The Nullification Crisis in 1832 was significant because all of the following actions occurred EXCEPT:

(A) Other states in addition to South Carolina were encouraged to secede.
(B) Vice President John C. Calhoun resigned.
(C) Calhoun argued that national laws must benefit each region of the United States.
(D) South Carolina drafted and issued the Ordinance of Nullification claiming that states had the final authority in laws passed by Congress.
(E) South Carolina claimed that the states gave the federal government its authority; therefore, the states retained the right to reject laws as unconstitutional, making the federal government subordinate to the states.

16. In the antebellum years, northern and southern states often disagreed on all of the following political issues EXCEPT

(A) the doctrine of states rights (Tenth Amendment)
(B) tariffs and trade restriction issues
(C) expansion of slavery
(D) suffrage for women and Black people
(E) nullification and secession

17. The message of the 18th-century Great Awakening directly challenged

(A) the belief that Christ was God's son sent to earth
(B) faith in individual self-reliance and economic mobility
(C) the belief that Native Americans could never be integrated into colonial society
(D) the established Puritan view of a coldly rational approach to God and religion
(E) the teachings of the Roman Catholic Church

GO ON TO THE NEXT PAGE.

18. "It is better to trust in the Rock of Ages than to know the age of rocks; it is better for one to know that he is close to the Heavenly Father than to know how far the stars in the heavens are apart."

These words reflect the 1920s campaign

(A) on behalf of farm relief
(B) in support of the fundamentalist religious movement
(C) to support teacher training colleges
(D) against the teaching of evolution in school science programs
(E) in support of Father Caughlin's weekly Sunday radio addresses

19. The major misconception about FDR's New Deal legislation claims is that

(A) the New Deal legislation was successful in ending the Great Depression
(B) the Great Depression did not end until after World War II
(C) the federal government and businesses worked together to end the depression
(D) FDR wasn't worried about creating a class of people becoming dependent upon the federal government for assistance programs
(E) FDR's New Deal programs were often deemed as being "too little, too late" in trying to solve the nation's problems

20. During the decade of the 1950s, all of the following forms of entertainment or amusement were popular EXCEPT

(A) movie theaters
(B) rock and roll music
(C) *I Love Lucy* and *American Bandstand* (along with a host of other television shows)
(D) drive-in theaters
(E) Disneyland

21. Under the system of triangular trade

(A) West Indies sugar and molasses were shipped to Africa and traded for slaves
(B) African slaves were traded in the West Indies for rum
(C) New England sugar and molasses were shipped to Africa and traded for slaves
(D) New England rum was shipped to England and traded for sugar and molasses
(E) New England rum was shipped to Africa and traded for slaves

22. "I long to hear that you have declared an independency—and by the way in the new Code of Laws you make I desire you would Remember the Ladies . . . [and] do not put such unlimited power into the hands of the Husbands. . . . if particular care and attention is not paid to the Ladies we are determined to foment a rebellion and will not hold ourselves bound by any Laws in which we have no voice or representation."

This significant quote, which expresses a great desire for women to benefit from the freedoms to be gained by the Revolutionary War, was written in 1776 by

(A) Martha Washington
(B) Abigail Adams
(C) Phyllis Wheatley
(D) Molly Pitcher
(E) Deborah Sampson

23. Which of the following was a reform movement of the 1840s?

(A) Abolitionism
(B) Temperance
(C) Public education
(D) Eliminating inhumane insane asylums
(E) All of the above

GO ON TO THE NEXT PAGE.

24. After the Civil War, radical Republicans in Congress sought to do all of the following EXCEPT

(A) remove President Andrew Johnson from office on the grounds of having committed "high crimes and misdemeanors"
(B) dictate the terms of Reconstruction
(C) punish the South
(D) use Lincoln's lenient ten percent plan
(E) use military occupation in the South

25. William Jennings Bryan in his famous "Cross of Gold" speech in 1896 gave strong support to

(A) higher tariffs to support the farmers and to protect domestic industry
(B) the restriction of the coinage of silver in favor of the gold standard
(C) the unlimited coinage of silver to inflate the currency in an effort to help the farmers with mild inflation to raise prices
(D) the limited use of the gold standard for a period of five years
(E) taking the United States off of the gold standard

26. The Seneca Falls Declaration called for

(A) humane treatment of those in insane asylums
(B) equal rights for women
(C) the immediate abolition of slavery
(D) universal public education
(E) prison reform

27. The effect of President Taft's "Dollar Diplomacy" foreign policy initiative was

(A) a reduction in tariffs
(B) increased suspicion and mistrust of the United States by Latin American countries
(C) Columbia received an additional $20 million payment for the Panama Canal
(D) the creation of a free trade zone in the Americas
(E) the removal of trade barriers with Mexico and Canada

28. The Zimmermann note in 1917 was significant in that it

(A) demanded that the U.S. continue its practice of neutrality or face continued retaliation
(B) warned of a German invasion of the U.S. in late 1917
(C) urged a resumption of unrestricted submarine warfare
(D) asked for a German payment for the sinking of the *Lusitania* two years earlier
(E) attempted to coerce Mexico into joining the war on the side of the Germans in return for land Mexico lost in the Treaty of Guadalupe Hidalgo in 1848 at the end of the Mexican-American War

29. The original purpose of NATO was to create a

(A) mutual defense pact against the Soviets
(B) free trade zone between Western Europe and the U.S.
(C) ten-year plan for the economic recovery of Europe
(D) financial mechanism to stabilize currency exchange rates of the Western nations
(E) line of defense for West Germany

30. Which of the following best characterizes the reason the U.S. sent ground troops to Vietnam and became involved in the Vietnam War?

(A) In the election of 1964, LBJ promised that if he were elected, he would commit land troops to battle.
(B) Johnson feared that spending for domestic programs would be at risk if the Communists succeeded in Vietnam (for fear that other Asian countries would also be at risk).
(C) The president and his advisors considered Vietnam strategically necessary to protect the Philippines and other U.S. holdings.
(D) The joint chief of staff assured LBJ that superior U.S. troops could easily win the war.
(E) Johnson wanted to follow through with JFK's plans for the war.

GO ON TO THE NEXT PAGE.

31. In earlier colonial times, a person who was a "separatist"

(A) lived outside the protection of the community
(B) earned his or her freedom after completing the mandatory years of service as an indentured servant
(C) was banished from the Puritan community for practicing witchcraft
(D) wanted to break away from the Church of England in search of a pure religion
(E) sought to earn wealth in the New World and then return to England

32. In the effort to ratify the Constitution, all the following were true EXCEPT:

(A) *The Federalist Papers* were a series of newspaper essays written to argue in favor of ratifying the Constitution
(B) New York would be the tenth state to ratify the Constitution, thereby making it a legal and binding document
(C) Supporters of ratification were generally more organized in their attempts to persuade the public
(D) There was never any doubt that the Constitution would be ratified
(E) Antifederalists warned about a government run without concerns for the rights of individuals

33. The War Hawks were successful in granting President Madison a declaration of war against the British in 1812 on the grounds of

(A) the continued impressment of U.S. sailors and economic problems
(B) convincing people living in the New England region that a war was beneficial for the entire nation
(C) bargaining with the French to secure a right of passage at the mouth of the Mississippi River
(D) a quick victory was assured against the British
(E) not securing any additional territory for the country

34. All of the following were efforts by reformers in the mid-nineteenth century EXCEPT

(A) the abolitionist movement
(B) prison reform
(C) temperance
(D) public school and deaf education
(E) labor reform

35. After the Lincoln-Douglas debates, Senator Stephen Douglas won his re-election bid, while Abraham Lincoln's actions in the debate served to

(A) diminish his political record as a viable candidate in the next election
(B) give rise to the Republican Party on a nation-wide scale
(C) give more support to the Democrat Party
(D) split the Republican Party into the Free Soil and Know-Nothing splinter groups
(E) diminish the record of Stephen Douglas

36. Booker T. Washington believed that the best way for Black people to improve their status in the U.S. was to

(A) acclimate themselves to segregation and disfranchisement, while, at the same time, work hard to prove their economic worth
(B) struggle militantly against all forms of racial discrimination in order to gain educational opportunities
(C) leave the U.S. and return to Africa
(D) form a nationwide council to work for the federal laws against lynching
(E) seek an immediate guarantee of their civil rights

GO ON TO THE NEXT PAGE.

37. Mother Jones once stated, "If you are too cowardly to fight for your rights then there are enough women in this country to come in and beat the hell out of you."

This statement was meant to encourage

(A) male workers to strike in favor of a labor union at Ludlow
(B) membership of women in the IWW
(C) the workers at Homestead
(D) business leaders from the Pullman strike
(E) the muckrakers working for McClure's Magazine

38. During the 1920s, the events in Rosewood, Florida, the race riots in Tulsa, Oklahoma, the increase in lynching, and the growth in membership in the Ku Klux Klan (KKK) membership illustrated that

(A) racism was finally ending in America
(B) legislation proved to be the key to fighting racism and injustice
(C) there were serious racial problems in America that had yet to be overcome
(D) the way to end racism was to appeal in the court system
(E) racist incidents were on the decline

39. The early years of the Cold War (1948–1953) were marked by all of the following EXCEPT

(A) the NSC-68 discussing the inadequacy of U.S. military programs, thus calling for a massive buildup and an increase in funding for the armed forces in an effort to contain the Soviets
(B) the USSR testing its first nuclear bomb
(C) the final resolution of the conflict in Korea
(D) the trials of Alger Hiss and Ethel and Julius Rosenburg
(E) the U.S. and USSR completing tests of H-bombs within months of each other

40. One of the major reasons for the failure of the ratification of the Equal Rights Amendment (ERA) was that

(A) affirmative action quotas gave women equality in the workplace, making the ERA unnecessary
(B) women leaders within the women's movement began to argue against the ERA claiming that it would destroy the traditional role of women
(C) the decision in the *Roe v. Wade* case in 1973 silenced the women's movement
(D) the "equality" language in the bill would apply only to women
(E) it was no longer necessary because of the Civil Rights Act of 1964

41. The Mayflower Compact is significant in that

(A) the people regarded themselves as the sole source of political power
(B) there were provisions for civil rights especially for women Black people
(C) it was also used for the Massachusetts Bay colony years later
(D) it spoke of the separation of church and state
(E) the people agreed to be bound by the will of the majority

42. All of the following are true about the experience of Black people in the Revolutionary War EXCEPT:

(A) They were freed after the signing of the Treaty of Paris in 1783
(B) Many slaves sought to escape during the war
(C) Some served in the Continental Army under Washington's command
(D) Several thousand were actually set free by the British
(E) Great Britain tried to entice some slaves to fight on the side of the British during the war

GO ON TO THE NEXT PAGE.

43. The transcendentalists spurred a literature movement that promoted the concepts of

(A) inner truth and individual self-reliance
(B) political community and economic progress
(C) personal guilt and redemption
(D) self-worth and determination
(E) discovery and the afterlife

44. The passage of the Alien and Sedition Acts in 1798 was intended to

(A) establish immigration quotas
(B) remove British loyalists
(C) force President John Adams to take a public stand on the XYZ Affair
(D) stop the harassment by the Barbary pirates
(E) silence Republican opposition to the Federalists

45. During the years of the Civil War, the North held the advantage over the South in all of the following areas EXCEPT

(A) more railroad mileage
(B) more production of materials for the war effort
(C) more abundant food resources for the war effort
(D) a larger and better equipped army
(E) more qualified military leaders (generally West Point graduates)

Carnegie Presents the Trust as a Trustworthy Beast Steel, oil, coal, lumber, sugar, and salt are all represented. (Harper's Weekly.)

46. The trusts in the steel and oil industries along with other trusts in the late 1800s believed that

(A) government intervention was necessary to keep their actions under control
(B) business owners could regulate themselves without government intervention
(C) a partnership between business owners and the government was feasible
(D) growing political scandals involving the formation of monopolies were false
(E) business owners were obliged to award kickbacks to Congressmen in order to prevent government regulation

47. Social Darwinism argued that human history witnessed

(A) the inevitable evolution of the weakest groups to the positions of highest power
(B) a struggle among the races with the strongest triumphing
(C) the evolution of humans from the ape
(D) the eventual disintegration of Western civilization
(E) the enslavement of weaker races

GO ON TO THE NEXT PAGE.

48. Which of the following is true about the Kellogg-Briand Pact of 1928?

(A) It created an alliance between the U.S. and France.
(B) It was a bilateral pact for naval disarmament.
(C) It was rejected by the Senate.
(D) It was a multilateral pact condemning a recourse to war to solve aggression.
(E) It contained provisions for enforcement.

49. Johnson's popularity began to wane and funding for the Great Society decreased after 1966 as

(A) American military leaders criticized the war effort
(B) media coverage began to create doubt about his credibility
(C) the UN and U.S. allies raised questions about winning the war
(D) Vietnam veterans themselves organized against the war
(E) China threatened to support North Vietnam

50. In July, 1974, the Supreme Court ruled that President Nixon had to give the subpoenaed tapes to the special prosecutor because

(A) the doctrine of executive privilege was unconstitutional
(B) failure to do so was a clear violation of the constitutional mandate of a separation of powers
(C) Nixon's rejection of the subpoena was based on the unconstitutional Bill of Attainder
(D) no person could withhold evidence that was demonstrably relevant in a criminal trial
(E) his use of executive privilege had expired

51. The British Navigation Acts used for the colonies had the express intent of

(A) limiting trade in the colonies to British or colonial merchants
(B) not allowing the colonies to issue any paper currency printed in the colonies
(C) allowing foreign goods to travel freely to the colonies
(D) encouraging a limited amount of "black market" smuggling in the colonies
(E) allowing the colonists to export goods that would be in direct competition with British goods

52. The first ten amendments to the Constitution were added in order to protect

(A) the power of the federal government over the states
(B) the rights of individuals from the power of state governments
(C) the rights of individuals from the power of the federal government
(D) the rights of minorities
(E) the formation of political parties

53. The Mexican-American War began after

(A) the U.S. annexed the Lone Star Republic
(B) Mexico expelled Slidell
(C) Zachary Taylor crossed the Nueces River and occupied Mexico City
(D) American and Mexican troops clashed in the disputed territory along the Nueces River and the Rio Grande
(E) Representative Abraham Lincoln issued the "Spot Resolution"

54. Which of the following Native American groups is incorrectly matched to its current geographical region?

(A) Maya—Yucatan Peninsula
(B) Aztecs—Mexico City
(C) Pueblo—American Southwest
(D) Wampanoag—Massachusetts
(E) Sioux—California

GO ON TO THE NEXT PAGE.

55. Following the terrorist attacks of September 11, 2001, Congress passed the USA Patriot Act, which
(A) allowed for the deportation of aliens without trial
(B) amended immigration, banking, and foreign intelligence laws in an attempt to more successfully identify terrorists
(C) was hailed by civil libertarians for its fairness and balance
(D) did not include wiretap authorizations
(E) was subsequently vetoed by President Bush

56. The United States overcame the Columbian refusal to approve a canal treaty by
(A) increasing the amount of money the U.S. was willing to pay for a canal zone
(B) encouraging Panamanian rebels to revolt and declare independence from Columbia
(C) looking for another canal site elsewhere in Central America
(D) seeking mediation of the dispute by other Latin American nations
(E) opening negotiations with the French Canal Company

57. The most popular stereotype of the rebellious and daring "flaming youth" among White people in the 1920s was Clara Bow, "the It girl," who was also a
(A) jazz musician
(B) alienated writer
(C) flapper
(D) jitterbug dance instructor
(E) radio soap opera star

58. When veterans of World War I demanded an early payment of their war pensions (to be paid in 1945), the Bonus Army March staged in 1932
(A) was a public relations disaster for Hoover
(B) brought about public relief for the unemployed
(C) discredited the demand for veterans' retirement benefits
(D) destroyed the military career of General Douglas MacArthur
(E) demanded public work projects for the unemployed

59. Which of the following is not associated with the youth culture of the 1960s?
(A) Popularity of the Beatles
(B) Free speech movement at the University of California at Berkeley
(C) The Woodstock Festival in 1969
(D) Hippies, love-ins, and communes
(E) The first appearance of beatniks

60. In 1955, the modern civil rights movement began when who refused to give up a bus seat to a White person in Montgomery, Alabama?
(A) Robert Moses
(B) Rosa Parks
(C) Fannie Hamer
(D) Stokely Carmichael
(E) Emmit Till

61. All of the following statements about the Salem Witchcraft Trials in 1693 are true EXCEPT:
(A) A large number of the accused women were "single women"—either widows who owned land or a sole female family survivor—who would inherit land that threatened the male-dominated Puritan society
(B) A geographic split had occurred in Salem and Salem Town over the selection and payment of a minister and economic differences in the two communities
(C) Although nineteen people died and many others were accused, it did not upset the political or social structure of the community
(D) The accused were mainly older women being charged with witchcraft by young girls in the community
(E) The entire incident occurred during unsettling political turmoil in the colony and presented a unique challenge to Winthrop's original vision of the Puritan community being a "city on a hill" model for the world

GO ON TO THE NEXT PAGE.

62. Most of the utopian movements, especially that of the Mormons, had as one of their founding ideas
    (A) cooperative efforts
    (B) rugged individualism
    (C) capitalism
    (D) opposition to the federal government
    (E) open marriage

63. The primary motivation for the Gadsden Purchase of 1853 was
    (A) to develop a place for freedmen to escape discrimination in the South
    (B) to find a haven for Mormons moving west
    (C) to create a slaveholding state in the West
    (D) to facilitate the building of a southern route for a transcontinental railroad
    (E) to renegotiate the treaty of Guadalupe Hidalgo

64. All of the following statements are true about the Gilded Age EXCEPT:
    (A) U.S. steel and textile production tapered off
    (B) Boom and bust cycles produced two major depressions (and many wealthy businessmen took advantage of business buyouts during these times)
    (C) Manufacturing output soared so that the U.S. became the leading industrial nation in the world by the end of the nineteenth century
    (D) The number of people engaged in manufacturing quadrupled
    (E) Union activity often turned violent

65. The primary cause of the panic of 1873 was
    (A) rising farm prices
    (B) competition for cheap prices for railroad transportation of goods
    (C) an all-time high protective tariff
    (D) overexpansion of commercial ventures
    (E) the collapse of the stock market with no intervention from the federal government

66. This image supports Teddy Roosevelt's desire to pursue the Open Door policy in China because
    (A) the U.S. would finally catch up with other nations in their imperialistic pursuits
    (B) the U.S. was being unfairly shut out of trade with China
    (C) Roosevelt saw it as a way to encourage U.S. participation in imperialism for U.S. interests
    (D) colonies around the world were being established by European powers and the U.S. was not a major factor in the colonization efforts
    (E) there was nothing left for the U.S. to obtain

67. The Harlem Renaissance on the 1920s was
    (A) an architectural revival of uptown Manhattan
    (B) an African American literary and artistic movement
    (C) a school of urban landscape painting
    (D) a group of urban planners trained in New York
    (E) the literary movement started by the "lost generation" authors

GO ON TO THE NEXT PAGE.

68. In addition to bringing a quick resolution to World War II, Truman made the decision to use the atomic bomb on Japan
(A) to demonstrate U.S. strength to the Soviet Union
(B) to destroy Japan
(C) to get the British involved in the war in the Pacific
(D) to follow through with FDR's original plans for ending the war
(E) to gain the support of the Chinese

69. "Operation Vittles," otherwise known as the Berlin Airlift, was significant for all of the following reasons EXCEPT:
(A) Materials were flown in twenty-four hours a day by U.S. and British troops
(B) It demonstrated a challenge to Soviet rule in Berlin
(C) It proved to be very successful after eleven months of flights
(D) It was a way to confront the spreading threat of communism right after the end of World War II
(E) The Russians copied it in a program known as "Operation Strudel"

70. The most dramatic evidence in the House of Representatives that the Cold War had a domestic side was the activities of the
(A) House Armed Services Committee
(B) House Ways and Means Committee
(C) House Un-American Activities Committee
(D) House Judiciary Committee
(E) House Red Scare Committee

71. Parliament passed the Proclamation Line of 1763 in order to
(A) negate the claims of Native Americans in the region
(B) set up a boundary for trade and taxation
(C) extend the colonist's claims west of the Appalachian Mountains
(D) allow for French occupation in the Northwest Territory
(E) prohibit colonists from moving and settling west of the Appalachian Mountains

72. Which of the following was presented as a warning in Washington's Farewell Address?
(A) Limiting trade with foreign nations
(B) Friendly relations with Europe
(C) Political entanglements in foreign affairs
(D) National growth in the U.S.
(E) The development of a two-party political system

73. Between 1965 and 1968 some urban African Americans around the country expressed their reaction to what they perceived as the slow pace of the civil rights movement by
(A) launching the most vigorous voter-registration drive in American history
(B) organizing a series of mass demonstrations and marches that paralyzed city affairs for days at a time
(C) looting, rioting and destroying property
(D) staging sit-ins at banks in order to get more loans for black-run businesses
(E) boycotting segregated city bus service

GO ON TO THE NEXT PAGE.

74. Great Plains farm communities in the post–Civil War period were characterized by

(A) cooperation among neighbors as a form of insurance in a rugged environment
(B) continual friendly relations with Indians
(C) deep suspicion of neighbors or any outsiders who were not blood relations
(D) homosexuality, because there were so few women on the frontier
(E) communal households as nuclear families were replaced with polygamous marriages

75. The result of the British-American conflict over Oregon in 1844–1846 was

(A) American success in winning the goal of a boundary at "fifty-four forty"
(B) an agreement to continue the joint occupation of Oregon for twenty more years
(C) a compromise agreement on a border at the forty-ninth parallel to the Puget Sound (with the exception of Vancouver Island and a few other islands in the area)
(D) an outbreak of war between the two nations known as the "Pig War"
(E) British Columbia's desire to seek U.S. statehood

76. In the Supreme Court's ruling in the *Dred Scott v. Sanford* case in 1857, the court maintained that

(A) poll taxes were legal
(B) Black people were denied U.S. citizenship; therefore, they could not sue in a court of law
(C) "separate but equal" could be a standard applied to the use of public facilities
(D) the Fugitive Slave Law was unconstitutional
(E) the practice of popular sovereignty was legal

77. "Brinksmanship, " the threat of "massive retaliation," and the "domino theory" reflected the belief in retaliation against Communist aggression as proposed by

(A) President Kennedy's administration
(B) President Truman's administration
(C) President Eisenhower's administration
(D) President Nixon's administration
(E) President Reagan's administration

78. In May 1970, the campus at Kent State in Ohio became a focal point of the conflict in Vietnam when

(A) students rallied in support of Nixon's actions to end the war
(B) four students were killed by National Guard troops during an anti-war demonstration
(C) two young Black men were killed by police gunfire and 12 other Black protesters were wounded during a campus protest
(D) students protested for "free speech"
(E) Nixon delivered a commencement address promising again to end U.S. involvement in Vietnam

79. In the *Bakke v. Regents of the University of California* case, the Supreme Court ruled that

(A) the Civil Rights Act of 1964 was unconstitutional
(B) quotas could be used in affirmative action matters
(C) race could still be considered as a factor in college admissions
(D) affirmative action programs were unconstitutional
(E) quotas and race would play a minor role in college admissions

GO ON TO THE NEXT PAGE.

80. A near-meltdown at a U.S. nuclear power plant, causing overheating and the release of radioactive gases, occurred at 4:00 a.m. on March 28, 1979, at a reactor

(A) owned by the PG & E power company in California
(B) at the Three Mile Island nuclear power facility near Harrisburg, Pennsylvania
(C) at a nuclear power plant at Love Canal in upstate New York
(D) at a power plant in Prince William Sound in Alaska
(E) in Los Alamos, New Mexico

END OF SECTION 1

GO ON TO THE NEXT PAGE.

AP* U.S. HISTORY
SECTION II
Time—2 hours and 10 minutes
Percent of total grade—50

General Instructions

Reading Period—15 minutes: All students should read and plan their answer to Part A, Question 1, the document-based essay question. If time permits, they may also read the essay questions in Part B and Part C.

Part A Suggested writing time—45 minutes: All students must answer Question 1.
Part B Suggested planning and writing time—35 minutes: Answer ONE question from Part B.
Part C Suggested planning and writing time—35 minutes: Answer ONE question from Part C.

Section II of this examination requires answers in essay form. The supervisor will announce the time for starting and ending the Reading Period. To help you use your time efficiently, the supervisor will also announce the time at which the writing for Part A should be completed. Be careful not to exceed the writing time suggested for Part A. If you do, you may endanger your grade on the whole examination. If you finish writing Part A before time is announced, you may go on to plan and write Part B. If you finish the examination in less than the time allotted, you may go back and work on either Part A, Part B, or Part C. Keep in mind that in an essay you should pay attention to the organization of your material, the validity and clarity of your general statements, and the intelligent and appropriate use of facts to support your generalizations.

You should write your answers with a pen, preferably one with black or dark blue ink. Be sure to write CLEARLY and LEGIBLY. Cross out any errors you make.

GO ON TO THE NEXT PAGE.

*AP is a registered trademark of the College Board, which was not involved in the production of, and does not endorse, this product.

AP U.S. HISTORY
SECTION II
PART A

(Suggested planning and writing time—45 minutes)

Percent of Section II score—45

Directions: The following question is based on the accompanying Documents A–K. (Some of the documents have been edited for the purpose of this excercise.) Write your answer on the lined pages of the essay booklet.

This question is designed to test your ability to work with historical documents. As you analyze the documents, take into account both the sources of the documents and the authors' points of view. Write an essay on the following topic that integrates your analysis of the documents. Do not simply summarize the documents individually. You may refer to relevant historical facts and developments not mentioned in the documents.

1. "The unparalleled growth of big business during the Gilded Age was challenged on many fronts by labor movements and government regulations during the Gilded Age through the reform movement of the Progressive era."

   For the time period 1875–1915, evaluate the growth of big business and the effectiveness of regulations and labor challenges at reining in various business practices.

Document A

Source: Eugene V. Debs, "How I Became a Socialist," *The Comrade*, April 1902

Next followed the final shock—the Pullman strike—and the American Railway Union again won, clear and complete. The combined corporations were paralyzed and helpless. At this juncture there was delivered, from wholly unexpected quarters, a swift succession of blows that blinded me for an instant and then opened wide my eyes—and in the gleam of every bayonet and the flash of every rifle the class struggle was revealed. This was my first practical lesson in Socialism, though wholly unaware that it was called by that name.

GO ON TO THE NEXT PAGE.

Document B

Source: Mother Jones, 1903 Children's March—New York City speech

We want President Roosevelt to hear the wail of the children who never have a chance to go to school but work 11 and 12 hours a day in the textile mills of Pennsylvania; who weave the carpets that he and you walk upon; and the lace curtains in your windows, and the clothes of the people. Fifty years ago there was a cry against slavery and men gave up their lives to stop the selling of black children on the block. Today the white child is sold for two dollars a week to the manufacturers. Fifty years ago the black babies were sold COD4. Today the white baby is sold on the installment plan.

In Georgia where children work day and night in the cotton mills they have just passed a bill to protect song birds. What about the little children from whom all song is gone?

I shall ask the President in the name of the aching hearts of these little ones that he emancipate them from slavery. I will tell the president that the prosperity he boasts of is the prosperity of the rich wrung from the poor and helpless.

Document C

Source: The Sherman Antitrust Act, July, 1890

SEC.1. Every Contract, combination in the form of trust or otherwise, or conspiracy, in restraint of trade or commerce among the several States, or with foreign nations, is hereby declared to be illegal. Every person who shall make any such contract or engage in any such combination or conspiracy, shall be deemed guilty of a misdemeanor, and, on conviction thereof, shall be punished by fine not exceeding five thousand dollars, or by imprisonment not exceeding one year, or by both said punishments, in the discretion of the court.

GO ON TO THE NEXT PAGE.

Document D

Source: President Theodore Roosevelt

"The captains of industry . . . have on the whole done great good to our people. Without them the material development of which we are so justly proud could never have taken place. . . . Yet it is also true that there are real and great evils. There is a widespread conviction in the minds of the American people that the great corporations known as trusts are uncertain of their futures and tendencies hurtful to the general welfare. This . . . is based upon sincere conviction that combinations and concentration should be, not prohibited, but supervised and within reasonable limits controlled; and in my judgment this conviction is right."

Document E

GO ON TO THE NEXT PAGE.

Document F

Source: Mr. Justice Brewer delivered the opinion of the Supreme Court in 1908 in the *Muller v. Oregon* case.

On February 19, 1903, the legislature of the state of Oregon passed legislation stating:

"Sec. 1. That no female (shall) be employed in any mechanical establishment, or factory, or laundry in this State more than ten hours during any one day. The hours of work may be so arranged as to permit the employment of females [Muller v. Oregon, 208 U.S. 412, 417] at any time so that they shall not work more than ten hours during the twenty-four hours of any one day."

Sec. 3 made a violation of the provisions of the prior sections a misdemeanor subject to a fine of not less than $10 nor more than $25. On September 18, 1905, an information was filed in the circuit court of the state for the county of Multnomah, charging that the defendant 'on the 4th day of September, A. D. 1905, in the county of Multnomah and state of Oregon, then and there being the owner of a laundry, known as the Grand Laundry, in the city of Portland, and the employer of females therein, did then and there unlawfully permit and suffer one Joe Haselbock, he, the said Joe Haselbock, then and there being an overseer, superintendent, and agent of said Curt Muller, in the said Grand Laundry, to require a female, to-wit, one Mrs. E. Gotcher, to work more than ten hours in said laundry on said 4th day of September, A. D. 1905, contrary to the statutes in such cases made and provided, and against the peace and dignity of the State of Oregon.

GO ON TO THE NEXT PAGE.

Document G

Caption: The trust giant's point of view—"What a funny little government."

GO ON TO THE NEXT PAGE.

Document H

Source: Rose Schneiderman, addressing audience at a memorial meeting held in the Metropolitan Opera House on April 2, 1911

I would be a traitor to these poor burned bodies if I came here to talk good fellowship. We have tried you good people of the public and we have found you wanting. The old Inquisition had its rack and its thumbscrews and its instruments of torture with iron teeth. We know what these things are today; the iron teeth are our necessities, the thumbscrews are the high-powered and swift machinery close to which we must work, and the rack is here in the firetrap structures that will destroy us the minute they catch on fire.

This is not the first time girls have been burned alive in the city. Every week I must learn of the untimely death of one of my sister workers. Every year thousands of us are maimed. The life of men and women is so cheap and property is so sacred. There are so many of us for one job it matters little if 146 of us are burned to death.

We have tried you citizens; we are trying you now, and you have a couple of dollars for the sorrowing mothers, brothers and sisters by way of a charity gift. But every time the workers come out in the only way they know to protest against conditions which are unbearable the strong hand of the law is allowed to press down heavily upon us.

Public officials have only words of warning to us—warning that we must be intensely peaceable, and they have the workhouse just back of all their warnings. The strong hand of the law beats us back, when we rise, into the conditions that make life unbearable.

I can't talk fellowship to you who are gathered here. Too much blood has been spilled. I know from my experience it is up to the working people to save themselves. The only way they can save themselves is by a strong working-class movement.

Document I

Source: Edward Bellamy, from *Looking Backward*, 1888

". . . The movement toward the conduct of business by larger and larger aggregations of capital, the tendency toward monopolies, which had been so desperately and vainly resisted, was recognized at last, in its true significance, as a process which only needed to complete its logical evolution to open a golden future to humanity."

GO ON TO THE NEXT PAGE.

Document J

Source: Wabash, *St. Louis & Pacific Railroad v. Illinois* (1886)

This question of whether the statute of Illinois, as applied to the case in hand, is in violation of the constitution of the United States, as set forth in the plea, was also raised on the trial by a request of the defendant, the railroad company, that the court should hold certain propositions of law on the same subject, which propositions are as follows: 'The court holds as law that, as the tolls or rates of compensation charged and collected by the defendant in the instance in question were for transportation service rendered in transporting freight from a point in the state of Illinois to a point in the state of New York, under an entire contract or undertaking to transport such freight the whole distance between such points, that the act of the general assembly of the state of Illinois, approved May 2, 1873, entitled 'An act to prevent extortion and unjust discrimination in the rates charged for the transportation of passengers and freight on railroads in this state, and to punish the same, and prescribe a mode of procedure and rules of evidence in relation thereto, and to repeal an act entitled 'An act to prevent unjust discrimination and extortion in the rates to be charged by the different railroads in the state for the transportation of freight on said roads' approved April 7, 1871,' does not apply to or control such tolls and charges, nor can the defendant be held liable in this action for the penalties prescribed by said act.

The court further holds as law that said act in relation to extortion and unjust discrimination cannot apply to transportation service rendered partly without the state, and consisting of the transportation of freight from within the state of Illinois to the state of New York, and that said act cannot operate beyond the limits of the state of Illinois.

The court further holds as matter of law that the transportation in question falls within the proper description of 'commerce among the states,' and as such can only be regulated by the congress of the United States under the terms of the third clause of section 8 of article 1 of the constitution of the United States.

GO ON TO THE NEXT PAGE.

Document K

Source: *The Saturday Globe*, a pro-union weekly, (Utica, New York), July 9, 1892

Caption: "Forty-Millionaire Carnegie in his Great Double Role. As the tight-fisted employer he reduces wages that he may play philanthropist and give away libraries, etc."

END OF DOCUMENTS FOR QUESTION 1

GO ON TO THE NEXT PAGE.

AP U.S. HISTORY
SECTION II
Part B and Part C
(Suggested planning and writing time—70 minutes)

Percent of Section II score—55

Part B

Directions: Choose ONE question from this section. The suggested writing time for this question is 30 minutes. You are advised to spend 5 minutes planning your answer in the area below. Reference historical evidence in support of your generalizations and make sure you present your arguments clearly and logically.

2. The political debate about slavery began at the Constitutional Convention in 1787 and continued to stir political debate until 1860. Evaluate the growing political debate about slavery and the rise in sectionalism from 1787 until 1860.

3. Improvements in transportation had tremendous economic, social, and political impact on America in the years 1815 to 1875. Choose *three* of the following and discuss the impact each one had on the economic, social, and political development in the country between the years 1815 and 1875.

   Canals

   Steamboats

   Overland trails

   Railroads

GO ON TO THE NEXT PAGE.

Part C

Directions: Choose ONE question from this section. The suggested writing time for this question is 30 minutes. You are advised to spend 5 minutes planning your answer in the area below. Reference historical evidence in support of your generalizations and make sure you present your arguments clearly and logically.

4. During the last third of the nineteenth century, America became involved in territorial expansion outside the continental United States. This acquisition of territory increased regional influence and affected United States foreign policy. Focusing on the period from 1865 to 1910, discuss U.S. foreign policy in relation to *three* of the following areas:

   Alaska

   Hawaii

   Puerto Rico

   Philippines

   Cuba

5. Discuss the changing role of the media and the impact it had on American society in *three* of the following conflicts:

   Civil War

   Spanish-American War

   World War I

   World War II

   Vietnam

STOP

END OF EXAM

PRACTICE EXAM 2: ANSWER KEY

No.	Answer	Right	Wrong	No.	Answer	Right	Wrong	No.	Answer	Right	Wrong
1	B	__	__	27	B	__	__	54	E	__	__
2	C	__	__	28	E	__	__	55	B	__	__
3	C	__	__	29	A	__	__	56	B	__	__
4	E	__	__	30	B	__	__	57	C	__	__
5	B	__	__	31	D	__	__	58	A	__	__
6	C	__	__	32	D	__	__	59	E	__	__
7	C	__	__	33	A	__	__	60	B	__	__
8	B	__	__	34	E	__	__	61	C	__	__
9	D	__	__	35	B	__	__	62	A	__	__
10	A	__	__	36	A	__	__	63	D	__	__
11	C	__	__	37	A	__	__	64	A	__	__
12	B	__	__	38	C	__	__	65	D	__	__
13	C	__	__	39	C	__	__	66	B	__	__
14	C	__	__	40	B	__	__	67	B	__	__
15	A	__	__	41	E	__	__	68	A	__	__
16	D	__	__	42	A	__	__	69	E	__	__
17	D	__	__	43	A	__	__	70	C	__	__
18	B	__	__	44	E	__	__	71	E	__	__
19	A	__	__	45	E	__	__	72	C	__	__
20	A	__	__	46	B	__	__	73	B	__	__
21	E	__	__	47	B	__	__	74	A	__	__
22	B	__	__	48	D	__	__	75	C	__	__
23	E	__	__	49	B	__	__	76	B	__	__
24	D	__	__	50	D	__	__	77	C	__	__
25	C	__	__	51	A	__	__	78	B	__	__
26	B	__	__	52	C	__	__	79	C	__	__
				53	D	__	__	80	B	__	__

HOW TO CALCULATE YOUR SCORE

Section I: Muliple Choce

[________ - ¼ × ________] × 1.125 = ________

Number Correct (out of 80) | Number Wrong | Multiple-Choice Score | Weighted Section I Score (Do not round.)

Section II: Free Response

4.50 × ________ = ________

Question 1 (0-9 ponts) | Question 1 Weighted Score

2.75 × ________ = ________

Question 2 (0-9 ponts) | Question 2 Weighted Score

2.75 × ________ = ________

Question 3 (0-9 ponts) | Question 3 Weighted Score

________ + ________ + ________ = ________

Question 1 Weighted Score | Question 2 Weighted Score | Question 3 Weighted Score | Weighted Section II Score (Do not round)

Composite Score

________ + ________ = ________

Weighted Section I Score | Weighted Section II Score | Composite Score (Round to the nearest whole #.)

Composite Score*	AP Grade	Interpretation
114-180	5	extremely well qualified
91-113	4	well qualified
70-94	3	qualified
49-73	2	possibly qualified
0-48	1	no recommendation

*Each year the Development Committee determines the formulas used to calculate the raw composite scores. The Chief Faculty Consultant determines how the composite scores fit into the 5-point AP scale.

SECTION I: MULTIPLE CHOICE

1. **B** Social Change, Cultural & Intellectual Developments: Pre-Columbian–1789 *Trend*
The Puritan leadership saw Anne Hutchinson as a threat because she challenged the traditional role of women by speaking to mixed audiences of men and women and openly challenged the preachers' messages. She also thought that a believer could be personally enlightened by God.

2. **C** Political Institutions, Behavior & Public Policy: Past–1789 *Fact*
The meeting approved continuing boycott measures against Great Britain and encouraged the individual colonies to begin training local militia for war. The delegates also expressed their support for Boston after passage of the Intolerable Acts closed the Port of Boston in retaliation for the Boston Tea Party.

3. **C** Political Institutions, Behavior & Public Policy: 1790–1914 *Fact*
The Missouri Compromise of 1820 sought to preserve the Senate's delicate balance between slave and free states by keeping the numbers even with the admission of Missouri as a *slave* state and Maine as a *free* state. This process worked until the Compromise of 1850 allowed the entry of California as a free state, undoing the delicate balance in favor of popular sovereignty.

4. **E** Political Institutions, Behavior & Public Policy: 1790–1914 *Fact*
Both the Wilmot Proviso of 1846 and the Compromise of 1850 dealt with extending slavery into the territories acquired from Mexico. The Wilmot Proviso sought to forbid extending slavery into any territory acquired in the Mexican-American War, while the Compromise of 1850 admitted California as a free state and allowed the concept of popular sovereignty in new territories, which allowed a territory to decide on the issue of slavery.

5. **B** Political Institutions, Behavior & Public Policy: 1790–1914 *Fact*
This railroad scandal involved inflated prices designed to get more money from lucrative government loans. It also involved kickbacks for members of Congress who voted in favor of railroad financing bills.

6. **C** Political Institutions, Behavior & Public Policy: 1915–Present *Fact*
This measure sought to limit immigration through quotas. Immigration numbers from 1880 were used as a baseline to determine the number of immigrants allowed from various countries. It severely limited immigration from southern and eastern Europe.

7. **C** Political Institutions, Behavior & Public Policy: 1915–Present *Trend*
Joseph McCarthy gained notoriety with his accusations of card-carrying Communists in the U.S. government. This began a wave of Red Scare hysteria in the early 1950s.

8. **B** Social Change, Cultural & Intellectual Developments: Pre-Columbian–1789 *Fact*
The most significant unit of 17th-century Puritan society was the family. Fathers were expected to oversee the religious and economic health of all members of their families.

9. **D** Political Institutions, Behavior & Public Policy: 1790–1914 *Fact*
This measure sought to regulate businesses deemed to be monopolies "in constraint of trade." In other words, the big monopolies were using unfair business practices to limit competition and raise prices.

10. **A** Political Institutions, Behavior & Public Policy: 1915–Present *Trend*
Women gained the right to vote with the passage of the Nineteenth Amendment in 1920.

11. **C** Social Change, Cultural & Intellectual Developments: Pre-Columbian–1789 *Fact*
Bostonians, in particular, had grown weary of the Townshend Duties, which were enacted to raise revenue with the intent of "making a more certain and adequate provision for defraying the charge of the administration of justice, and the support of civil government, in such provinces as it shall be found necessary; and towards further defraying the expenses of defending, protecting and securing the said dominions." In other words, Great Britain was using these revenues to pay for troops and royal commissioners in the colonies.

12. **B** Political Institutions, Behavior & Public Policy: Pre-Columbian–1789 *Fact*
Shays's Rebellion persuaded many Americans that the weak government under the Articles of Confederation wasn't working and that a stronger federal government was necessary.

13. **C** Social Change, Cultural & Intellectual Developments: 1790–1914 *Trend*
The mills in Lowell, Massachusetts, relied on young girls from surrounding rural areas for their labor supply. These workers became known as the infamous Lowell Girls.

14. **C** Social Change, Cultural & Intellectual Developments: 1790–1914 *Fact*
Settlement houses, such as Jane Addams' Hull House in Chicago, provided a myriad of social services for poor immigrants in inner cities. Hull House was the first of many such settlement houses.

15. **A** Political Institutions, Behavior & Public Policy: 1790–1914 *Fact*
John C. Calhoun and South Carolina openly protested the "Tariff of Abominations" and even threatened secession over the crisis. But no other state was willing to follow South Carolina's lead in seceding. Calhoun claimed that the states had the final authority in laws passed by Congress and that a state could nullify a law it didn't agree with. Twenty-eight years later in 1860, South Carolina would take the lead in the secession movement and in the formation of the Confederacy.

16. **D** Political Institutions, Behavior & Public Policy: 1790–1914 *Fact*
Suffrage for women was discussed during the antebellum years, but the message was lost in the discussion of abolition. Black men would get the right to vote with the Fifteenth Amendment in 1870, while women would be forced to wait another fifty years until the Nineteenth Amendment was ratified in 1920.

17. **D** Social Change, Cultural & Intellectual Developments: Pre-Columbian–1789 *Fact*
The Great Awakening, which began in the 1730s, reinvigorated American Puritanism by emphasizing immediate, personal religious experience.

18. **B** Social Change, Cultural & Intellectual Developments: 1915–Present *Fact*
This statement supported the 1920s fundamentalist movement, which stressed acceptance of the literal word of God in the Bible. The statement was made in reference to the Bible's claims of creation and not evolution.

19. **A** Political Institutions, Behavior & Public Policy: 1915–Present *Fact*
Many people tend to credit the New Deal legislation with bringing an end to the Great Depression. Although the New Deal legislation offered relief from the effects of the depression, it was actually the United States' involvement in World War II and the economic boom it created that ended the Great Depression.

20. **A** Social Change, Cultural & Intellectual Developments: 1915–Present *Trend*
As other forms of entertainment gained in popularity in the 1950s, movie theaters experienced a dramatic decline.

21. **E** Economic Developments: Pre-Columbian–1789 *Trend*
New England rum was shipped to Africa in return for slaves. The triangular trade route involved the shipment of fish, lumber, and other goods from New England to the West Indies. In the West Indies, ships picked up the sugar and molasses that was used to make rum. From the West Indies, merchants carried the rum, along with guns, gunpowder, and tools, to West Africa. Here they traded these items for slaves and transported the slaves to the West Indies, where they, in turn, were sold. Traders would take the profits and buy more molasses.

22. **B** Social Change, Cultural & Intellectual Developments: 1790–1914 *Fact*
This is the infamous quote from a letter that Abigail Adams wrote to her husband, John Adams.

23. **E** Social Change, Cultural & Intellectual Developments: Pre-Columbian–1789 *Fact*
Reform movements of the 1840s included abolitionism, temperance, public education, and the elimination of cruel and inhumane insane asylums.

24. **D** Political Institutions, Behavior & Public Policy: 1790–1914 *Fact*
The radical Republicans sought to firmly dictate the terms of Reconstruction themselves—even if it meant ignoring Lincoln's Ten Percent Plan and removing President Johnson from office by impeaching him.

25. **C** Economic Developments: 1790–1914 *Fact*
William Jennings Bryan advocated the free coinage of silver in his 1896 presidential campaign.

26. **B** Social Change, Cultural & Intellectual Developments: 1790–1914 *Fact*
The 1848 Seneca Falls meeting issued an early strong statement of women's rights and declared "All men and women are created equal."

27. **B** Diplomacy and International Relations: 1790–1914 *Fact*
As the United States became more involved in Latin American affairs, Latin American countries grew more suspicious of America's intentions. "Dollars would be a more effective means of achieving national goals than bullets," they often said.

28. **E** Diplomacy and International Relations: 1915–Present *Fact*
The Germans sent the Zimmermann telegram to Mexico in 1917, attempting to coerce Mexico into joining the war effort on Germany's side. The Germans also issued the telegram in an attempt to anger the United States, to eventually draw the country into the war effort. Within the next three months, the United States would become openly involved in the war.

29. **A** Diplomacy and International Relations: 1915–Present *Fact*
The North Atlantic Treaty Organization (NATO) was a mutual defense pact of several nations of Western Europe, the United States, and Canada in response to the Soviet threat.

30. **B** Diplomacy and International Relations: 1915–Present *Fact*
Lyndon Johnson was in the midst of promoting his Great Society of economic programs, but he felt those programs would be threatened if the conflict in

Vietnam weren't addressed. If Communist North Vietnam succeeded in defeating South Vietnam, it was widely believed that other Asian countries would be at risk of Communist domination (thus, the domino theory—if one falls, all fall).

31. **D** Social Change, Cultural & Intellectual Developments: Pre-Columbian–1789 *Fact*
A separatist sought to break away (separate) from the Church of England in pursuit of a pure church not tainted by worldly things.

32. **D** Political Institutions, Behavior & Public Policy: Pre-Columbian–1789 *Except*
The Antifederalists mounted a convincing campaign against ratification. So, to secure enough votes for ratification, concessions were made to later add a Bill of Rights to the Constitution to secure the rights of individuals. This was done two years after the ratification of the Constitution.

33. **A** Diplomacy and International Relations: 1790–1914 *Fact*
The major reasons the War Hawks sought a declaration of war were the issue of impressment and the lingering recession that was causing economic problems, especially to people in the South and West.

34. **E** Social Change, Cultural & Intellectual Developments: 1790–1914 *Except*
The labor reform movement was part of the labor union movement. It started with the Knights of Labor in 1869 and was later continued by the Progressive Movement in the early twentieth century.

35. **B** Political Institutions, Behavior & Public Policy: 1790–1914 *Fact*
Even though Lincoln lost the debates to Douglas, his popularity increased, as did the popularity of the Republican Party on a national scale. Lincoln would then run as the Republican candidate for president in the 1860 election.

36. **A** Social Change, Cultural & Intellectual Developments: 1790–1914 *Trend*
Booker T. Washington took a more subdued approach to civil rights for Black people through accommodation. He felt that Black people must receive job training and prove their worth to a White society while they worked for civil rights.

37. **A** Social Change, Cultural & Intellectual Developments: 1790–1914 *Fact*
Mother Jones was an ardent supporter of unions and strikers. She sought to rally the men in Ludlow, Colorado, in April 1914 in their strike against the Colorado Fuel and Iron Company, which was owned by J. D. Rockefeller.

38. **C** Social Change, Cultural & Intellectual Developments: 1915–Present *Fact*
These events proved that there were serious racial problems to address. Rosewood, Florida, was burned in 1923 as a result of a Black man being accused of raping a White woman. In 1921, the race riots that resulted in the destruction of a thirty-five-acre site in the Greenwood district of Tulsa, Oklahoma, also

involved accusations of an assault on a White woman by a Black man. The membership of the KKK rose to an estimated 4 million by the mid-1920s.

39. **C** Diplomacy and International Relations: 1915–Present *Except*
The conflict in Korea has never been fully resolved. There has been only a cease-fire—no formal peace settlement has ever been reached between North and South Korea.

40. **B** Social Change, Cultural & Intellectual Developments: 1915–Present *Trend*
Leaders within the women's movement began to disagree openly about the merits of the ERA. Many began to feel it would undermine the traditional role of women.

41. **E** Political Institutions, Behavior & Public Policy: Pre-Columbian–1789 *Fact*
The passengers on the *Mayflower* agreed to be bound by the decision of the majority in establishing the settlement at Plymouth in 1620.

42. **A** Social Change, Cultural & Intellectual Developments: Pre-Columbian–1789 *Except*
Black people failed to gain their freedom after the Revolutionary War ended in 1781. It was not until after the Civil War ended in 1865 that they gained their freedom.

43. **A** Social Change, Cultural & Intellectual Developments: 1790–1914 *Trend*
The transcendentalist authors promoted the concepts of inner truth and individual self-reliance. Transcendentalists such as Ralph Waldo Emerson believed that people should live life to the fullest and seek to reach their potential. Emerson felt that a person could achieve this transcendence through his ability to be an individual and through his relationship with nature by rising above the material world. Emerson also believed that the meaning of life could be discovered only within oneself.

44. **E** Political Institutions, Behavior & Public Policy: 1790–1914 *Fact*
The Alien and Sedition Acts were an attempt to silence opposition from the Republicans (Antifederalists) to the Federalist president John Adams. This put Vice President Thomas Jefferson, an Antifederalist, at odds with the president.

45. **E** Political Institutions, Behavior & Public Policy: 1915–Present *Except*
The South clearly had the early advantage in military leadership during the Civil War.

46. **B** Political Institutions, Behavior & Public Policy: 1790–1914 *Cartoon/Chart/Map*
As businesses began to grow and form monopolies in the Gilded Age, business owners decided that they could best regulate themselves without government intervention. Business leaders had their company's interests at stake and felt that

self-regulation was the best way for the industries to survive and work together in the marketplace. During the era of laissez-faire, businesses tried to avoid government intervention.

47. **B** Social Change, Cultural & Intellectual Developments: 1790–1914 *Fact*
Social Darwinism promoted the concept of the fittest—the strong in society will triumph and survive over the weaker members of society

48. **D** Diplomacy and International Relations: 1915–Present *Fact*
The Kellogg-Briand Pact in 1928 sought to outlaw the use of war to resolve conflicts between nations.

49. **B** Political Institutions, Behavior & Public Policy: 1915–Present *Trend*
President Johnson's popularity began to suffer when media coverage started to suggest a lack of credibility in what the president was saying about the war effort. Johnson claimed the United States was winning the war, but the media portrayed the escalating death and destruction in Vietnam. Body-bag counts became very important in media reporting.

50. **D** Political Institutions, Behavior & Public Policy: 1915–Present *Fact*
Not even the president was above the law when it came to matters involving a criminal investigation. Nixon's use of executive privilege was denied, forcing him to turn over the infamous Watergate tapes requested by the Senate committee.

51. **A** Political Institutions, Behavior & Public Policy: Pre-Columbian–1789 *Fact*
Great Britain sought to control trade with the colonies and to keep them subordinate by requiring goods to be transported on British ships or to pass first through British ports for taxation purposes.

52. **C** Political Institutions, Behavior & Public Policy: Pre-Columbian–1789 *Fact*
The Bill of Rights (the first ten amendments to the Constitution) was intended to protect the rights of individuals from the power of the federal government.

53. **D** Diplomacy and International Relations: 1790–1914 *Fact*
The Mexican-American War began in 1845 after Mexican troops crossed the Rio Grande and killed Americans on "American soil" in the disputed region between Texas and Mexico. On December 22, 1847, Whig congressman Abraham Lincoln questioned whether the spot to which President Polk had referred in his call for a declaration of war against Mexico in 1846 was really U.S. (and Texas) soil. Lincoln issued the "Spot Resolution" demanding to know the exact spot where the conflict actually began. Whigs in Congress didn't support Polk's claims about the war's necessity.

54. **E** Social Change, Cultural & Intellectual Developments: Pre-Columbian–1789 *Except*
The Sioux tribes were nomads living in the Great Plains of the United States.

55. **B** Political Institutions, Behavior & Public Policy: 1915–present *Fact*
The Patriot Act gave broad powers to the federal government in an attempt to counter terrorism within the United States.

56. **B** Political Institutions, Behavior & Public Policy: 1790–1914 *Fact*
When Colombia rejected the U.S. offer to build a canal across Panama, the United States "encouraged" Panama to revolt against Colombian rule and declare its independence. After the successful revolt, the United States then negotiated the canal with the newly formed country of Panama.

57. **C** Social Change, Cultural & Intellectual Developments: 1915–Present *Trend*
The flapper represented a sexual revolution for women, becoming one of the endearing cultural icons of the 1920s. This new female image was of a thin, flat-chested, and boyish-looking female with bobbed hair, who wore fashions that exposed more flesh and reveled in dancing, drinking, and smoking. The flapper image took its cue from such stars as "the It girl," Clara Bow, and Harlem Renaissance blues singer Bessie Smith.

58. **A** Political Institutions, Behavior & Public Policy: 1915–Present *Fact*
The Bonus Army March in Washington, D.C., became a political nightmare for President Hoover as U.S. troops under the command of Douglas MacArthur forced the World War I veterans out of Anacostia Flats.

59. **E** Social Change, Cultural & Intellectual Developments: 1915–Present *Except*
Beatniks (or the Beat Generation) first gained notice during the 1950s. All of the other choices were aspects of 1960s youth culture.

60. **B** Social Change, Cultural & Intellectual Developments: 1915–Present *Fact*
Rosa Parks is credited with beginning the modern civil rights movement when she refused to give up her bus seat to a White person. This action led to the bus boycott by Black citizens in Montgomery, Alabama.

61. **C** Social Change, Cultural & Intellectual Developments: Pre-Columbian–1789 *Except*
The Salem witchcraft trials greatly upset the political and social structure of the community. They demonstrated serious problems with John Winthrop's original intent for the colony to be a model community for the entire world.

62. **A** Social Change, Cultural & Intellectual Developments: 1790–1914 *Trend*
Cooperation was a major tenet of many of the utopian religious movements in the mid-1800s; many of them practiced communal lifestyles.

63. **D** Economic Developments: 1790–1914 *Fact*
The Gadsden Purchase in 1853 was made in order to secure land for a southern route for a transcontinental railroad.

64. **A** Economic Developments: 1790–1914 *Except*
U.S. steel and textile production skyrocketed during the Gilded Age. By the beginning of the twentieth century, the United States had become the world's number-one producer of goods. U.S. Steel, founded in 1901, became the first billion-dollar corporation in U.S. history.

65. **D** Economic Developments: 1790–1914 *Trend*
Overexpansion of commercial ventures ultimately led to the panic of 1873. When U.S. railroads began to go bankrupt and Europe's economic problems reached the United States, the result was a serious economic crisis. Ultimately, unregulated growth was the major cause of the panic.

66. **B** Political Institution, Behavior, and Public Policy: 1790–1914 *Cartoons/Charts/Maps*
Teddy Roosevelt was concerned about the lack of open U.S. trade in China. All of the other major nations, including Great Britain, Germany, and Russia, were pursuing their national interests in imperialism, and the United States was being left behind. This led to the negotiation of the Open Door policy, which allowed the United States to open up trade negotiations with China.

67. **B** Social Change, Cultural & Intellectual Developments: 1915–Present *Trend*
The Harlem Renaissance was a major literary and artistic movement in the 1920s, centered in the Harlem district of New York.

68. **A** Diplomacy and International Relations: 1915–Present *Fact*
Truman wanted to demonstrate U.S. military strength to the Russians when he made the decision to drop atomic bombs on Japan, in order to bring a quick end to the war. Truman was growing concerned about the Russians and their activities in Eastern Europe and had begun to distrust this World War II ally.

69. **E** Diplomacy and International Relations: 1915–Present *Except*
The Russians didn't copy the Berlin Airlift, known as Operation Vittles. It was a successful U.S. project to supply Germans in West Berlin with necessities for eleven months.

70. **C** Political Institutions, Behavior & Public Policy: 1915–Present *Trend*
The House Un-American Activities Committee (HUAC) was an important part of the Cold War in America in the late 1940s and early 1950s. Representative Richard Nixon served on this investigative committee searching for Communist infiltration in America. The HUAC investigated the Alger Hiss case, which involved an accusation by journalist Whittaker Chambers identifying Hiss as a Communist who was involved in espionage. The committee also investigated

producers and actors in Hollywood, seeking "Communist infiltration" in the movie industry.

71. **E** Political Institutions, Behavior & Public Policy: Pre-Columbian–1789 *Fact*
King George III sought to limit colonists' movement with his Proclamation Line of 1763, which curtailed the movement of colonists west of the Appalachian Mountains. In addition, after Pontiac's rebellion in the Ohio country, King George III sought to minimize any further conflicts between colonists and Native Americans. By limiting colonial movement west of the Appalachians, Great Britain could maintain further control over the colonists.

72. **C** Diplomacy and International Relations: Pre-Columbian–1789 *Trend*
In 1796, George Washington warned the young nation about becoming entangled in foreign affairs. He encouraged friendly ties and economic trade measures, but cautioned against becoming involved in other countries' affairs.

73. **B** Social Change, Cultural & Intellectual Developments: 1915–Present *Fact*
Following the early successes of the non-violent demonstrations and protests organized by Martin Luther King Jr. and other civil rights leaders, a number of demonstrations and marches took place that tied up city affairs.

74. **A** Social Change, Cultural & Intellectual Developments: 1790–1914 *Fact*
The isolation and sparse population of farm families on the Great Plains led to a spirit of cooperation and mutual assistance. Communal trade organizations such as the Grange had their roots in this cooperative spirit.

75. **C** Diplomacy and International Relations: 1790–1914 *Fact*
This dispute in the Oregon country was resolved with an agreement that the forty-ninth parallel would be a dividing line between Canada and the United States, extending to the Puget Sound. Vancouver Island and a few other islands would remain part of British Columbia.

76. **B** Political Institutions, Behavior and Public Policy: 1790–1914 *Fact*
Chief Justice Taney ruled in the *Dred Scott v. Sandford* case that Black people were not U.S. citizens, so they had no right to sue in a court of law.

77. **C** Diplomacy and International Relations: 1915–Present *Fact*
Eisenhower's secretary of state, John Foster Dulles, promoted the concepts of brinksmanship and massive retaliation by openly challenging the Russians.

78. **B** Social Change, Cultural & Intellectual Developments: 1915–Present *Fact*
Kent State was the site of a student protest against the Vietnam War on May 4, 1970. National Guard troops opened fire on a group of students, wounding nine

and killing four. Two days earlier, the Army ROTC building on the Kent State campus had been burned.

79. **C** Political Institutions, Behavior & Public Policy: 1915–Present *Fact*
Race could still be used in college admissions, but the use of quotas was challenged. In this case, Bakke had been barred from admission because he was the eighty-sixth applicant for eighty-five slots. Out of the total 100 slots for students entering the medical program, fifteen slots were kept open for minorities. Bakke sued on the basis of discrimination—he had higher test scores than the minority applicants but because he was a White male (and number 86 on the list of applicants) he was denied admission. He won his case.

80. **B** Social Change, Cultural & Intellectual Developments: 1915–Present *Fact*
The nuclear near-meltdown occurred at Three Mile Island near Harrisburg, Pennsylvania, on March 28, 1979.

SECTION II: SAMPLE DBQ AND FREE-RESPONSE QUESTIONS

A note about the sample essays: We've included sample answers to each of the questions included in the Free-Response section. These essays would receive a top score from graders. It is possible to receive an equally high score without mentioning all of the facts and themes included here. If your essay is well-crafted and supported but all of the points and themes below aren't included, a top score may still be given. Since the DBQ and Free-Response Essays are graded by humans instead of machines, and these humans usually have somewhere between 2 and 4 minutes to read and grade your essay, it is harder to pin down what will constitute a high-scoring response.

Question 1

President Theodore Roosevelt astutely observed both the "great good" and the "great evils" produced by the Gilded Age (Doc D). During the period between Reconstruction and 1900, the United States experienced a phase of unparalleled industrial and technological growth. In an attempt to maximize efficiency, entrepreneurs created industries that increased the scale of business to staggering proportions. The emergence of monopolies and trusts resulted in a disproportionate concentration of wealth and power. The federal government did little to regulate corporate expansion, and workers became increasingly vulnerable. Tired of and frustrated by deplorable working conditions, workers developed unions and waged massive strikes of protest. Social organizations made some headway, but actual reform remained elusive until the Progressive Movement.

In the decades following the Civil War, the country experienced an unparalleled growth of big business. Technological advances fueled productivity and instilled an appreciation of efficiency. Entrepreneurs like Jay Gould, Andrew

Carnegie, J. P. Morgan, and J. D. Rockefeller combined technology with cunning business practices to revolutionize the scale of industry and epitomized the growing sense of entitlement produced by success. National railroads, such as Gould's Union Pacific, were forged from the consolidation of smaller regional lines. In order to maximize efficiency, industry leaders agreed to standardize basic equipment and even went as far as to establish four separate time zones across the country in order to maintain scheduling consistency. Such decisions inevitably affected everyone, yet the federal government did little to intervene. The only check of growth occurred during the panic of 1893, but, even then, monopolies were preserved as the railroad industry was taken over by investment bankers like J. P. Morgan. In fact, the Supreme Court actually sided in favor of the railroad companies when Illinois passed a law regulating transportation rates (Doc J).

As the railroads expanded, they created a demand for other industries, such as steel and oil. Andrew Carnegie used his background in railways to pioneer development in the steel industry. His Carnegie Steel Company utilized the newest technology to maximize cost-effectiveness. Carnegie also used vertical integration to gain control of all phases from refinement to production. His only competition came from J. P. Morgan's Federal Steel Company; however, Morgan bought out Carnegie Steel in 1901. Morgan paid over a half-million dollars and created the United States Steel Corporation, the nation's first billion-dollar corporation.

The oil industry also reached gargantuan proportions. J. D. Rockefeller's Standard Oil Company also used new technology and refining techniques to achieve unparalleled success. Rockefeller believed that competition wasted resources, so he used vertical and horizontal integration to found the Standard Oil Trust. The new trust controlled ninety percent of the refining capacity in the United States. Horace Taylor's cartoon conveys the scale of Standard Oil Trust, which literally towered over that of the government (Doc G).

The railroad, steel, and oil industries justified their success as a triumph of capitalism. In Carnegie's "Gospel of Wealth," he endorsed laissez-faire policies limiting government interference in the growth of business. He believed that competition was necessary for progress. Although offered as a critique, Edward Bellamy captured the essence of the capitalist argument, namely that capitalism was a "logical evolution to open a golden future to humanity" (Doc I). That reasoning, along with the word *evolution*, echoed the beliefs of Social Darwinism. Business leaders claimed that the emergence of monopolies and trusts amounted to a "survival of the fittest" and strengthened American business and benefited society on the whole. One of the by-products of success was philanthropy. Carnegie felt that his wealth imposed certain social responsibilities. He founded the Carnegie Foundation and contributed to charities and social organizations. While his generosity seemed contradictory to some, it was widely recognized nonetheless (Doc K).

There were some states that attempted to regulate the practices of national corporations, but they had very limited success. When Illinois enacted a law that adjusted interstate transportation rates for the railways, the law was immediately appealed by the St. Louis & Pacific Railroad. In the Supreme Court case *Wabash,*

St. Louis & Pacific Railroad v. Illinois, the Court sided in favor of the railroads on the grounds that "such [issues] can only be regulated by the congress of the United States" (Doc J). Congress did respond in 1887 by passing the Interstate Commerce Act, but this act did little more than establish the Interstate Commerce Commission (ICC) to investigate and monitor railroad operations. The most defining legislation came three years later with the passage of the Sherman Antitrust Act. This act was the first attempt to rein in monopolies and trusts, as it declared that practices aimed at the "restraint of trade or commerce among the several States" were illegal (Doc C). Although the Sherman Antitrust Act was a positive step, it failed to define "trust" and "restraint of trade," and likewise, it remained largely ineffective. In the 1895 Supreme Court case *United States v. E.C. Knight Co.*, the Court ruled that E.C. Knight, a trust controlling over ninety percent of sugar refining, was not in violation of the Sherman Antitrust Act. As suggested by Taylor's cartoon, the industry leaders literally seemed to have the government in the palm of their hands (Doc G).

Without effective government intervention, workers became increasingly susceptible to exploitation. As corporations sought to maximize efficiency, women, children, and immigrants were hired as a source of cheap labor. These workers were subjected to deplorable working conditions, including workdays of 12–14 hours, monotonous assembly lines, and fluctuating wages. In an effort to combat these unscrupulous practices, workers banded together in labor unions such as the American Federation of Labor. The Haymarket Square riot and the strike against Carnegie Steel in Homestead, Pennsylvania, indicated growing tension, but the most emblematic confrontation occurred during the Pullman strike in 1894.

The Pullman Palace Car Company established a combination factory/town in Illinois. After the panic of 1893, Pullman reduced wages but did not adjust employee rent. Outraged by the perceived injustice, workers found support in the American Railway Union. Under the leadership of Eugene Debs, the Pullman workers organized an effective strike in which "the combined corporations were paralyzed and helpless" (Doc A). However, even in this instance, the government sided with railroad executives and accused the workers of violating the Sherman Antitrust Act. After federal troops intervened, the final outcome of the Pullman strike left Debs in jail, several workers dead, and hundreds of railroad cars burned and destroyed.

Despite the various challenges presented by labor movements, true reform did not occur until the Progressive Era. Progressives picked up on some of the success of the Populist Movement but ultimately appealed to a broader base, the urban middle class. Social organizations emerged promoting the regulation of business and the protection of workers. Mother Jones spoke on behalf of working children and the need to "emancipate them from slavery" (Doc B). Similarly, in response to the Triangle Shirtwaist fire that claimed the lives of hundreds of young women, Rose Schneiderman called for "working people to save themselves" (Doc H). Their pleas did not go unnoticed by the federal government. Even the Supreme Court made a decision in favor of a shorter workday in the case of *Muller v. Oregon* (Doc F) . The true lift of the Progressive Movement came with the presidency of Theodore Roosevelt. Roosevelt earned a reputation as “the Trustbuster” because he was the first to use the Sherman Antirust Act to break up monopolies. He advocated labor mediation, ethical business, and conservation. He helped pass the Hepburn Act of 1906, which finally gave the Interstate Commerce Commission the authority to set maximum rates for railroads. Roosevelt’s success was continued by William Taft and Woodrow Wilson. Taft actually prosecuted even more trust suits than Roosevelt, and Wilson was instrumental in the passing the Federal Trade Commission Act and the Clayton Antitrust Act.

The Progressive Era came to an end with the onset of World War I. Thanks to the strong leadership of Roosevelt, Taft, and Wilson, along with the constant determination of social activists, business practices and labor standards underwent important reformation. At last, in 1911, the Supreme Court forced Standard Oil Trust to break up. The unparalleled and unrestricted growth of big business during the Gilded Age had finally been reined in by the federal government. While there were still improvements to be made, the average worker had achieved substantial progress.

Question 2

The first African slaves were brought to Virginia in 1619, just twelve years after the founding of Jamestown. Slaves were imported as a source of labor for the cultivation of tobacco, indigo, and rice. The introduction of slavery did not stir much controversy then, nor would it during the early colonial period. Despite the lack of objection from the North, slavery was almost exclusively practiced in the South. The political debate about slavery did not even begin until the Constitutional Convention of 1787, but, from that point onward, it would be the subject of growing concern. In its earliest stages, the discussion revolved around political principles, and both sides worked towards compromise. However, as the North and South developed distinct economies, the debate became clouded by economic issues. The previous harmony gradually dissolved, and sectional divisions became apparent. The territorial expansion accompanying manifest destiny furthered the sectional divide. Finally, the debate took on a moral dimension, and both sides became increasingly intolerant as the nation moved toward civil war.

Although slavery had been in practice for well over a century, its political debate did not begin until the Constitutional Convention of 1787. The delegates in attendance shared a common viewpoint that the country needed a stronger national government. The emphasis on unity helped shape the early discussion of slavery and paved the way for compromise. More than a third of the convention’s delegates were slaveholders; yet, in deciding the issue of congressional representation and how slaves would be counted, the debate emphasized political principle over personal interest. The delegates carefully deferred decisions that would have broad consequences for slavery, including a ban on the importation of slaves. Even the final agreement to count three-fifths of all slaves towards a state’s population represented a political compromise.

While both sides made difficult concessions, the spirit of compromise continued to characterize the early stages of the political debate about slavery

through the 1820s. The Missouri Compromise confirmed the desire to maintain balance. The admission of Missouri as a slave state was offset by the admission of Maine as a free state; furthermore, both sides agreed that slavery would be prohibited in the remainder of the Louisiana Territory north of the southern Missouri border.

As the United States began to follow two separate paths of economic development, the debate about slavery proceeded accordingly. The invention of the Cotton Gin in 1793 revolutionized the agrarian South and furthered southern resolve about agriculture and slavery (since the vitality of southern agriculture was also dependent upon slavery as a necessary source of labor) as the foundation of its economy. Meanwhile, the North pursued the path of industrialization and urbanization. As these two regions moved in distinct directions, the North harbored a feeling that the South was clinging to tradition and resisting the movement towards progress. The regional differences came to a head in 1828 with the "Tariff of Abominations." On behalf of the South, Vice President John Calhoun argued that the high protective tariff favored industry in the North at the expense of the South. Likewise, he believed that the tariff was unconstitutional because it did not advance the good of the country as a whole. If the government was capable of promoting sectional interest, Calhoun implied that slavery might be next. Southern anxiety about slavery was compounded by Nat Turner's rebellion in 1831 and the rise of the abolition movement in the North. Amidst talk of secession, the Compromise of 1833 reminded both sides of the viability of political solutions and staved off civil war for the time being.

The ability to reach true compromise ended as morality became the central element of the political debate about slavery. The abolition movement, led by David Lloyd Garrison, adamantly maintained that slavery was immoral and that all slaves should be liberated. The growing political voice of the abolition movement, which culminated in the formation of the Free-Soil Party, understandably caused concerns in the South. Many southerners justified slavery as a positive institution that actually provided for an inferior race. Southerners accurately understood the cultural and economic implications of abolition and viewed the North with increasing suspicion. The sectional differences reached new heights during the debate about expansion and manifest destiny. After gains in Oregon and Texas, spoils from the Mexican-American War aroused fierce sectional debate about slavery, as each side hoped to secure a majority representation in Congress. The Compromise of 1850 provided some success by restoring the balance between free states and slave states, but it also introduced the idea of popular sovereignty. Ultimately, the tenuous harmony was dealt a final blow with the Kansas-Nebraska Act, which basically nullified the Missouri Compromise. With both sides fighting for a very way of existence, political compromise was no longer an option, and the stage was set for civil war.

Prior to the Missouri Compromise, the political debate about slavery transcended sectional difference. The delegates at the Constitutional Convention deliberately omitted specific provisions regulating slavery, and they set a precedent for the political compromise illustrated in the Missouri Compromise, the Compromise of 1833, and the Compromise of 1850. However, when the Kansas-Nebraska Act stipulated that both territories could decide the issue of slavery via popular sovereignty, it effectively undermined the boundary that was agreed to in the Missouri Compromise. In the three decades separating those two acts, the North, South, and newly emerged West had developed distinct regional differences. The sectional difference became increasingly difficult to overcome, and, by 1860, it was so pronounced that the Civil War was all but inevitable.

Question 3

The combined development of steamboats, canals, and railroads during the nineteenth century has been proclaimed as the Transportation Revolution. Prior to this time, national transportation was characterized by horse-drawn carriages traveling the Cumberland and Coastal roads. The Louisiana Purchase extended the borders of the country and helped expose the limitations of the existing system. Following the invention of the steam engine, the introduction of the steamboat drastically transformed transportation. The success of steamboats supported the development of a canal system, which in turn fostered growing interest in railroads. These three methods of transportation collectively revolutionized American culture and commerce between the years of 1815 and 1875.

Since flatboats, keelboats, and rafts were only useful floating downstream, steamboats solved the longstanding problem of upstream navigation. In the early 1800s, the technology of the steam engine was applied to shipping, which produced early steamboats like the *Clermont*. The initial technology was modified to enhance efficiency, and steamboats became increasingly advantageous for transporting goods. The result was the rise of a market economy since the transportation improvements provided new markets that were previously inaccessible. In that sense, steamboats also accelerated the growth of important river towns like New Orleans, Cincinnati, Pittsburgh, and St. Louis. Because of their popularity, steamboats became a cultural symbol of the West. While the national usefulness of steamboats would eventually be replaced by railroads, steamships continued to play an important role in international transportation.

Steamboats were integral in facilitating the development of an extensive canal system by opening up America's waterways. While initially dismissed as being financially unrealistic, canals had certain obvious appeals. Steamboat traffic was primarily limited to north-south travel along the Ohio and Mississippi Rivers. The desire to connect those river systems to the Northeast led to the creation of the Erie Canal. The project was funded by the New York State government, and it took seven years to complete. The canal indirectly connected New York City with the Great Lakes Region, which meant that goods from the Midwest could now reach European markets. The Erie Canal was able to turn a profit within seven years, and its success inspired similar projects like the Blackstone Canal in New England and the Main Line Canal in Pennsylvania.

As the network of canals expanded, shipping costs dropped exponentially and the Northeast became the center of American commerce. Despite the thousands of miles of canals that were built, the rapid expansion came to an end with the Panic of 1893. By 1850, the Canal Era was completely over, but it had played an irreversible role in the rise of industry and manufacturing throughout the North.

Even while the use of canals was waning, railroads were opening up even more of the country. The growth of the railroad industry was slow in its initial stages because railroads required large amounts of capital to fund the expenses of buying land, laying tracks, and building cars. Unlike canals, the bulk of the financing was left to private corporations. The fact that railroads were not dependent upon waterways meant that the possibilities for growth were virtually endless. The railroads were twice as fast as canals, and they could be operated year-round, which made them even more indispensable for the transportation of freight. Railroad investments gradually surpassed those in canals during the 1830s, but the real boom took place in the 1850s. Networks of smaller railroads sprang up throughout the Northeast and Midwest (which would prove to be of great advantage to the North during the Civil War). Railways connected economic centers and enabled the small towns in between to prosper. The railroad industry also fostered the growth of other industries like lumber and flour mills. Soon discussion about a transcontinental railroad began. The completion of the first transcontinental railroad in 1869 connected the country in unprecedented ways. In the coming decades, the railroad industry continued to expand, and as it did, the economic, social, and political ramifications became increasingly significant.

By 1875, the U.S. transportation system had transformed dramatically. The first phase of the Transportation Revolution featured the development of steamboats and the canal system. The second phase was dominated by the massive expansion of railroads. The overall transformation improved the transport of goods by reducing shipping costs and times and helped to create a market economy. Even more significantly, the construction of a national infrastructure connected the country during a period that was otherwise characterized by sectional strife.

Question 4

The spirit of expansion that characterized the manifest destiny movement resumed after the Civil War, only in global terms. The acquisition of Alaska in 1867 paved the way for American expansion beyond the continental borders, and many in the United States seemed ready to participate in the international trend of imperialism. The arguments for expansion were justified on political, economic, military, and moral grounds, each of which played varying roles in the development of American foreign policy at the turn of the century. American involvement in Hawaii, Cuba, and the Philippines revealed an eagerness to redefine foreign policy along imperialistic principles, as well as an uncertainty about occupation and the other consequences of expansion.

Hawaii was a natural target for American expansion. Its strategic location and plentiful harbors appealed to commercial and military interests. Historically, Hawaii was also a trading connection for the United States and a large number of American sugar plantations. As interest increased, the American government negotiated terms with the Hawaiian government in 1887 and began to construct a naval base at Pearl Harbor. Some Hawaiians, including Queen Liliuokalani, who inherited the Hawaiian throne in the early 1890s, began to resent the growing American presence. Tension escalated after the Hawaiian economy collapsed; the U.S. reinstated an import tax on Hawaiian sugar. A group of American plantation owners, led by Sanford Dole, staged a revolt and overthrew the Queen. They immediately applied for annexation to the United States. The bill was stalled by Democrats in Congress until Grover Cleveland took office in 1893. Cleveland ordered an investigation of the Hawaiian situation and rescinded his support after it became clear that Hawaiians did not universally desire annexation. Cleveland's caution was harshly criticized by Republican expansionists. They were forced to wait until he was succeeded by William McKinley. Under the new administration, Hawaii was annexed as an American territory in 1898; thus, beginning a quick period of rampant international expansion.

Having secured a stronghold in the Pacific, America turned its attention to the Caribbean. Since 1895, Cuba had been in a state of revolt against Spain. Cuban independence did not arouse much support from the American government at first, but it was becoming a popular cause among the American people. Americans responded to the sensational headlines published by the yellow journalists and were increasingly convinced that American intervention was a moral imperative. The outcry peaked in 1898 when an explosion devastated the USS *Maine*, which had been ordered to Havana harbor. Although the Spanish government had indicated an initial willingness to negotiate peace in Cuba, President McKinley could not ignore the public outrage. He asked Congress for a declaration of war and set extreme demands for Spain. Spain responded with its own declaration of war, and the Spanish-American War ensued. America quickly prevailed, and Cuba was granted its independence.

With respect to foreign policy, two important amendments revealed the haziness of American objectives. The Teller Amendment of 1898 declared that the United States did not have an interest in controlling Cuba after the war. Three years later, however, the Platt Amendment stipulated the right to intervene at any time deemed necessary and the right to construct a naval base. According to those terms, the United States did reoccupy Cuba for three years and also established a naval base at Guantanamo Bay in 1912.

On the eve of the Spanish-American War, Theodore Roosevelt, then the assistant secretary of the navy, ordered Commodore Dewey's Pacific Fleet to prepare for action in the Philippines. His request, which was unauthorized, serves as further evidence of the expansionist agenda. After the Philippines were ceded to the United States by Spain, a debate about annexation followed, and the various motivations for expansion became increasingly clear. Business interests were enticed by the Philippines as a way of accessing the profitable markets of China. Others worried about the political and military consequences of relinquishing control, namely that the Philippines would quickly fall to another foreign power. Finally, the moral argument, embraced by McKinley himself, was that America needed to educate and Christianize the Filipino population (apparently not accomplished by centuries of Spanish colonization). The Philippines desired their own independence prior to the Spanish-American War, and they continued to wage a guerilla war against America for three more years. Finally in 1902, Congress passed an act that promised the Philippines eventual self-government, which did not come about until 1946.

During his time in office, McKinley was often criticized for lacking political convictions. His concern for public approval was particularly apparent in the area of foreign policy. Without clear objectives regarding expansion, America rushed into Hawaii and the Spanish-American War generally unprepared for the consequences. Despite the various challenges of occupation, the United States was able to extend its military and commercial interests internationally between the years of 1865 and 1910.

Question 5

The media has made a major impact on American society by effectively shaping public opinion. In its earliest form, newspapers were the most common medium of delivering information to the public. Advances in technology, like the creation of television, have dramatically transformed the media; but, even today, newspapers remain an important source of information. One of the most defining moments in the history of media occurred prior to the Spanish-American War. The reporting of yellow journalism roused public support and thrust the country towards war. Forty years later, the government took steps to control media influence and forged an alliance with the media in the coverage of World War II. That alliance was shattered during the Vietnam War, as the media inspired passionate antiwar sentiment. Towards the end of the nineteenth century, the popularity of newspapers surged, much to the credit of Joseph Pulitzer, William Randolph Hearst, and yellow journalism. The term yellow journalism was inspired by the comic strip *The Yellow Kid*, which was featured in Hearst's newspaper. Yellow journalism referred to a new style of sensational reporting. Both Pulitzer and Hearst ran their papers out of New York City. Both newspapers were in a circulation war prior to the Spanish-American War. American entry into that war was precipitated by events surrounding the Spanish colony of Cuba, which was in a state of revolt. Each newspaper published scandalous stories about the atrocities being committed by the Spanish government and resorted to increasingly outrageous headlines in order to boost sales. Their plan worked, and Americans were convinced that the United States should intervene. In 1898, Hearst published a private letter from a Spanish diplomat who expressed the uncertainty about the Spanish position on Cuba and described President McKinley as being weak. The story produced a massive outcry, which was then magnified by the news about an explosion on board the USS *Maine*, a battleship stationed off the coast of Havana. Without conclusive evidence, both newspapers alleged that the explosion had been caused by a Spanish torpedo. Although McKinley was on the verge of peaceful negotiations with Spain, he bowed to the overwhelming public demand for war. Shortly thereafter, the United States declared war on Spain. While there were certainly other factors at work, yellow journalism had an undeniable impact on the country's readiness for war.

Recognizing the vast influence of the media, President Roosevelt took steps to regulate the coverage of World War II. In an effort to bolster public support and to prevent compromising leaks of information, the government established the Office of Censorship in 1941. This agency employed fourteen-thousand people to screen all letters being sent abroad to American troops. The Office of Censorship also worked with the media to suppress any information that might be damaging to the war effort. The first photograph of dead American soldiers was not published until two years after the United States entered the war, and only a few others were released after that. Roosevelt also commissioned the Office of War Information to counter enemy propaganda. This office glorified the patriotism and service of American soldiers while vilifying the Axis powers. Hollywood responded and produced war-oriented movies that increased morale. The general interest in the war led to the increased popularity of magazines and the radio. *Time* was just one of several magazines that offered news and analysis. Radio broadcasts reached record levels of eager listeners, providing the most recent updates from the war. While Americans were receiving more news than ever before, the news was carefully censored by the alliance between the government and media.

The cooperation between the government and the media came to an abrupt end during the Vietnam War. The emergence of television dramatically changed the media's coverage of the war, as well as the public's perception. Many refer to Vietnam as a "living room war" because of the immediate access to the news. Televisions relayed graphic images of American and Vietnamese casualties, and the equally vivid revelation of the destruction caused by napalm and defoliation agents. The media's coverage also dispelled the government's claims of success. After the Tet Offensive, for example, the government declared that the defense of Saigon was to be a pivotal turning point. However, the media focused on the number of American casualties and argued that the very ability to stage an offensive proved that little had been accomplished. The media was instrumental in rallying antiwar sentiment because it forced the American government to be accountable in unprecedented ways.

In all three wars—the Spanish-American War, World War II, and Vietnam—the media significantly influenced public attitudes. Popular opinion motivated the United States to enter the Spanish-American War and to leave Vietnam. Roosevelt appreciated the enormous impact of the media and manipulated it to the country's advantage, but, in doing so, he raised issues about censorship. As the media has diversified, the one constant has been its ability to captivate and inspire the public.

A

B

C

G

M

N

O

P

S

X

Y

Z